Insan al Kamil
The Universal Perfect Being

SHAYKH NURJAN MIRAHMADI

PUBLISHED BY THE
SUFI MEDITATION CENTERS SOCIETY

Insan al Kamil
The Universal Perfect Being

Copyright © 2020

by Shaykh Nurjan Mirahmadi

ISBN: 978-1-989602-02-7

All rights reserved.

No part of this book may be used or

reproduced in any manner whatsoever

without written permission.

Published and Distributed by:

Sufi Meditation Center Society
3660 East Hastings
Vancouver, BC V5K 2A9 Canada
Tel: (604) 558-4455

nurmuhammad.com

Special thanks to the Publishing Team for making these books possible

❧❦❧

Mrs. Amina K. ❧ Ms. Wida M. ❧ Mrs. Nadia H. ❧ Ms. Aumbrine K.
❧ A Dedicated Team of Transcribers

First Edition: July 2020

TABLE OF CONTENTS

About the Author i
Universally Recognized Symbols vii

CREATION OF NUR MUHAMMAD ﷺ

First of Creation was Nur Muhammad ﷺ (Hadith Jabir) 2

Seven Heavens and Universes in Prophet Muhammad ﷺ
(Hadith of Sayyidina Uwais al-Qarani ؓ and Sayyidina 'Ali ؓ) 4

Creation of Nur Muhammad ﷺ 7

Secrets of the Name Muhammad ﷺ - Meem, Ha, Meem, Daal 25

Sultanate of Sayyidina Muhammad ﷺ and the
Naqshbandi Taweez 49

THE CROWN OF CREATION

Opening the 7 Points of the Head
A Gateway to the 9 Points of the Body 63

7 Divinely Attributes Dress the 7 Holy Openings 83

Secrets of the Eyes – Light and Eternity (An Nur, Al Hay) 111

Reality of Eyes – Compassion and Mercy
Imam Hassan ؓ & Imam Hussain ؓ 129

THE HOLY TONGUE

Divinely Pen - Qaf of Qur'an al Majeed and Qalam 153

God's Voice is Like Thunder - Power of Qalam (Pen) –
Writing Knowledge 165

Noon wal Qalam – Our Life is in Search of
These Divine Lights 179

THE HOLY FACE

Ayat al Kursi About WajhAllah (Face of God) 203

The Secret Book of Hu Perfection of the Holy Face 221

Insan al Kamil - Book of Realities 259

Realities of the Face, Presence, Essence 283

Realities of Insan (Perfect Human) The Sun and the Moon 289

THE HOLY CHEST

Allah 🕊 Wanted to be Known, He Created
Nur Muhammad ﷺ (Misbah) 313

Malik al Hayat, Malik al Dunya – Meem, Ha, Meem, Daal 335

THE ALL-ENCOMPASSING OCEAN - BAHRUL MUHEET

Ma'rifah of Allah 🕊 - Enter Hey, Lam, Lam, Alif 353

Real Ka'bah in the Heart of Muhammad ﷺ 379

Reality of Hu, From the Ocean of La Ilaha IllAllah,
Muhammad RasulAllah ﷺ 393

19 Letters of Bismillahir Rahmanir Raheem and
19 Letters of Ahlul Bayt 🕊 407

Hidden Things Will Be Revealed Drinking From Kawthar 431

GUIDANCE

Spiritual Internet Wi-Fi Signal From God For Soul 443

Realities of a Zawj (Mate) on Earth, Within, and in the Heavens .469

A Seed is Annihilated in the Soil to Become a Tree –
The Tree is a Manifestation of the Soil 493

ABOUT THE AUTHOR

PROFILE

For the past two decades, Shaykh Nurjan Mirahmadi has worked hard to spread the true Islamic teachings of love, acceptance, respect and peace throughout the world and opposes extremism in all its forms. An expert on Islamic spirituality, he has studied with some of the world's leading Islamic scholars of our time.

Shaykh Mirahmadi has also founded numerous educational and charitable organizations. He has travelled extensively throughout the world learning and teaching Islamic meditation and healing, understanding the channeling of Divine energy, discipline of the self, and the process of self-realization. He teaches these spiritual arts to groups around the world, regardless of religious denomination.

BACKGROUND

Shaykh Nurjan Mirahmadi studied Business Management at the University of Southern California. He then established and managed a successful healthcare company and imaging centers throughout Southern California. Having achieved business success at a remarkably young age, Shaykh Nurjan Mirahmadi shifted his focus from the private sector to the world of spirituality. In 1994 he pursued his religious studies and devoted himself to be of service to those in need. He combined his personal drive and financial talents to work for the less fortunate and founded an international relief organization, a spiritual healing center, and a religious social group for at risk youth.

In 1995, he became a protégé of Mawlana Shaykh Hisham Kabbani for in-depth studies in Islamic spirituality known as Sufism. He studied and accompanied Shaykh Kabbani on many tours and learned about Sufi practices around the world. Together with Shaykh Kabbani, he has established a number of other Islamic educational organizations and relief programs throughout the world.

Shaykh Nurjan Mirahmadi has received written *ijazas* (authorization) to be a Spiritual guide, from two of the World Leaders of the Naqshbandi Sufi Order; Sultan al-Awliya Shaykh Muhammad Nazim al-Haqqani ق and Mawlana Shaykh Muhammad Hisham Kabbani. He is authorized to teach, guide, and counsel religious students around the world to Islamic Spirituality.

IJAZAS (AUTHORIZATION)

Shaykh Nurjan Mirahmadi has taught and travelled extensively throughout the world from Uzbekistan to Singapore, Thailand, Indonesia, Cyprus, Argentina, Peru, and North America. He teaches the spiritual sciences of Classical Islam, including meditation (*tafakkur*), subtle energy points (*lataif*), Islamic healing, the secrets of letters and numbers (*ilm huroof*), disciplining the self (*tarbiya*), and the process of self-realization (*ma'rifah*). He teaches the Muslim communities the prophetic ways of being kind, respectful and live in harmony with people. He emphasizes on good manners and respect, and often reminds his students that the spiritual journey begins from within and "You can't give what you don't have."

ACCOMPLISHMENTS

One of Shaykh Nurjan's greatest accomplishments has been the worldwide dissemination of the spiritual teachings of Classical Islam through his books and online presence. The Prophet Muhammad ﷺ has told us, "Speak to people according to their levels." In an era of social media, Shaykh Nurjan's ability to reach a new generation of spiritual seekers through the Internet has been remarkable. His *NurMuhammad.com* website alone has over 1,500 unique visitors each day, and since its inception has seen more than 200,000 downloads of the book *"Dailal Khairat"*, 1.5 Million free downloads of *Naqshbandi Muraqabah*, and another 700,000 downloads of the *Naqshbandi Book of Devotions (Awrad)*, as well as many more articles. His Facebook pages "Shaykh Nurjan Mirahmadi" and "Nur Muhammad" combined have over 1.1 million likes and followers. Furthermore, his YouTube Channel "The Muhammadan Way" has over 2.5 million views, and his Google page, "Shaykh Sayed Nurjan Mirahmadi" has over 2.7 million views.

Shaykh Nurjan Mirahmadi focuses on the worldwide social media presence working on ways to bring knowledge to all seekers around the world. In 2015 he launched an Online University, called *SimplyIman.org*, to spread these traditional Spiritual Islamic teachings even further and make it accessible to all seekers around the world.

For over 20 years Shaykh Nurjan has dedicated his life to spreading the true Islamic teachings of love, acceptance, respect and peace. He has established several non-profit organizations since the early 1990s and has founded numerous educational and charitable organizations. In the Greater Vancouver region alone, he has established the following:

Divine Love: Hub-E-Rasul TV Series – launched in May 2017, this weekly half-hour Islamic television show covers a wide range of topics, focusing on spreading Prophet Muhammad's ﷺ message that Islam is a religion based on peace, love, and acceptance.

The show airs every Saturday at 1:30 pm (PST) on Joytv, reaching 7 million viewers Canada-wide. It reaches the online community through social media and through its website **huberasul.net**. For a full channel listing please visit **www.huberasul.net/schedule**.

Muhummadan Way App (over 20,000 Users Worldwide) – a comprehensive resource of Islamic information for all mobile devices. Created for both Muslims and non-Muslims, it provides users with a wealth of knowledge including access to books, supplications, prayer times, month-specific practices, a media library of audio and video files, an events calendar, and much more.

Ahle Sunnah wal Jama of BC – this organization is a resource for authentic content, books, and articles from the Qur'an & Sunnah from around the world. It works in collaboration with the well-known international organizations, Al Azhar University of Cairo, Dar al Ifta of Egypt and Islamic Supreme Council of North America.

Hub-E-Rasul ﷺ Conference – monthly Mawlid & Mehfil-e-Dhikr events are organized and held throughout the Lower Mainland. The aim is to revive the teachings of the Qur'an and *Sunnah* by celebrating holy events in true Islamic spirit (*Isra wal Mi'raj, Lailatul Bara'h, Lailatul Qadr, Mawlid an-Nabi* etc.)

Naqshbandi Islamic Center of Vancouver – this Center is a place for people of all faiths and beliefs to attend weekly *zikr* programs (circles of remembrance) three times a week (Thursdays, Fridays, and Saturdays). Shaykh Nurjan teaches above and beyond the principles of Islam including the deep realities of *maqam al-iman* (belief) and *maqam al-ihsan* (excellence of character).

SMC – an outreach organization that spreads teachings to the Western audience including concepts such as meditation and charity. It reaches out to other faiths to increase peace, love, and acceptance in the interfaith environment.

Simply Iman Cloud University – an international online platform allowing people from around the world to pursue studies in various aspects of faith and spirituality from a classical Islamic perspective. Students have the opportunity to learn at their own pace and engage in an open dialogue with a teacher in real-time.

Fatima Zahra Helping Hand – this charity organization runs a food program every two weeks which feeds more than 500 less fortunate people in the downtown eastside of Vancouver. It also collects clothing and non-perishable food items for the BC Muslim Food Bank and the Burnaby Homeless Shelter.

Shaykh Nurjan's Published Books – these titles are available at all major retailers and online.

- Rising Sun of the West
- YASEEN – Prophet is the Walking Qur'an
- Divinely Praising Upon the Pearl of Creation
- In Pursuit of Angelic Power
- Levels of the Heart – Lataif al Qalb
- Secret Realities of Hajj
- The Healing Power of Sufi Meditation

Shaykh Nurjan has established an international presence through many social media outlets including:

- FaceBook **(Shaykh Nurjan Mirahmadi)** with over 1.1 million followers
- YouTube Channels
  - **The Muhummadan Way** – over 5 million views with a library of over 1,000 videos
  - **Divine Love: Hub-E-Rasul** – based on the acclaimed TV series with over 27,000 views and 173 videos
  - **Shaykh Talks** – video series of short, powerful talks focusing on Spiritual Reminders and Motivational Topics
- **NurMuhammad.com**, a comprehensive website containing many resources covering the deep realities of classical Islam.

Shaykh Nurjan's sincere mission is to spread the love of Sayyidina Muhammad ﷺ throughout the city for our families and children. If you would like to be a shareholder in all these blessings, we invite you to support our Center by any means possible. We hope to strengthen our efforts by joining our hands in raising the Honourable Flag of Sayyidina Muhammad ﷺ.

UNIVERSALLY RECOGNIZED SYMBOLS

The following Arabic and English symbols connote sacredness and are universally recognized by Muslims:

The symbol ﷻ represents *Azza wa Jal*, a high form of praise reserved for God alone, which is customarily recited after reading or pronouncing the common name Allah, and any of the ninety-nine Islamic Holy Names of God.

The symbol ﷺ represents *sall Allahu 'alayhi wa salaam* (Short Form: *saws*) (God's blessings and greetings of peace be upon the Prophet), which is customarily recited after reading or pronouncing the holy name of the Prophet Muhammad ﷺ. It commonly appears as *pbuh (peace be upon him)* in English translations.

The symbol ؑ represents *'alayhi 's-salam* (peace be upon him/her), which is customarily recited after reading or pronouncing the sanctified names of prophets, Prophet Muhammad's ﷺ family members, and the angels.

The symbol ؓ represents *radi-allahu 'anh/ 'anha* (may God be pleased with him/her), which is customarily recited after reading or pronouncing the holy names of Prophet Muhammad's ﷺ Companions.

The symbol ق represents *qaddas-allahu sirrah* (may God sanctify his or her secret), which is customarily recited after reading or pronouncing the name of a saint.

Creation of Nur Muhammad ﷺ

FIRST OF CREATION WAS NUR MUHAMMAD ﷺ
(HADITH JABIR)

عَنْ جَابِرٍ ، قَالَ : قُلْتُ : يَا رَسُولَ اللَّهِ صَلَّى اللهُ عَلَيْهِ وَسَلَّمَ ، "بِأَبِي أَنْتَ وَأُمِّي ، أَخْبِرْنِي عَنْ أَوَّلَ شَيْءٍ خَلَقَهُ اللَّهُ قَبْلَ الْأَشْيَاءِ؟

قَالَ رَسُولَ اللَّهِ صَلَّى اللهُ عَلَيْهِ وَسَلَّمَ: يَا جَابِرٍ ، إِنَّ اللَّهَ خَلَقَ قَبْلَ الْأَشْيَاءِ نُورُ نَبِيِّكَ مِنْ نُورِهِ ، فَجَعَلَ ذَلِكَ النُّورَ يَدُورُ بِالْقُدْرَةِ حَيْثُ شَاءَ اللَّهُ ، وَلَمْ يَكُنْ فِي ذَلِكَ الْوَقْتِ لَوْحٌ وَلَا قَلَمٌ، وَلَا جَنَّةٌ وَلَانَارٌ، وَلَا مُلْكٌ، ولاسَمَاءٌ وَلَا أَرْضٌ، ولاشَمْسٌ وَلَا قَمَرٌ، وَلَإِنْسٌ وَلَا جِنٌّ. فَلَمَّا أَرَادَ اللَّهُ تَعَالَى أَنْ يَخْلُقَ الْخَلْقَ قَسَّمَ ذَلِكَ النُّورَ أَرْبَعَةَ أَجْزَاءٍ: فَخَلَقَ مِنَ الْجُزْءِ الْأَوَّلِ الْقَلَمَ، وَمِنِ الثَّانِي اللَّوْحَ، وَمِنِ الثَّالِثِ الْعَرْشَ،...(وَمِنْ الاربعة كُلَّ شيء."

[رواية عَبْدِ الرَّزَّاقِ فِي مُصَنَّفَةٍ]

'An Jabir (ra) Qala: Qultu: Ya RasulAllah (saws), "Bi Abi anta wa Ummi, Akhberni 'an awwala shayin Khalqahu Allahu qablal ashyayi?"

Qala RasulAllah (saws):

"Ya Jabir, in Allah khalaqa qablal Ashiya e Nooru Nabiyika min Noorehi. Faj'ala dhalikan Noore yadoro bil Qudrati haithu sha Allahu, wa lam yakun fi dhalikal waqti lawhun wa la qalamun, wa la Jannatun wa la Narun, wa la Mulkun, wa la samaun wa la ardun, wa la Shamsun wa la Qamarun, wa la insun wa la jinnun.

Falama arada Allahu ta'ala an yakhluqal Khalqi qasama dhalikan Nooru arba'a ajza: a: fakhalaqa minal juzil awwalu al Qalamu, wa minath thaniul Lawhu, wa minath thalithul 'Arshu, [minal Aba'ahu kuli shayin]."

Jabir ibn 'Abdallah (ra) said to the Prophet (pbuh):

"O Messenger of Allah (pbuh), may my father and mother be sacrificed for you, tell me of the first thing Allah created before all things."

He (Prophet Muhammad (pbuh)) said: "O Jabir, the first thing Allah created was the light of your Prophet from His (Allah's) light, and that light remained (lit / 'turned') in the midst of His Power for as long as He wished, and at that time, there was no Tablet and no Pen, and no Paradise and no Fire, and no angel, and no heaven and no earth, and no Sun and no Moon, and No Human being and no jinn.

And when Allah wished to create creation, he divided that Light into four parts and from the first made the Pen, from the second the Tablet, from the third the Throne, [and from the fourth everything else].

SEVEN HEAVENS AND UNIVERSES IN PROPHET MUHAMMAD ﷺ
(HADITH OF SAYYIDINA UWAIS AL-QARANI (as) AND SAYYIDINA 'ALI (as))

We went to that place and we saw in the distance a man sitting with his back to us. We approached. When we came near, without turning around, he said, "O 'Ali, O 'Umar, give me my trust." Immediately we handed him the robe of the Prophet ﷺ. He stood up, kissed the robe, put it on his head, then put it to his heart and said, "I accept, I accept, I accept."

We wondered why he was kissing the robe and saying these words, because he had never seen the Prophet ﷺ in all his life. But we were hesitant to ask.

Then he turned to Sayyidina 'Umar and said to him, "Ya 'Umar, how many times have you seen the Prophet ﷺ?" 'Umar was astonished at this question. He said, "That is a strange question. I spent my whole life in the company of the Prophet." Sayyidina Uwais said, "I am asking for a reason. How many times did you actually see him?" Sayyidina 'Umar said, "How do you mean? I was with him all the time!" Sayyidina Uwais al-Qarani said, "Describe him to me." Sayyidina 'Umar began to describe the Prophet, his eyes, his features, his appearance. Then Sayyidina Uwais said, "Ya 'Umar, this description is known to everyone, including those who disbelieved in him."

Then he looked at me and said, "Ya 'Ali, how many times did you see the Prophet ﷺ?" I knew what he meant, and I said, "Ya Uwais, in my life I only saw the Prophet ﷺ one time." Sayyidina 'Umar was looking at me in amazement. I said, "I saw him one time. The Prophet ﷺ called me and told me, 'Look at me from my navel and above.' I looked and I saw that the Prophet ﷺ from his navel up filled the universes and the Seven Heavens. From his neck and up, I was unable to see, but it was above the *Sidratul Muntaha* (Furthermost Limit). Then he told me, 'Look from my navel and down.' I looked and I saw all these universes, all these worlds, stars and planets had disappeared and all that I saw was the Prophet ﷺ, from his waist to his knees filling up that entire space. And from his knees down to his feet I was unable to see. Then he ﷺ said, 'Look at all of me, from top to bottom.' I looked at him, and the *Sidratul Muntaha* and all these universes disappeared, and all I saw was Muhammad ﷺ, everywhere. At that time I knew that Muhammad ﷺ is the Heart of the Divine Presence *(al-Haqiqat al-Muhammadiyya)*."

Then Sayyidina Uwais looked at me and said, "You really saw the Prophet ﷺ one time. And that is why he ﷺ said about you, 'I am the City of Knowledge and 'Ali is its Door.' Allah has also given this Divine Knowledge to Abu Bakr as-Siddiq, as the Prophet ﷺ mentioned, 'Whatever Allah poured into my heart, I poured into the heart of Abu Bakr as-Siddiq.'"

In this state of wonderment, Sayyidina 'Umar asked Sayyidina Uwais, "What is the significance of that robe we brought to you?" He said, "O 'Umar, that is one of the biggest secrets, which will not be revealed to people until the Last Days of his Nation. While the Prophet ﷺ was passing away, he was asking for intercession for his Nation."

Then he said, "His Nation includes all human beings. And that is why Allah said, 'Say [O Prophet]: O mankind! I am a Messenger to you all from Allah, to Whom belongs the Kingdom of the heavens and the earth.' [7:158]. The Prophet asked for intercession and Allah gave permission. He was interceding for every individual that Allah created. As he was asking, he was sweating, and each drop of sweat represented one human being. He took on the burdens of each person. Until he was satisfied that Allah had forgiven everyone, then he left this world. And the symbols of that forgiveness are the drops of sweat which soaked this robe."

"This robe was given to me because the Prophet ﷺ wanted to tell me, 'O Uwais, I am passing to you the Divine Knowledge to clean the Nation after they make sins. You must pass that power to your successors, from me to you and from you to them.'"

And Sayyidina 'Ali said that Sayyidina Uwais al-Qarani said, "I didn't see the Prophet ﷺ physically, but in every moment, of every day, I was with him during his life. I received from him every matter of importance for his Nation. I am going to transmit this secret to the many successors and inheritors among Allah's saints. Without a physical connection but through a spiritual connection, they will receive the secret of the cleansing power and revive it in every century, until the Day of Judgment."

CREATION OF NUR MUHAMMAD ﷺ

Adapted from the book: Muhammad ﷺ - The Messenger of Islam
By Hajjah Amina Adil ق

The First Thing Allah ﷻ Created Was Nur Muhammad ﷺ

One day, Sayyidina 'Ali ؓ, *karam Allahu wajhahu* (may Allah ﷻ ennoble his face), asked, 'O Muhammad ﷺ, I pray you tell me what the Lord Almighty created before all other beings of creation. This was his blissful reply: 'Verily, before your Lord made any other thing, He created from His own Light the light of your Prophet ﷺ. And that Light rested, *haithu mashaAllah*, where Allah ﷻ willed it to rest. And at that time there existed aught else – not the Preserved Tablets, not the Pen, not Heaven nor Hell, not the Angelic Host, not the heavens nor the earth. There was no sun, no moon, no star, no *jinn* nor man, nor angel – none was as yet created, only this Light.

All Creation is From the Light of Prophet Muhammad ﷺ

1. The 'Arsh, Pen, and Preserved Tablet Were Created from Nur Muhammad ﷺ

Then Allah, glorified be He, by Divine decree willed the Creation to be. He therefore divided this Light of the Prophet ﷺ into four:

1. From the first part He created the Pen;
2. From the second the Tablets;
3. From the third the Divine Throne.

First the Pen Was Ordered to Write Kalima Tayyabah

Now it has become known that when the Lord had created the Tablets and the Pen, the Pen had on it one hundred nodes, the distance between two nodes being that of two years wayfaring. The Lord then commanded the Pen to write. And the Pen asked, 'Oh Lord, what shall I write?' The Lord said, 'Write: *La ilaha illAllah* (there is no deity but Allah).' 70,000 years, the pen wrote. Then ordered to write for 70,000 years *"Muhammadun RasulAllah"* (Muhammad ﷺ is the messenger of Allah).

Thereupon the Pen exclaimed, 'Oh, what a beautiful, great name is that of Muhammad that it is to mention in one with Thy hallowed Name, oh Lord.' The Lord then said, 'Oh Pen, mind your manners! This name is the name of My Beloved. From his light, I have created the Throne and the Pen and the Tablets. You too, are created from his light. Had it not been for him, I would not have created a single thing.'

When Allah Almighty ﷻ had spoken these words, the Pen split in two from awe of the Lord, and the place from which its speech issued became blocked. So that to this very day, its nib remains cloven in two and clogged up, so it does not write, which is the sign of this great divine secret. Therefore, let no one fail in veneration and honouring of the holy Prophet ﷺ, or become lax in following his shining example, or contravene the noble custom he has taught us.

Then the Pen Wrote Bismi Allah Ar Rahman Ar Raheem

Then again, the Lord commanded the Pen to write. 'What shall I write, oh Lord?' asked the Pen. The Lord of the Worlds then said, 'Write that which will be until the Day of Judgment!' Said the Pen, 'Oh Lord, with what shall I begin?' Said the Lord, 'With these words you shall commence: *Bismi Allah ar-Rahman ar-Raheem* (in the name of Allah, the Most Compassionate, the Most Merciful).' In perfect respect and deference, the Pen then set out to write these words upon the Tablets, and it completed writing them in 700 years.

When the Pen had written these words, the Almighty spoke and said, 'It has taken you seven hundred years to write three of My Names; the

Name of My Majesty, My Mercy and My Compassion. These blessed words I have made as a present to the nation of My Beloved Muhammad.' By My Majesty, I pledge that whenever any servant from this nation pronounces the words of the *Bismillah* with a pure intention, I will write seven hundred years of countless reward for this servant, and seven hundred years of sins I will erase.'

2. From The 4th Part of Nur Muhammad ﷺ Was Created: The Angels and The Divine Court

Now, the fourth part of this light of Prophet ﷺ I have again divided into four parts:

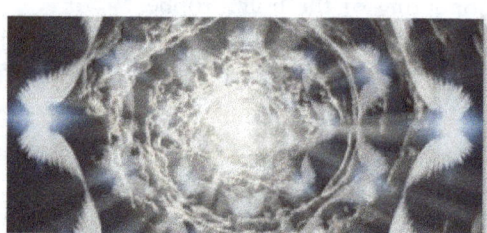

1. From one part I have created the Throne-bearing Angels *(hamalat al-'Arsh)*
2. From the second I have created the *Kursi*, the Divine court (the upper Heaven supporting the Divine Throne, the *'Arsh*);
3. From the third I created all the other heavenly angels;
4. And the fourth part I have partitioned once more into four.

3. The 4th Part was Divided Again to Create: The Skies, Earths, Jinn

1. From its first part, I made the skies;
2. From its second, I made the earths;
3. From its third, I made the jinn (unseen beings) and the fire;
4. Its fourth part I have again divided into four parts.

4. From the Last Section Was Created: The Light on Faces, Hearts, and Tongues of the Believers

1. From one part, I made the light upon the faces of the believers;

2. From the second part, I made the light within their hearts, imbuing them with Knowledge of the Divine;

3. From the third, the light upon their tongues which is the light of *Tawheed* (oneness);

4. From the fourth part, I made the different lights of the soul of Muhammad ﷺ

Description of the Soul of Sayyidina Muhammad ﷺ – Insan al Kamil

This lovely soul came into being 360 thousand years before the creation of the world. And it was shaped most beautifully and made of incomparable matter. Its head was made from guidance, its neck from humility, its eyes from modesty, its forehead from closeness (to Allah ﷻ), its mouth from patience, its tongue from truthfulness, its cheeks from love and admonition, its belly from abstemiousness and other worldliness, its feet and knees from following the straight path, and its noble heart was filled with mercy.

This much-honoured soul was taught with mercy and equipped with all manner of wondrous powers. It was given its message and its prophetic qualities were installed. Then the Crown of Divine Proximity was placed upon its blessed head, eminent and exalted above all else, embellished with Divine Pleasure and given the pure, holy name of *Habibullah* (Beloved of Allah ﷻ).

Allah ﷻ Dressed the Light of Sayyidina Muhammad ﷺ With Twelve Veils

After this, the Lord Almighty, blessed be He, created twelve Veils. Each month is a dress of Allah's ﷻ *Tajalli* (manifestation) on the Lights of Creation. (Starting from the first month Muharram).

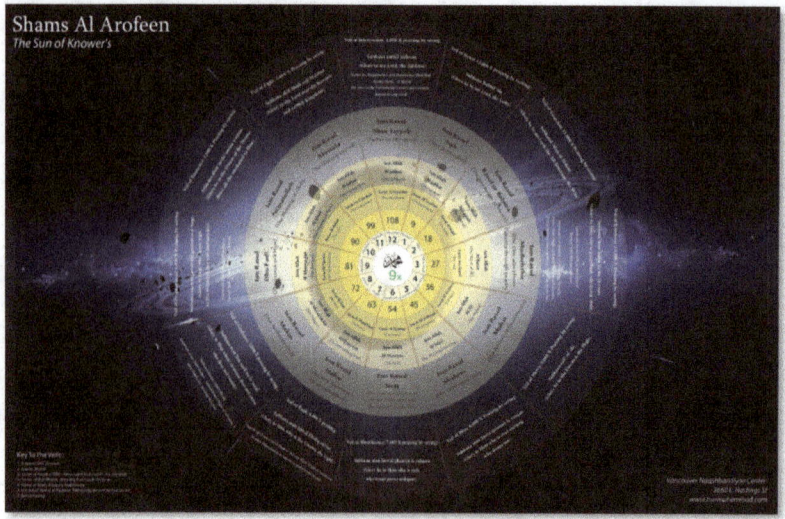

1. **Veil of Power** – The first of these was the Veil of Power within which the Prophet's ﷺ soul remained for twelve thousand years, reciting, *"Subhana rabbil 'ala"* (Glory be to my Lord, the Lofty). (Muharram)

2. **Veil of Grandeur** – The second was the Veil of Grandeur in which he was veiled for eleven thousand years, saying, *"Subhanal 'Alim al-Hakim"* (Glory be to my Lord, the All-Knowing, the Wise).

3. **Veil of Kindness** – Ten thousand years, he remained shrouded in the Veil of Kindness, saying, *"Subhana man huwa dayim, la yaqta"* (Glory to Him who is perpetual, who never ends).

4. **Veil of Mercy** – The fourth veil was the Veil of Mercy, therein the noble soul remained for nine thousand years, praising Allah ﷻ, saying, *"Subhana Rafi' al-'ala"* (Glory be to the Elevated, the High).

5. **Veil of Bliss** – The fifth veil was the Veil of Bliss, and therein he remained for eight thousand years, glorifying the Lord and saying, *"Subhana man huwa qayimun la yanam."* (Glory to Him who is ever existent, who sleeps not).

6. **Veil of Munificence** – The sixth veil was the Veil of Munificence; he remained enfolded in it for seven thousand years, praising, *"Subhana man huwal ghaniyu la yafqaru"* (Glory be to Him who is rich, who never grows indigent).

7. **Veil of Rank** – Then followed the seventh veil, the Veil of Rank. Here, the enlightened soul remained for six thousand years, praising the Lord and saying, *"Subhana man huwal Khaliq an-Nur"* (Glory to Him who is the Creator, the Light). (Rajab)

Creation of Nur Muhammad ﷺ

8. **Veil of Guidance** – Next, He veiled him in the eighth veil, the Veil of Guidance where he remained for five thousand years, praising Allah ﷻ and saying, *"Subhana man lam yazil wa la yazal"* (Glory to Him whose existence does not cease, who does not vanish).

9. **Veil of Prophethood** – Then followed the ninth veil, which was the Veil of Prophethood where he stayed for four thousand years, glorifying the Lord, *"Subhana man taqarrab bil qudrati wal-baqa"* (Glory to Him who draws nigh to His Omnipotence and Immortality). (Ramadan)

10. **Veil of Eminence** – Then came the Veil of Eminence, the tenth veil where this enlightened soul remained for three thousand years, reciting praises on the Creator of all Causes, saying, *"Subhana dhil 'arshi 'amma yasifun"* (Glory be to the Owner of the Throne, above all else attributed to Him).

11. **Veil of Light** – The eleventh veil was the Veil of Light. There he remained for two thousand years, praying, *"Subhana dhil Mulk wal Malakut"* (Glory to the Lord over the heavenly and earthly Kingdoms).

12. **Veil of Intercession** – The twelfth veil was the Veil of Intercession, and there he remained for one thousand years, saying, *"Subhana Rabbil 'azheem"* (Glory to my Lord, the Sublime). (Dhul Hijjah)

The Blessed Soul of Habibullah ﷺ Gazed at Himself in the Mirror

Thereafter, the Lord created a tree which is known as the Tree of Certainty. This tree has four branches. He placed this blessed soul upon one of its branches, and it continued to praise Allah ﷻ for forty thousand years, saying, *"Allahu dhul-Jalali wal-Ikram."* (Allah ﷻ, Possessor of Might and of Kindness). After it had thus praised Him with many and varied praises, the Almighty ﷻ created a mirror, and He placed it so as to face the soul of *Habibullah* (Beloved of Allah), and commanded his soul to gaze into this mirror. The soul looked into the mirror and saw itself reflected as possessing the most comely and perfect form.

- He then recited five times, *"Shukran lillahi ta'ala"* (thanks be to Allah ﷻ, Exalted be He), and fell down in prostration before his Lord.

- He remained in each *sajda* (prostration) for one hundred years, saying, *"Subhanal 'Aliyyul 'Azheem, wa la yajhalu."* (Glory be to the High, the Sublime, who ignores nothing);

- *Subhanal Halim alladhi la yu'ajjalu.* (Glory be to the Mild One who hastens not);

- *Subhanal Jawad alladhi la yabkhalu.* (Glory be to the Generous who is unstinting).

Therefore, the Causer of all Being obliged the nation of Muhammad ﷺ to perform *sajda* (prostration) five times a day. These five prayers in the course of one day and night were a gift of honour to the nation of Muhammad ﷺ.

Nur Muhammad ﷺ Placed Inside a Misbah

Next, the Lord created a lamp of green emerald (Bible, Book of Revelations describes the Emerald Throne of the Heavenly King) from the Light and attached it to the tree by a chain of light. Then He placed the soul of Muhammad ﷺ inside the lamp.

اللَّهُ نُورُ السَّمَاوَاتِ وَالْأَرْضِ ۚ مَثَلُ نُورِهِ كَمِشْكَاةٍ فِيهَا مِصْبَاحٌ ۖ الْمِصْبَاحُ فِي زُجَاجَةٍ ۖ الزُّجَاجَةُ كَأَنَّهَا كَوْكَبٌ دُرِّيٌّ يُوقَدُ مِنْ شَجَرَةٍ مُبَارَكَةٍ زَيْتُونَةٍ لَا شَرْقِيَّةٍ وَلَا غَرْبِيَّةٍ يَكَادُ زَيْتُهَا يُضِيءُ وَلَوْ لَمْ تَمْسَسْهُ نَارٌ ۚ نُورٌ عَلَىٰ نُورٍ ۗ يَهْدِي اللَّهُ لِنُورِهِ مَنْ يَشَاءُ ۚ وَيَضْرِبُ اللَّهُ الْأَمْثَالَ لِلنَّاسِ ۗ وَاللَّهُ بِكُلِّ شَيْءٍ عَلِيمٌ ﴿٣٥﴾

24:35 – "Allahu noorus samawati wal ardi. mathalu noorehi kamishkatin feeha misbahun, almisbahu fee zujajatin, azzujajatu kaannaha kawkabun durriyyun yoqadu min shajaratim mubarakatin zaytoonatil la sharqiyyatin wa la gharbiyyatin yakadu zaytuha yudeeo wa law lam tamsashu narun. noorun 'ala noorin. yahdellahu linoorihi man yashao. Wa yadribullah ul amthala linnasi, wallahu bikulli shayin 'Aleem." (Surat An-Nur)

"Allah is the Light of the heavens and the earth. The Parable of His Light is as if there were a Niche and within it a Lamp: the Lamp enclosed in Glass: the glass as it were a brilliant star: Lit from a blessed Tree an Olive, neither of the east nor of the west, whose oil is well-nigh luminous, though fire scarce touched it: Light upon Light! Allah guides whom He will to His Light: Allah present examples for the people: and Allah knows all things." (The Light, 24:35)

Zikr of Ar-Rahman and Creation of All Prophets From Nur Muhammad ﷺ

And commanded it to praise Him with the Most Beautiful Names *(Asma ul-Husna)*. This it did, and it began to recite each one of the Names for one thousand years. When it reached the name *ar-Rahman* (the Most Compassionate), the gaze of mercy fell upon it, and the soul began to sweat from modesty. Drops of sweat fell from it, as many as there were to be prophets and messengers, each drop of rose-flavoured sweat turning into the soul of a prophet. They all assembled around that lamp in the tree, and the Almighty ﷻ addressed the soul of the Prophet Muhammad ﷺ, 'See here this multitude of prophets whom I have created from the pearl-like drops of your sweat.' Obeying this command, he gazed upon them.

The Covenant of All Prophets to Believe in RasulAllah ﷺ

And as the light of the eye enfolds the object, so the souls of all these prophets were suddenly engulfed in the light of Muhammad ﷺ and they cried, 'Oh Lord, who has wrapped us in light?' The Lord answered them, 'This is the light of My Beloved Muhammad ﷺ, and if you will believe in him and confirm his prophetic message, I will grant you the

honour of prophethood.' Thereupon, all the souls of the prophets declared their belief in his prophethood, and the Lord said, 'I bear

Creation of Nur Muhammad ﷺ

witness to your acknowledgment,' and they all assented. As it is declared in the Holy Qur'an:

وَإِذْ أَخَذَ اللَّهُ مِيثَاقَ النَّبِيِّينَ لَمَا آتَيْتُكُم مِّن كِتَابٍ وَحِكْمَةٍ ثُمَّ جَاءَكُمْ رَسُولٌ مُّصَدِّقٌ لِّمَا مَعَكُمْ لَتُؤْمِنُنَّ بِهِ وَلَتَنصُرُنَّهُ ۚ قَالَ أَأَقْرَرْتُمْ وَأَخَذْتُمْ عَلَىٰ ذَٰلِكُمْ إِصْرِي ۖ قَالُوا أَقْرَرْنَا ۚ قَالَ فَاشْهَدُوا وَأَنَا مَعَكُم مِّنَ الشَّاهِدِينَ ﴿٨١﴾

3:81 – "Wa iz akhazal laahu meesaaqan Nabiyyeena lamaaa aataitukum min Kitaabinw wa Hikmatin summa jaaa'akum Rasulum musaddiqul limaa ma'akum latu'minunna bihee wa latansurunnah; qaala 'aaqrartum wa akhaztum alaa zaalikum isree qaalooo aqrarnaa; qaala fashhadoo wa ana ma'akum minash shaahideen"
(Surat Al-Imran)

"Behold! Allah took the covenant of the prophets, saying: 'I give you a Book and Wisdom; then comes to you a messenger, confirming what is with you; do ye believe in him and render him help.' Allah said: 'Do ye agree, and take this my Covenant as binding on you?' They said: 'We agree.' He said: 'Then bear witness, and I am with you among the witnesses.'" (The Family of Imran, 3:81)

From the Pearls of Sweat of RasulAllah ﷺ, Creation Came to Existence

Then this pure, holy soul (of Prophet Muhammad ﷺ) took up its recital of the Most Beautiful Names again. When it came to the name *al-Qahhar* (The Subduer) its head began to sweat once more from the intensity of His Divine Majesty and Awe. And from these beads of sweat, the Almighty ﷻ the souls of the blessed angels.

- From the sweat on his ﷺ face, the Almighty created the Throne and the Divine Court, the Tablets and the Pen, the sun, the moon and the stars.

- From the sweat of his chest, He created the scholars, the martyrs and the righteous believers.

- From the sweat on his back were made the *Bayt al-Ma'mur* (the heavenly house) (Qur'an 52:4), the *Kabatullah* (the Ka'bah), and the *Bayt al-Muqaddas* (the sanctified house, Haram in Jerusalem), and the *Rawda-e-Mutahhara* (the purified resting Place of the Holy Prophet ﷺ at Madina), as well as all other mosques in the world.

- From the sweat on his brows were made the souls of all the believers, and;

- From the sweat of his lower back (the coccyx) were made the souls of all the unbelievers, fire worshippers, and idolaters.

- From the sweat of his feet was made all the ground from east to west, and all that is within it.

Sayyidina Muhammad ﷺ is Abu Arwah – The Father of the Souls

From every drop of sweat, the soul of one believer or unbeliever was created. That is the reason the holy Prophet ﷺ is referred to as *"Abu Arwah,"* Father of Souls. All these souls gathered round the soul of Muhammad ﷺ, circling round him with praise and glorification for one thousand years.

Creation of Nur Muhammad ﷺ

قَالَ اِبْنُ عَرَبِيٍّ: أَصْلُ الْأَرْوَاحَ: هُوَ رُوْحُ مُحَمَّدْ ﷺ فَهُوَ أَوَّلَ الْأَبَاءِ رُوحاً

Qala Ibn 'Arabi: "Aslul arwaha: Huwa rohu Muhammad ﷺ, fahuwa awwalal aabayi rohan."

Imam Ibn Arabi said: *"The essence of all souls is the soul of Prophet Muhammad ﷺ, he is the first father of souls."*

The Souls Gazed to the Soul of Sayyidina Muhammad ﷺ

Then the Lord commanded these souls to look at the soul of Sayyidina Muhammad ﷺ. The souls all obeyed.

Who Gazed Upon His Holy Face?

- Now, those among them whose gaze fell upon his head were destined to become kings and heads of state in this world.

- Those who gazed at his forehead became just chiefs.

- Those who gazed at his eyes would become hafiz (one who memorizes) of the Word of Allah ﷻ (Qur'an).

- Those who saw his eyebrows became painters and artists.

- Those who saw his ears were to be of those who accept admonition and advice.

- Those who saw his blessed cheeks became performers of good and reasonable works.

- Those who saw his face became judges and perfumers, and

- Those who saw his blessed lips became ministers.

- Whoever saw his mouth was to be of those who fast much.

- Whoever looked at his teeth would be of comely appearance, and

- Whoever saw his tongue was to become the ambassador of kings.

- Whoever saw his blessed throat was to become a preacher and muezzin (one who calls to prayer).

- Whoever looked at his beard was to become a fighter in the way of Allah ﷻ.

Who Gazed Upon His Holy Hands?

- Whoever looked at his upper arms was to become an archer or a diver in the sea, and

- Whoever saw his neck became a merchant and a trader.

- Whoever saw his right hand became a leader, and who saw his left hand became a dispenser (who holds the scales and measures out provisions).

- Whoever looked at the palms of his hands became a generous person;

- Whoever looked at the backs of his hands became a miser.

- Whoever saw the inside of his right hand became a painter;

- Who saw the fingertips of his right hand was to be a calligrapher, and

- Who saw the tips of his left hand would be an ironworker.

Who Gazed Upon His Holy Body?

- Whoever saw his blessed chest would be of the learned, ascetic and scholarly.

- Whoever saw his back would be a humble person and obeying the laws of the *Shari'ah* (Divine Law).

- Whoever saw his blessed sides would be a warrior.

- Whoever looked at his belly would be of the contented ones, and

- Whoever looked at his right knee would be of those who perform *ruku* (bowing) and *sujud* (prostration)

- Whoever looked at his blessed feet became a hunter, and

- Who saw the bottom of his soles became one of those who take to the road.

- Who saw his shadow were to become singers and *saz* (lute/instrument) players.

All those who looked but saw nothing were to become unbelievers, fire worshippers and idolaters. Those who didn't look at all were to become those who would declare themselves to be gods, such as Nimrod, Pharoah and his like.

All the Waiting Souls Lined Up in Four Rows

In the first row stood the souls of the prophets and messengers, on whom be peace; in the second row were placed the souls of the holy saints, the Friends of God; in the third row stood the souls of the believing men and women; in the fourth row stood the souls of the unbelievers. All these souls remained in the world of spirits in the presence of Allah Almighty until their time had come to be sent into the material world.

No one but Allah Almighty knows how much time elapsed from the time of the creation of the Prophet Muhammad's blessed soul to his descent from the spiritual world into his physical form.

When Was Sayyidina Jibreel Created?

It is narrated that the holy Prophet Muhammad asked the angel Jibreel, 'How long is it since you were created?' The angel answered, 'Oh *RasulAllah*, I don't know the number of years, all I know is that every seventy thousand years a tremendous light shines forth from behind the Canopy of the Divine Throne. Since the time of my creation this light has appeared twelve thousand times.'

Creation of Nur Muhammad ﷺ

'Do you know what this light is?' asked Sayyidina Muhammad ﷺ.

'No, I don't know,' said the angel.

'It is the light of my soul in the world of the spirit,' replied the holy Prophet ﷺ. Consider then, how immense a number it must be if 70,000 is multiplied by 12,000!

Subhana rabbika rabbal 'izzati 'amma yasifoon, wa salaamun 'alal mursaleen, walhamdulillahi rabbil 'aalameen. Bi hurmati Muhammad al-Mustafa wa bi siri Surat al-Fatiha.

SECRETS OF THE NAME MUHAMMAD ﷺ
MEEM, HA, MEEM, DAAL

Every Reality Lies in La Ilaha IllAllah Muhammadun RasulAllah ﷺ

Alhamdulillah, in the holy month of Rabi al-Awwal, in the holy month of *Mawlid an Nabi* (celebration of Prophet's ﷺ birth), it means who knows himself. Every holy *hadith* has an ocean of realities. And Mawlana Shaykh teaches, always a reminder for myself, that who knows himself will know his Lord.

مَنْ عَرَفَ نَفْسَهُ فَقَدْ عَرَفَ رَبَّهُ

"*Man 'arafa nafsahu faqad 'arafa Rabbahu*"

"*Who knows himself, knows his Lord.*" Prophet Muhammad (pbuh)

As soon as we take the path of knowing the self that where I come from? What's my reality? What's my purpose in life so that I can find that reality? And they begin to teach us that every reality, its core is in *la ilaha illAllah Muhammadun RasulAllah* ﷺ.

لَا إِلَهَ إِلاَّ اللهُ مُحَمَّدًا رَسُولُ الله

"*La ilaha illAllahu Muhammadun RasulAllah.*"

"There is no deity but Allah, Prophet Muhammad is the messenger of Allah."

Every reality is born from that reality. That, that is where the two rivers meet. That is where Nabi Musa ﷺ was seeking his *ma'rifah* (gnosticism). That, 'I will not stop, in all my life until I reach that point at where the two rivers meet.'

وَإِذْ قَالَ مُوسَىٰ لِفَتَاهُ لَا أَبْرَحُ حَتَّىٰ أَبْلُغَ مَجْمَعَ الْبَحْرَيْنِ أَوْ أَمْضِيَ حُقُبًا ﴿٦٠﴾

18:60 – *"Wa idh qala Mosa lefatahu laa abrahu hatta ablugha majma'a albahrayni aw amdiya huquba."* (Surat Al-Kahf)

"Behold, Moses said to his attendant, I will not give up until I reach the junction of the two seas or (until) I spend years and years in travel." (The Cave, 18:60)

And *alhamdulillah, Muhammadun RasulAllah* ﷺ is a river and the reality of *la ilaha illAllah* is a huge river of the Divinely Presence where it comes in *la* is the reality of the opening of every reality.

Prophet Muhammad ﷺ is From Allah's ﷻ Light

The story of creation begins from *Bismillahir Rahmanir Raheem*. But Prophet ﷺ describes that, 'I was created from the light of Allah ﷻ and all creation created from My Holy Light.'

قَالَ رَسُولُ اللهِ صَلَّى اللهُ عَلَيْهِ وَسَلَّمَ: "أَنَا مِنَ اللهِ ، وَالْمُؤْمِنُونَ مِنِّي" (حديث مرفوع)

Qala Rasulullahi ﷺ: *"Anna minAllahi, wal muminoona minni."*

The Messenger of Allah, Prophet Muhammad (pbuh) said:" I am from Allah, and the believers are from me." (Hadith Marfo')

For us to understand the reality of that light, that what is Allah ﷻ granting to this holy name of Muhammad ﷺ? That, in understanding the *huroof* and understanding these words, we understand what Allah ﷻ is dressing us with.

Everything is Based on Hamd (Praise)

That everything is based on *hamd*. Everything is based on praise. We  only now know scientifically there must be a sound. That sound produces an energy. That energy produces a light. That light produces a form. It means that everything in creation, its origin is the sound. That's why all the holy books described was the word of God came first. It means the *hamd* and praise, "*Yusabbihu bihamdi.*" 'For verily everything exists within the *hamd* (praise).'

تُسَبِّحُ لَهُ السَّمَاوَاتُ السَّبْعُ وَالْأَرْضُ وَمَن فِيهِنَّ ۚ وَإِن مِّن شَيْءٍ إِلَّا يُسَبِّحُ بِحَمْدِهِ وَلَٰكِن لَّا تَفْقَهُونَ تَسْبِيحَهُمْ ۗ إِنَّهُ كَانَ حَلِيمًا غَفُورًا ﴿٤٤﴾

17:44 – "*Tusabbihu lahus samawatus sab'u wal ardu wa man fee hinna wa in min shayin illa yusabbihu bihamdihi wa lakin la tafqahoona tasbeehahum innahu kana haleeman ghafoora.*" (Surat Al-Isra)

"The seven heavens and the earth and whatever is in them exalt [praises] Him. And there is not a thing except that it exalts [Allah] by His praise, but you do not understand their [way of] exalting. Indeed, He is ever Forbearing and Forgiving." (The Night Journey, 17:44)

La Ilaha IllAllah is Nothing But Allah

To understand the greatness of Muhammad, the *meem, ha, meem, daal*. What Allah wants us to understand is that we have to be from the reality of *la ilaha illAllah Muhammadun RasulAllah*. And *awliyaullah* (saints) come into our lives that you are not in *la ilaha illAllah*. It means that we first clarify that there is no way that you are in the reality of *la ilaha illAllah*.

La ilaha illAllah means, no, nothing but Allah. It would be a *sharik*, it would be a partner. It would be breathing and taking the space, sharing the form of that reality which is impossible. So then they clarify that you are not in *la ilaha illAllah*. *La ilaha illAllah*, is a very clear phrase; nothing but Allah.

We Come From Bahrul Muheet (All-Encompassing Ocean)

So where are we from, *ya Rabbi*? What ocean do we come from and what ocean are we returning to? Because if I don't know myself, I don't understand what my Lord wanted me to understand. He said, 'No, you are from the ocean of *Muhammadun RasulAllah*.'

Then they begin to explain that this *meem* of Sayyidina Muhammad is an all-encompassing circle of creation. It's a *Bahrul Muheet*, that within that *meem*, all creation is inside that, like a sun. What do you get from the example of a sun is that it's a source like a star? It's a source of power. It's not Allah, but it has an eternal flame. It's not of the east and not of the west and producing a light of its own. Light upon light! That's not *sharik*, Allah ﷻ saying, 'I'm not the sun. That's all My creation. I am the *Izzah* and the Power of that. That sun exists within this ocean of creation.' That's why when we begin to study the creation of *Nurul Muhammadi* ﷺ, Allah ﷻ took from His Divinely Light and brought the soul of Prophet ﷺ.

اللَّهُ نُورُ السَّمَاوَاتِ وَالْأَرْضِ ۚ مَثَلُ نُورِهِ كَمِشْكَاةٍ فِيهَا مِصْبَاحٌ ۖ الْمِصْبَاحُ فِي زُجَاجَةٍ ۖ الزُّجَاجَةُ كَأَنَّهَا كَوْكَبٌ دُرِّيٌّ ... يَكَادُ زَيْتُهَا يُضِيءُ وَلَوْ لَمْ تَمْسَسْهُ نَارٌ ۚ نُّورٌ عَلَىٰ نُورٍ ... ﴿٣٥﴾

24:35 – "Allahu noorus samawati wal ardi. mathalu noorehi kamishkatin feeha misbahun, almisbahu fee zujajatin, azzujajatu kaannaha kawkabun durriyyun ... yakadu zaytuha yudee o wa law lam tamsashu naarun. noorun 'ala noorin..." (Surat An-Nur)

"Allah is the Light of the heavens and the earth. The Parable of His Light is as if there were a Niche and within it a Lamp: the Lamp enclosed in Glass: the glass as it were a brilliant star: ... though fire scarce touched it: Light upon Light!..." (The Light, 24:35)

Everything Comes From the Ocean of Hamd

From the light of Prophet ﷺ, everything is born. *Malaika* (angels) are from the light, *Nur Muhammadi* ﷺ, Ka'bah from *Nur Muhammadi* ﷺ, the Throne, *'Arsh ar-Rahman*, is from *Nur Muhammadi* ﷺ, otherwise where is it from, *la ilaha illAllah*? This means every creation; every paradise is within this ocean. Every *malaika* (angels) because  they have the *meem*. Meem is, do you see the big *meem* here? *Malaika* (angels) because they are from this ocean. *Baitul Mamur*, the house in the Divinely Presence, from this ocean. Ka'bah? From this ocean. *Insan* (human being)? From this ocean. Prophets? From this ocean. What other creation are we missing? Everything from this ocean!

So when Allah ﷻ begins to teach, 'This ocean is what you should be understanding and studying.' This is the ocean of *hamd* and praise. This is the ocean in which praises Allah ﷻ. The only praise Allah ﷻ wants is the praise of Sayyidina Muhammad ﷺ. The only praise that Allah ﷻ cares for is the praising of Prophet ﷺ on Divinely Presence. So he is *Liwal Hamd*, the Flag of Praise (one of the names of Prophet Muhammad ﷺ). That Prophet ﷺ praises Allah ﷻ, Prophet's ﷺ *zikr* of *la ilaha illAllah*. That is the *zikr* that Allah ﷻ is interested in. Everything else is a much lesser reality.

Each Letter in Hamd is Symbolic

	حمد	
	Hamd	
د	م	ح
Daal	Meem	Ha
دلائل الخيرات	محمداً	حياة
Dalail al Khayrat (Best of Guides for Creation)	Muhammadan ﷺ (Muhammadan Realities ﷺ)	Hayat (Ever-Living)

*Note: Please read English from right to left to coincide with Arabic.

Then Allah ﷻ begins to teach that because of that *hamd*, that is dressing the Prophet ﷺ with that this is *daal* of guidance, the *daleel* (guide) for all of the *dawam* (continuity), all of creation. This *meem* is the Muhammadan reality. This is the *ha* of *hayat* (life) and the ocean of *hayat*. Everything is alive in that ocean. Allah ﷻ dressed it from its *hayat* (life). In the *meem*, everything is under that *mulk* and the kingship of this *Malik* (King). This *daal* is the guide for all creation. *Dalail Khayrat*, the best of guidance. When we understand this is the ocean of power, this is the ocean of all realities. From that sound, energy is coming out. That's how creation is coming. From that energy, light is coming.

Our Atomic Reality Consists of Light

So when they study the atomic reality and the atoms and molecules, they understood. It's a sound, what they call string theory. From its sound, it produces an energy. From its energy, it's producing a light. That which Allah ﷻ gives a light, it manifests; that which yet not understood by us, they call dark matter. Then from the light, we're given a form.

So it means then in our atomic reality, we're just light. You see yourself with a form, it's all an illusion. But this is all the ocean of *hamd*. *Hamd*, because of that and because of Allah's ﷻ love, it's Muhammad ﷺ. So the *meem* is the ocean of *muheet* that is all-encompassing. Inside the ocean, the nucleus where they want us to start to make our *mi'raj* (ascension), you're making your *mi'raj*, you're making your *ma'rifah* (gnosticism) towards the center. But you are never going to know *la ilaha illAllah*. So in *tafakkur* and contemplation, don't contemplate Allah ﷻ.

لا تَتَفَكَّرُوا فِي ذَاتِ اللهِ.

"*La tatafakkaru fi zatillah.*"

"*Do not contemplate upon the Essence (of God).*"

Secrets of the Name Muhammad ﷺ – Meem, Ha, Meem, Daal

Don't ask where Allah ﷻ comes from, where Allah ﷻ is, *astaghfirullah*, this takes you out of belief. It's not for creation to know who the Creator and where the Creator and when the Creator, this takes us out of belief. But what Prophet ﷺ contemplates is the best of creation. What's the best of creation? Sayyidina Muhammad ﷺ!

Our Salah is in the Form of the Name of Sayyidina Ahmad ﷺ

So *awliyaullah* (saints) begin to teach us that this *meem* is the key of all realities. That's why they wear a turban. The turban is the *meem*. The *meem* is the turban. Your *sajda* (prostration) is in the form of the *meem*. Your belly, your head goes down. The secret between you and other nations is your *meem*. So what Allah ﷻ wanted? Wear your turban upon your head, wear the *meem* of Sayyidina Muhammad ﷺ that you are

Muhammadiyoon. You make a *sajda*, prostration because this is your head, right? This is your legs, your head is in here (pointing to the *sajda*), this is your belly. When it goes down, it's forming the *meem*. So the secret of your reality is in this *meem*.

Your *salah* (prayer) is in the name of Sayyidina Muhammad ﷺ. You stand, it's *alif*. Your *ruku*, it's the *ha*. The secret of your reality is in this *meem*. Your *salah* (prayer) is in the name of Sayyidina Muhammad ﷺ. In his name in heaven, Ahmad. That Allah ﷻ teaching that, 'Come to Me. Even when you come to Me, you are making the form of Sayyidina Ahmad *(alayhi salatu salaam)*, dressing from these realities because you are from this ocean, and this reality.' You stand is *alif*. Your *ruku* is the *ha*. Your *sajda* (prostration) is the *meem*. Your *attahiyat* is the *daal*. You are sitting on your knees.

Allah's ﷻ Alif Turns Hamd to Ahmad

They begin to teach this is the ocean of *hamd* and praise. So much praising upon the Divine, so much praising upon the Divine that Prophet's ﷺ hadith that, '*Ya Rabbi, ya Allah,*' that, 'nothing can praise You as You deserve to be praised.'

So when the Holy Qur'an reveals, *InnAllaha wa malaikatahu yusalluna 'alan Nabiyi* ﷺ, it means Allah ﷻ gave this an *alif*. (*Alif* beside the *lillah* becomes Allah ﷻ).

إِنَّ اللَّهَ وَمَلَائِكَتَهُ يُصَلُّونَ عَلَى النَّبِيِّ يَا أَيُّهَا الَّذِينَ آمَنُوا صَلُّوا عَلَيْهِ وَسَلِّمُوا تَسْلِيمًا ﴿٥٦﴾

33:56 – "InnAllaha wa malaikatahu yusalluna 'alan Nabiyi yaa ayyuhal ladhina aamanu sallu 'alayhi wa sallimu taslima." (Surat Al-Ahzab)

"*Allah and His angels send blessings upon the Prophet [Muhammad (pbuh)]: O you that believe! Send your blessings upon him, and salute him with all respect.*" *(The Combined Forces, 33:56)*

Allah ﷻ is giving from His *Alif* to Sayyidina Ahmad ﷺ (the *Alif* beside *Hamd* becomes Ahmad). It is the nucleus of this circle of creation.

The Real Hamd of Abd Allah is the Hamd of Sayyidina Muhammad ﷺ

The ocean is Muhammad and Sayyidina Muhammad ﷺ makes *zikr* of Allah ﷻ. Mine and your *zikr* of Allah ﷻ is imitated on the outside. It is not *wahid* (one), it is not in the ocean of witnessing and real *tawheed* (oneness). We have many different beliefs, many different submissions. We are imitating that *zikr* (remembrance). But the real *hamd* of the *Abd Allah* (servant of Allah ﷻ) is the *hamd* of Sayyidina Muhammad ﷺ. That *meem* and *hamd* is Muhammad ﷺ.

When Sayyidina Muhammad ﷺ is making *zikr* of *"Allah, Allah, Allah."* '*Ya Rabbi*, nobody can praise You, this power cannot be completed by creation. That give me from Your *Izzah*, give me from Your Might and Majesty. *Izzatu wa li Rasuli hi wa lil Mumineen*.'

وَلِلَّهِ الْعِزَّةُ وَلِرَسُولِهِ وَلِلْمُؤْمِنِينَ وَلَكِنَّ الْمُنَافِقِينَ لَا يَعْلَمُونَ ﴿٨﴾

63:8 – *"...Wa Lillahil 'izzatu wa li Rasuli hi wa lil Mumineena wa lakinnal munafiqeena la y'alamoon.."* (Surat Al-Munafiqoon)

"...And to Allah belongs [all] honor, and to His messenger, and to the believers, but the hypocrites do not know." (The Hypocrites, 63:8)

Izzatullah means Allah ﷻ gives the *alif*. That *izzah* is the source of Divinely Power. The *izzah* is the source of Divinely power. From that *alif* springs the fountain of power. That's why in paradises and in heavens is Sayyidina Ahmad ﷺ is the king. The king of praise is given the *alif* of Allah ﷻ. All might and majesty, all Divinely power, every Divinely light emanating from that reality because Allah ﷻ gives this *alif*.

When we understand that *alif*, we understand this reality that Allah ﷻ dressing this reality, Allah ﷻ blessing this reality.

Meem, Ha Symbolizes Malik al Hayat

محمد ﷺ	
Muhammad ﷺ *- MHMD*	
مد	مح
Meem Daal	*Meem Ha*
مَالِكُ الدُّنْيَا	مَالِكُ الْحَيَاة
Malik al Dunya (King of Manifested Worlds)	Malik al Hayat (King of Oceans of Eternity)

*Note: Please read English from right to left to coincide with Arabic.

Then when they want us to understand the name of Muhammad ﷺ. It is that *meem, ha* (first two letters) – *Malik al Hayat*. The *meem, ha* is closest to the paradise reality. The *meem, ha* is *Malik al Hayat*, that he is the King of the all *Hayat* (life) *(alayhis salatu salaam)* because everything is in his ocean. You cannot say Allah ﷻ is in the ocean of *hayat* because then you will be inferring that Allah ﷻ has a death, *astaghfirullah*. Allah ﷻ has no *hay* (life) and no *mayt* (dead). There is no life and no death for Allah ﷻ.

It is like the computer thinking that, 'Oh, at night the operator gets unplugged'. No, no, you have no way of understanding what the operator is doing. The computer is merely a computer. We are just Allah's ﷻ creation. And Allah ﷻ wants us to know that you are born and you die. But that doesn't mean the same for Allah ﷻ, *astaghfirullah* (seek forgiveness from Allah ﷻ). So, it means Allah ﷻ is far beyond this understanding. In this ocean of all universes, all paradises, all creation of *samawati wal ard* (heavens and earth) and beyond is in the ocean of *Muhammadun RasulAllah* ﷺ.

Muhammad is the 'Most Praised'

Then they want us to understand it is the ocean of praise. All testaments talk about that first came the word of God. Who is the word of God? *Hamd*. That is why he came as the Most *Hamd* (praised). Muhammad ﷺ. That he came saying that I am confirming your books. Your books said that, 'First came the word of God and the praise.' I am the praise of the Divinely Presence, that my name means praise – *Liwal al Hamd*. Surat al Hamd (first chapter of Qur'an, Al-Fatiha (the Opener)) is the description of that reality.

We Will Return To the Ocean of Hamd

Allah ﷻ is giving that the grant I gave you of Surat al Fatiha is that I give you Sayyidina Muhammad ﷺ as your *imam*, as your reality.

That you are from that ocean of reality and to that ocean you will return. It means that we manifest and we think we are something. Then in the end, when you lose your body, you return back into this ocean of *hamd* (praise). And that ocean of *hamd* returns back to Allah ﷻ because of *tawheed* (oneness).

$$ \text{إِنَّا لِلَّهِ وَإِنَّا إِلَيْهِ رَاجِعُونَ... ﴿١٥٦﴾} $$

2:156 – *"Inna lillahi wa inna ilayhi raji'oon."* (Surat Al-Baqarah)

"Indeed we belong to Allah, and indeed to Him we will return."
(The Cow, 2:156)

Everything has to be from *la ilaha illAllah Muhammadun RasulAllah*, since we're on the outside (of the *meem* ocean) we go back *Muhammadun RasulAllah* ﷺ and return back to *la ilaha illAllah*.

لَا إِلَهَ إِلاَّ اللهُ مُحَمَّدًا رَسُولُ الله

"*La ilaha illAllahu Muhammadun RasulAllah.*"

"*There is no deity but Allah, Prophet Muhammad is the messenger of Allah.*"

This means as you collapse and unfold, you have to return back the way you were unfolding. You don't go directly to Allah ﷻ. You go back into the ocean in which you came. You came from this ocean of praise; you came from this ocean of manifestation. Where this ocean ends is where the praise ends and moves into the Divinely Presence. This is time. This reality of light is timeless, the reality within the heart of Prophet of Allah ﷺ is timelessness where Allah's ﷻ *Irada*, Allah's ﷻ Will is in the heart of Prophet ﷺ.

Prophet Muhammad ﷺ is the Walking Holy Qur'an

Allah's ﷻ *Irada*, Allah's ﷻ Will is in the heart of Prophet ﷺ. That is why they describe Prophet ﷺ is Holy Qur'an, walking Holy Qur'an. Surah YaSeen is the heart of the Holy Qur'an. Surah YaSeen, Sayyidina YaSeen ﷺ is the name of Prophet Muhammad ﷺ and he is called *Habibullah* (beloved of Allah ﷻ). Sayyidina YaSeen ﷺ is *habibullah* because it's the heart of the Divinely Presence and the heart of Holy Qur'an. He is the *habib* (beloved) of Allah ﷻ.

Secrets of the Name Muhammad ﷺ – Meem, Ha, Meem, Daal

صَلَاةُ الله، سَلَامُ الله،   عَلَى طٰهَ رَسُوْلِ الله
صَلَاةُ الله، سَلَامُ الله،   عَلَى يٰسٓ حَبِيْبِ الله

Salatullah salamullah 'ala Taha Rasullillah
Salatullah salamullah 'ala Yasin Habibillah

Allah's praise, Allah's blessing Upon Taha, Messenger of Allah
Allah's praise, Allah's blessing Upon the YaSeen, Beloved of Allah

Sayyidina TaHa ﷺ is RasulAllah ﷺ. These are all the names of Prophet ﷺ. So the name of Sayyidina TaHa ﷺ is the messenger for all of creation. The name of Sayyidina YaSeen ﷺ is the heart for all creation. Because of this holy heart, Allah ﷻ is revealing His Divinely Book through the tongue of Prophet ﷺ. This *meem* is the source of Holy Qur'an emanating.

Holy Qur'an Came From the Heart of Sayyidina Muhammad ﷺ

Where did Holy Qur'an come from? It didn't come from here and there (outside the *meem* ocean). It came from the heart of Sayyidina Ahmad ﷺ. From the heart of the Prophet ﷺ, Allah ﷻ spoke. There is no direction for Allah ﷻ in a circle of creation. You cannot find Allah ﷻ. Then this creation would be holding Allah ﷻ. *La sharik* (no partner), *la shabeh*, nothing is like onto Allah ﷻ. Allah ﷻ says, 'You will never find Me. I am a hidden treasure.'

كُنْتُ كَنْزاً مخفيا فأحْبَبْتُ أَنْ أُعْرَفَ، فَخَلَقْتُ خَلْقاً فَعَرَّفْتُهم بِي فَعَرَفُوني

"Kuntu kanzan makhfiyya, fa ahbabtu an a'rafa, fa khalaqtu khalqan, fa 'arraftahum bi fa 'arafonee."

Allah (AJ) said, "I was a hidden Treasure then I desired to be known, so I created a creation to which I made Myself known; then they knew Me." (Hadith Qudsi)

My *Izzah*, My *Alif* (*Alif* of Allah ﷻ) is the power for Sayyidina Ahmad ﷺ (*alif* of Ahmad). Within the heart of Sayyidina Ahmad ﷺ is the *zikr* of Allah ﷻ. That *zikr* of Allah ﷻ is the source of *Qaf, wal Quranil Majeed*.

$$ق ۚ وَالْقُرْآنِ الْمَجِيدِ ﴿١﴾$$

50:1 – *"Qaf, wal Quranil Majeed." (Surat Qaf)*

"Qaf. By the honored Qur'an." (The Letter Qaf, 50:1)

It is the *qalb* (heart) of Divinely Presence. *Qaf wal Quranil Majeed*. Ba (of the word *qalb*) is the *Bahrul Qudra* (Ocean of Power). This is an ocean of power. *Meem, ha* was *Malik al Hayat*.

Meem, Daal Represents Malik al Dunya and Malik al Dawam

محمد ﷺ	
Muhammad ﷺ - MHMD	
مد	مح
Meem Daal	Meem Ha
مَالِكُ الدُّنْيَا	مَالِكُ الْحَيَاة
Malik al Dunya (King of Manifested Worlds)	Malik al Hayat (King of Oceans of Eternity)

*Note: Please read English from right to left to coincide with Arabic.

Meem, daal (second part of the name of Muhammad ﷺ is for *Malik al dunya* and *Malik al dawam*. That all of this *dunya* (material world), the *sultan* (king) of it is Sayyidina Muhammad ﷺ.

Secrets of the Name Muhammad ﷺ – Meem, Ha, Meem, Daal

Under *sifat ar-Rahman* (attribute of the Most Compassionate), all creation is manifesting. The created and manifested world is under *sifat ar-Rahman*. *Malik al Dunya* means Sayyidina Muhammad ﷺ is the King of that creation.

Sifat ar-Raheem (attribute of the Most Merciful) in which all the *lateef* or subtle creation is existing. *Baitul Mamur* (the Sacred house in Heaven), *malaika* (angels), everything of paradises and heavens is under *malik al hayat*. His *sultanate* (kingship) is complete. He is *sultan* of everything created in the world of form and sultan of everything in the world of light.

Prophet Muhammad ﷺ is the Only Authorized Representative of Allah ﷻ

And because of that *sultanate*, Allah ﷻ gave the *Izzah*, gave the *alif*. That you sit upon the chair and I sit upon your heart. It means this position of authority, the throne of authority, the throne of guidance – Allah ﷻ says, there is no chair that is going to hold me. *Mujasimiyun*, they say no, Allah ﷻ has a chair. He sits and in *Salatul Tahajjud* (night prayer), He comes down. *Astaghfirullah* (seek forgiveness from Allah ﷻ)! They give a form to the Creator.

Allah ﷻ says, 'No, no, you are very wrong. The chair represents My Authority. That direct yourself to My Authority. My authorized one, my only *khalif* (representative) is Sayyidina Muhammad ﷺ. All other *khalifs* (representatives) are below the representation of Prophet ﷺ. My only messenger, there is only one messenger of Allah ﷻ, it is Sayyidina Muhammad ﷺ.' There is only one message. All those who were delivering, they were within the *risalat* and messengership of Sayyidina Muhammad ﷺ. There can't be multiple signs going out. Allah ﷻ says, 'You have been given everything complete. You are *RasulAllah*. I gave you the guidance.'

Then the *Nur Muhammadi* ﷺ in their soul allow them to guide people, brought them the laws that were necessary for them for their time. Under the light of what? Sayyidina Muhammad ﷺ! *Malaika* are from Sayyidina Muhammad ﷺ. The Throne of the Divine is from light of *Nur Muhammad* ﷺ. That is why all the *naats* (praises on Muhammad ﷺ) you sing. When the people begin to understand what they are reciting and what they are praising when everything is from that light.

Paradise Lies Under Our Mother's Feet

Why Allah ﷻ asking you to respect your mother? Your paradise is under your mom's feet. Why? Because what kind of creature would you be that you don't respect the one who brought you into this world? You don't respect the one who brought you into this world. Allah ﷻ says you want paradise with that type of character? Respect the one who brought you. Kiss her hand. Be kind and gentle to her. She brought you through difficulty and with tremendous love, brought you into this world. You owe it to her. Prophet ﷺ says, 'Under the feet of your mother is the paradise.'

عَنْ أَنَسَ بْنِ مَالِكٍ رَضِيَ اللهُ عَنْهُ قَالَ رَسُولُ اللهِ صَلَّى اللهُ عَلَيْهِ وَ سَلَّمَ: "الْجَنَّةُ تَحْتَ أَقْدَامِ الْأُمَّهَاتِ"

'An Anas bin Maliku ﷺ, *Qala Rasulullahi* ﷺ *"Al Jannatu tahta aqdamil ummahati." (Sunan bin Maja)*

Secrets of the Name Muhammad ﷺ – Meem, Ha, Meem, Daal

Narrated by Annas bin Malik that the Messenger of Allah, Prophet Muhammad (pbuh) said: "Paradise is under the feet of the mothers."

What do you think from the reality of Sayyidina Muhammad ﷺ? When everything is from that light? You don't owe a love? You don't owe him an admiration and respect? *Ya Rabbi*, if not for the birth of this light, if not for the destiny of this light, if not for the creation of this light (within *meem* ocean), we are non-existent. You are *abtar*, you are cut off, you are nothing.

Our Light Came From Sayyidina Muhammad ﷺ

That when you don't remember or where you came from, what type of people are you? When you don't respect your mother, Allah ﷻ said to respect your mother. What you put now in *darajat* (level) of your mother and Sayyidina Muhammad ﷺ? Allah ﷻ says, your soul is coming from here (*meem* ocean) and then you choose not to remember this holy birthday? Your soul is coming from Prophet ﷺ. When you do something wrong and when they are oppressor to themselves, they have to come to you, *ya RasulAllah*.

وَلَوْ أَنَّهُمْ إِذ ظَّلَمُوا أَنفُسَهُمْ جَاءُوكَ فَاسْتَغْفَرُوا اللَّـهَ وَاسْتَغْفَرَ لَهُمُ الرَّسُولُ لَوَجَدُوا اللَّـهَ تَوَّابًا رَّحِيمًا ﴿٦٤﴾

4:64 – *"Wa law annahum idh zhalamoo anfusahum jaooka fastaghfaro Allaha wastaghfara lahumur Rasulu lawajado Allaha tawwaban raheema." (Surat An-Nisa)*

"And if, when they had wronged themselves, they had but come to you and asked forgiveness of Allah, and asked forgiveness of the messenger, they would have found Allah Forgiving, Merciful." (The Women, 4:64)

We Owe Our Love and Gratitude to Sayyidina Muhammad ﷺ

Why? Because you think you did a *gunah* (sin). What you think you do a sin against Allah ﷻ? Can you make a *gunah* (sin) against Allah ﷻ? How? Allah ﷻ says, 'I have nothing to do with this creation. You didn't do anything against Me. But you owe your forgiveness to the one whom you took your light from. You took your light from Sayyidina Muhammad ﷺ.' From the drops of sweat that all creation is coming to the existence. One drop of that is your soul! It has nothing to do with *shirk* (polytheism) because all of this worships *la ilaha illAllah*. Just like it's not *shirk* (polytheism) to have a mother. Your mother brought you to this world. You owe her respect. You owe her love and gratitude. Allah ﷻ said no difference. Then if you understand where your soul came from, you owe him love, you owe him gratitude, you owe him thankfulness.

Seek Forgiveness From the Source of Our Light

When you do something wrong, you are doing something wrong against the light that was given by Allah ﷻ to Prophet ﷺ. When we are making *astaghfirullah* (seeking forgiveness). 'Ya Rabbi, forgive me I am asking Prophet ﷺ that I am an oppressor to myself. I am coming to you, *Sayyidi ya RasulAllah* ﷺ, forgive me. Then you feel ashamed for the light he gave to us and what we're doing against it, what we do bad for it. Why we are not praising upon it? Why we are not cleansing and nourishing it? Then we begin to understand that no, I ask forgiveness from Allah ﷻ and ask forgiveness form Sayyidina Muhammad ﷺ. I am an oppressor to myself, *ya Sayyidi* (O my master), *ya RasulAllah* (O messenger of Allah ﷻ), represent us to Allah's ﷻ Divinely Presence, cleanse us and purify us. That if your *du'a* (supplication) goes, Allah ﷻ will accept that *du'a* and begin to clean.

Secrets of the Name Muhammad ﷺ – Meem, Ha, Meem, Daal

The Fountains of Kawthar Flow From Bismillahir Rahmanir Raheem

They teach that is *Malik al Hayat* and *Malik al Dunya*. This is the circle of creation (referring to the encompassing *meem* that has Allah ﷻ and Ahmad ﷺ written in it). *Meem, ha, meem* is *Muhamma*. *Muhamma* means the spinning ocean of power. *Muhamma*, it's the spinning ocean of power. It means everything in this ocean of creation is ocean of power.

Then when you want to look at *Bismillahir Rahmanir Raheem*, these were the fountains of *Kawthar*. These are the streams of paradise. From the *meem* of the *Bismi* is a fountain that is flowing in. From the *ha* of Allah ﷻ and *hidayat* is a fountain that is flowing in. From the *meem* of *Rahman* is a fountain that is flowing in. From the *meem* of *Raheem* is a fountain that is flowing in. All these fountains are flowing into the *meem* (the Ocean of existence). All these fountains are described that its pond is the pond of *Kawthar*. That is what Allah ﷻ describes in Surat al-Kawthar. I gave you the fountain of *Kawthar*. I gave you the fountain of abundance.

إِنَّا أَعْطَيْنَاكَ الْكَوْثَرَ ﴿١﴾

108:1 – "*Inna 'atayna kal kawthar.*" (Surat Al-Kawthar)

"*To thee (O Muhammad) we have granted the Fount (of Abundance).*" (The Abundance, 108:1)

It means that within this ocean, everything is manifesting. As much as Allah ﷻ is expanding this creation, as much as Allah ﷻ is giving. Allah ﷻ expands the creation and gives, expands the creation and gives. That is *katheer* (abundance). This fountain that I have given to you will never end! 'If all the trees were pens and all the known oceans were ink, My Words would never finish.'

وَلَوْ أَنَّمَا فِي الْأَرْضِ مِن شَجَرَةٍ أَقْلَامٌ وَالْبَحْرُ يَمُدُّهُ مِن بَعْدِهِ سَبْعَةُ أَبْحُرٍ مَّا نَفِدَتْ كَلِمَاتُ اللَّهِ ۗ إِنَّ اللَّهَ عَزِيزٌ حَكِيمٌ ﴿٢٧﴾

31:27 – "Wa law annamaa fil ardi min shajaratin aqlaamunw wal bahru yamudduhoo mim ba'dihee sab'atu abhurim maa nafidat Kalimaatul laah; innal laaha 'azeezun Hakeem." (Surat Al-Luqman)

"And if all the trees on earth were pens and the ocean (were ink), with seven oceans behind it to add to its (supply), yet would not the words of Allah be exhausted (in the writing): for Allah is Exalted in Power, full of Wisdom." (Luqman, 31:27)

That is the *izzah* (might) Allah ﷻ has given to the reality of *hamd*. What we know of the physical is Muhammad ﷺ. In the Divinely Presence, they begin to teach this is the heart of the direction, that you direct yourself is known as Sayyidina Ahmad ﷺ. That's why they write that in the *huroof* (letters). When they write that style of *huroof* (each letter is written separately), they want us to understand.

Secrets of the Name Muhammad ﷺ – Meem, Ha, Meem, Daal

Letters in the Name of Allah ﷻ

الله				
Allah ﷻ				
ه	ل	ل	ا	
Hey	Lam of Dunya	Lam of Akhirah	Alif
هداية	مُلك	مَلَكوت	عزّتُ الله
Hidayat (Guidance)	Mulk (Material World)	Malakut (Heavens)	'Izzatullah (Allah's ﷻ Might)

*Note: Please read English from right to left to coincide with Arabic.

This Allah ﷻ is in the heart of that reality (refers to *meem* of *hamd* in the circle). That is the source of that power. Mawlana Shaykh, *alhamdulillah*, gave a *tafsir* (interpretation) on the realities of *lam, lam, hey* (part of the name of Allah ﷻ). The *alif* is always floating.

This *hey* describes the *hey* of *hidayat*. This is the *lam* of *dunya* (material world). This is the *lam* of *akhirah* (hereafter). *Lam* represents a *mulk*, a manifestation, *mulk wa malakut* (earthly and heavenly realms). *Hey* is the *hidayat* (guidance) to take us to that reality. *Alif* is *Izzatullah* and the *alif* is always moving. You cannot grab the *alif* as Allah ﷻ moves the *alif*. That My Might and My Support is with Sayyidina Muhammad ﷺ.

Meem of Sayyidina Muhammad ﷺ is the Key to Achieving Maqamul Iman

We pray on this holy month that they take us deeper into that reality of importance of being the *Muhammadiyun*. This is the source of Islam because you cannot be Muslim without this *meem* (*meem* ocean). It means if you don't know the key – how can you be Muslim and have *iman* (faith) without the

meem of Sayyidina Muhammad ﷺ? You can't have faith and be *mu'min* or *mukhlis* and a *muhsin*. You can't be anything without the understanding of this *meem*.

To come to Islam and be a Muslim, you have to accept Sayyidina Muhammad ﷺ. To have *maqamul iman* (station of faith), and be *muhsin* (believer), you have to have the *meem* and you have to love Sayyidina Muhammad ﷺ more than you love yourself.

Every *maqam* (spiritual station) is based on the *maqam* of Sayyidina Muhammad ﷺ. You can't have Islam, Mawlana Shaykh is teaching, without accepting Sayyidina Muhammad ﷺ. It means you accept it; you got the *meem*, they give you the turban – you say *alhamdulillah*. You are now a Muslim. You got the *meem*, you got the turban, and you walk around and say I am *Muhammadiyun*.

Love Prophet ﷺ More Than Yourself

Maqamul iman – where is *maqamul iman*? *Maqamul iman* is here. *Maqamul iman* is the heart of this reality. What did Prophet ﷺ tell the Companions that you can't have faith until you love me more than you love yourself.

لَا يُؤْمِنُ أَحَدُكُمْ حَتَّى أَكُونَ أَحَبَّ إِلَيْهِ مِنْ وَالِدِهِ وَوَلَدِهِ وَالنَّاسِ أَجْمَعِينَ

"*La yuminu ahadukum hatta akona ahabba ilayhi min walidihi wa waladihi wan Nasi ajma'yeen.*"

"*None of you will have faith till he loves me more than his father, his children and all mankind.*" (Prophet Muhammad (pbuh))

Secrets of the Name Muhammad ﷺ – Meem, Ha, Meem, Daal

Why? Because if you love yourself, you'll always choose yourself. To love Sayyidina Muhammad ﷺ more than we love ourselves. Why? Because now you are in the center (inside the *meem* ocean).

Even being a *muhsin*, you have to love Prophet ﷺ more. *Mukhlis*, their whole life is how to serve Sayyidina Muhammad ﷺ. Don't worry about being *Abdullah* (servant of Allah ﷻ). That is a high title. That is the title that Allah ﷻ is giving to this reality (of Prophet ﷺ). This is My *Abd Allah. Abd Allah*! You are not *Abdullah*. That's why there is only one *AbdAllah*. It is humiliating to think that you are *Abd Allah*. You can't attach your name with Allah's ﷻ name.

But Allah ﷻ says that Prophet ﷺ can. He is *Rasul Allah*. He is *Habib Allah*. He is *Abd Allah*. You? *Ubaid. Ubaidullah*. Serve the one who serves Allah ﷻ. That is how we become *mukhlis. Mukhlis* is to serve Prophet ﷺ with our life, with our death, with our being, with our wealth, with everything to make Prophet ﷺ happy with us. If Prophet ﷺ is happy with us, no doubt Allah ﷻ is happy with us, *inshaAllah*.

Subhana rabbika rabbal 'izzati 'amma yasifoon, wa salaamun 'alal mursaleen, walhamdulillahi rabbil 'aalameen. Bi hurmati Muhammad al-Mustafa wa bi siri Surat al-Fatiha.

SULTANATE OF SAYYIDINA MUHAMMAD ﷺ AND THE NAQSHBANDI TAWEEZ

The Haq (Truth) Has Come

وَ قُلْ جَاءَالْحَقُّ وَزَهَقَ الْبَطِلُ، إِنَّ الْبَطِلَ كَانَ زَهُوقًا ﴿٨١﴾

17:81 – *"Wa qul jaa alhaqqu wa zahaqal baatil, innal batila kana zahoqa." (Surat Al-Isra)*

"And say, Truth has come, and falsehood has perished. Indeed falsehood, [by its nature], is ever perishing/ bound to perish."
(The Night Journey, 17:81)

Who Has Seen Prophet Muhammad ﷺ Has Seen Haq

Hadith of Prophet ﷺ is that, 'Who has seen me (Muhammad ﷺ) has seen the truth.'

قَالَ أَبُو قَتَادَةَ قَالَ رَسُولُ اللَّهِ ﷺ " مَنْ رَآنِي فَقَدْ رَأَىٰ الْحَقَّ
[متفق عليه البُخَارِي 6996، مُسْلِم 2267]

Qala Abu Qatadah qala Rasulullahi (saws): "Man ra aani, faqad ra'aa alHaq."

Abu Qatada reported that Allah's Messenger (pbuh) said: "Who has seen me, has seen the truth."
(Imam Al Bukhari 6996, Imam Muslim 2267)

Allah ﷻ Gives the Kingdom to Whom He Wills

قُلِ اللَّهُمَّ مَالِكَ الْمُلْكِ تُؤْتِي الْمُلْكَ مَن تَشَاءُ وَتَنزِعُ الْمُلْكَ مِمَّن تَشَاءُ ۖ وَتُعِزُّ مَن تَشَاءُ وَتُذِلُّ مَن تَشَاءُ ۖ بِيَدِكَ الْخَيْرُ ۖ إِنَّكَ عَلَىٰ كُلِّ شَيْءٍ قَدِيرٌ سُورَةُ آلِ عِمْرَان ﴿٢٦﴾

3:26 – "Qulillahumma Malikul mulki, tu'til mulka man tashaau wa tanzi'ul mulka mimman tasha'u, wa tu'izzu man tasha'u, wa tudhillu man tasha'u, bi yadikal khayr, innaka 'ala kulli shay'in qadir."
(Surat Ali-Imran)

"Say: O Allah, Master of the Kingdom, You give the Kingdom to whom You will, and You Take away the Kingdom from whom You will, You honor whome You will and You humble whom You will; in Your hand is [all] the good, Indeed, You are over all things Powerful."
(Family of Imran, 3:26)

The Taweez is a Top View of the Divine Court

The Divinely Throne and the Naqshbandi Taweez

- The Throne (al-'Arsh) is the Kingdom.
- The Pillars of the Throne are the Four Main Supports.

- Those brought near are the *muqarabeen* who circumambulate the Throne and Praise the King.

- The bearer of this heavenly seal proudly displays their love for the King of the Heavens and the Earth and seeks His Protection.

- Image in center *"Allah Haq"* is the hand of truth: four fingers and thumb with *ha*.

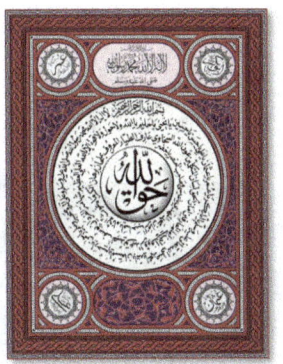

The Understanding of the Divine Court

Allah ﷻ is in The Heart of His Habib ﷺ Who Sits on the Throne

- Allah ﷻ can never be seen and nothing may encompass Allah ﷻ.

- Creation sits upon a Throne and Allah ﷻ sits upon his heart.

مَا وَسِعَنِيْ لَا سَمَائِيْ ولا اَرْضِيْ وَلَكِنْ وَسِعَنِيْ قَلْبِ عَبْدِيْ الْمُؤْمِنْ

"Maa wasi'anee laa Samayee, wa la ardee, laakin wasi'anee qalbi 'Abdee al Mu'min."

"Neither My Heavens nor My Earth can contain Me, but the heart of my Believing Servant."
(Hadith Qudsi conveyed by Prophet Muhammad (pbuh))

Prophet Muhammad ﷺ is the Eternal Messenger

That is why Prophet Muhammad ﷺ said, 'I was a *Nabi* before Adam عليه السلام was between water and clay.'

قَالَ رَسُولُ اللهِ صَلَّى اللهُ عَلَيْهِ وَسَلَّمَ:
"كُنْتُ نَبِيًّا وَآدَمُ بَيْنَ الْمَاءِ وَالطِّينِ"

Qala Rasulullahi ﷺ: *"Kuntu Nabiyan wa Adama baynal Maa e wat Teen."*

"I was a Prophet and Adam was between water and clay."
(Prophet Muhammad (pbuh))

He is teaching us that his eternal position in the Divine Presence is in the world of souls and light. This is a timeless dimension. He is the Messenger of Allah ﷻ. The messenger, the one who speaks on Allah's ﷻ behalf to all creation, eternally. Who is created before the physical creation of the form known as Adam عليه السلام. The Divine Kingdom was created first. The Divine Kingdom has no time! Time is only relevant to earthly life based on the sun, moon, and Earth.

Nothing Can Come Between Ahad and Sayyidina Ahmad ﷺ

Between Ahad ﷻ and Sayyidina Ahmad ﷺ, there is no created being between them.

فَكَانَ قَابَ قَوْسَيْنِ أَوْ أَدْنَىٰ ﴿٩﴾

53:9 – *"Fakana qaaba qawsayni aw adna." (Surat An-Najm)*

"And was at a distance of two bow lengths or nearer [to the Divine Presence]." (The Star, 53:9)

All heavenly beings must go to Sayyidina Muhammad ﷺ. He is the *shafi*, the intercessor. He hears Allah's ﷻ Holy Command, *"Qul."* Nothing in creation can carry the power in the *qaf* of *Qul*, except the Messenger of Allah ﷺ.

وَمَا كَانَ لِبَشَرٍ أَن يُكَلِّمَهُ اللَّهُ إِلَّا وَحْيًا أَوْ مِن وَرَاءِ حِجَابٍ أَوْ يُرْسِلَ رَسُولًا فَيُوحِيَ بِإِذْنِهِ مَا يَشَاءُ ۚ إِنَّهُ عَلِيٌّ حَكِيمٌ ﴿٥١﴾

42:51 – *"Wa maa kaana libasharin any yukallimahul laahu illaa wahyan aw minw waraaa'i hijaabin aw yursila Rasulan fa yoohiya bi iznihee maa yashaaa'; innahoo 'Aliyyun Hakeem."* (Surat Ash-Shura)

"It is not fitting for a man that Allah should speak to him except by inspiration, or from behind a veil, or by the sending of a messenger to reveal, with Allah's permission, what Allah wills: for He is Most High, Most Wise." (The Consultation, 42:51)

وَمَا يَنطِقُ عَنِ الْهَوَىٰ ﴿٣﴾ إِنْ هُوَ إِلَّا وَحْيٌ يُوحَىٰ ﴿٤﴾

53:3-4 – *"Wa ma yantiqu 'anil hawa. (3) In huwa illa wahyun yooha. (4)"* (Surat An-Najm)

"Nor does he (Prophet Muhammad (pbuh)) speak from [his own] desire. (3) He is not but a revelation revealed. (4)" (The Star, 53:3-4)

In Arabic the 'Arsh (Throne) Represents Kingdom

Know that in Arabic, 'the Throne' is a designation by which the kingdom is meant.

By: Shaykh Al-Akbar Sayyidina Ibn Arabi
(The Throne and its Angelic Inhabitants)

- Then Allah ﷻ brought into existence the pure darkness which is opposite this light, which is in the position of absolute non-existence, opposite absolute existence.

- When He brought it into existence, that light flowed onto it with an essential out flowing with the help of nature.

- So that light repaired its disarray and the body appeared which is designated as the Throne.

- Then the name the Rahman settled on it by the name, the Outwardly Manifest. That was the first of the world of creation to appear.

الرَّحْمَٰنُ عَلَى الْعَرْشِ اسْتَوَىٰ ﴿٥﴾

20:5 – "ArRahmanu 'alal 'arshi istawa." (Surat Taha)

"The Most Merciful [who is] above the Throne established." (Taha, 20:5)

The Angels Surrounding the Throne of Haq

- From that mixed light, which is like the light of dawn, He created the angels which encircle the seat. That is His words, 'You will see the angels encircling the Throne proclaiming the praise of their Lord.'

- They have no other occupation than to encircle the Throne, proclaiming His praise. We explained the creation of the universe in our book, 'Uqla al-Mustawfiz.' We have used the principles for this chapter.

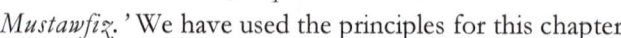

وَتَرَى الْمَلَائِكَةَ حَافِّينَ مِنْ حَوْلِ الْعَرْشِ يُسَبِّحُونَ بِحَمْدِ رَبِّهِمْ ۖ وَقُضِيَ بَيْنَهُم بِالْحَقِّ وَقِيلَ الْحَمْدُ لِلَّهِ رَبِّ الْعَالَمِينَ ﴿٧٥﴾

39:75 – *"Wa taral malaaa'ikata haaaffeena min hawlil 'Arshi yusabbihoona bihamdi Rabbihim wa qudiya bainahum bilhaqqi wa qeelal hamdu lillaahi Rabbil 'aalameen"* (Surat Az-Zumar)

"And thou wilt see the angels surrounding the Throne on all sides, singing Glory and Praise to their Lord. The Decision/judgement between them will be in truth/justice, and the cry (on all sides) will be, 'Praise be to Allah, the Lord of the Worlds!'" (The Troops, 39:75)

Understanding the Haq (Truth)

The Word Haq in Ilm Huroof (Knowledge of Letters)

حق	ق	ح
Haq	Qaf	Ha
١٠٨ =	١٠٠ +	٨
108 =	100 +	8

*Note: Please read English from right to left to coincide with Arabic.

- *Haq* (truth): Ha – 8, *Qaf* – 100 = *Haq* – 108
- 108th Surat is *Kawthar* (Abundance), Fountain of life and knowledge, source of *zamzam*.

How the Word Allah ﷻ Relates to Haq ﷻ

الله	ه	ل	ل	ا
Allah	Hey	Lam	Lam	Alif
٦٦ =	٥ +	٣٠ +	٣٠ +	١
66 =	5 +	30 +	30 +	1

*Note: Please read English from right to left to coincide with Arabic.

- *Kalima* Allah ﷻ in *abjad* adds up to 1 + 30 + 30 + 5 = 66
- 66th Name of Sayyidina Muhammad ﷺ in *Dalail al Khayrat* is *Haq* (the Truth)
- Allah's ﷻ Reflection in Divine Mirror is Sayyidina *Haq* ﷺ

Sayyidina Muhammad ﷺ is the Light and Reflection of the Haq

If Allah ﷻ cannot be seen, then His proofs and signs must be visible. The greatest of His signs is *Muhammadur RasulAllah* ﷺ. He is Allah's ﷻ Light and a reflection of the truth. Allah ﷻ in *abjad* value equals 66. The 66th name of Sayyidina Muhammad ﷺ is *Haq*! In Holy Qur'an, Surat al-Qalam, "*Khuluq Azeem*."

وَإِنَّكَ لَعَلَىٰ خُلُقٍ عَظِيمٍ ﴿٤﴾

68:4 – *"Wa innaka la'ala khuluqin 'azheem."* (Surat Al-Qalam)

"Truly, You (O Muhammad!) are of a magnificent character."
(The Pen, 68:4)

Four Known Things of Existence

By: Shaykh Al-Akbar Sayyidina Ibn Arabi

Know that known things are four:

- The Real *Al-Haqq* (truth) who is described with absolute existence because He is neither caused by anything nor the cause of anything.

- He is the Creator of causes and exists by His Essence from own His Essence. Knowledge of Him refers to knowledge of His existence, and His existence is not other than His essence. However, His Essence is not known, but the attributes ascribed to Him are known.

- This means the attributes of meanings, which are the attributes of perfection. Knowledge of the reality of the Essence is impossible since it is not known by either proof or logical demonstration and is untouched by definition. Allah  is not like anything and nothing is like Him.

- So, how can the one who is like things be like the One who resembles nothing and nothing resembles Him? Gnosis of Him is that, 'There is nothing like Him and Allah cautions you about Himself.' The *shari'ah* (Divine Law) includes the prohibition against reflection about the Essence of Allah. Reflect upon His Creation, best of Creation is *Muhammad RasulAllah* 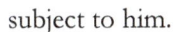.

Allah Subjected Heavens and Earth to Prophet Muhammad

Finally, there is the fourth known which is the man, Muhammad, the *khalif* (representative) appointed by Allah in this world which is subject to him.

Allah said, 'He has subjected to you (Muhammadan Kingdom) whatever is in the heavens and whatever is in the earth, all together, from Him.'

Sultanate of Sayyidina Muhammad ﷺ and the Naqshbandi Taweez

وَسَخَّرَ لَكُم مَّا فِي السَّمَاوَاتِ وَمَا فِي الْأَرْضِ جَمِيعاً مِّنْهُ إِنَّ فِي ذَلِكَ لَآيَاتٍ لَّقَوْمٍ يَتَفَكَّرُونَ ﴿١٣﴾

45:13 – *"Wa sakhkhara lakum ma fis Samawati wa ma fil Ardi jamee'an minhu, inna fee dhalika la ayatin liqawmin yatafakkaron." (Surat Al-Jathiya)*

"And He has subjected/gave the authority to you [*Sayyidina Mahmood (pbuh)*], as from Him, all that is in the heavens and on earth: Behold, in that are Signs indeed for those who reflect/Contemplate [Meditate]." *(The Crouching, 45:13)*

Sayyidina Muhammad ﷺ is the Truth and the Greatest Sign of Allah ﷻ

محمد ﷺ	
Muhammad ﷺ - MHMD	
مد	مح
Meem Daal	**Meem Ha**
مَالِكُ الدُّنْيَا	مَالِكُ الْحَيَاة
Malik al Dunya (King of Manifested Worlds)	**Malik al Hayat (King of Oceans of Eternity)**

*Note: Please read English from right to left to coincide with Arabic.

Now understands that seeking Allah ﷻ and pursuing *ma'rifah* (gnosticism). Allah ﷻ will not be seen. Allah's ﷻ greatest of signs is to be witnessed. When one arrives to the Divine Court, the Truth will be witnessed. That Truth is *Muhammad RasulAllah* ﷺ. *Malik al Hayat* (King of Oceans of Eternity), *Malik al Dunya* (King of Manifested World)

This Ayah is Upon the Entrance to the Presence of the King

This *ayah* (verse) is upon your entrance to the Presence of The King; enter from the door of truth and exit from the door of truth.

وَقُل رَّبِّ أَدْخِلْنِي مُدْخَلَ صِدْقٍ وَأَخْرِجْنِي مُخْرَجَ صِدْقٍ وَاجْعَل لِّي مِن لَّدُنكَ سُلْطَانًا نَّصِيرًا ﴿٨٠﴾

17:80 – *"Wa qul Rabbi adkhelni mudkhala Sidqin wa akhrejni mukhraja Sidqin waj'al li min ladunka Sultanan NaSeera." (Surat Al-Isra)*

"Say: O my Lord! Let my entry be by the Gate of Truth and Honour, and likewise my exit by the Gate of Truth and Honour; and grant me from Your Presence a Victorious King to aid (me)."
(The Night Journey, 17:80)

Subhana rabbika rabbal 'izzati 'amma yasifoon, wa salaamun 'alal mursaleen, walhamdulillahi rabbil 'aalameen. Bi hurmati Muhammad al-Mustafa wa bi siri Surat al-Fatiha.

The Crown of Creation

OPENING THE 7 POINTS OF THE HEAD A GATEWAY TO THE 9 POINTS OF THE BODY

Shaykh al-Kamil: The Complete Guide

Example of Complete Perfection – Look to Him to See Your Example

When God wants to manifest Himself, He looks at His creation. His first attention goes to human beings because they resemble him. Those who resemble Him the most among them are the saints; hence the Prophet ﷺ said of them, 'They remind you of the Divine.'

عَنْ أَبِي هُرَيْرَةَ رَضِيَ اللهُ عَنْهُ قَالَ: قَالَ رَسُولُ اللهِ ـ صَلَّى اللهُ عَلَيْهِ وَسَلَّمَ ـ: إِنَّ مِنْ عِبَادِ اللهِ عِبَادًا يَغْبِطُهُمُ الْأَنْبِيَاءُ وَالشُّهَدَاءُ.

قِيلَ: مِنْ هُمْ يَا رَسُولَ اللهِ، لَعَلَّنَا نَحْبُهُمْ؟

قَالَ: هُمْ قَوْمٌ تَحَابُّوا فِي اللهِ مِنْ غَيْرِ أَمْوَالٍ وَلَا أَنْسَابٍ. وُجُوهُهُمْ نُورٌ عَلَى مَنَابِرَ مِنْ نُورٍ. لَا يَخَافُونَ إِذَا خَافَ النَّاسُ، وَلَا يَحْزَنُونَ إِذَا حَزِنَ النَّاسُ. "ثُمَّ قَرَأَ:" أَلَا إِنَّ أَوْلِيَاءَ اللهِ لَاخَوْفٌ عَلَيْهِمْ وَلَا هُمْ يَحْزَنُونَ." (يُونُسَ، ٦٢)
[رَوَاهُ ابْنُ جَرِيرٍ وَغَيْرَهُ]

'An Abi Huraira (ra) qala: Qala Rasulullahi (saws): "Inna min 'ibadillahi 'ibadan yaghbituhumul Anbiyayi wash Shuhada a."

Qila: "Min hum ya Rasulullahi, la'allana nahbuhum?"

Opening the 7 Points of the Head
A Gateway to the 9 Points of the Body

Qala: "Hum qawmu tahabo fillahi man ghaire amwalin wa la ansabin. Wujuhahum noorun 'ala manabere man noorin. La yakhafona iza khafan nasu, wa la yahzunona iza haznan naas. "Thuma qara'a: "alaa inna Awliya Allahi la khawfun 'alayhim wa laa hum yahzunoon." (Surat Yunus 10:62) (Rawahu Ibnu Jaririn wa ghayrahu)

Narrated by Abi Huraira (ra) that, the Prophet (pbuh) said: "There are servants among Allah's servants who are envied by the prophets and the martyrs."

The Prophet's companions said: "Who are they, O' Messenger of Allah, we wish to receive their love."

The Prophet (pbuh) said: "They are those who love each other for the sake of Allah, not for money or family lineage and status. Their faces are full of lights, and they stand on a pulpit of light. They are not afraid when everyone else is, and they are not sad when everyone else is." Then the Prophet (pbuh) read: "No doubt, [for] the friends of Allah there is no fear, nor will they grieve" (Qur'an, Jonah 10:62)
(Based on the book of Ibn Jarir and others)

"We also pity you because human beings are unwilling to open themselves to attract the angelic power by which they reach the state of heavenly knowledge that is their inheritance. That makes us appear in your human form in varying shapes and degrees of light, in different places and to different ages of human life, to remind you that you have been honored with an angelic power and a divine likeness."

Keep the likeness! Use the angelic power! It shall elevate you to that luminous station without which God said, 'Verily, those for whom God did not appoint light, they will never inherit light!' and He said, 'Light upon light!'

وَمَن لَّمْ يَجْعَلِ اللَّهُ لَهُ نُورًا فَمَا لَهُ مِن نُورٍ ۚ ﴿٤٠﴾

24:40 – "… Wa mal lam yaj'a lillahu lahu noora famaa lahu min noor." (Surat An-Nur)

"…And he to whom Allah has not granted light – for him there is no light." (The Light, 24:40)

&

اللَّهُ نُورُ السَّمَاوَاتِ وَالْأَرْضِ ۚ مَثَلُ نُورِهِ كَمِشْكَاةٍ فِيهَا مِصْبَاحٌ ۖ الْمِصْبَاحُ فِي زُجَاجَةٍ ۖ الزُّجَاجَةُ كَأَنَّهَا كَوْكَبٌ دُرِّيٌّ … يَكَادُ زَيْتُهَا يُضِيءُ وَلَوْ لَمْ تَمْسَسْهُ نَارٌ ۚ نُّورٌ عَلَىٰ نُورٍ ۗ … ﴿٣٥﴾

24:35 – "Allahu noorus samawati wal ardi. mathalu noorehi kamishkatin feeha misbahun, almisbahu fee zujajatin, azzujajatu kaannaha kawkabun durriyyun … yakadu zaytuha yudeeo wa law lam tamsashu naarun. noorun 'ala noorin…" (Surat An-Nur)

"Allah is the Light of the heavens and the earth. The Parable of His Light is as if there were a Niche and within it a Lamp: the Lamp enclosed in Glass: the glass as it were a brilliant star: … though fire scarce touched it: Light upon Light!…" (The Light, 24:35)

Opening the 7 Points of the Head
A Gateway to the 9 Points of the Body

He declared that the light of the heart's vision must be connected with the light of angelic power, ensuring success and guidance to all human beings. That light shall then appear over the entire human realm like a rising sun and a rising moon over all of creation, without ever setting. The light of this power, at that time, will make every individual like a moon.

That is, a heavenly body that will reflect the original light for the rest of creation. By this light, this world will be preserved, the love of nature will rule the earth, and everyone will live in peace and love, swimming in the ocean of angelic beauty and harmony.

7 0 0 7

7 Eternal Attributes that Dress, 7 Noble Openings on the Crown of Creation are the Gateway to the 9 Sacred Points

The Crown of Creation is the Holy Head

The seeker must safeguard this grant from the Divine.

- 2 ears in which to hear with
- 2 eyes in which to see with

- 2 nostrils in which to breathe with
- 1 mouth/tongue in which to taste/speak with.

These are 7 blessed openings on human creation. Many recitations are in numbers of 7 for this reason.

The 5 senses are hear, see, touch, smell, taste. If guarded, these points are the opening for all your spiritual energies. If harmed, these will be the source of all miseries.

Images are ugly to show the extent of harm that is being done to this noble creation.

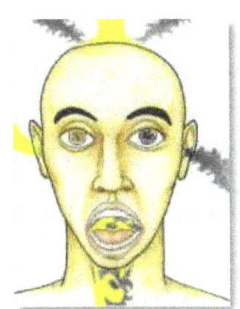

- Point of energy on crown
- Eyes: window to the soul
- Ears: door to the soul
- Nose: breath of mercy
- Mouth: tongue of truth

Protect Crown of the Head

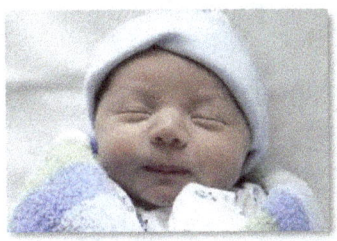

The head is soft when newborn, this is a source of great emanations of light and energy from the Divine. Safeguard this point to protect against negative energies that are trying to draw that energy away from you.

Protection for this Point

- Ablution and head cover or cap.
- During sleep try to sleep with a cap.
- Long hair takes away from men's spiritual energy.
- For women long hair increases energy.

وَلَقَدْ ذَرَأْنَا لِجَهَنَّمَ كَثِيرًا مِّنَ الْجِنِّ وَالْإِنسِ ۖ لَهُمْ قُلُوبٌ لَّا يَفْقَهُونَ بِهَا وَلَهُمْ أَعْيُنٌ لَّا يُبْصِرُونَ بِهَا وَلَهُمْ آذَانٌ لَّا يَسْمَعُونَ بِهَا ۚ أُولَٰئِكَ كَالْأَنْعَامِ بَلْ هُمْ أَضَلُّ ۚ أُولَٰئِكَ هُمُ الْغَافِلُونَ ﴿١٧٩﴾

7:179 – "Wa laqad zara'naa li jahannama kaseeram minal jinni wal insi lahum quloobul laa yafqahoona bihaa wa lahum a'yunul laa yubisiroona bihaa wa lahum aazaanul laa yasma'oona bihaa; ulaaa'ika kal an'aami bal hum adall; ulaaa'ika humul ghaafiloon."
(Surat Al-Ar'af)

"Many are the Jinn's and men we have made for Hell: They have hearts wherewith they understand not, eyes wherewith they see not, and ears wherewith they hear not. They are like cattle – nay more misguided: for they are heedless (of warning)." (The Heights, 7:179)

Openings 1 & 2 – Ears: Door to the Soul

Harmful Effects
- Approach your Lord from the door.
- Hearing is the first order.
- We heard the message and we accept.
- This is the Divine doorway to the soul. Evilness knows this, so what is so prevalent now.
- Horrible sounds that are being pumped into the ears and blocking the doorway to the soul. Everyone has a walkman like pouring cement on the doorway.
- Attempting to darken and harm that reality.

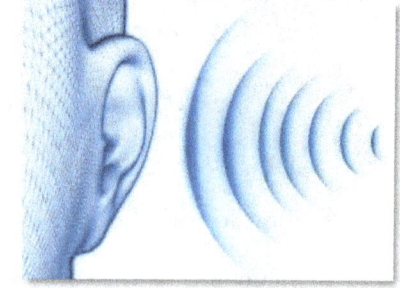

Protection for Ears

- Approach the Divine by the door not the window.
- Protection for this opening is to listen to your inner voice or conscious is most important first step towards inner realities is to hear your angelic beings assisting you.
- Hear only Qur'an or *salawat* – holy recitation or praising of the prophets of the Divine, melodies that remind you of love and tranquility.
- Love and holy recitations are rocket fuel for the soul.

Openings 3 & 4 – Eyes: Window to the Soul

Harmful Effects
- Eyes are desire for *dunya* or materialism.
- Have you heard the expression your eyes are 'hungry'?
- The Divine showing us through our technology.
- If you allow your computer to endlessly capture images especially negative ones, your hard drive will 'crash'.
- Your heart is already crashing with endless negative, horror, violence, pornographic, or vulgar images.
- All images are saved and difficult to purge. Forgetting images is very difficult.

Protection for Eyes

To take away *dunya* or materialism, one must:
- Close the eyes often and meditate.
- Protection of this opening is to reduce the intake of harmful images.
- See only good, read holy scriptures – those are images to remember.
- Close your eyes to the material world and ask for the Divine to open eyes of the heart.

Openings 5 & 6 – Nostrils: Divine Breath, Nafas ar-Rahmah, Divine Gift of Life in the Breath

The most important mission for the seeker in this order is to safeguard his breath, and he who cannot safeguard his breath, it would be said of him, 'he lost himself.'

Shah Naqshband ق said, 'This order is built on breath. So, it is a must for everyone to safeguard his breath in the time of his inhalation and exhalation and further, to safeguard his breath in the interval between the inhalation and exhalation.'

Don't be heedless. The Gift of Life is '24,000 breaths in each day.' Our lives on Earth are one breath away. All the planning in the world won't change when it is our last breath. Praise the Divine life which is in each breath. *Hu Allah* inhale and *Hu* exhale. Evilness wishes to fill this channel with cigarettes or drugs to come against this Divine gift of breath.

Opening 7 – The Mouth and Tongue of Truth (Lisanul Haq)

Mawlana Bistami ق said, 'For thirty years, when I wanted to remember Allah ﷻ and do *zikr*, I used to wash my tongue and my mouth for His glorification.' The Tongue of Truth is the holy passage of sustenance and power for human beings.

That is why the Divine orders fasting:
- It is the highest action one can do with highest reward from the Divine.
- When you decide to really fast.
- Purify all hearing, seeing, breathing, touching.

- All your 5 senses are submitting to your Lord, then your 5 levels of the heart will be also submitting to the Divine.
- He will open for you from the 'Tongue of Truth.'

وَوَهَبْنَا لَهُم مِّن رَّحْمَتِنَا وَجَعَلْنَا لَهُمْ لِسَانَ صِدْقٍ عَلِيًّا ﴿٥٠﴾

19:50 – "Wa wahabna lahum min rahmatina wa ja'alna lahum lisana Sidqin 'Aliya." (Surat Maryam)

"And We bestowed of Our Mercy on them, and We granted them lofty honour from/on the tongue of truth." (Mary, 19:50)

The Divine's highest gift is the gift of wisdom. The one who has the power to revive the dead – the dead souls, that are in need of heavenly realities.

يُؤْتِي الْحِكْمَةَ مَن يَشَاءُ ۚ وَمَن يُؤْتَ الْحِكْمَةَ فَقَدْ أُوتِيَ خَيْرًا كَثِيرًا ۗ وَمَا يَذَّكَّرُ إِلَّا أُولُو الْأَلْبَابِ ﴿٢٦٩﴾

2:269 – "Yu'til Hikmata mai yasha o; wa mai yutal Hikmata faqad otiya khairan kaseeraa; wa maa yazzakkaru illaa ulul albaab." (Surat Al-Baqarah)

"He gives wisdom to whom He wills, and whoever has been given wisdom has certainly been given abundant goodness. And none will remember except those of understanding." (The Cow, 2:269)

Protection for the Mouth and Tongue

Safeguarding the mouth:
- This is a holy opening where the tongue testifies to the Lord's Oneness.
- The Tongue of Truth and power of speech.
- Eating only Divinely prescribed foods.
- Abstaining from forbidden beverages and foods.

- Speaking good words – truthfulness.
- Reduce anger.
- Keeping tongue moist in *zikrullah* or essential remembrance.
- Secret of *siwak*, tooth stick, is the grounding wood for taking negative energies out of the mouth.

Because He said, *"Wa in min shayyin illa yusabbih bihamidiwa laakin laa tafqahoona tasbihahum…"* It means everything is existing in it's praise – even a rock is praising. It has atomic energy.

تُسَبِّحُ لَهُ السَّمَاوَاتُ السَّبْعُ وَالْأَرْضُ وَمَن فِيهِنَّ ۚ وَإِن مِّن شَيْءٍ إِلَّا يُسَبِّحُ بِحَمْدِهِ وَلَٰكِن لَّا تَفْقَهُونَ تَسْبِيحَهُمْ ۗ إِنَّهُ كَانَ حَلِيمًا غَفُورًا ﴿٤٤﴾

17:44 – *"Tusabbihu lahus samawatus sab'u wal ardu wa man fee hinna wa in min shayin illa yusabbihu bihamdihi wa lakin la tafqahoona tasbeehahum innahu kana haleeman ghafoora." (Surat Al-Isra)*

"The seven heavens and the earth and whatever is in them exalt [praises] Him. And there is not a thing except that it exalts [Allah] by His praise, but you do not understand their [way of] exalting. Indeed, He is ever Forbearing and Forgiving." (The Night Journey, 17:44)

Harmful Effects

The mouth is the canal for energy and sustenance for the maintenance of your being. As soon as you eat, 32 teeth are crunching down on the food filled with energies.

- Then that energy is divided amongst 16 teeth take the good energy.
- 16 teeth take the bad energy.
- That energy is then dispersed into the body mainly sent to the heart and the stomach.
- Garbage foods, forbidden beverages, and bad words: cursing, yelling, shouting, anger are poisons in the mouth and then sent to all the body.

- Leading cause of heart disease and all illnesses of the intestines.
- The Prophet's ﷺ prayer for *siwak* in mouth, 'O my Lord, protect my heart from bad character, anger and associating anything with you.' This was the prayer when he used the toothstick showing that too much badness enters from the mouth.

اَللَّهُمَّ طَهِرْ قَلْبِيْ مِنَّ الشِّرْكِ الْخَفِيْ وَالنِفَاق

"Allahumma tahhir qalbi minash shirk khafi wan nifaaq."

"O Allah! Purify my heart from hidden polytheism and hypocrisy."

The Crown of the Head is Safeguarded With a Cover

The process of submission will return humans to the image of the Divine. It is the image of honour, love, respect and chivalry. That energy is directed to the crown of the head. It is safeguarded with a cover. The Shaykh's head cover stresses the importance of covering the top and the triangle *taj* or hat under the turban cloth is pointing to the heavens showing that *Islam* and *Iman* lead to *Ihsan* (Religion + Faith = Moral Excellence)

You can imagine an energy connection into the spiritual heart of the universe from your crown *lataif*/chakra while intending that you be aligned with the highest soul purpose while staying well connected to the physical plane.

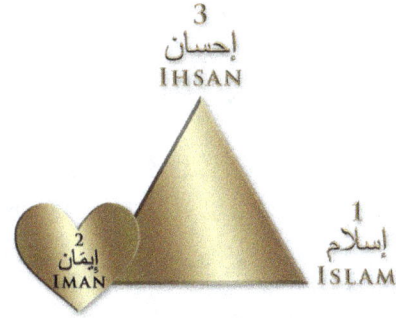

Opening the 7 Points of the Head
A Gateway to the 9 Points of the Body

Imagine energy from above all focusing to one point on the top the turban and like a condensed laser light entering the crown *lataif* or chakra. You are contained within yourself and connected to Earth and the physical and to spiritual source at the same time in a harmonious balance with the universe.

Focusing energy from heavens to crown of head. Turban cloth is the burial shroud of the seeker to remind him that this life is temporary and that the hereafter is the permanent eternal abode.

Hair on head: For men, hair on the head diminishes spiritual power and increases vanity and pride as in the jungle where male animals adorn themselves to attract females. Humanity is not like animals, the Divine role for men is to serve the Divine Kingdom. The nobility of a man is in the crown upon his head.

Beard: This is the spiritual power of heavenly men. Angels will flock to the beard and anoint those hairs with angelic powers.

The Secrets of the Mouth

The mouth is the holy opening for sustenance, breathing, and speaking. The Prophet's ﷺ teaching that controlling the opening of the mouth is of highest concern can earn tremendous reward or eternal doom.

عَنْ نَافِعٍ عَنْ ابْنِ عُمَرَ قَالَ، قَالَ رَسُولُ اللهِ: رَحِمَ عَبْداً تَكَلَّمَ فَغَنِمَ، أَوْ سَكَتَ فَسَلِمَ. إِنَّ اللِّسَانَ أَمْلَكُ شَيْءٍ لِلْإِنْسَانِ. أَلَا وَ إِنَّ كَلَامَ الْعَبْدِ كُلَّهُ عَلَيْهِ، إِلَّا ذِكْرُ اللهِ تَعَالَى، أَوْ أَمْرٌ بِمَعْرُوفٍ، أَوْ نَهْىٌ عَنْ مُنْكَرٍ، أَوْ إِصْلَاحٌ بَيْنَ الْمُؤْمِنِينَ.

'An nafi' 'an ibn 'Umara qala, qala Rasulullahi (saws): "Rahima 'abdan takallama faghanema, aw sakata fasalem. Innal lisana amlaku

shayin li insane, ala wa inna kalamal 'abde kullahu 'alayhi, illa zikrullahi ta'ala, aw amrun be ma'ruf, aw nahi 'an munkar, aw islahun baynal mumineen."

It has been narrated from Nafi' from B. 'Umar that he said, the Messenger of Allah (pbuh) said, "May (Allah) have mercy on that servant who gains benefit when he speaks, or one who is protected through maintaining silence. Surely the tongue is the thing which wields the most authority over a person. Be aware that everything that servant speaks is against him, except for the remembrance of Allah, the High, or the commanding of others to that which is right or preventing them from that which is evil or setting the affair right between two believers."

Safeguarded Your Mouth With Siwak (Toothstick)

The food we eat is filled with energy. Radio waves, electromagnetic radiation, whatever is in the atmosphere and emitting from creation is absorbed in the food we eat and air we breathe. This energy collects in the mouth and will try to be absorbed by the teeth and then sent into the body where it will go to the heart and into the blood and then to the stomach area. If this energy is bad or overwhelming negative energy, then physical and spiritual sickness occur. Enmity destroys teeth. Bad energies darken and weaken the heart and poison the body.

The *siwak* is a grounding stick that will draw out negative energy from the mouth. If negative energy is in the mouth, one's words are like fire. When positive energy in the mouth, it is like sweetness that people may take benefit from. The Prophet's ﷺ prayer was, 'O my Lord, clean my heart from bad thoughts and action and anger.'

Opening the 7 Points of the Head
A Gateway to the 9 Points of the Body

اَللَّهُمَّ طَهِرْ قَلْبِيْ مِنَّ الشِّرْكِ الْخَفِيْ وَالنِّفَاق

"*Allahumma tahhir qalbi minash shirk khafi wan nifaaq.*"

"*O Allah! Purify my heart from hidden polytheism and hypocrisy.*"

When we use the *siwak* (toothstick), it is made from the root of certain trees. Later, we will find that the highest reward from the Divine is the 'fast.' The Divine is showing us that this mouth that testifies to His Oneness and the tongue that sings His praise is a tremendous opening safeguard it for the highest opening of the heart is based on its preservation.

The Power of the Ring and Safeguarding It

The blessed ring is worn on the right hand on the second finger near pinky. The purpose of the ring is a protection against enmity, which is a very powerful negative force. Unfortunately, human creation does not understand the gift of energy or what we call life that was given to us. This atomic energy is always flowing. When we feel good, others in our ocean of energy will feel good. 'Be with the righteous,' for they are the best of company because they will enlighten you.

يَا أَيُّهَا الَّذِينَ آمَنُوا اتَّقُوا اللَّهَ وَكُونُوا مَعَ الصَّادِقِينَ ﴿١١٩﴾

9:119 – "*Ya ayyuhal ladheena amanoo ittaqollaha wa kono ma'as sadiqeen.*" (*Surat At-Tawbah*)

"*O you who have believed, have consciousness of Allah and be with those who are truthful/ Pious /sincere (in words and deed).*"
(*The Repentance, 9:119*)

But if someone is negative, they will send out the negativity to people causing many sicknesses. Prophet Muhammad ﷺ taught that the use of the ring on the right hand takes away enmity.

عَنْ جَابِرِ بْنِ عَبْدِ اللهِ: أَنَّ النَّبِيَّ صَلَّى اللهُ عَلَيْهِ وَسَلَّمَ كَانَ يَتَخَتَّمُ فِي يَمِينِهِ.

'An Jabir bin 'Abdullahi (as): "Annan Nabi (saws) yatakhattamu fi yaminihi."

Narrated by Jabir bin Abdullah (as), "The Prophet of Allah (pbuh) wore the ring on the right hand."

People of the Right are *Ashab al Yamin*, they are blessed. Preferable stones for rings are amber or turquoise. For men, silver or steel base rings with no gold. The left hand is used for cleaning the unclean (restroom).

عَنِ الْإِمَامِ جَعْفَرَ الصَّادِقِ (عَلَيْهِ السَّلَامُ) أَنَهُ قَالَ :
قَالَ رَسُولُ اللهِ (صَلَّى اللهُ عَلَيْهِ وَآلِهِ)" : تَخَتَّمُوا بِالْعَقِيقِ فَإِنَّهُ مُبَارَكٌ ، وَ مَنْ تَخَتَّمَ بِالْعَقِيقِ يُوشِكُ أَنْ يُقْضَىٰ لَهُ بِالْحُسْنَىٰ."

'Anil Imami Ja'far asSadiq (as) anahu qala: "Qala Rasulullahi (sallallahu 'alayhi wa aalihi): "Takhattamo bil 'aqiqi fainnahu mubarakun, wa man takhattama bil 'aqiqi yusheku an yuqday lahu bilhusna."

Narrated by Imam Jafar asSadiq (as), the Prophet (pbuh) said: "Wear an Aqiq ring as it is full of blessings, and this who wears it, is granted victory over his opponents."

Amber – an electromagnetic gem that opens the solar plexus *lataif* chakra and can aid in enhancing and balancing moods, obtaining mental clarity, and confidence. It can also be used to purify or detoxify.

Turquoise – general healer, multi-purpose, relieves many negative emotions, increases psychic connections, divination, communication, creativity, serenity, uplifting, soothes and calms.

The Cane and Grounding Your Energy

It is your grounding mechanism to take from heavens and send negative to the Earth. 'Grounding' – two feet and one cane like modern day electrical prong. This was the way of all Divine Messengers.

By now, we are seeing that the Divine Presence sent messengers to teach scriptures, laws, morals but most of all how to reach perfection to return to the angelic state in which we were created. You are undoubtedly familiar with electrical grounding energy and its properties, through your experience with sunshine. It is a warming, expansive kind of energy, which can make you feel open, contented, and encompassed or held.

On the other hand, too much electrical energy coming in can make you feel lightheaded, disoriented, burned out (fried), or jumpy and irritable. Too much (or not enough) heavenly energy may make you crave sugar. Too much (or not enough) earth energy may announce itself through cravings for salt.

The Eternal Struggle Between Energy of the Heavens & Energy of the Earth

How to Balance and Safeguard Oneself

This symbol expresses a continuous flow of *qudra* or power in a circular direction as it generates the two opposing forces of positive and negative, darkness and light, heaven and earth, man and woman. (Binary: Active 1, Passive 0). These forces interact to balance each other's excesses and to bring into existence the physical and metaphysical realms.

The yin and yang represent all the opposite principles one finds in the universe.

- Under yang (Active or 1) are the principles of maleness, the sun, creation, heat, light, heaven, dominance, and so on, and;
- Under yin (Passive 0) are the principles of femaleness, the moon, completion, cold, darkness, material forms, submission, and so on.
- Each of these opposites produce the other.

Grounding in the Elemental Self

Your body is a transformer of energy. You bring in electrical energy from the cosmos. You bring in magnetic energy from the earth, and your body mixes and uses these two energies, generally within the areas of the naval button and heart.

Opening the 7 Points of the Head
A Gateway to the 9 Points of the Body

The lower part of the body is the entryway for a lot of the magnetic energy. That is what you might consider to be 'earth grounding' energy. And the top of your head and back of the neck is the usual doorway for the electrical or 'sky grounding' energy.

In you, earth and heavens meet and mingle. It is your nature to blend these two as fuel for your life here on the planet. That is why you have a physicality that requires earthly energy. You also have a soul that requires heavenly energy.

Earth energy is also something we are sure you know well. It is heavy and solid. It is slow, stately and reassuring. If you lie on the ground for a while, feeling the solidity of earth, the support of the ground beneath you, the heaviness of being a physical creature – that is magnetic energy. Too much of it can make you feel confused, lazy, logy, or sleepy.

Heavenly Emanation Raining Down Upon You

Earthly energies coming through the contact with the earth are forces clashing within the abdomen. The Prophet ﷺ warned us that all sickness starts from the stomach for both males and females.

اَلْمِعْدَةُ بَيْتُ الدَّاءِ وَالْحِمْيَةُ رَأْسُ اَلدَّوَاءِ

"Al mi'datu baytud daaye, wal Himyatu rasu addawaa."

"The stomach is the house of disease and abstinence is the head of every remedy."

Above we covered protection for the head, mouth, hands, and grounding aspect of the cane in Sufi healing. All of this is now showing how to bring energy into your being, how to preserve that energy, and how to release negative unwanted energy.

A big secret within the womb of a woman is called the *rahem (ra, ha, meem)*. The mercy and secret of creation is a gift of the Divine. Without this, we would not be born, and the cycle of life would not continue. Protecting that point, meditating on it and covering it 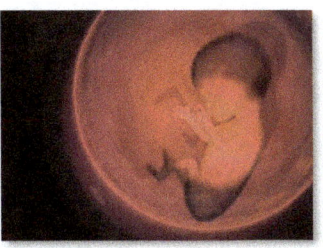 with clothing is essential in its safeguarding. Evilness wishes to expose that point and pull from the secret of life from women. They feed on that energy that they don't have.

Subhana rabbika rabbal 'izzati 'amma yasifoon, wa salaamun 'alal mursaleen, walhamdulillahi rabbil 'aalameen. Bi hurmati Muhammad al-Mustafa wa bi siri Surat al-Fatiha.

7 DIVINELY ATTRIBUTES DRESS THE 7 HOLY OPENINGS

Allah ﷻ Gives Knowledge to 'IbadAllah From the Ocean of 'Aleem

InshaAllah, from the realities of guidance, there are different levels of guidance. And in the oceans of *irshad* (guidance), and real guidance from soul to soul, that there's a guidance from a level of *Rijalullah* (men of God). *Rijalullah* are those whom Allah ﷻ have put into the schools of training in *tarbiyah* (discipline). Above the *rijal* are *ibadAllah* (servants of God).

IbadAllah, Allah ﷻ dress them from his ancient *ayn* and gave them to be from the oceans of *'Aleem*. As a result, they are from the oceans of *ibadAllah*, that Allah ﷻ dress them with a guidance and with a knowledge.

WajhAllah Reflects to Wajhi hil Kareem of Prophet ﷺ and He ﷺ Reflects to Awliya

The associations are not normal associations in the presence of those *ibadAllah*, that their face is lit. That the reality of guidance through their face that they inherit, where Allah ﷻ describes everything shall perish,

7 Divinely Attributes Dress the 7 Holy Openings

except the Holy Face. The *WajhAllah*, the Holy Face of Allah ﷻ, is a reflection to *Wajhi hil Kareem* of Sayyidina Muhammad ﷺ. And these *awliyaullah* (saints) who have been trained to take from that reality of the face of Sayyidina Muhammad ﷺ. That the ear, *as-Sami* (All-Hearing) and *al-Basir* (All-Seeing).

وَلَا تَدْعُ مَعَ اللَّهِ إِلَٰهًا آخَرَ ۘ لَا إِلَٰهَ إِلَّا هُوَ ۚ كُلُّ شَيْءٍ هَالِكٌ إِلَّا وَجْهَهُ ۚ لَهُ الْحُكْمُ وَإِلَيْهِ تُرْجَعُونَ ﴿٨٨﴾

28:88 – *"Wala tad'uo ma'Allahi ilahan aakhara la ilaha illa huwa kullu shayin halikun illa wajha hu la hul hukmu wa ilayhi turja'oon." (Surat Al-Qasas)*

"...Everything (that exists) will perish except His holy Face. To Him belongs the Command, and to Him you will be returned." (The Stories, 28:88)

That when they describe, it's not you that can do anything. Our responsibility is to attend, whether it's in person, whether it's via whatever transmission Allah ﷻ is opening. That you do what Allah ﷻ asked of you as an obligation. But our training was that don't think that, that obligation will be able to lift you from anything. If you think your *salah* (prayer) can lift you out of difficulty, that your *zakat* (charity) will clean you from your bad characters, then look at 99.9% of the people who do that and still have all the bad character. It means if you fall into quicksand, there is no way for you to lift yourself out.

Guidance of 'Waliyun Murshid' is a Gift From Allah ﷻ

So, Allah ﷻ describes whom we guide, we guided. Whom we have not given guidance, they can never be guided. And guidance of *waliyun murshidun* from Surat al-Kahf, where Allah ﷻ is giving a very specific type of guidance.

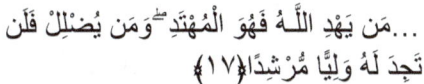

18:17 – "…Man yahdillahu fahuwal Muhtadi, wa man yudlil falan tajida lahu waliyyan murshida."
(Surat Al-Kahf)

"… He whom Allah, guides is rightly guided; but he whom Allah leaves to stray - for him you will never find Saintly Guide to the Right Way."
(The Cave, 18:17)

This *hidayat*, this guidance is a gift from Allah ﷻ. That their face is lit. And for us to even understand is that don't look at only the physical face but imagine a face that is in all 360 dimensions of light. That, from the right ear, an energy light comes out, *sifat as-Sami* (attribute of hearing). And when that energy hits the student, *as-Sami* is to bring you into the perfection of listening.

Most People Only Listen to Their Ego and Submit to Their Desires

Our way is based on *itibah* and obedience. Our way is based on *samina wa atana*. I hear, and I obey.

2:285 – "Sam'ina wa ata'na, ghufranaka Rabbana wa ilaykal masir."
(Surat Al-Baqarah)

"*...We hear, and we obey: (We seek) Thy forgiveness, our Lord, and to Thee is the end of all journeys.*" (The Cow, 2:285)

Ninety-nine percent of people, they hear their *nafs* (ego) and they obey. And Allah ﷻ describes them, 'Have you seen those who make their desires, their Lord?' Because the *nafs* (ego) only wants the desire. As a result, they follow all their desires and it becomes *ilah*, it becomes a God for them. That they bow down to their desires, they submit themself to their desires.

أَرَأَيْتَ مَنِ اتَّخَذَ إِلَٰهَهُ هَوَاهُ أَفَأَنتَ تَكُونُ عَلَيْهِ وَكِيلًا ﴿٤٣﴾

25:43 – "*Ara'aita manit takhaza ilaahahoo hawaahu afa anta takoonu 'alaihi wakeelaa.*" (Surat Al-Furqan)

"*Have you seen the one who takes as his god his own desire?*"
(The Criterian, 25:43)

7 Awliya Support the 7 Holy Points of the Face

So, what Prophet ﷺ wanted, and didn't leave the nation to themselves. But these *awliyaullah* (saints), these pious souls, and again the different *darajat* (level). These that they're describing tonight, their guidance is from the power of the face. And what Allah ﷻ dressed their face, and what they take from the holy face of Sayyidina Muhammad ﷺ. That this *sifat as-Sami – as-Sami* is the perfection of hearing. When they direct their energy upon the students, and those whom are looking at their face, this *sifat* (attribute), its purpose to come out and to destroy; destroy the energies that are blocking the student from listening to the correct inspiration.

Through all their teachings, through all their writings, through all their *zikrs*, through all their association, these 7 points upon them, are continuously in movement. Behind these 7 points are 7 huge *awliyaullah* (saints). And each of those *awliya* are supporting that attribute, that  essence from Allah ﷻ, and sending their *madad* (support) upon the face of that shaykh.

1. Sifat as-Sami' (All-Hearing) Perfects the Hearing

Hear Your Higher Conscience From Heavens, Not the Lower Conscience in Your Body

So, this *sifat as-Sami* – S, A, M, I – it's for hearing. This energy that comes has to keep hitting the student, hitting the student, hitting the student, that stop listening to your bad character. Stop listening to your bad desire and hear the message that Allah ﷻ wants you to hear. It means to hear your higher conscience. You have a lower conscience hidden within the body, there's a higher conscience that's always with Allah ﷻ. Your soul is not given all to you; only a drop of your soul was given to you. The bulk, the amount of the soul is always with Allah ﷻ, only a drop came into this body. That part, that higher reality, that higher soul, is trying to communicate with the lower soul that is imprisoned within the *nafs* (ego).

Sayyidina YaSeen ﷺ is Yaqeen us Sami', He ﷺ Hears and Speaks for Allah ﷻ

Their job is they're inheriting from YaSeen, Yaqeen ul Sami (Certainty of Hearing). This means the most perfected of creation, Sayyidina Muhammad ﷺ, that Allah ﷻ described that the name of Prophet ﷺ is YaSeen.

عَنْ عَلِيِّ بْنِ أَبِي طَالِبٍ (عَلَيْهِ السَّلَامُ) – قَالَ: سَمِعَتُ رَسُولُ اللهِ - (صَلَّى اللهُ عَلَيْهِ وَسَلَّمَ) يَقُولُ: إِنَّ اللهَ تَعَالَى أَسَمَّانِي فِي الْقُرْآنِ سَبْعَةَ أَسْمَاءٍ:مُحَمَّدٌ، وَأَحْمَدُ، وَطَهَ، وَيَس، وَالْمُزَّمِّلَ، وَالْمُدَّثِّرَ، وَعَبْدُ اللهِ

'An 'Ali bin Abi Talib (as) Qala: Sami'at Rasulullah (saws) yaqulo: "InnAllaha ta'ala asammani fil Quraani sab'ata asmayin: Muhammadun ﷺ, wa Ahmadu, wa Taha, wa Yaseen, wal Muzzammila, wal Muddaththira, wa 'Abdullahi ﷺ."

Imam 'Ali (as) said, "I heard the Messenger of God (pbuh) say, "Verily God has named me by seven names in the holy Quran: Muhammad (the Praised one) [3:144; 33:40; 47:2; 48:29], Ahmad (the Most Praised one)[61:6], TaHa [20:1], YaSeen [36:1], al-Muzammil (Enwrapped One) [73:1], al-Mudaththir (Covered/ Cloaked One) [74:1], and 'Abdullah (Servant of Allah) [72:19]."

He is *YaSeen, Yaqeen us Sami'*, and as a result, he's *Habibullah* (beloved

of Allah ﷻ). It has to do with this heart of the Divinely Presence. The one who hears is the one who speaks. The one who hears Allah ﷻ, speaks for Allah ﷻ. And that's why Prophet ﷺ described, 'I'm a *Rasul* before this body of Adam and clay and water.' It means the eternal position of Prophet ﷺ is the messenger of Allah (AJ), created to hear the Divine and speak for the Divine.

صَلَاةُ اللهِ، سَلَامُ اللهِ عَلَى طَهَ رَسُوْلِ اللهِ
صَلَاةُ اللهِ، سَلَامُ اللهِ عَلَى يٰسٓ حَبِيْبِ اللهِ

Salatullah salamullah 'ala Taha Rasullillah
Salatullah salamullah 'ala Yaseen Habibillah

Allah's (AJ) praise and blessing is upon Taha (Purified Guide), Messenger of Allah (AJ). Allah's (AJ) praise and blessing is upon the Yaseen, Beloved of Allah (pbuh)

and

كُنْتُ نَبِيًّا وَآدَمُ بَيْنَ الْمَاءِ وَالطِّينِ

"*Kuntu Nabiyan wa Adama baynal Maa e wat Teen.*"

"*I was a Prophet and Adam was between water and clay.*"
(Prophet Muhammad (pbuh))

Awliya's Hearing is Perfected and Their Talks Are a Pocket of Truth From Janab al Haq

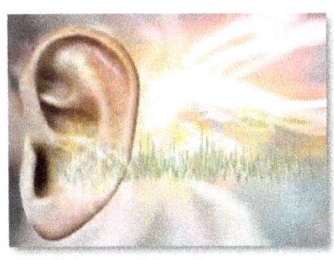

As a result of this name of *YaSeen* dress upon these shaykhs, their hearing is brought into perfection. The energy, which is emanating from them, is an energy that goes out and hits the student's light. That stop listening to your *waswas* (whispering) and bad desires and begin to listen to your heart and a higher consciousness, a higher reality. It means that their talks are not like the talks from people at different places. Their talks are activated energies. Whether you hear it now or you hear it ten years later on the internet, it's a pocket of reality. It's a pocket of truth from *Janab al Haq*, from the Owner of all truth. As a result, that pocket of truth stays eternally in its place.

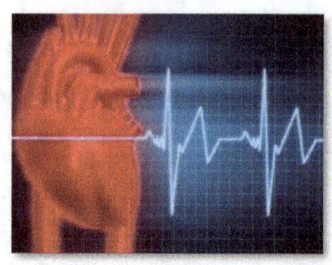

It means that anytime you listen to these *awliyaullah* (saints) who've been dressed by that level of *irshad* and guidance, their all, their face is lit. As soon as you listen to their talk, this *sifat as-Sami* is coming and hitting the heart destroying all the obstacles and idols within the heart, that stop listening to the *waswas* (whispering), stop listening to the devil.

Listen to what's true, listen to your heart, listen to your consciousness and enter into your reality. What you're looking for is not outside. Outside is imagination, inside is the reality. Outside is your imagination. Everybody imagines God is something, whatever their crazy thoughts can be. You want the real? You go inside. Inside is where we find Allah ﷻ. Prophet ﷺ described, 'Who knows himself will know his Lord.'

مَنْ عَرَفَ نَفْسَهُ فَقَدْ عَرَفَ رَبَّهُ

"Man 'arafa nafsahu faqad 'arafa Rabbahu."

"Who knows himself, knows his Lord." (Prophet Muhammad (pbuh))

2. Sifat al-Basir (All Seeing) Perfects Our Vision

The next attribute that they dress from is *Sami al-Basir*, which means *sifat al-Basir* (attribute of seeing) comes to perfect the vision of the student. That was the *hadith*, that, that vision that you're using of your eyes, you're not going to find Allah ﷻ anywhere on this Earth, but yet you see him everywhere. All His signs are everywhere. But what you're looking for is not from the physical eyes. It's from the spiritual eyes. So, it means

they're *Ahlul Basirah* (people of spiritual vision), they're not blind people. Allah ﷻ opened, it's unimaginable what Allah ﷻ opened within their heart. That attribute dresses the servants that watch them, listen to them, follow that guidance. That begins to dress and bless them.

عَنْ أَبِي سَعِيدٍ الْخُدْرِيِّ، قَالَ قَالَ رَسُولُ اللَّهِ صلى الله عليه وسلم: " اتَّقُوا فِرَاسَةَ الْمُؤْمِنِ فَإِنَّهُ يَنْظُرُ بِنُورِ اللَّهِ." ثُمَّ قَرَأَ : (إِنَّ فِي ذَلِكَ لَآيَاتٍ لِلْمُتَوَسِّمِينَ)

'An Abi Sa'yidel Khudriyi, qala Rasulullahi (saws): "Ittaqoo Firasatal Mu'min, Fa Innahu yanzuru Bi Nurillah. Thumma Qara'a: "Inna fee dhalika la ayaatun lil mutawassimeen." (Surat al Hijr)"

Narrated by Sa'yidel Khudri that the Messenger of Allah (pbuh) said: "Beware/be conscious of the true believer's spiritual vision, for indeed he sees with Allah's Light." Then he recited from holy Qur'an: "Surely in this are signs for those who see." (The Rocky Tract 15:75). (Tirmidhi, Book 47, #3419)

7 Divinely Attributes Dress the 7 Holy Openings

Strive to Practice Mawt Qablil Mawt, We Don't Live Forever

Then they begin to train them, that, that what you're looking for, close your eyes. Take a life in which you practice *mawt qablil mawt* (death of desires before physical death). You practice the arrival of your death. Don't think your death is way off, that this life is for you to be entertaining yourself only. But think that your death could come at any

moment. You live as if you have to live forever, pay your bills. But you pray as if you're going to die by morning. So, you work hard all day long to make your sustenance and feed your family, and all night long you're concerned that, 'Ya Rabbi, is this going to be the moment

that I won't make it to my Fajr and I'm going to die?' And then when they train with that understanding, they take a way of *tafakkur* and contemplation. That they, in their meditating and contemplating, that these eyes have played an illusion upon me. And that I want the eyes of my soul, *ya Rabbi*. That open the eye of my soul and begin to open the eye of truth and all realities.

Focus on Fixing Our Own Bad Characteristics, Not Others

So, *sifat al-Basir* has to be dressing. Otherwise, the student will never leave the imaginal world and the world of illusions to enter into the world of *haqqaiqs* (realities). 'Who knows himself will know his Lord.'

مَنْ عَرَفَ نَفْسَهُ فَقَدْ عَرَفَ رَبَّهُ

"*Man 'arafa nafsahu faqad 'arafa Rabbahu.*"

"*Who knows himself, knows his Lord.*" (Prophet Muhammad (pbuh))

The self can only be known by going inside. As soon as I go inside, I see all my bad characteristics, I see all my bad desires. I see that I can't change anybody until I change myself. So, I don't go around changing people so that it better suits me. You, you be like that, you be like that, you be like that, because it makes me happier when I come. You can't change anyone. So, Prophet ﷺ wanted us first, change ourself. As soon as I begin to work and change myself, everything around me by its nature begins to change. Because I'm the one who is changed. So, *sifat al-Basir* has to dress the student. That take a path in which we're looking into the heart. That which we're searching for is not out here.

When Reciting Salawats, Visualize Yourself in the Rauza Sharif

This means that when you're even doing these *nasheeds* and *salawats* (praisings), you're not thinking I'm sitting next to this guy, next to the cushion, and oh wow, this is so nice. But you close your eyes and see that you're in the presence of Sayyidina Muhammad ﷺ. Is he not the best of character, *Khuluq al Azeem*? That you think that you're praising upon Prophet ﷺ and Prophet ﷺ is not present, to take your salutations and take your greetings back? Allah ﷻ described, 'He's the immense character, the beatific character.' One *Salaam* and Prophet ﷺ said I will come and give you back ten *Salaams*.

$$وَإِنَّكَ لَعَلَىٰ خُلُقٍ عَظِيمٍ ﴿٤﴾$$

68:4 – *"Wa innaka la'ala khuluqin 'azheem." (Surat Al-Qalam)*

"Truly, You (O Muhammad!) are of a magnificent character."
(The Pen, 68:4)

and

7 Divinely Attributes Dress the 7 Holy Openings

عَنْ أَنَسِ بْنِ مَالِكٍ رَضِيَ اللهُ عَنْهُ، قَالَ: قَالَ رَسُولُ اللَّهِ – صلى الله عليه وسلم -: " مَنْ صَلَّى عَلَيَّ صَلَاةً وَاحِدَةً، صَلَّى اللَّهُ عَلَيْهِ عَشْرَ صَلَوَاتٍ، وَحُطَّتْ عَنْهُ عَشْرُ خَطِيئَاتٍ، وَرُفِعَتْ لَهُ عَشْرُ دَرَجَاتٍ "

Qala Rasulullah (saws): "Man Salla 'alaiya Salatan wahidatan, Sallallahu 'alayhi 'ashra Salawatin, wa Huttat 'anhu 'ashru khaTeatin, wa ruf'at lahu 'ashru darajatin."

Prophet Muhammad (pbuh) said: *"Whoever sends blessings (Praises) upon me, God will shower His blessings upon him ten times, and will erase ten of his sins, and elevate (raise) his (spiritual) station ten times."* (Hadith recorded by Nasa'i)

So, imagine whole three hours of praising upon Sayyidina Muhammad ﷺ. Don't you think that the presence of Prophet ﷺ is present? But then why don't you see it? It means then *Ahlul Basirah* (people of spiritual vision) train you, keep your eyes closed. Visualize yourself in the *Rauza Sharif*. You never been to Madina? Then Google it. *MashaAllah*, now the whole world can see Madina, where it was just for those who made the *Hajj* (pilgrimage) or *Umrah* (nonmandatory pilgrimage). Now everyone, you Google, look at the *Rauza Sharif*, and see the bars and say, 'Ya Rabbi I'm just locked onto those bars until Prophet ﷺ gazes at me.' I am at your *Rauza Sharif, Ya Rasulul Kareem* ﷺ, you're the *habib* (beloved) of Allah ﷻ. I cannot leave here until your *nazar* (gaze) dresses me and that you bless me, and that you take away my sicknesses and bad character. And a life, you sit like that, lifelong at the *Rauza Sharif* from *Ahlul Basirah*.

3. Sifat al-'Alim (All Knowing) Dresses the Tongue From Lisan Siddiq al 'Aliya

'Alim al Qadir means then Allah (ﷻ) dresses, they've been dressed by these realities. Then they teach that these associations are not empty. That when Allah (ﷻ) dresses their tongue with *sifat al-'Alim*, I'm going to give you from *Lisan as-Siddiq al 'Aliya*.

﴿وَوَهَبْنَا لَهُم مِّن رَّحْمَتِنَا وَجَعَلْنَا لَهُمْ لِسَانَ صِدْقٍ عَلِيًّا ٥٠﴾

19:50 – "Wa wahabna lahum min rahmatina wa ja'alna lahum lisana Sidqin 'Aliya." (Surat Maryam)

"And We bestowed of Our Mercy on them, and We granted them lofty honour from/on the tongue of truth." (Mary, 19:50)

In Surah Maryam, Allah (ﷻ) says, those whom we gave *hikmah* and wisdom, we have given them an immense reward. And they inherit from *Lisan as-Siddiq al 'Aliya*. The *siddiq* whose name is 'Ali (ؑ). Don't need too much interpretation. Oh, does this mean elevator, what does this mean? The most high tongue of the *siddiqs* (truthful). Allah (ﷻ) said you're going to inherit; I'm going to make your tongue from *al-'Alim*. It means we'll be flowing off your tongue from the oceans of reality, Allah's (ﷻ) ancient knowledges. That's why they're not *rijal*, they're *ibadAllah*. That the *rijal*, they were in training.  Those whom are above that training, Allah (ﷻ) granted them Allah's (ﷻ) ancient knowledges, that *abd*. They carry that *ayn*, Allah's (ﷻ) ancient knowledges. When their tongue speaks, it speaks with the power and *qudra* from their soul. They can shatter all falsehood in their talk and all the energy they're trying to affect upon the soul. And in its place put every perfection that Allah ﷻ wants. Whether it's in person, whether its live, or whether its via YouTube, ten years later, it doesn't matter.

When Awliya Speak the Haq, They Destroy Falsehood and Revive the Hearts

The energy still dressing, still dressing. And that's when Allah ﷻ describes, when the truth comes, falsehood perishes.

وَ قُلْ جَاءَالْحَقُّ وَزَهَقَ الْبَاطِلُ، إِنَّ الْبَاطِلَ كَانَ زَهُوقًا ﴿٨١﴾

17:81 – *"Wa qul jaa alhaqqu wa zahaqal baatil, innal batila kana zahoqa." (Surat Al-Isra)*

"And say, Truth has come, and falsehood has perished. Indeed falsehood, [by its nature], is ever perishing/ bound to perish."
(The Night Journey, 17:81)

And falsehood by its nature is ever crumbling and perishing. They don't occupy the same space. That's why *shaitan* tries to block them, don't listen to them, don't, don't hear them, don't turn onto that channel, don't read from that book, because it's filled with *haqqaiqs* (realities) that begin to emanate out. Like a laser beam, it hits and every falsehood that people have built upon themself will come shattering down. Not only it shatters all the falsehood, all the incorrect, all the bad characteristic, but the soul that feels that it's dying and losing its faith, losing its course, losing its purpose, they're *muhyil qulub* (revivers of the hearts). As soon as they speak from the heart of Prophet ﷺ, *mahidh dhunubi, muhyil qulub*.

يَا مُحْيِي الْقُلُوبِ، سَلَامٌ عَلَيْك
يَا مَاحِي الذُّنُوبِ ، سَلَامٌ عَلَيْك

Ya Muhyil qulubi, Salaam 'Alayk
Ya Mahidh dhunubi, Salaam 'Alayk

O the reviver of the hearts, O the eraser of the sins, Peace be upon you

The Fish in the Story of Sayyidina Musa ﷺ Symbolizes the Soul

They crush all the wrong and the light that comes from Prophet ﷺ, revives the dead. That was the sign between Sayyidina Musa ﷺ and Sayyidina Khidr ﷺ. He was looking for Sayyidina Khidr ﷺ. He said, 'Where, where was the sign when the fish came to life and went into the water?'

قَالَ أَرَأَيْتَ إِذْ أَوَيْنَا إِلَى الصَّخْرَةِ فَإِنِّي نَسِيتُ الْحُوتَ وَمَا أَنْسَانِيهُ إِلَّا الشَّيْطَانُ أَنْ أَذْكُرَهُ ۚ وَاتَّخَذَ سَبِيلَهُ فِي الْبَحْرِ عَجَبًا ﴿٦٣﴾

18:63 – "Qala araayta idh awayna ilas sakhrati fa-innee naseetu alhoota wa ma ansaneehu illash shaytanu an adhkurahu, wat takhadha sabeela hu fee al bahri 'ajaba." (Surat Al-Kahf)

"He said, Did you see when we retired to the rock? Indeed, I forgot [there] the fish. And none made me forget it except Satan – that I should mention it. And it took its course into the sea amazingly."
(The Cave, 18:63)

The fish, we said many times, is the soul. It's a symbol of the soul. The soul is like a fish, looking for its water, looking for its sustenance. The sign of these *rijal* (holy men) is they can revive the dead hearts. The hearts that are losing hope, Allah ﷻ sends to them, just look at them. As soon as you look at them, the energy will begin to dress upon the soul, dress upon the heart. How many people say that they saw pictures and their hearts felt revived, that their energy comes back? The nation of Sayyidina Muhammad ﷺ been given many gifts. Allah ﷻ didn't leave them alone to be in the hands of *shayateen* (demons). And even more power coming now for what these *shaitans* are trying to do upon this Earth.

4. Sifat al-Qadir (All Powerful) Opens the Nafas ar-Rahmah

Their faces are powerful. From that *'Alim al Qadir* means these knowledges that are coming from their tongue, from the oceans of Allah's ﷻ ancient knowledges, Allah ﷻ begin to open for them *nafas ar-rahmah* (breath of mercy). In their training, Allah ﷻ opened for them. So, it means their dressing now from the reality of the breath. Through their breath, because the *Qadir* is upon their nose, *'Alim* upon the tongue.

Hu is the Power of Every Atom That Makes It Move

So, that *Qadir* that Allah ﷻ opened for them in their training, that everything in its atomic reality. Within every atom, the power of every atom is '*Hu.*' Whatever the atom is, the power within its nucleus, like a power plant. Like cells, you know like battery charging cells everywhere. What is making that atom to move, is the power of *Hu. Qul Hu,* then *Allah,* then *huhad,* then *Ahad* after. But the *Hu* is the power for everything.

﴿١﴾ قُلْ هُوَ اللَّـهُ أَحَدٌ

112:1 – "*Qul Huw Allahu Ahad.*" (Surat Al-Ikhlas)

"*Say, He is Allah, [who is] One.*" (The Sincerity, 112:1)

Allah ﷻ begins to unlock for them every breath they bring in; the secret of the *Hu* is unlocked, and that breath becomes like an energized fuel upon their breath. They breathe the reality of *zikr Hu* into their soul. As a result, they heat up. They can heat everybody up, anybody watching them will be heated up. Even deeper in that reality is that if you imagine this whole room filled with souls. Don't look at the *mulk* (earthly realm) of just the bodies. The body makes you think that you're all separated. But for you to be sitting here, your soul is bigger than this Earth. And his soul is bigger, so it's just an ocean of light. When they breathe, they can breathe all the light in.

They breathe all the light in through their heart, stamps and purifies that light and they exhale out all the light. So, with every breath they're able to clean. Whatever contamination coming upon the students, with every breath that they bring in, is purified within their heart. Because they have a Muhammadan heart. That Allah ﷻ granted them from a reality of their heart, all their faculties have been changed. So, this *nafas* (breath) that's coming in, is from *'Alim al Qadir*. This *Qadir* that begins to dress the breath, means that Allah ﷻ give them like a power that coming through every atom. Otherwise, they can't survive on this Earth with what Allah ﷻ wants their soul to do, without that energy coming to them.

Like Awliya, the Sun Takes in Waste, Uses it as a Fuel to Emit Light

One of the by-products of that energy is the amount of the lights they can bring in from people's lights, and they begin to filter. You study the sun – this is not so far off. The sun is actually a filter within our galaxy. It brings in all the waste, uses that as a fuel and produces light. The light then comes out and nourishes you. Comes from where? Allah ﷻ made the whole of our galaxy a food source for the sun. It pulls, it has a gravitational pull that pulls elements, eats it, uses it for fuel, and produces an energy, electromagnetic power. A light. That light nourishes the entire galaxy. Allah ﷻ said, 'Look, I show you my signs upon the horizon, but the one inside you, more powerful, and I show it within yourself.'

سَنُرِيهِمْ آيَاتِنَا فِي الْآفَاقِ وَفِي أَنفُسِهِمْ حَتَّىٰ يَتَبَيَّنَ لَهُمْ أَنَّهُ الْحَقُّ ۗ ... ﴿٥٣﴾

41:53 – *"Sanureehim ayatina fil afaqi wa fee anfusihim hatta yatabayyana lahum annahu alhaqqu…" (Surat Al-Fussilat)*

"We will show them Our signs in the horizons and within themselves until it becomes clear to them that it is the truth…"
(Explained in Detail, 41:53)

Allah ﷻ Wages War on Those Who Come Against Awliya

Wa laqad karramna bani adam (Holy Qur'an, 17:70). *Bani Adam's* gift is much higher than the sun on the outside. Said you have this entire creation and reality within yourselves.

وَلَقَدْ كَرَّمْنَا بَنِي آدَمَ وَحَمَلْنَاهُمْ فِي الْبَرِّ وَالْبَحْرِ وَرَزَقْنَاهُم مِّنَ الطَّيِّبَاتِ وَفَضَّلْنَاهُمْ عَلَىٰ كَثِيرٍ مِّمَّنْ خَلَقْنَا تَفْضِيلًا ﴿٧٠﴾

17:70 – *"Wa laqad karramna banee adama, wa hamalna hum filbarri wal bahri wa razaqnahum minat tayyibati wa faddalnahum 'ala katheerin mimman khalaqna tafdeela." (Surat Al-Isra)*

"And We have certainly honored the children of Adam and carried them on the land and sea and provided good and pure sustenance and bestow upon them favours, and preferred them over much of what We have created, with [definite] preference." (The Night Journey, 17:70)

If Allah is empowering that servant's heart, Allah is telling you that, *Qalb al Mu'min Baytullah*. I'm talking about Allah's house on your heart. That's the *Azimah* (greatness). That's the *Azimah*! Allah didn't say my house is in the sun. My house is in your heart. If you purify and listen to what they're teaching, your talking about Allah's heart on the servant.

قَلْبَ الْمُؤْمِنْ بَيْتُ الرَّبْ

"Qalb al mu'min baytur rabb."

"The heart of the believer is the House of the Lord." (Hadith Qudsi)

That's why they said, don't break somebody's heart. Because if it should be Allah's heart, Allah declares war against you. Because these *ahadith*, for *jahal* (ignorant) people, they're just beads. All over the place, beads. For *awliya* (saints), they're like a *tasbih* (prayer beads). The *ahadith*, they all come together. Why Allah said, 'I am going to make war if against *awliya*? If you come against my *awliya*, I make war against you.'

عَنْ أَبِي هُرَيْرَةَ رَضِيَ اللهُ عَنْهُ قَالَ: قَالَ رَسُولُ اللهِ صلى الله عليه و سلم إِنَّ اللَّهَ تَعَالَى قَالَ

"مَنْ عَادَى لِي وَلِيًّا فَقَدْ آذَنْتُهُ بِالْحَرْبِ" – رَوَاهُ الْبُخَارِيُّ

"Man 'ada li waliyan faqda adhantahu bil harbe..."
(*'An Abi Huraira, Rawa e Bukhari*)

Narrated by Abu Huraira (ra), that Prophet Muhammad (pbuh) said that, "Allah (AJ) said, 'I will declare war against him who shows

hostility to a waliy (saint) of Mine..."
(Hadith Qudsi, Narrated by Abu Huraira, in Sahih Bukhari)

And all the *ulama* (scholars) came and said there's very few things that Allah ﷻ would make war against anyone. Why war against if you come against His *awliya*? Because it's Allah's ﷻ heart. If they reach *wilayat* (sainthood), they reach the station in which Allah ﷻ, I am the heart, My house is in their heart. This is the house of Allah ﷻ within the heart of that *wali* (pious servant). Of course, you come against them, you came against Allah ﷻ.

The Shaykh's Energy Ignites the Heart of the Student

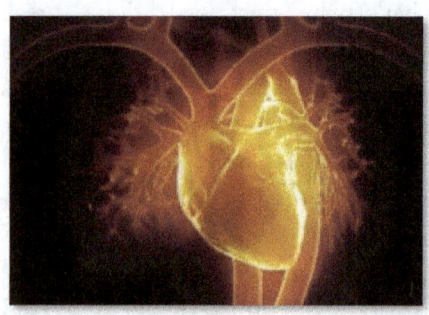

So, it means this *qudra* and this power that's emanating through the breath, then that shaykh has to be able to dress the breath. So, when you want to catch somebody on fire, you keep igniting them, you keep igniting them, you keep igniting through the breath. So, the *qudra* (power) the people feel, they're heated up in the *zikr* (remembrance). Even from a distance they're heating up, heating up, they're catching fire. Because if you ever watch somebody make a campfire, you throw sparks at it, right? When the student, the time is right, they ignite. Because they're continuously under the spark of the shaykh. They ignite and immediately they start to feel the energy, because the shaykh has to turn their reality into what he has been made. He is a walking sun.

Prophet Muhammad ﷺ is the Star Maker and the Black Hole

That's why Prophet ﷺ described that follow any of my companions, they're *najm*. They are stars, stars on a dark night.

أَصْحَابِيْ كَالنُّجُـومْ بِأَيِّهِمْ اَقْتَدَيْتِمْ اَهْتَدَيْتِمْ

"*Ashabi kan Nujoom, bi ayyihim aqta daytum ahta daytum.*"

"*My companions are like stars. Follow any one of them and you will be guided.*" *(Prophet Muhammad (pbuh))*

Prophet ﷺ is the 'star maker.' But yet they didn't understand the reality of the black hole. They saw something black with orange and they're astonished. Oh wow, it's a black hole with a circle with the orange. But the black hole is Prophet ﷺ and is the reality of every star. You cannot have a star manifest without entering into the black hole. The *fana* and the annihilation is the black hole, the *baqa* and that which appears after it was annihilated in the black hole, it appears as a sun. That's '*mawt qablil mawt*' (death of desires before physical death). When you approach them with who you are and say, 'No, I don't want to be this. I want to enter into the reality of what you created me for, to be a star, to be eternal.' Then say, go to the 'star maker.' Go to the presence of Sayyidina Muhammad ﷺ, he is going to annihilate you. If he annihilates you, it means he takes all your elements and breaks them down. That's what they saw of the black hole, that all the elements broke down.

7 Divinely Attributes Dress the 7 Holy Openings

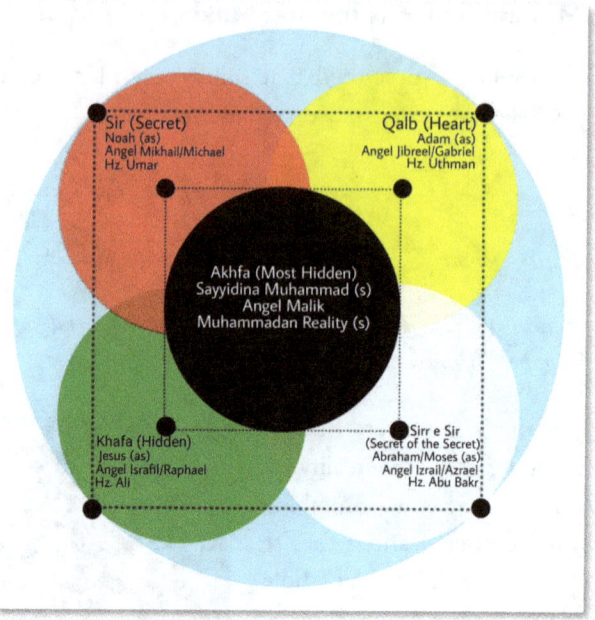

If you watch the *lataif* teachings, that the *Akhfa* reality, is the center. The *Qalb*, *Sir*, *Sirr e Sir*, *Khafa*, *Akhfa*. The *Akhfa* holds all the realities. Because once they annihilate, they come back as the Sun and they appear as a sun. They annihilate again and come back as the *Sir*. They annihilate again, they come back as *Sirr e Sir*. They have to keep annihilating with Prophet ﷺ. Each level of their annihilation, they come back now and manifest as a more powerful reality. That's why he said that all my *Sahabi* are stars. He ﷺ is the 'star maker.' And it goes even deeper.

أَصْحَابِيْ كَالنُّجُـــومْ بِأَيِّهِمْ اَقْتَدَيْتِمْ اَهْتَدَيْتِمْ

"Ashabi kan Nujoom, bi ayyihim aqta daytum ahta daytum."

"My companions are like stars. Follow any one of them and you will be guided." (Prophet Muhammad (pbuh))

Real Shaykhs Take the Burdens of People and Give Light

This *'Alim al Qadir* means their breath has power. They want to dress the student with power. Enough of the dress, enough of the dress, the student will be lit. That their soul will be ignited, they begin to heat up at every association. Their hands are hot, their neck is hot because their heart is now alive. It's burning like a sun and it needs a fuel source. It takes the burdens and bad character of people and gives light. They  never harm anyone, never talk bad. There are shaykhs online, I heard that they're bad, they throw things, they yell at people. Run from crazy people, run from crazy people. That's not a shaykh, that's a clown. The shaykh, he takes the burdens, he takes the sour and produces everything sweet. He takes their burdens and the difficulty is a fuel for him. Those burdens and difficulty come, and he produces more light, because Allah ﷻ made his heart like the alchemy. Like the sun, it takes the elements and produces light. *The 'Alim al Qadir.*

5. Sifat an-Nur (The Light) Dresses Awliya's Right Eye

The *Nurul Hayy* means then, the right eye, Allah ﷻ dress them from  *Sifat an-Nur*. That through their right eye, is a light that comes out and dresses. Dresses from *Sifat ar-Rahman* and *bi Haqqi* Imam al Hassan ؑ, and Allah ﷻ, where Prophet ﷺ described that Imam al Hassan ؑ, Imam al Hussain ؑ, *wa qurrato 'aini*, they're my beloved eyes.

7 Divinely Attributes Dress the 7 Holy Openings

أَسْيَادِي الْحَسَنْ وَالْحُسَيْنْ
إِلَى النَّبِيْ قُرَّةُ الْعَيْنْ
وَيَا شَبَابَ الْجَنَّتَيْنْ
جَدُّكُمْ صَاحِبُ الْقُرْآنْ

Asyadil Hassan wal Hussaini
Ilan Nabi qurrato 'aini
Wa Ya shabaa bal janna'taini
Jaddukum, saahibul Qur'ana

Our Masters, Imam Hassan ؑ and Imam Hussain ؑ, They are the coolness of Prophet's ﷺ eyes. O the Youth of the Paradises, Your Grandfather (Prophet Muhammad ﷺ) is the owner of the Holy Qur'an.

This is from *Insan al Kamil* of Prophet ﷺ, that describing that these two realities of my eyes are from their inheritance. That, you have to inherit from them. When Allah ﷻ wants to dress the right eye of the shaykh, it means then in the association from his eye, when you look into his face, his eye sends out a light. And that light goes into everyone's soul. It revives whatever is deficient, whatever is incorrect, whatever bad actions, that light has to dress upon them. And that's why Mawlana Shaykh ق described, Mawlana Shah Naqshband Fard ul Alam wa Shah e Qul ق, fills four paradises with the intercession of his right eye. That he saved his eyes, and when they would look at his eyes, they would roll. He would roll his eyeballs so that you couldn't see his eyes, and that you couldn't look at his *nazar* (gaze). So, that he could save that gift and that power, when Allah ﷻ grants, 'Whom do you want to intercede?' *Ya Nur Ya Rahman bi Haqqi* Mawlana Shah Naqshband ق. It means when you ask, '*Ya Nur Ya Rahman bi Haqqi*

Mawlana Shah Naqshband ق,' this light is ignited and begin to go around.

6. Sifat al-Hay (The Ever-Living) Dresses the Left Eye of Awliya

From the light of *Al-Hay* (Ever-Living), *sifat Al-Hay*, their left eye takes from *sifat ar-Raheem*. The *Raheem* is the attribute that governs *Rahman*, because *Raheem* is *malakut* (heavenly realm), *Rahman* is *mulk* (earthly realm). The *malakut* runs the *mulk*, not the *mulk* runs the *malakut*, right? The world of light, it runs the world of form. Anything manifesting is the world of form. The spiritual world, *sifat ar-Raheem*, "*Salamun Qawlam mir Rabbir Raheem.*"

سَلَامٌ قَوْلًا مِّن رَّبٍّ رَّحِيمٍ ﴿٥٨﴾

36:58 – "Salamun qawlam mir Rabbir Raheem." (Surat YaSeen)

"'Peace,' a word from a Merciful Lord." (YaSeen, 36:58)

That attribute is what dresses from the Oceans of *Al Hayat*. So, from their left eye, is coming out the ocean of *Hayat* and reviving and making everything to come to life. All with whatever Allah ﷻ wants. This is not outside of Allah ﷻ. When Allah ﷻ controls their movement, they don't move left and right without Allah's ﷻ permission.

7. Sifat al-Muqtadir (The Powerful Determiner) – Dresses the Entire Face of Awliya and Make Them Full Moons

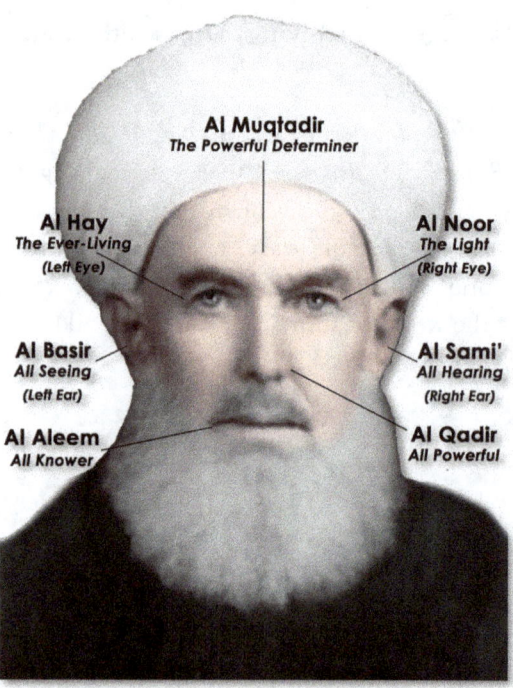

Whatever Allah ﷻ wants to dress and open that *sifat* (attribute), their face become ignited and these realities begin to dress. It's not an empty association. It's not a hollow face. As a result of these faculties being opened, that the *nur* coming from the right, oceans of *hayat* coming from their left eye.

When all of these 7 points are opened, Allah ﷻ opened *Al Qadir* and *Al Muqtadir*. *Sifat al Muqtadir* begin to dress their entire face, and Allah ﷻ make them to be *qamarun*. So, it means what? That the *Muqtadir*, they have the *Muhammadan Qadir*, that their faces are full moons. Full moons of guidance, not just somebody keep saying these are *qamarun, qamarun*. They have to know this reality and understand it because then they don't know what they've been dressed with. That *Qadir* and *Muqtadir*, that their heart is lit, ignited, Allah ﷻ opens the 7 faculties. As a result of the dress of *Muqtadir* upon their forehead, and all these names upon their reality, that face is filled with light and guidance. And at every moment, all of these attributes are dressing upon the souls of the student.

We pray that Allah ﷻ open for us more and more understanding of guidance, real guidance, not imitated guidance and playing around, *inshaAllah*.

Subhana rabbika rabbal 'izzati 'amma yasifoon, wa salaamun 'alal mursaleen, walhamdulillahi rabbil 'aalameen. Bi hurmati Muhammad al-Mustafa wa bi siri Surat al-Fatiha.

SECRETS OF THE EYES – LIGHT AND ETERNITY (AN NUR, AL HAY)

Balanced Vision vs. Dajjal System

The way of *ma'rifah* (gnosticism) and the way to realities is the fountain flowing from the heart of Prophet ﷺ to the heart of Sultanul Awliya Mawlana Shaykh Nazim Haqqani ق, and his representatives. We are asking for their *madad* and support for the realities. These realities are important for the last days.

Allah ﷻ Has Honored Human Beings

From every holy *hadith* of Prophet ﷺ, *awliya* (saints) can open tremendous understandings. One in the way of *ma'rifah* (gnosticism) is that, 'Who knows himself, will know his lord.'

مَنْ عَرَفَ نَفْسَهُ فَقَدْ عَرَفَ رَبَّهُ

"Man 'arafa nafsahu faqad 'arafa Rabbahu"

"Who knows himself, knows his Lord." (Prophet Muhammad (pbuh))

Secret of the Eyes – Light and Eternity (An Nur, Al Hay)

The knowing of the self is an understanding towards the reality which Allah ﷻ is dressing *insan* (human being). "*Wa laqad karramna bani Adama.*"

وَلَقَدْ كَرَّمْنَا بَنِي آدَمَ وَحَمَلْنَاهُمْ فِي الْبَرِّ وَالْبَحْرِ وَرَزَقْنَاهُم مِّنَ الطَّيِّبَاتِ وَفَضَّلْنَاهُمْ عَلَىٰ كَثِيرٍ مِّمَّنْ خَلَقْنَا تَفْضِيلًا ﴿٧٠﴾

17:70 – "*Wa laqad karramna banee adama, wa hamalna hum filbarri wal bahri wa razaqnahum minat tayyibati wa faddalnahum 'ala katheerin mimman khalaqna tafdeela.*" (Surat Al-Isra)

"And We have certainly honored the children of Adam and carried them on the land and sea and provided good and pure sustenance and bestow upon them favours, and preferred them over much of what We have created, with [definite] preference." (The Night Journey, 17:70)

What an honor and dress Allah ﷻ has given to human being. In the understanding of just the eyes of *insan* (human being), what lights emanate from the holy eyes and the reality in which the eyes serve? Everything about ourselves is a sign of the Divinely Presence, and everything within ourselves is a sign of the Divinely Presence. To gain an understanding Allah ﷻ says, 'I will teach you about my signs upon the horizons and within yourself.'

سَنُرِيهِمْ آيَاتِنَا فِي الْآفَاقِ وَفِي أَنفُسِهِمْ حَتَّىٰ يَتَبَيَّنَ لَهُمْ أَنَّهُ الْحَقُّ ۗ ... ﴿٥٣﴾

41:53 – "*Sanureehim ayatina fil afaqi wa fee anfusihim hatta yatabayyana lahum annahu alhaqqu...*" (Surat Al-Fussilat)

"We will show them Our signs in the horizons and within themselves until it becomes clear to them that it is the truth..."
(Explained in Detail, 41:53)

You Need Both Eyes for a Balanced Vision and Balanced Path

Awliyaullah (saints) and pious people come to teach us to reflect and contemplate and begin to understand. One example in the secret of the eyes is the understanding of living a balanced life and what is the difference between a balanced life and imbalanced life. For example, we are holding something holy such as this Holy Qur'an. We hold the Holy Qur'an here and you point to it. This is a hands-on demonstration.

1. Point your finger towards the Holy Qur'an (or another stationary object).
2. Focus both your eyes on your finger and the finger pointing towards the Qur'an. You have to have the focus of your finger between two eyesights and the Holy Qur'an so they are all lined up.
3. Now close your right eye. You will see that the point that you were focusing on moves.
4. Open your eyes.
5. Close your left eye. The point moves again.

The Qur'an didn't move, your perception of it moved. Depending on whether you see with the right eye, there will be a different understanding. Whether you see with the left eye, there is an understanding. It means the truth is one and the truth is there. How we are perceiving it is the way of *ma'rifah* (gnosticism) and the way of reality. Allah ﷻ says the truth doesn't keep changing between people, based on their level of understanding and their level of realities. The truth is not

Secret of the Eyes – Light and Eternity (An Nur, Al Hay)

changing, but their perception of the truth is either expanding or contracting. The truth remains one.

They begin to teach us that the truth is right there in the center. If life is imbalanced and one eye is not functioning, it is as if the target moves. If the other side is not balanced, again the target moves. It requires both eyes to look on and to keep the center way and to keep the balanced path. Then in our physiology of the self, Allah ﷻ is describing, your two eyes are responsible for keeping your path balanced. If you are using one eye (right eye), it will have a different imbalance. If you are using the left eye, it will have a different imbalance.

An Nur (Light) and Al Hay (Ever-Living) Give Spiritual Vision

Then they begin to teach us from Allah's ﷻ attributes, which are the essences. *Al Hay* (Ever-living) *wa an Nur* (Light). They first teach us in the way of the *ma'rifah* (gnosticism), then we come to the understanding of the disbelief and unbeliever and great deceiver that is opening within *dunya* (material world).

In the way of the belief, they begin to teach us that Qur'an and *hadith* are one. But how you perceive it is going to be based on the light within your heart. The light within your heart that emanates a *nur* (light) and the light within your heart that emanates from the *sifat al Hayat* (ever-living). It means these two divinely attributes are responsible for the quality of your *firasah*, your divinely vision, and your physical vision. It means everything has to be balanced.

عَنْ أَبِي سَعِيدِ الْخُدْرِيِّ، قَالَ رَسُولُ اللهِ صلى الله عليه وسلم: اتَّقُوا فِرَاسَةَ الْمُؤْمِنِ فَإِنَّهُ يَنْظُرُ بِنُورِ اللهِ. ثُمَّ قَرَأَ : "إِنَّ فِي ذَٰلِكَ لَآيَاتٍ لِلْمُتَوَسِّمِينَ

'An Abi Sa'yidel Khudriyi, qala Rasulullahi (saws): "Ittaqoo Firasatal Mu'min, Fa Innahu yanzuru Bi Nurillah. Thumma Qara'a: 'Inna fee dhalika la ayaatun lil mutawassimeen.' (Surat al Hijr, 15:75)"

Narrated by Sa'yidel Khudri that the Messenger of Allah (pbuh) said: "Beware/be conscious of the true believer's spiritual vision, for indeed he sees with Allah's Light. Then he recited from holy Qur'an: 'Surely in this are signs for those who see.' (The Rocky Tract, 15:75)"
(Tirmidhi, Book 47, #3419)

An Nur (The Light)

Like Light Reads a CD, You Read Qur'an Through the Light of Your Heart

There are people who are coming to belief. Immediately, Allah ﷻ grants them a *nur* (light). It is a *nur* but not yet from the ocean of realities of *hayat* (life), complete. These are like two cups and we are asked to fill them. As much as we fill them from Allah's ﷻ attributes, it's endless. It is

never enough. It never takes anything from Allah ﷻ. But they begin to teach us the perception and understanding. Somebody comes to belief. They are granted a *nur* (light). Within their eye, they have a light. They read Holy Qur'an and they only understand something very basic.

Where we understand that in technology? In a CD. CD is a plastic, like a mirror but encoded with millions of information. There is a reader that hits the CD to get the information. Based on the quality of that light, it hits that mirror (CD) and retrieves information. They begin to teach

Secret of the Eyes – Light and Eternity (An Nur, Al Hay)

when Allah ﷻ begins to send a *nur* (light) into the heart and that *nur* begins to reflect through the eyes. When the eye looks, at the entry level, the eye has very little light. It is still struggling just to flicker. It pulls information, reads Holy Qur'an and mainly at the level of *furqan*. *Furqan* is right and wrong, right and wrong.

Then they become, maybe *mu'min* (believer) and maybe *imam* (leader). They have more light into their hearts. If they don't keep the way of *tazkiya* (purification), *tasawwuf* (mysticism), and the ways of purification, they won't be drinking from the oceans of *Hayat* (ever-living). But, because of their *amal* and their action, they will be granted *nur, nur, nur* (light). Again, they look and their perception of Holy Qur'an and holy *hadith* and everything else is at a different *darajat* (level). Because there is a light reflecting and that light is hitting the letters, Allah ﷻ is reflecting back to the level of their heart and their beliefs. It can't be more than the level of beliefs because it crashes. It's a power, it is *qudra* (power) from Allah's ﷻ Divinely Presence.

What Differentiates Awliyaullah (Saints) From Regular Scholars

They begin to teach so we understand that there are *darajats* and levels. These levels are based on the *nur* (light) in their hearts. It means you come across very pious scholars. Again, their practices, their *amal* (action) has been granting them light and maybe little bit of *Hayat*. Because *Hayat* (ever-living) then we go into is a completely different practice. The *amal* and actions grant you a light. They speak again as if they read the interpretations of Qur'an and they speak nicely and give you out the interpretations. Not from the oceans of realities. They mainly mix the English, the Arabic, and give you back an explanation with a little bit of knowledge here and there. You can see them throughout YouTube – every type of scholar and knowledgeable person. Again, it is based on the light within their heart.

Now the perception, like the test we gave at the beginning of this *suhbah* (association). When working only with one eye and the light of faith is entering that heart and the eye is shining a *nur* (light), their perception of reality is a bit off-center. They are pulling out information but not at the level of *awliyaullah* (saints).

It's not at the level of pious saints who are drinking from the fountain of *hayat* (ever-living). It means their whole life is in *zikrullah* (remembrance of Allah ﷻ) and in praising upon Sayyidina Muhammad ﷺ. Their whole life is in *tazkiya* (purification). As a result of that, they are drinking from the oceans of *Kawthar* (fountain of  abundance), they are drinking from the Oceans of *Hayat* (ever-living). They are now two winged. What is emanating from their hearts is the Ocean of *Hayat*, the oceans of the ever-living reality and the oceans of *nur* (light). When the Ocean of *Hayat* and *nur* begin to look at something, it means they pull out the reality in which Allah ﷻ wants to dress them. They speak at the levels of realities that are far beyond the abilities of others.

When people say I haven't heard those realities and other people speak from different realities and at different levels. They begin to teach, those who know themselves, they know that if the practices of that one (regular scholars) is not strong enough and not opening the Ocean of *Hayat*. They are merely through their *amal* (actions) have been granted *nur*. Their *nur* (light) can only retrieve so much information.

Al Hay (The Ever-Living)

Real Ashabul Kahf are the People of Hayat

Then you have *furqan* (book of right and wrong). You have now Qur'an. Qur'an is from the heart of the Arabic messenger. It means that the light and love of Sayyidina Muhammad ﷺ must be emanating within your heart. That is the Ocean of *Hayat*. He ﷺ is the servant of *Al-Hay* (the ever-living). When Allah ﷻ wants to describe *hayat*, it is not through Allah ﷻ. Allah ﷻ is *la sharika la* (without any partner);

don't make example of Allah ﷻ. Allah ﷻ is not *hay* (life) and He is not *mayt* (dead), He is not life and He is not dead. Allah ﷻ is beyond the ocean of understanding. But when we want to describe, who is the ever-living servant of Allah ﷻ? It's Sayyidina Muhammad ﷺ.

It means then the lovers and *ashiqeen* of Sayyidina Muhammad ﷺ are the people of *hayat*. Allah ﷻ describes them as *Ashabul Kahf* (people of the cave). That's why the number 18. Next month is the month of Safar.

This is the reality of *Ashabul Kahf*. The real *Ashabul Kahf* are the ones who accompanied Prophet Muhammad ﷺ to the holy cave. It means the *Ashabul Kahf* from before were the imitation for the arrival of Muhammad ﷺ. They are the exemplars to teach us that the characteristics of *Ashabul Kahf* are the people of *hayat* (ever-living).

We know that every *amal* and every action has a *nur* (light). Therefore, people of *nur* will be granted a light but it doesn't mean they will be granted *hayat* (ever-living). They don't reach to those oceans of eternity. The example of that servant was Sayyidina Khidr ﷺ. Sayyidina Khidr ﷺ was asking, '*Ya Rabbi* (O my lord), let me drink from the fountain of the ever-living and to reach eternity.' The eternal ocean of ever-living is oceans of holy *Kawthar*. He reached the holy *Kawthar*, drank from that reality, and now he reached eternity.

Awliya Have Nur of Rahman and Hay of Raheem

It means *Al-Hayat* is never dying. The souls that are dressed from the *Al Hayat* (ever- living) swim in the *zikr* of *Hay* (ever-living); under the *sifat Ar-Raheem* (The Merciful), *ra, hay, meem*. Who are the *meem*? These are the Muhammadan whose hearts are *hay* (ever-living). They have been granted *nur* (light) from *Rahman* (the Most Compassionate), because of *noon* (representing *nur*). They have *nur* (light) of *Rahman*, *hay* of *Raheem*. *Salamun Qawlam mir Rabbir Raheem*.

سَلَامٌ قَوْلًا مِّن رَّبٍّ رَّحِيمٍ ﴿٥٨﴾

36:58 – "Salamun qawlam mir Rabbir Raheem." (Surat YaSeen)

"Peace, a word from a Merciful Lord." (YaSeen, 36:58)

Why? Because they are in the heart of YaSeen ﷺ. It means they love Prophet ﷺ. They follow the way and the example, the *sunnah* of Muhammad ﷺ. Not only the external *amal* (action) but their internal *tazkiya* (purification), their internal *adab* (manners), and their internal characteristics. They don't talk, they are very quiet, and they are very pious, very humble. They are in constant *zikr* (remembrance) and constant purification – never glorifying themselves but constantly

Secret of the Eyes – Light and Eternity (An Nur, Al Hay)

humiliating and humbling themselves. As a result, Prophet ﷺ grants them an access towards that ocean and they become from the *Ashabul Kahf* (People of the Cave).

Awliya (Saints) are People of the Kaaf and Kawthar

Then Mawlana Shaykh ق teaches that *Ashabul Kahf* is to be from the people of *kaaf* (letter of Arabic alphabet). What is *kaaf*? It is *Kawthar*; to be from the people of the *Kawthar* (fountain of abundance), from the *Katheer* (abundant). Allah ﷻ says, 'We have given you from the fountain of abundance and *kabeer* (great), the Ocean of greatness.'

﴿١﴾ إِنَّا أَعْطَيْنَاكَ الْكَوْثَرَ

108:1 – *"Inna 'atayna kal kawthar."* (Surat Al-Kawthar)

"To thee (O Muhammad) we have granted the Fount (of Abundance)." (The Abundance, 108:1)

They drink, they bathe, and they nourish their souls from that ocean. Everything about them is how much their souls can move into the *Kawthar* (fountain of abundance) and how much they can swim in the ocean of *Kawthar*. Like a fish, they try to absorb as much as they can from Prophet ﷺ, from what Allah ﷻ is dressing Sayyidina Muhammad ﷺ. The owner of the holy *Kawthar* that flows to the *zamzam* is Sayyidina Muhammad ﷺ. *"Atayna kal kawthar."* Allah ﷻ said, 'We have given you the fountain of abundance.' It means everything within it and every life emanating from it. And be from the *Ashabul Kahf* (People of the Cave) and be from the people who are seeking the *Kawthar*. They drink *zamzam* in *dunya* (material world) to reach the reality of *Kawthar* of *akhirah* (afterlife), to reach to the ocean of *hayat* (ever-living).

$$\text{إِنَّا أَعْطَيْنَاكَ الْكَوْثَرَ ﴿١﴾}$$

108:1 – *"Inna 'atayna kal kawthar."* (Surat Al-Kawthar)

"To thee (O Muhammad) we have granted the Fount (of Abundance)." (The Abundance, 108:1)

People of Hayat (Ever-Living) Are Taught by Light of Rahman

They begin to teach us that people of *hayat* are different from the people who have certain *amal* (action). That *amal* has a perception that is off target but it is still good. But when the heart is filled with the Ocean of *Hayat* and filled with ocean of *nur*, they are looking with *Al-Hay wan Nur*, like a CD, that whatever they focus their heart on, begin to retrieve information. Why? Because they are now under the reality of *Ar-Rahman*. What Allah ﷻ describes them in Surat Ar-Rahman? *Alamal Qur'an. Khalaqal insaan.*

$$\text{عَلَّمَ الْقُرْآنَ ﴿٢﴾ خَلَقَ الْإِنْسَانَ ﴿٣﴾}$$

55:2-3 – *"Allamal Qur'an (2). Khalaqal Insaan (3)."* (Surat Ar-Rahman)

"It is He Who has taught the Qur'an. (2) He has created Mankind. (3)." (The Beneficent, 55: 2-3)

It means, that which you are looking for of the realities; that your soul is dressed from *Al-Hayat*, your soul has reached My *Nur*. Whatever your soul looks at, it's going to now remember what I taught you when you were in the world of souls. I taught you Qur'an *(alamal Qur'an)*. Allah ﷻ is saying anciently, I taught you these realities. I burned them all onto your soul like your CD. Your duty was to come into this world and to reflect, to reflect, to reflect. Take your vision from outside and look inside. Outside is the filthiness of *dunya* (material world). What you are looking for? God in the market and in the shops? You are not going to find Allah ﷻ anywhere.

One Hour of Contemplation is Worth More Than 70 Years of Worship

That's why Prophet ﷺ said to *tafakkur* (contemplate). One hour contemplation is like a lifetime of *'ibadah* (worship).

تَفَكُّرْ سَاعَةٍ خَيْرٌ مِنْ عِبَادَةِ سَبْعِينْ سَنَةً

"Tafakkur sa'atin khairun min 'Ibadati sab'een sanatan."

"One hour of contemplation is more valuable than seventy years of worship." (Prophet Muhammad (pbuh))

One hour of *tafakkur* like 70 years of worship. Why? Because you just have *nur* (light). But the servant who has *nur* and *hayat* is like an ocean and mountain of difference in their reality. All that reality within their heart, whatever they contemplate to their ability and the strength of their soul, Allah ﷻ would remind them what Allah ﷻ has taught them. Now their *darajats* (levels) is going higher, higher, and higher. It's unimaginable what Allah ﷻ has taught. Nobody can put a limit on Allah ﷻ. Nobody can come and say that, 'No, Allah ﷻ didn't teach that.'

Khidr ؏ Attained Love of Prophet ﷺ, Then His Heart Became Eternally Alive

Sayyidina Khidr ؏ steps forward and describes to us that Allah ﷻ described in Holy Qur'an that, 'He (Khidr ؏) attained a *rahmah* (mercy) and then we taught him.' Not he was taught and then he attained a mercy. He attained a *rahmah* (mercy). Who is *Rahmah* (mercy) of Allah ﷻ? *Rahmatal Lil'alameen* (mercy to the worlds) is Sayyidina Muhammad ﷺ.

فَوَجَدَا عَبْدًا مِّنْ عِبَادِنَا آتَيْنَاهُ رَحْمَةً مِّنْ عِندِنَا وَعَلَّمْنَاهُ مِن لَّدُنَّا عِلْمًا ﴿٦٥﴾

18:65 – *"Fawajada 'abdan min 'ibadinaa ataynahu rahmatan min 'indina wa 'allamnahu mil ladunna 'ilma."* (Surat Al-Kahf)

"So they found one of Our servant from among Our servants, on whom We had bestowed Mercy from Ourselves and whom We had taught [unseen/heavenly] knowledge from Our own Presence..."
(The Cave, 18:65)

وَمَا أَرْسَلْنَاكَ إِلَّا رَحْمَةً لِّلْعَالَمِينَ ﴿١٠٧﴾

21:107 – *"Wa maa arsalnaka illa Rahmatal lil'alameen."*
(Surat Al-Anbiya)

"And We have not sent you, [O Muhammad (pbuh)], except as a mercy to the worlds/creation." (The Prophets, 21:107)

He (Khidr ؏) attained the love and the nearness of Prophet ﷺ; as a result, We taught him. Because he is near the *habib* (beloved), he is in

Secret of the Eyes – Light and Eternity (An Nur, Al Hay)

the divine heart of *YaSeen* ﷺ. And he was granted, *Salamun Qawlum mir Rabbir Raheem*.

سَلَامٌ قَوْلًا مِّن رَّبٍّ رَّحِيمٍ ﴿٥٨﴾

36:58 – "*Salamun qawlam mir Rabbir Raheem.*" (Surat YaSeen)

"'Peace', a word from a Merciful Lord." (YaSeen, 36:58)

A *salaam* (peace) from *Raheem* (the Merciful) means the activation of the heart of *hayat* (ever-living). That heart now is alive, eternally alive. That which Allah ﷻ gives eternal life is never dead. It can never go wrong. It is *mahfuz* (safeguarded), Allah ﷻ guards it. Allah ﷻ doesn't take away what he gives. We give a gift; we may take it back. Allah ﷻ waits, waits, waits but when Allah ﷻ gives, He never takes it back. They are now *Hay wa Nur*. What they say and what they teach are oceans apart (from other scholars). What they say and what they teach through their eyes will dress you from the Ocean of *Hayat* and dress you from the ocean of *An Nur*. Because they are alive! There is a frequency and energy being transmitted from their souls. It's very different; there is energy moving.

Sayyidina Muhammad ﷺ Wants Us to Drink From Kawthar

This is a balanced life. This is the life that *turuq* (spiritual paths) comes to teach; that seek the reality of Prophet ﷺ, reach to his nearness. He ﷺ is going to grant the ever-living fountain and quench our thirst at the *Kawthar* (fountain of abundance). The whole creation was looking for that fountain. It is held in the hand of Sayyidina Muhammad ﷺ.

They make movies looking for a special cup. The whole world is flipping around for a cup. Prophet ﷺ says, 'I have it in my hand, come! That which you seek is not from this world but it's the Divinely Presence. Drink from the *zamzam*. Drink from my *Kawthar*.'

"Fasali li rabbika wanhar." Pray onto your lord and sacrifice yourself (not physically but sacrifice your desires). *"Inna shani-aka huwal abtar."* And Allah ﷻ will obliterate everything that begins and tries to stop you from that reality. If you sacrifice, sacrifice, sacrifice, Allah ﷻ dresses you from *Hayat* and Allah ﷻ dresses you from *Nur*. At that time, He obliterates anything of the *shayateen* (satans) that is coming to take us from that because they become *mahfuz*, they've become guarded by Allah ﷻ.

إِنَّا أَعْطَيْنَاكَ الْكَوْثَرَ ﴿١﴾ فَصَلِّ لِرَبِّكَ وَانْحَرْ ﴿٢﴾ إِنَّ شَانِئَكَ هُوَ الْأَبْتَرُ ﴿٣﴾

108:1-3 – *"Inna 'atayna kal kawthar. (1) Fasali li rabbika wanhar. (2) Inna shani-aka huwal abtar. (3)"* (Surat Al-Kawthar)

"To thee (O Muhammad) we have granted the Fount (of Abundance). (1) So pray to your Lord and Sacrifice. (2) Indeed, your enemy is the one cut off. (3)" (The Abundance, 108:1-3)

People of Hayat Are Always in Zikr of Hay

This is the reality that they are asking us to seek. When we begin to understand that reality, we understand why certain people; even with belief, they speak at different level. They have *nur* (light), but they are not from people of *Hay*. The people of *Hay* are busy with saying *Hay, Hay, Hay*. It's not a question. You see the little kids of *Hay*. They go home and keep saying *Hay, Hay, Hay*. How can someone say I am from *Hayat* but never make *zikr* of *Hay*? It means their whole existence is *Hay, Hay, Hay*. Their whole reality is in that ocean.

Dajjal's System of Deception

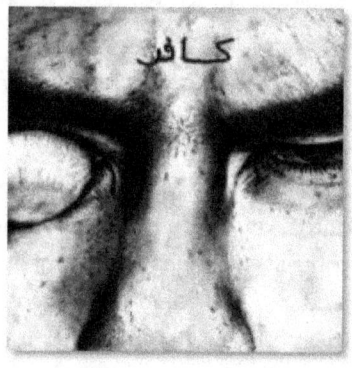

Now we look at the other side. To understand how this is implemented is the *Dajjal's* (the deceiver) system. Whether the people say the *Dajjal* is here or that he is coming, that doesn't matter. The system which Prophet ﷺ wants us to understand is that the *Dajjal* (the deceiver) has a corrupt vision of *dunya* (material world). His one eye is damaged. It means the eye that is damaged is the eye that has no *nur*, light of faith, *Hayat* (ever-living). As a result, the light from his other eye doesn't emanate but it pulls the light of faith. To understand the importance of the *Dajjal* system in *dunya* (material world) is that there is no *hayat*.

The men of God come to increase the ever-living. That you think about your soul and live for eternity in Allah's ﷻ Ocean of Power. And *Dajjal* (the deceiver) comes and says there is no *hayat* (ever-living). Live life to the fullest. Isn't that his logo on every commercial? You see somebody is running. Where are you running to? You are not going to live five minutes longer. You are wasting your time and you are hurting your knees. He says live life to the fullest! What full? *Dajjal's* system says don't believe in heavens. You live life here, you enjoy here, you celebrate here, and here the party ends. Everything from that system is based on only focusing here.

Dajjal's System is to Take Away Faith Brick by Brick

His other eye is to take away all faith. Every TV show that comes out, you look at it; you lost your faith. Every movie that comes out, you watch it; you lost your faith. Every music that you hear, you listen to it; you lost your faith. Brick by brick, *shaitan* (satan) takes away faith, takes away faith, takes away faith until they are faithless people.

Take away the light and now you have darkness. It is opposites. Either you are moving to the light and you feel the warmth of the light or you have turned away from the light, and you feel now a coldness of darkness. The *Dajjal* system is to take away the light; don't let anybody who speaks, speak of the faith. Have them speak and question the Divine and take away faith. Have them curse and take away faith. Everything from the *Dajjal* system is to take away faith. Take away the concept of *hayat*. I should just live life and party and do everything. Then I am going to die and it is finished. They begin to teach, that is the system that is moving on this earth now. Everything is based on that reality.

To seek the *hayat* of the heavens and seek the *Nur* of the heavens is our way. And to understand the deceiver's system is very much active. Its understanding is to take away all concept of *hayat* and you live life to the fullest. Take away all signs of faith; that everything to be based on darkness. As a result, the eye is corrupt and there is an imbalance in the formula. It's not the middle way.

Keep the Middle Way to Have a Balance in Life

Where Allah ﷻ said you live life on the middle way. It means your both eyes. Your both realities are focused. When they are focused, you will find your life at very even keel. If you follow his (satan's) example of *hayat* of *dunya* (material world), you will fall and become blindsided because your whole desire would be *dunya* (material world) and you will be devoid of any light and you will find yourself tipping.

It means the concept of a balanced life and the understanding of this life and the understanding of *darajats* (levels). Even amongst the pious people, how they speak at a level that other people don't speak. Their characteristics are beyond the characteristics of other people because they are men and women of *hayat* and the oceans of reality. They are in existence to prepare people for the difficulties that are opening in *dunya* (material world). And the extreme amount of power that now *Dajjal* is emanating in this *dunya* (material world) to take away these lights, to take away faith, to take away all of it.

Pray that Allah ﷻ grant us from these lights and these blessings; and love of Sayyidina Muhammad ﷺ, love of *Ahlul Bayt Nabi* ﷺ and *Ashabun Nabi* ﷺ, and love of *awliyaullah* (saints).

Subhana rabbika rabbal 'izzati 'amma yasifoon, wa salaamun 'alal mursaleen, walhamdulillahi rabbil 'aalameen. Bi hurmati Muhammad al-Mustafa wa bi siri Surat al-Fatiha.

REALITY OF EYES – COMPASSION AND MERCY
IMAM HASSAN ؑ & IMAM HUSSAIN ؑ

We Live in a Time of Deception

We're asking that Allah ﷻ allow us to enter oceans of mercy and *rahmah*. We are in days of difficulty and days of great deceit. That these are a time that we call the days of a great mischief and a great deceit is upon the earth and moving. And no nation is going to be safe. Every nation is filled with that deceit and with that deception, like a tremendous magic show. And what is happening is related to the world of light. Understanding the world of light, the reality of light, opens our heart to move towards that.

Light Always Extinguishes Darkness

We were saying before that the greatness of light, the greatness of *nur* (light), just to understand always by example, is that if we blacken the room as much as we can and make it to be black. If one candle and one light is lit, that light begins to push away darkness. And if 5,000 more darknesses enter into that room, it cannot extinguish

that light which Allah ﷻ is allowing. It means this is the greatness of light. Light, *"Qul ja al haq, wa zahaqal batil."* The light always extinguishes darkness.

Reality of Eyes – Compassion and Mercy
Imam Hassan ؑ & Imam Hussain ؑ

وَ قُلْ جَاءَالْحَقُّ وَزَهَقَ الْبَطِلُ، إِنَّ الْبَطِلَ كَانَ زَهُوقًا ﴿٨١﴾

17:81 – *"Wa qul jaa alhaqqu wa zahaqal baatil, innal batila kana zahoqa." (Surat Al-Isra)*

"And say, Truth has come, and falsehood has perished. Indeed falsehood, [by its nature], is ever perishing/ bound to perish."
(The Night Journey, 17:81)

Allah ﷻ describes, it obliterates darkness. But all we need is light. That's why a true knowledgeable one is as if 1,000 men. Now imagine the heart of an *'arifeen*, of a lover of Sayyidina Muhammad ﷺ. That heart is like 1,000 men. If there is a dark time entering this earth and darkness is wishing to spread upon this earth, then they most definitely don't appreciate anyone becoming *'arifeen* (knowers). Because they know that as much as they want the room to be as dark, so that they can do their magic. They want this earth like a room; we talk by example because we don't want to talk too big. They want the room to be dark, so that they can begin a magic show because in darkness, all sorts of deceit that can be happening. But if all of sudden somebody comes in with a spotlight, what happens? You immediately begin to uncover all the deceit.

So, then darkness by its nature doesn't like the light, wants nothing to do with the light. It also realizes that it cannot put out light. But what it can try to do is to kill. It kills and destroys the light. It extinguishes the heart and the light that is entering within the heart, through darkness. It tries to take the lives of people, to take away light and increase darkness, and increase darkness, and increase darkness.

Everything Will Perish Except the Holy Face

It means this is a tremendous reality that Allah ﷻ is dressing from *Insan al Kamil* and the perfected being. That Allah ﷻ says, 'Everything perishes but My Holy Face.'

كُلُّ شَيْءٍ هَالِكٌ إِلَّا وَجْهَهُ ۚ ﴿٨٨﴾

28:88 – "...*kullu shayin halikun illa wajha.*" (Surat Al-Qasas)

"...Everything (that exists) will perish except His Holy Face..."
(The Stories, 28:88)

Everything in creation, from all of its paradises, everything will vanish, will cease to exist, except the Holy Face. And every reality is based on *la ilaha illAllah Muhammadun RasulAllah* ﷺ.

لَا إِلَهَ إِلَّا اللهُ مُحَمَّدًا رَسُولُ الله

"*La ilaha illAllahu Muhammadun RasulAllah*"

"There is no deity but Allah, Prophet Muhammad is the messenger of Allah."

If you don't know *la ilaha illAllah*, and we can never know the reality of *la ilaha illAllah*; that reality must be reflecting in *Muhammadun RasulAllah* ﷺ. That's why all the calligraphy you see, *Hu wa Hu*.

Reality of Eyes – Compassion and Mercy
Imam Hassan ؓ & Imam Hussain ؓ

When they begin to mirror calligraphy, Allah ﷻ is showing. If you want to know *la ilaha illAllah*, enter the ocean of *Muhammadun RasulAllah* ﷺ. It is the reflection. Every reality, Allah ﷻ will reflect to *Muhammadun RasulAllah* ﷺ.

These realities that we want is dressing the light of Prophet ﷺ. When we want to know the holy face, the holy face of Sayyidina Muhammad ﷺ is the dress of that reality. All the prophets are in that dress. So, there must be a tremendous reality.

Right Eye is From Sifat Ar-Rahman (The Most Compassionate)

Just the understanding of what's happening with the eyes because the eyes are the window of the soul. The ears are the door for the soul. It means that the window of the soul and the reality of the soul must be in the secret of the eyes. The right eye is *sifat ar-Rahman*. When you say *Bismillahir Rahmanir Raheem*, (in the name of Allah, the Most Compassionate, the Most Merciful) the right eye is from the reality of *ar-Rahman*. The left eye is from the reality of *ar-Raheem* (the Most Merciful). It means in *dunya* (material world), *sifat ar-Rahman* (attribute of the Most Compassionate). We have said in other teachings of Mawlana Shaykh's teachings, that *ha* is the ocean of *hayat* (ever-living). The *meem* has to do with the reality of *Bahrul Muheet*, the all-encompassing ocean of Sayyidina Muhammad ﷺ. As a result, it gives a *noon* and gives a *nur* (light).

So, it means that right eye that Allah ﷻ is dressing the believers, dressing the reality in what He wants for all creation. He wants His attribute to be dressed upon your right eye, upon our right eye. He wants to dress it from *nur ar-Rahman*. So that with the right eye,

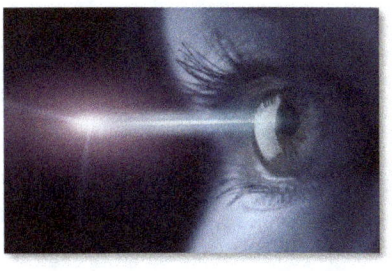

you look with a *nur*. That *nur* (light) extinguishes darkness. That *nur* enlightens because it is able to see the reality of everything that it looks at.

Left Eye is From Sifat Ar-Raheem (The Most Merciful)

The left eye is the *Bahrul Hayat* (Ocean of Ever-living), the oceans of *al-Hayat* because *sifat ar-Raheem*, means ra, hay, meem. What Allah ﷻ gives us *nur* in *dunya* (material world), what is the result in *akhirah* (afterlife)? If Allah ﷻ dresses us with *nur* (light) in *dunya*, it means what were we granted in *akhirah* is the oceans of *Hayat*, ever-living, ever-eternal. If Allah ﷻ gives you *nur* (light), it means He is now granting you from the ocean of *al-Hay*, of *al-Hayat*. It means for your soul to reach its eternity and your soul to be dressed from its eternity.

That's why the *ahlul hayat* (people of ever-living), *al-hay*. These are the people of *zikrullah* (remembrance of Allah ﷻ) and the people of *hay, hay, hay*. It describes in the *sifat* (attribute) of *Raheem* – *hay, meem*, which means *hay Muhammad, hay Muhammad*. It means the love of Sayyidina Muhammad ﷺ is carrying the ocean of *al-Hayat* (ever-living). The love of Sayyidina Muhammad ﷺ is carrying the *nur* (light).

Nabi Musa ﷺ Sought the Ocean of Hayat

Because every reality, its highest level is in the understanding of Muhammadan reality. You can never know *la ilaha illAllah*. But the reflection of these two rivers is where Nabi Musa (Moses) ﷺ wanted, 'I want where the two rivers meet.'

وَإِذْ قَالَ مُوسَىٰ لِفَتَاهُ لَا أَبْرَحُ حَتَّىٰ أَبْلُغَ مَجْمَعَ الْبَحْرَيْنِ أَوْ أَمْضِيَ حُقُبًا ﴿٦٠﴾

18:60 – "Wa idh qala Mosa lefatahu laa abrahu hatta ablugha majma'a albahrayni aw amdiya huquba." (Surat Al-Kahf)

"Behold, Moses said to his attendant, I will not give up until I reach the junction of the two seas or (until) I spend years and years in travel." (The Cave, 18:60)

Not only from the *Bismillahir Rahmanir Raheem* and out, 'Ya Rabbi, I want from your realities where the two rivers meet.' From the *Qalam al Qudra* (the Pen of Power), Mawlana Shaykh said many times that the Pen of Power was writing *La ilaha illAllah Muhammadun RasulAllah* before it was writing *Bismillahir Rahmanir Raheem*. That is what Nabi Musa ﷺ wanted from the realities. That reality has to do with the left eye. So, the left eye is under *sifat ar-Raheem* and the oceans of *al-Hayat* (ever-living).

Imam Hassan ؑ Symbolizes the Right Eye and He's Granted Sifat Ar-Rahman

Then they begin to inspire us that the right eye is Imam Hassan ؑ. That the family of Prophet ﷺ are the ones carrying first the reality of Sayyidina Muhammad ﷺ. That it's coming as an inheritance from Prophet ﷺ to the family of Sayyidina Muhammad ﷺ. That he ﷺ is granting him *bi sifat ar-Rahman. Ya Rabbi, bi Haqi Rahman wa bi Haqi Imam al-Hassan al-Mujtaba, bi Haqi Rahman.* From the reality of *sifat ar-Rahman,* and by the name of Imam al-Hassan al-Mujtaba ؑ, grant me from that light, grant me from that *sifat* (attribute). That *sifat (Rahman)* is dressing the light.

That is why Allah ﷻ describes in Qur'an, *"Fid dunyaa hasanat wa fil aakhirati hasanat wa qinaa azaaban Naar."*

وَمِنْهُم مَّن يَقُولُ رَبَّنَا آتِنَا فِي الدُّنْيَا حَسَنَةً وَفِي الْآخِرَةِ حَسَنَةً وَقِنَا عَذَابَ النَّارِ ﴿٢٠١﴾

2:201 – "Wa minhum mai yaqoolu rabbanaaa aatina fid dunyaa hasanatawn wa fil aakhirati hasanatanw wa qinaa azaaban Naar." (Surat Al-Baqarah)

"Our Lord, give us in this world [that which is] good and in the Hereafter [that which is] good and protect us from the punishment of the Fire." (The Cow, 2:201)

It means to whom I have given *hasanat* (goodness) in *dunya* (material world) and I gave *hasanat* in *akhirah* (afterlife), it will save them from punishment. Because Hassan and Hussain is the same. Hussain means 'little Hassan.' It has also a secret within that reality.

*Reality of Eyes – Compassion and Mercy
Imam Hassan (as) & Imam Hussain (as)*

Imam Hassan (as) and Imam Hussain (as) Carry the Secret of Prophet Muhammad (pbuh)

It means then the grandchildren of Prophet (pbuh) are holding that reality. That is why in the *salawats* (praisings), we say, "*Ilan Nabi qurrato 'aini, Jaddal Hassan wal Hussaini.*"

أَسْيَادِي الْحَسَّنْ وَالْحُسَّيْنِ   النَّبِيِّ قُرَّةُ الْعَيْنِ
وَيَا شَبَابَ الْجَنَتَيْنِ   جَدُّكُمْ صَاحِبُ الْقُرْآنَ

Asyadil Hassan wal Hussaini   *Ilan Nabi qurrato 'aini*
Ya shabaa bal janna'taini   *Jaddukum saahibul Qur'ana*

Our Masters, Imam Hassan (as) and Imam Hussain (as),
They are the coolness of Prophet's (pbuh) eyes.
O the Youth of the Paradises,
Your Grandfather (Prophet Muhammad (pbuh)) is the owner of the Holy Qur'an.

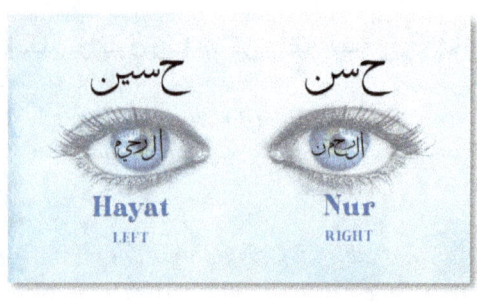

They are reciting from that reality. They know they are the owners of the paradise. They are owners, *Sahibul Qur'an*. It means everything of Holy Qur'an is in Surat al-Fatiha (1st chapter of Quran). All of al-Fatiha is in *Bismillahir Rahmanir Raheem. Bismillahir Rahmanir Raheem*, all of that Allah (swt) is dressing in *Bismillahir Rahmanir Raheem. Ar-Rahman, Ar-Raheem.* Dressing from that reality; it means that by loving *Ahlul Bayt* (as), by understanding their reality, they are the oceans of *al-Hayat*. And they carry the *seen* and the secret of Sayyidina Muhammad (pbuh) (referring to the letter *seen* in the names of Imam Hassan (as) and Hussain (as)). That is their inheritance.

What Does It Mean to Have Hasanat in Dunya?

Ya Hassan bi Haqq Al Rahman. Ya Rabbi, by the reality of Imam Hassan ؑ, grant me from *sifat ar-Rahman*. They are carrying that reality. They begin to dress us from their *nur* (light) (*noon* in Hassan ؑ). That's why Allah ﷻ described to have *hasanat* in *dunya* and *hasanat* in *akhirah* and save us from difficulty.

وَمِنْهُم مَّن يَقُولُ رَبَّنَا آتِنَا فِي الدُّنْيَا حَسَنَةً وَفِي الْآخِرَةِ حَسَنَةً وَقِنَا عَذَابَ النَّارِ ﴿٢٠١﴾

2:201 – "Wa minhum mai yaqoolu rabbanaaa aatina fid dunyaa hasanatawn wa fil aakhirati hasanatanw wa qinaa azaaban Naar." (Surat Al-Baqarah)

"Our Lord, give us in this world [that which is] good and in the Hereafter [that which is] good and protect us from the punishment of the Fire." (The Cow, 2:201)

The *hasanat* that they are describing is not just any good deed, but accompany them, love them, be with them, eat with them, pray with them, have a respect for them. That's why the celebration of *Mawlid an Nabi* ﷺ, respecting all *Ahlul Bayt* ؑ, respecting all *Ashabi Nabi* ﷺ. Living a life of trying to be of service to Prophet ﷺ and the *Ahlul Bayt Nabi* ﷺ (Family of Prophet ﷺ), respecting all *Ashabi Nabi* ﷺ (companions of Prophet ﷺ) and *awliyaullah* (saints). All of this is to be dressed from *hasanat* of *dunya* (material world).

Reality of Eyes – Compassion and Mercy
Imam Hassan & Imam Hussain

Be With Pious People in Dunya, So You Will Be With Them in Paradise

Allah describes and says, 'If you are eating with them in *dunya* (material world), praying with them in *dunya*, traveling and accompanying them in *dunya*, what type of *hasanat* (goodness) I have? What type of *hasanat* I have in store for you in *akhirah*?' If this is your *dunya*, imagine where you are eating in *akhirah* (afterlife). Because everything is a reflection. But if I am accompanying crazy people in *dunya* and say, 'No, my *akhirah* will be good.' How is that possible?

It means that everything is a reflection. If we are eating in the circles of *zikr* (remembrance), and we are praying in the circles of *zikr*, and we are being visited by the big family of Sayyidina Muhammad. And when we visit, we visit the family of Sayyidina Muhammad. And we learn and read and been taught by the big family members of Sayyidina Muhammad. What Allah is then describing? What will be your paradise? It means you will be with that reality in paradise. They are carrying the *sifat ar-Rahman* and that *nur* (light).

قَالَ رَسُولُ اللهِ صلى الله عليه و سلم: الْمَرْءُ مَعَ مَنْ أَحَب

Qala Rasulullah (saws): "Almar o, ma'a man ahab."

Prophet Muhammad (pbuh) said: "One is with those whom he loves."

Ahlul Bayt Taught Us to Live a Life of Sacrifice

If we live by that *nur* (light) (*noon* of Hassan), and live by that reality, the *Ahlul Bayt* (Family of Prophet) begin to teach us that you want *Atayna kal kawthar, Fasali li rabbika wanhar.*

$$\text{إِنَّا أَعْطَيْنَاكَ الْكَوْثَرَ ﴿١﴾ فَصَلِّ لِرَبِّكَ وَانْحَرْ ﴿٢﴾}$$

108:1-2 – *"Inna 'atayna kal kawthar. (1) Fasalli li rabbika wanhar. (2)" (Surat Al-Kawthar)*

"To thee (O Muhammad) we have granted the Fount (of Abundance). (1) So pray to your Lord and Sacrifice. (2)" (The Abundance 108:1)

Fasalli li Rabbika. It means pray onto your lord and live a life of sacrifice. Sacrifice yourself, sacrifice your property, and sacrifice your character. Not sacrifice other people, like *shaitan* (satan) is doing. He (satan) is doing everything the opposite of that reality, sacrificing every other person but himself. What *Ahlul Bayt* ؏ taught us? No, you sacrifice yourself. You put yourself first on the block. You first judge yourself. You look at all your bad characteristics and say it all has to go. Nobody else has to go, nobody else is bad; I am the bad one. I have to sacrifice all my character. I have to sacrifice all my property. I have to sacrifice everything from me. *"Fasalli li rabbika wanhar"* (Holy Qur'an, 108:2).

Sayyid Shuhada Imam Hussain ؏ is Granted Sifat Ar-Raheem

Sayyid Shuhada, sifat ar-Raheem, Sayyid Shuhada dresses the *Sayyid Shuhada* (Imam Hussain ؏). The attribute dresses their character, who they are. So, the *hasanat* (goodness) and beauty was Imam Hassan ؏. *Sifat ar-Rahman* and the majestic, beatific oceans dress the eye.

Sifat ar-Raheem is your paradise reality. Paradise is not an easy entrance where in many, many books that Allah ﷻ describes, 'My Paradise is not easy to enter.' You must sacrifice. You must struggle in the way of Allah ﷻ. You make a discipline upon yourself to enter into those

Reality of Eyes – Compassion and Mercy
Imam Hassan ﷺ & Imam Hussain ﷺ

---

realities. The life of Imam Hussain ﷺ is then the symbol of that reality. He sacrificed himself and 72 family members. 72 is a tremendous key, a tremendous reality. Because of that reality, Allah ﷻ is dressing from *sifat ar-Raheem*.

Decoding the Name of Imam Hussain ﷺ

حسين (عليه السلام)			
Hussain (as)			
ن	ي	س	ح
Noon	Ya	Seen	Ha
نور	يقين	سر	حياة
Nur (Light)	Yaqeen (Certainty)	Sir (Secret)	Hayat (Ever-Living)

Note: Please read English from right to left to coincide with Arabic.

These are ancient names. Allah ﷻ doesn't pick and choose as He goes. He knows that that ancient *sifat* (attribute), that ancient name will dress a very ancient reality known as Hussain ﷺ. He will be from the oceans of *hayat* (ever-living), as the grandchildren of Prophet ﷺ. He will carry the *seen* and the secret of Sayyidina Muhammad ﷺ, *nurul anwar wa sirratul asrar* (light of every secret and secret of every light). They are all the carriers of the light and the reality of that secret. But he carries the *ya* of *yaqeen*, that what we are asking for is the *yaqeen* and certainty. With that *yaqeen* and that certainty, every reality opens. It means the *hasanat* of good character opens the *nur* (light).

When Allah ﷻ begins to dress you with the *nur* (light), He wants to dress us from the realities of *al-Hayat* (ever-living). The people of *hayat*, the *ahlul zikr*, who make the *zikr* of *hay, hay, hay*. Their whole reality is that they are swimming in that ocean of *hayat*. Their reality is based on that sacrifice. Imam Sayyid Shuhada (Hussain ﷺ) begins to come to them that you sacrifice all your character, sacrifice all these things so that you become a big *mujahid*, the one who struggles in Allah's ﷻ way. Not hurting people but coming against yourself so that you can begin to witness these realities.

With that *nur* (*noon* of Hussain ؑ) is a *nur* of *yaqeen* (certainty). It's a different light. That *nur* of *Rahman* (*noon* of Hassan ؑ) is a *nur* (light). This *nur* of *Raheem* is from the *yaqeen* and the certainty. It means the *shuhada* (witnesses) is a different level. It means the *Saliheen, Shuhada, Siddiqeen, wa Nabiyeen* – these are the oceans of reality that Imam Hussain ؑ wants to dress us and make the left eye to be from *Bahrul Hayat* (ocean of ever-living).

وَمَن يُطِعِ اللَّهَ وَالرَّسُولَ فَأُوْلَئِكَ مَعَ الَّذِينَ أَنْعَمَ اللَّهُ عَلَيْهِم مِّنَ النَّبِيِّينَ وَالصِّدِّيقِينَ وَالشُّهَدَاءِ وَالصَّالِحِينَ وَحَسُنَ أُولَئِكَ رَفِيقًا ﴿٦٩﴾

4:69 – *"Wa man yuti' Allaha war Rasola faolayeka ma'al ladheena an'ama Allahu 'alayhim minan Nabiyeena, was Siddiqeena, wash Shuhadai, was Saliheena wa hasuna olayeka rafeeqan."*
(*Surat An-Nisa*)

"And whoever obeys Allah and the Messenger (pbuh) are in the company of those on whom Allah has bestowed His Favours/Blessings - of the prophets, the sincere Truthful, the witnesses (who testify), and the Righteous, and excellent are those as companions." (*The Women, 4:69*)

That if I open your two eyes, from your right eye will begin to emanate *Rahman* and from your left eye will become the oceans of *al-Hayat*. You will become a balanced creation in this *dunya* (material world). That's why the face of *awliyaullah* (saints) are so powerful. They are dressed with 7 holy attributes that are from Divine Essences.

*Reality of Eyes – Compassion and Mercy
Imam Hassan ﷺ & Imam Hussain ﷺ*

Three Levels of Yaqeen (Certainty)

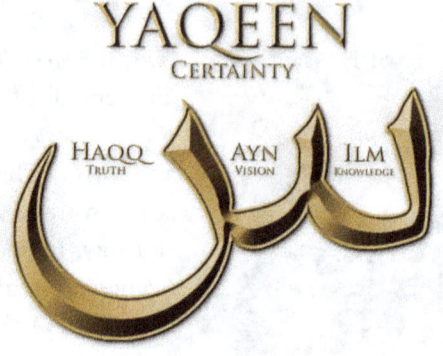

This light, this reality, Imam Hussain ﷺ is teaching, if I begin to open that *yaqeen* (ya of Hussain ﷺ), then the reality of that *seen* begins to open. The *seen* has the three (spaces): *ilm ul-yaqeen* because He is granting *yaqeen*. What kind of *yaqeen* (certainty) do you want? I'm going to make the knowledge that you know because these are paradise realities. It's not only *sifat ar-Rahman* for *dunya* (material world). The *sifat ar-Raheem* means your paradise reality begins to dress you, so that you will have a *yaqeen* and certainty; *ilm ul-yaqeen* (knowledge of certainty), *ayn ul-yaqeen* (vision of certainty), *haqq ul-yaqeen* (certainty of truth). These three *yaqeens* begin to dress the soul and dress the reality and begin to perfect the *nur* and the *hayat*.

Imam Hassan ؑ and Imam Hussain ؑ Are the Eyes of Prophet ﷺ

That is why in *salawats* (praisings) you have, *"Ilan Nabi qurrato 'aini"* (the coolness of Prophet's ﷺ eyes), *"Jaddal Hassan wal Hussaini."*

النَّبِيُّ قُرَّةُ العَيْنِ	أَسْيَادِي الْحَسَنْ وَالْحُسَّيْنْ
جَدُّكُمْ صَاحِبُ الْقُرْآنْ	وَيَا شَبَابَ الْجَنَّتَيْنْ
Asyadil Hassan wal Hussaini	*Ilan Nabi qurrato 'aini*
Ya shabaa bal janna'taini	*Jaddukum saahibul Qur'ana*

Our Masters, Imam Hassan (as) and Imam Hussain (as),
They are the coolness of Prophet's (pbuh) eyes.
O the Youth of the Paradises,
Your Grandfather (Prophet Muhammad (pbuh)) is the owner of the Holy Qur'an.

These are the eyes of Prophet ﷺ. Every reality is a reality of Sayyidina Muhammad ﷺ. On the *ma'rifah* (gnosticism) of Prophet ﷺ, moving towards the *ma'rifah* of Prophet ﷺ, that the reality of Prophet ﷺ is dressed from Allah ﷻ. You will never know Allah ﷻ, but what you will know is the dress of Prophet ﷺ. He begins to teach you that my right eye is the reality of Imam Hassan ؑ and dressed from *sifat ar-Rahman*. My left eye is Imam Hussain ؑ and dressed from the *sifat ar-Raheem*. Through which I look at *Rahmanir Raheem*, I look through that 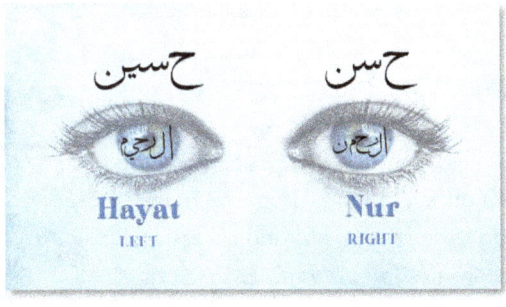 reality and I dress everything from that reality. And every reality is in the hands of that reality of these *Ahlul Bayt Nabi* ﷺ. That is the reality.

Reality of Eyes – Compassion and Mercy
Imam Hassan ؓ & Imam Hussain ؓ

Shaitan is Devoid of Nur and Wants to Take Away Our Light

What in *dunya* (material world) now? *Shaitan*, the anti-Christ comes. You have seen their signs everywhere? Why is he making his sign like  that (covering one eye)? Because he is teaching that I don't have anything from *Rahman*, because I am not working for *Rahman*. I'm working for *shaitan* (satan). And we don't have light. Allah ﷻ made us devoid of light. Because we don't follow Allah ﷻ we have no light. We are those who bring darkness. Either we are going to obliterate you to take away your light or we are going to send darkness into your heart to take away your light. So, everything from their signs is to take away your *Rahman*, take away your *Rahman*, take away *nur* (light), take away *nur* until what happens? No *nur*, and then if no light, no *hayat* (ever-living), no ocean of reality. Then what they have? [Shaykh makes gesture of the triangle on his eye]. They have just the *hayat* of *dunya*.

Hayat is the oceans of ever-living. If you have light of heaven, then you come to the *zikr*. They begin to give you the ever-living of eternity of the soul. Make your soul ever-living. Let your soul to swim in the oceans of eternity, so that it will be eternal.

What does Anti-One, the person of deceit comes and says, 'No, there is no light and you live for today and enjoy everything.' Because there is no tomorrow, he has no access to it. So just *hayat al-dunya*. Everything is about live life today to the fullest. This is their term. Live to the fullest. 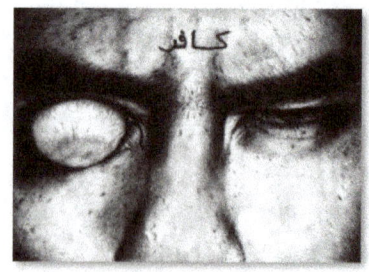 Fullest of what? To fill your belly with *dunya* (material world)? Why? Why he wants to fill you with *dunya*? So that your heart becomes darker and darker, and darker until you detach from *Rahman* and then he has covered your eye.

The one of deceit is coming with a smashed right eye, bulging, as a sign from Allah ﷻ that he is not inheriting from this reality and he is not inheriting from *Rahman* and he has no *nur* (light) whatsoever. His whole purpose is to take *nur* from *dunya*. By music, by TV, by internet, by every means possible, take away *nur,* take away all of these blessings.

If No Nur, There is No Balanced Judgment

Everything from Allah ﷻ is to bestow *nur* upon us. Allah ﷻ asks from us, 'Do good deeds and I am going to shower you with mercy.' *Shaitan* comes, 'No, no. Do bad things so I can throw burdens of people upon you.' And you will be crushed with burdens and sins until you have absolutely no *nur* (light).

What Prophet ﷺ described somebody who's backbiting and doing bad things? That he is bankrupt. Why? Because absolutely no light in their account. If there is no light in the account, it means the right eye is beginning to shut. They see the world no longer balanced. And their judgement is not a balanced judgement because there is no *nur* (light). They are not able to see with *nur* (light). The choices that they are making are making everything to be darkened and darkened and darkened until there is no more light. And they begin to choose only *hayat dunya* (life of material world). Let me go to the casino, let me go out and play, and do all these things that make Allah ﷻ to be angry so that I move farther and farther and farther away from the light. And that is the role of *shaitan.*

*Reality of Eyes – Compassion and Mercy
Imam Hassan ؑ & Imam Hussain ؑ*

Dajjal's Deception is Upon Everyone

It means from the highest reality of *Rahman*, and the dress upon Prophet ﷺ, the reality of *Ahlul Bayt* ؑ, the love of Imam Hassan ؑ and Imam Hussain ؑ, *"Fid dunya Hasana wa fil akhera hasana wa qina adhab an Naar."* To keep that reality is the highest.

وَمِنْهُم مَّن يَقُولُ رَبَّنَا آتِنَا فِي الدُّنْيَا حَسَنَةً وَفِي الْآخِرَةِ حَسَنَةً وَقِنَا عَذَابَ النَّارِ ﴿٢٠١﴾

2:201 – *"Wa minhum mai yaqoolu rabbanaaa aatina fid dunyaa hasanatawn wa fil aakhirati hasanatanw wa qinaa azaaban Naar."* (Surat Al-Baqarah)

"Our Lord, give us in this world [that which is] good and in the Hereafter [that which is] good and protect us from the punishment of the Fire." (The Cow, 2:201)

And to know what's happening in this *dunya* now is that he (Satan) wants only to extinguish this reality. That's why the right eye. He doesn't want *sifat ar-Rahman*, nor is he working for *Rahman*. And everything you see on TV and on internet; any religious practice that is based off of darkness, based on horrific acts, based on deceit and deception, there is no *nur* in it. You can't put people in a trench and kill them. There is no *nur* (light) in that action. You cannot even sacrifice a goat, with the goat seeing it, more or less other goats watching what you're doing.

It's impossible. There is no *nur* in that action. So it means that every action that is happening, when you look at that action, you say there is no light in that action.

Who is doing that then? The anti-Christ. We say anti-Christ because it's not only for Christians. His biggest followers will be the whole world. He is *Dajjal*, the man of deceit. His deception will be upon everyone on earth, every race, every religion, every creed.

Do Your Actions Bring Light To Your Eyes Or Pull It Away?

All we do is look with *tafakkur* and contemplation. People of *zikr*,  people of contemplation, people of good deeds, they look with *nur ar-Rahman* through the right eye. They look through the ocean of *hayat* with their left eye, and they can see it balanced. They say this action is not based on *nur*. What they are doing has no light. If it has no light, its purpose then is exact opposite. There is no grey. There is no middle ground.

When we listen to something, we are choosing. Are you choosing something that is bringing light upon you or are you choosing something that is taking your light? You cannot play and keep your life always on the middle; I do all these things. Because they tell us keep a *hisaab* (account) and a balance of yourself. What you are doing, is it bringing light into your eyes or it is pulling light from your eyes? Most likely you will have headaches. Many shaykhs have tremendous amount of headaches because the light coming out is pulling all the sins of people coming back, because every positive *"Qul jaa al haqu wa zahaqal batil."* It means the positive energy that comes out, gets hit by every type of negativity and comes back to them and causes tremendous difficulty and sickness.

Reality of Eyes – Compassion and Mercy
Imam Hassan ؑ & Imam Hussain ؑ

وَ قُلْ جَاءَالْحَقُّ وَزَهَقَ الْبَطِلُ، إِنَّ الْبَطِلَ كَانَ زَهُوقًا ﴿٨١﴾

17:81 – *"Wa qul jaa alhaqqu wa zahaqal baatil, innal batila kana zahoqa." (Surat Al-Isra)*

"And say, Truth has come, and falsehood has perished. Indeed falsehood, [by its nature], is ever perishing/bound to perish."
(The Night Journey, 17:81)

But for our lives and for our *hisaab* (account), they teach us. That what I am doing, is that going to increase my light or is it satanic influence and deception to take away my light? If he takes away enough light, I feel myself no longer guided. And I begin to make choices that don't bring *hayat* (ever-living) and bring only the desire of the material world and no longer the desire from my soul. We pray that Allah ﷻ protect us. Allah ﷻ guides us and grants us light within our eyes from *sifat ar-Rahman*.

Ya Rabbi bi Haqil Imamil Hassan alMujtaba wa bi haqi sifate Rahman.
Ya Rabbi bi Haqi Imamil Hussain wa sifat e Raheem.

Oh my Lord for the sake of Imam Hassan al Mujataba and for the sake of the attribute of Rahman.
Oh my Lord for the sake of Imam Hassain and for the sake of the attribute of Raheem.

بِسْمِ اللهِ الرَّحْمَنِ الرَّحِيمِ

يَا حَمِيدُ بِحَقِّ مُحَمَّدٍ ﷺ، يَا عَلِيُّ بِحَقِّ عَلِي (عَلَيْهِ السَّلَامُ)، يَا خَالِقُ بِحَقِّ فَاطِمَةُ الزَّهْرَاءِ (عَلَيْهِ السَّلَامُ)، يَا رَحْمَنُ بِحَقِّ حَسَنْ (عَلَيْهِ السَّلَامُ)، يَا رَحِيمُ بِحَقِّ حُسَّيْنِ (عَلَيْهِ السَّلَامُ)

Bismillahir Rahmanir Raheem

Ya Hamidu bi Haqqi Muhammad ﷺ, Ya 'Aliyu bi Haqqi 'Ali ؏, Ya Khaliqu bi Haqqi Fatimatuz Zahra ؏, Ya Rahmanu bi Haqqi Hassan ؏, Ya Raheemu bi Haqqi Hussain ؏."

In the name of Allah, the Most Compassionate, the Most Merciful

O' Most praised one for the sake of Prophet Muhammad (pbuh), O' the Most High for the sake of Imam 'Ali (as), O' the Creator for the sake of Fatima Zahra (as), O the Most Compassionate for the sake of Imam Hassan (as), O' the Most Merciful for the sake of Imam Hussain (as).

Subhana rabbika rabbal 'izzati 'amma yasifoon, wa salaamun 'alal mursaleen, walhamdulillahi rabbil 'aalameen. Bi hurmati Muhammad al-Mustafa wa bi siri Surat al-Fatiha.

The Holy Tongue

DIVINELY PEN - QAF OF QUR'AN AL MAJEED AND QALAM

The Holy Qur'an is Allah's ﷻ Speech

InshaAllah, that we are entering the holy month of Ramadan, and the holy month of *Qur'an al-Majeed*, that we are reading Holy Qur'an, that memorizing Holy Qur'an, meditating and contemplating upon Holy Qur'an. And understand that each word, especially in reference to Allah's ﷻ Qur'an, which is Allah's ﷻ 'not created' Divinely Speech. It means we have to keep always that in the heart that its Qur'an is not created. It's Allah's ﷻ Divinely Speech. And to just understand or towards the understanding of what the *huroof* (Arabic letters) of the Holy Qur'an is. It gives us an understanding of what is it that is going to be dressing us, what lights are going to be dressing us, what is the benefit and the power upon the soul from the Holy Qur'an.

Letters of the Word Qur'an

Qaf in the Word of Qur'an Represents Allah's ﷻ Qudra (Divinely Power)

قرآن			
Qur'an			
ن	آ	ر	ق
Noon	Alif	Ra	Qaf

*Note: Please read English from right to left to coincide with Arabic.

Then we look to Qur'an – *qaf, ra, alif, noon*. That the power, *Qaf wal Qur'an al-Majeed*. This means that the *qaf* is holding the power. That that *qaf* and Allah's ﷻ Divinely *Qudra*, Allah's ﷻ Divinely Oceans of Power is the source of this energy and this light, moving. Later we go into where that's moving from, but to understand we are being dressed by the *qaf*. Allah ﷻ in Holy Qur'an says, *"Qaf wal Qur'an al Majeed."* It means that to draw our attention to the *qaf* and that this is the source of Oceans of Power that we want to be dressed by these lights.

ق ۚ وَالْقُرْآنِ الْمَجِيدِ ﴿١﴾

50:1 – *"Qaf, wal Quranil Majeed."* (Surat Qaf)

"Qaf. By the honored Qur'an." (The Letter Qaf, 50:1)

Shaykh Nurjan Mirahmadi

Noon Represents the Nur (Light) Coming From That Qudra

That *qaf* is dressing the *noon* of Qur'an. That *nur* (light) that's coming from that *noon* is not like any other *nur*, that we have many different layers and levels of *nur*. But this *noon* and this *nur* is coming from the *qaf*. That is the  light that we are asking to be dressed by. That is the light in which dresses the soul of its eternal realities.

Then Mawlana Shaykh is directing us to understand because we want to be dressed by these realities. Not just you hold the Qur'an and keep  reading it and not understanding. Year after year, year after year, you are reading it but not thinking and contemplating with the heart that what are these letters? What are these words? What are these powers? What are these oceans of power? What type of *nur* and light and how am I going to reach to that light, to the secret of Holy Qur'an? Why are *awliyaullah* (saints) carrying the secret of Holy Qur'an? Because me, you, we all read the same *kitab* (book), but why are we not getting that reality, understanding that reality? It means they teach us that make your *tafakkur* and your contemplation. You want to be dressed by that "*Qaf wal Qur'an al Majeed*," (Qur'an, 50:1). It's coming to the *noon*, that *nur* (light) is dressing us.

Noon wal Qalam

Allah Testifies By the Pen – Qalam is the Secret of Manifestation

Then how to understand that noon in Surat al-Qalam, *"Noon. Wal qalam."*

ن ۚ وَالْقَلَمِ وَمَا يَسْطُرُونَ ﴿١﴾

68:1 – "Noon. Wal Qalami wa ma yasTuroon." (Surat Al-Qalam)

"Noon. By the pen and what they inscribe." (The Pen, 68:1)

It means now that becomes a big ocean that you want the *noon*; Allah testifies by the *Qalam* (pen). So one, in our life they say, 'The pen is mightier than the sword.' So take a life of *qalam*, take a life of being a student. Take a life of seeking knowledge and realities. As much as you are using the *qalam* (pen) to reach realities, as much as we are becoming a seeker. As we use the *qalam*, it begins to teach us the *qalam* is the secret of manifestation. The nobility of our creation is in the thumb. What

separates us from a monkey or baboon is the thumb so that we can hold a *qalam*. The *qalam*, as soon as you write, something is manifesting. As soon as you draw something, something is manifesting. It means that reality of the *qalam* is in the physical. So we take a life of seeking, a life of reaching and asking to reach towards realities, to be always a student of realities, to move towards that.

What Does Allah ﷻ Mean By Qalam (Pen)?

Then Mawlana Shaykh begins to teach that always contemplate beyond the physical into the timeless reality. What is Allah ﷻ meaning by *qalam*? There is no hand up there in the sky drawing something. It means that each of the *huroof* (Arabic letters) must be standing for something. Because we said it before, you say cake, and everybody says, 'Oh, I have had that cake before.' No, but what makes the cake is important because we have the flour, has salt, has sugar. What are the elements that is making that to be powerful? So, when we go towards a timeless reality, the *qalam* (pen) is no longer the importance of the physical pen but must have a reality and a secret within it.

The Word Qalam is Made of Qaf, Lam, Meem

Qaf is the Qudra and the Source of Power That Manifests the Qur'an

Then Mawlana Shaykh is teaching, begins to teach, okay *qalam*, because we're trying to understand how to reach to that "*Noon; wal qalam*" (Holy Qur'an, 68:1). That that *qalam* has a *qaf*. Again, this *qaf* is appearing, "*Qaf wal Qur'an al Majeed.*"

﴿ق ۚ وَالْقُرْآنِ الْمَجِيدِ ﴾١﴿

50:1 – "*Qaf, wal Quranil Majeed.*" (Surat Qaf)

"*Qaf. By the honored Qur'an.*" (The Letter Qaf, 50:1)

Divinely Pen – Qaf of Qur'an al Majeed and Qalam

This means Allah's ﷻ directing us that when you see that *qaf*, it's a *qudra* (power). It's Allah's ﷻ Divinely *Qudra*. It is the source of power that is making this Qur'an to come out. And that's why the Holy Qur'an, it is the source of power that encompasses everything. Allah ﷻ says, 'If it's living or dead, if it can bring the dead to life, everything is in that.' Not in the book, but in the *qudra* and the oceans of power of Allah's ﷻ uncreated Divinely Speech. We always remember within our hearts it's uncreated Divinely Speech.

Lam Signifies Lisanul Haq - Tongue of Truth

That *qaf* is moving to a *lam*. *Lam* signifies the tongue, *lisanul haq* (tongue of truth) because Allah ﷻ is a hidden treasure wanting to be known.

كُنْت كَنْزاً مخفيا فَأُحْبَبْت أَنْ أُعْرَفَ؛ فَخَلَقْتُ خَلْقاً فَعَرَّفْتهمْ بِي فَعَرَفُونِي

"*Kuntu kanzan makhfiyya, fa ahbabtu an a'rafa, fa khalaqtu khalqan, fa 'arraftahum bi fa 'arafonee.*"

Allah (AJ) said, "I was a hidden Treasure then I desired to be known, so I created a creation to which I made Myself known; then they knew Me."
(Hadith Qudsi)

Allah ﷻ is not just speaking from a place in the universe that is manifesting sound. But Allah ﷻ is directing us that, 'There must be a *lisan*. There must be a tongue for Me that manifests My realities.'

If Qur'an Was Revealed On a Mountain, It Would Turn To Dust

Just between the *qaf* and the *lam*, Allah ﷻ begins to describe in Holy Qur'an, 'If I revealed My Qur'an to the mountain,' because we are in creation small. We think of Mount Everest and how many thousands of feet in the air. Allah ﷻ says, 'If I revealed My Qur'an to the mountain, *khashi'a*, it would be dust.' But, comes to the heart of Sayyidina Muhammad ﷺ and nothing, nothing affects that.

لَوْ أَنزَلْنَا هَٰذَا الْقُرْآنَ عَلَىٰ جَبَلٍ لَّرَأَيْتَهُ خَاشِعًا مُّتَصَدِّعًا مِّنْ خَشْيَةِ اللَّهِ وَتِلْكَ الْأَمْثَالُ نَضْرِبُهَا لِلنَّاسِ لَعَلَّهُمْ يَتَفَكَّرُونَ ﴿٢١﴾

59:21 – "*Law anzalna hadha alQurana 'ala jabalin laraaytahu, khashi'an mutasaddi'an min khashyatillahi, wa tilkal amthalu nadribuha linnasi la'allahum yatafakkaroon.*" (Surat Al-Hashr)

"*Had We sent down this Qur'an on a mountain, verily, you would have seen it obliterated to dust (from its power) And these examples We present to the people that perhaps they will Contemplate...*"
(The Exile, 59:21)

Divinely Pen – Qaf of Qur'an al Majeed and Qalam

Only Sayyidina Muhammad ﷺ Can Hold Allah's ﷻ 'Qul' – Divinely Speech

Now we're beginning to understand that greatness of Prophet ﷺ for revealing Holy Qur'an to creation, revealing it in the physical, but what did he reveal in the world of light? Allah ﷻ is teaching that that *qaf* and *lam*, when they come together, it denotes *"Qul."* Qul means 'Say.' Allah's ﷻ Divinely *Qul* – nothing can hold it. There is not an angel that can  hold Allah's ﷻ *Qul*. There's not a prophet that can hold Allah's ﷻ *Qul*. There's not a human being or anything in creation that can contain or hold Allah's ﷻ *Qul*, except the heart of Sayyidina Muhammad ﷺ.

ق + ل = قل

Qul = Lam + Qaf

*Note: Please read English from right to left to coincide with Arabic.

Qalam is Qul to the Meem – Say, O Muhammad ﷺ

Allah ﷻ clarifies that because the *qalam* is *Qul* to the *meem*. *"Qul"* is directing itself to the *meem*. The *meem*, if you look, is a *qalam*. The *meem* that sticks down is the pen of Allah ﷻ, is the ocean of manifestation of Allah ﷻ. When Allah ﷻ wants to manifest and wants creation to manifest, merely *"Qul"* into the heart of Prophet ﷺ in the world of souls. And Sayyidina Muhammad ﷺ, *"kun faya kun."* It means immediately it's manifesting by the order of Allah ﷻ.

قلم	
Qalam	
م	قل
Meem	*Qul*
محمد ﷺ	قل
Muhammad ﷺ (Prophet Muhammad ﷺ)	*Qul* (Say)

*Note: Please read English from right to left to coincide with Arabic.

إِنَّمَا أَمْرُهُ إِذَا أَرَادَ شَيْئًا أَن يَقُولَ لَهُ كُن فَيَكُونُ ﴿٨٢﴾

36:82 – "*Innama AmruHu idha Arada shay an, an yaqola lahu kun faya koon.*" (*Surat YaSeen*)

"His Command is when He Wills/Intends a thing, He says to it, 'Be,' and it is!" (YaSeen, 36:82)

Qalam al Qudra, the Pen of Might, the Pen of Power. It is the manifestation through the heart of Prophet ﷺ. That is the *nur* (light), that is the Muhammadan *nur*. We are trying to reach to that *nur* (referring to *noon* of Qur'an) trying to reach to the Holy Qur'an.

Neither Heavens Nor Earth Contains Allah's ﷻ Power, But the Heart of Sayyidina Muhammad ﷺ

And Allah ﷻ is directing us that, 'What you want, I'm not in heavens and I'm not on the earth, but I'm in the heart my believer.' And who's Allah's ﷻ believer? It's Sayyidina Muhammad ﷺ.

مَا وَسِعَنِيْ لَا سَمَائِيْ ولا أَرْضِيْ وَلَكِنْ وَسِعَنِيْ قَلْبِ عَبْدِيْ الْمُؤْمِنْ

"*Maa wasi'anee laa Samayee, wa la ardee, laakin wasi'anee qalbi 'Abdee al Mu'min.*"

Divinely Pen – Qaf of Qur'an al Majeed and Qalam

"Neither My Heavens nor My Earth can contain Me, but the heart of my Believing Servant."
(Hadith Qudsi conveyed by Prophet Muhammad (pbuh))

This means they begin to direct us that what you are looking for of Allah ﷻ, what you are looking for of realities is in the heart of Sayyidina Muhammad ﷺ. There must be a *tashreef*, a respect, a love, salutations constantly upon Prophet ﷺ, to enter into the heart of Sayyidina Muhammad ﷺ, to enter into the *nazar* (gaze) of Sayyidina Muhammad ﷺ because it begins to dress us from that light.

When we begin to understand the greatness of Prophet ﷺ, and how is the soul of Prophet ﷺ able to manifest Allah's ﷻ Divinely Speech that is not created. This is *azimat an-Nabi* ﷺ. Allah's ﷻ Uncreated Power, His not created Holy Qur'an, His Ocean of Power is moving through the heart of Prophet ﷺ. How is it possible? It's beyond imagination.

If You Want Oceans of Divinely Power, Follow Sayyidina Muhammad ﷺ

When Allah ﷻ wants to be known, be known through the heart of Sayyidina Muhammad ﷺ. So, they begin to direct us that, that's the power of the *salawats* (praisings). That's the power of *Mawlid an-Nabi* ﷺ. That's the power of the love of Prophet ﷺ. That's why throughout Qur'an, *"Qul in kuntum tuhibbonAllah, fattabioni."*

$$\text{قُلْ إِنْ كُنْتُمْ تُحِبُّونَ اللَّهَ فَاتَّبِعُونِيْ يُحْبِبْكُمُ اللَّهُ وَيَغْفِرْ لَكُمْ ذُنُوبَكُمْ ۗ وَاللَّهُ غَفُورٌ رَّحِيمٌ ﴿٣١﴾}$$

3:31 – *"Qul in kuntum tuhibbon Allaha fattabi'oni, yuhbibkumullahu wa yaghfir lakum dhunobakum wallahu Ghaforur Raheem."*
(Surat Ali-Imran)

"Say, [O Muhammad], "If you should love Allah, then follow me, [so] Allah will love you and forgive you your sins. And Allah is Forgiving and Merciful." (Family of Imran, 3:31)

Allah ﷻ says, 'You want to reach to that love, you want to reach to My Divinely Love, you want to reach to My Oceans of Power – direct yourself to Prophet ﷺ.'

Sayyidina Muhammad ﷺ Brings Us to Islam, Iman, and Ihsan

As you direct yourself to Prophet ﷺ, he's going to fix our *Islam*, bring us into submission. Then he's going to fix our *iman* (faith). When he taught his *Sahabi* (Companions), 'Your *iman* is based on love. If you don't love me more than you love yourself, you are deficient in your faith.'

$$\text{لَا يُؤْمِنُ أَحَدُكُمْ حَتَّى أَكُونَ أَحَبَّ إِلَيْهِ مِنْ وَالِدِهِ وَوَلَدِهِ وَالنَّاسِ أَجْمَعِينَ}$$

"La yuminu ahadukum hatta akona ahabba ilayhi min walidihi wa waladihi wan Nasi ajma'yeen."

"None of you will have faith till he loves me more than his father, his children and all mankind."
(Prophet Muhammad (pbuh))

It means then Prophet ﷺ directs us towards our *iman*, that we have to love Sayyidina Muhammad ﷺ more than we love ourselves. With our *Islam* and our *iman* perfecting, it becomes *dar al ihsan*, the abode of perfection, to worship as if you see Allah ﷻ. If you don't see Allah ﷻ, know that He sees you.

أَنْ تَعْبُدَ اللَّهَ كَأَنَّكَ تَرَاهُ، فَإِنْ لَمْ تَكُنْ تَرَاهُ فَإِنَّهُ يَرَاك

"*An Ta'bud Allaha, Ka annaka tarahu, fa in lam takun tarahu fa innahu yarak.*"

"*It (Ihsan – Station of Excellence) is to serve/worship Allah as though you behold [See] Him; and if you don't behold [See] him, (know that) He surely sees you.*" (Prophet Muhammad (pbuh))

Subhana rabbika rabbal 'izzati 'amma yasifoon, wa salaamun 'alal mursaleen, walhamdulillahi rabbil 'aalameen. Bi hurmati Muhammad al-Mustafa wa bi siri Surat al-Fatiha.

GOD'S VOICE IS LIKE THUNDER POWER OF QALAM (PEN) – WRITING KNOWLEDGE

If You Don't Write Knowledges, Don't Speak

...أَطِيعُواللَّهَ وَأَطِيعُواْ ٱلرَّسُولَ وَأُوْلِي ٱلْأَمْرِ مِنكُمْ... ﴿٥٩﴾

4:59 – "...Atiullaha wa atiur Rasula wa Ulil amre minkum..." (Surat An-Nisa)

"... Obey Allah, Obey the Messenger, and those in authority among you..." (The Women, 4:59)

And always a reminder for myself *ana abdukal 'ajeez, wa dayeef, wa miskin, wa zhalim, wa jahl*. And but for the Grace of God kept us alive, that Allah ﷻ forgive us and keep us within His oceans of mercy. And that this way, this way of reality is based on writing. And Imam 'Ali ؑ and the inheritance of Imam 'Ali ؑ was writing the revelations of Sayyidina Muhammad ﷺ. And the one whom teaches and is the gate of all knowledges into the heart of  Sayyidina Muhammad ﷺ is then reminding for us that, 'If you don't write, don't speak.'

Because what you're speaking could be from left to right and every other understanding that you can imagine. That the first principle of *tariqah* (spiritual path), you have to have written the *haqqaiqs* (realities). That pen is a pen that has a double action. As you write on paper, it's writing into your heart. If you don't write, don't speak.

Speaking Without Writing the Realities Can Cause Sickness

There were nine who wrote in the time of Sayyidina Muhammad ﷺ and as a result, those were the nine who spoke and described and taught because Allah ﷻ, "*Alam bil Qalam*."

اقْرَأْ وَرَبُّكَ الْأَكْرَمُ ﴿٣﴾ الَّذِي عَلَّمَ بِالْقَلَمِ ﴿٤﴾ عَلَّمَ الْإِنسَانَ مَا لَمْ يَعْلَمْ ﴿٥﴾

96:3-5 – "*Iqra, wa rabbukal akram (3). Alladhee 'allama bil Qalam (4). 'Allamal insana ma lam ya'lam. (5)*" (Surat Al-Alaq)

"*Recite, and your Lord is the most Generous. (3) Who taught by the pen. (4) Taught man that which he knew not. (5)*" (The Clot, 96:3-5)

"*Alam bil Qalam,*" that whatever knowledges were coming, they were writing. And as a result, it was burning into the heart. When one doesn't write and try to speak of the realities of *tariqah*, it's left and right like a soup. Two words of the shaykh, ten words of their own, three of imagination and now you've got a dish that can make everybody sick. Because it's not what the shaykh said; it's not what even he taught. Until the degree becomes such that when they learned, they learned, they learned, and the shaykh opened their heart and gave their trust. It doesn't have 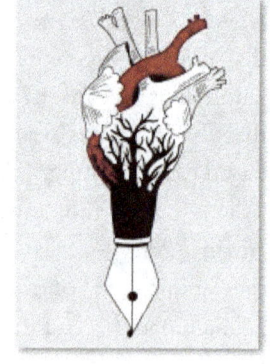 to be the full trust or what you understand of a trust, but a trust was given in which the heart is open and now receiving their *isharats* (signs) and their knowledges.

Keep Ihtiram of the Realities By Writing Them

But that was only achieved by the struggle through the first door of writing, to be a student in the way to one who keeps the understanding of the way and the *ihtiram* (respect) of the knowledges coming from the holy heart of Sayyidina Muhammad ﷺ in which they were raised to be higher than *Kiraman Katibin* (noble scribes). They are higher than the station of angels and the only reason these angels are *kiram*, are honoured, because they document the realities and *haqqaiqs* of Sayyidina Muhammad ﷺ because all this creation is a gift for Sayyidina Muhammad ﷺ.

So, for us to raise in our honour then, the reminder is then be a student of the way. Not everyone is a student of the way. Many are coming for the enjoyment, for the food, for the *zikr* (remembrance), for whatever their entertainment purposes are. But for the seeker of the way and the student of realities and those whom praying for their hearts to open, this key of opening is in the *qalam* (pen).

The Pen is Mightier Than the Sword

It's very simple. This *qalam* (pen) is *qaf, lam, meem* because you are inheriting from the *qalam* of Sayyidina Muhammad ﷺ and he ﷺ is the *Qalam* of Allah ﷻ. When Allah ﷻ speaks, the Holy Pen writes and documents what Allah ﷻ wants. And in the heavens, they've described there's no pen.

	قلم	
	Qalam	
م	ل	ق
Meem	Lam	Qaf
محمد ﷺ	لسان الحق	قدرة
Muhammad ﷺ (Prophet Muhammad ﷺ)	Lisanul Haq (Tongue of Truth)	Qudra (Divinely Power)

*Note: Please read English from right to left to coincide with Arabic.

So, this *qaf, lam, meem*, it stands for *qaf* and all *qudra* and power. *"Qaf wal Quran al-Majeed"* to the *lam* and the *lisanul haq* (tongue of truth).

$$ق ۚ وَالْقُرْآنِ الْمَجِيدِ ﴿١﴾$$

50:1 – *"Qaf, wal Quranil Majeed."* (Surat Qaf)

"Qaf. By the honored Qur'an." (The Letter Qaf, 50:1)

The tongue and soul that created to speak in truth and for the truth, and then known as *meem, Muhammadun RasulAllah* ﷺ. So, it's a tremendous inheritance. That's why, 'the pen is mightier than the sword' because the inheritance of this *qaf*, this *lam*, and this *meem* comes to the one who carries the pen in their life. 'Ya Rabbi, let me to inherit from this *qaf*. Let me to inherit from this *lam*. Let me to inherit from this *meem*.'

The Qalam is Powerful and Brings Knowledge To Set You Free

So, that Allah ﷻ dresses the servants with the light of Holy Qur'an. Gives them the inheritance from *Lisan as-Siddiq*. *Lisanul Haq* of Allah ﷻ giving to Sayyidina Muhammad ﷺ. *Lisan as-Siddiq al-Aliya*, the highest of the *Siddiqiya* tongues and then they inherit from that reality of that tongue. And then they become *Muhammadiyun*.

So, then this *qalam* (pen) that we carried in our life is more powerful than a sword, more powerful than taking a way in which to fight. This was the most powerful weapon of Allah ﷻ – knowledge. The knowledge will set you free. The knowledge will set all creation free. And the knowledge comes with an abundance of power. This means the *ahle zikr* (people of zikr), Allah's ﷻ dressing them, blessing them; blessing them with so much energy, so much lights, so many *malaika* (angels) that its by-product that's coming out is the knowledges because of the abundance of angelic power that's flowing in a fountain. And its by-product is coming out by the secret of this *qalam* (pen). We pray Allah ﷻ give us more and more understanding of this reality and how to reach of it.

God's Voice is Like Thunder
Power of Qalam (Pen) – Writing Knowledge

We Encompass Nothing from the Knowledge of Prophet ﷺ

When we talk from *Ayatul Kursi* about the reality of Sayyidina Muhammad ﷺ, 'Man zallazee yashfa'u illa bi-iznih; ya'lamu maa baina aydeehim wa ma khalfahum...'ilmihee illaa bimaa shaa.'

...وَلَا يُحِيطُونَ بِشَيْءٍ مِّنْ عِلْمِهِ إِلَّا بِمَا شَاءَ... ﴿٢٥٥﴾

2:255 – "...Ya'lamu maa baina aydeehim wa maa khalfahum wa laa yuheetoona bishai'im min 'ilmihee illaa bimaa shaaa..." (Surat Al-Baqarah)

"...They do not compass anything from His knowledge except what He wills/permits..." (The Cow, 2:255)

Of their knowledge, of His knowledge, you encompass nothing. This was when we talked about Prophet's ﷺ light like the wi-fi and only now they're barely understanding it. They don't even understand what the photon is but they found it everywhere. Even you can Google, still they're not understanding the photon. The photon coming from our sun, for this galaxy reaches the farthest planet out of the galaxy, in this galaxy out. Reaches into the depth of the earth through every nighttime and every rock and every cave, every ocean, the photon of the sun is reaching.

By means of that photon, it's just for an analogy to understand, it's a wireless wi-fi hitting all your cells. So, you can have this device (Shaykh picks up his mobile) all you want. If the wi-fi signal is not broadcasting, it's not of any use. Every cell is in need of the command coming from that photon. And these suns are like satellite offices for the central sun that orbits all around the circle. The center of the entire created universe is a huge sun. It sends its signal to all the other suns. Those suns send out their photons to their galaxy under their command.

Every Cell of the Body Does What It's Commanded To Do

It is, "*Malaikatu war ruh bi izni-rab bihimin kulli amr.*"

$$ تَنَزَّلُ الْمَلَائِكَةُ وَالرُّوحُ فِيهَا بِإِذْنِ رَبِّهِم مِّن كُلِّ أَمْرٍ ﴿٤﴾ $$

97:4 – "*Tanazzalul malaikatu war Ruh, fiha beizne Rabbihim min kulle amr.*" (Surat Al-Qadr)

"*The angels and the Spirit descend therein by permission of their Lord for every Command/affair.*" (The Power 97:4)

So, the *malaika* (angels) and the *ruh* (soul) are taking the command because the *ruh* is the Muhammadan representative of that sun, takes the command from *Atiullaha wa atiur Rasula wa Ulil amre minkum.*

$$ ...أَطِيعُوا اللَّهَ وَأَطِيعُوا الرَّسُولَ وَأُولِي الْأَمْرِ مِنكُمْ... ﴿٥٩﴾ $$

4:59 – "*...Atiullaha wa atiur Rasula wa Ulil amre minkum...*" (Surat An-Nisa)

"*... Obey Allah, Obey the Messenger, and those in authority among you...*" (The Women, 4:59)

Take that command, give to the *malaika* (angels) and all the spiritual beings, and these photons are moving with commands from Allah ﷻ. Every cell is being hit by that photon and been told exactly

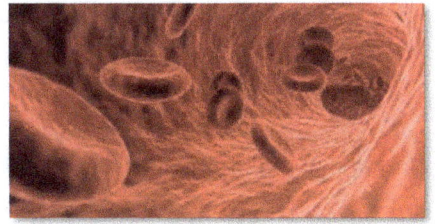

what the cell is supposed to do and not to do, which beyond comprehension that you could even think it's possible. It's not anything random in your body operating.

That's why you watch medical shows, you get scared. These emergency medical shows they show that some one thing in the body is off by a little thing and everything swells up, everything goes out of control. The frailty of how fragile we are is frightening. Because we like to think ourself as very tough and very strong. If one thing goes one percentage, two percentage this way, the *insan* (human being) is falling apart, swelling up, blowing up, stomach collapsing, skin falling apart, all defense mechanisms of the body.

Sayyidina Muhammad's ﷺ Knowledges Are Infinite

Who's sending these commands? If it was random, good God, what life would look like? Everyday you'd see somebody deformed and skin falling off and blisters and boils and tumors. Nothing's random. Every cell is under a command. Every defense mechanism of the body is under command and that's when Allah ﷻ said, 'Of this knowledge, you comprehend nothing.'

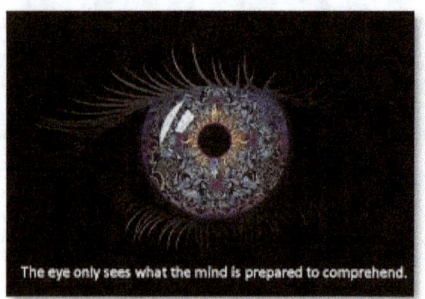
The eye only sees what the mind is prepared to comprehend.

What the cells receive of knowledges is one way. But does the cell understand the one whom is sending them the knowledges? Allah ﷻ says, 'Of it, you understand nothing.' Of what you receive from Sayyidina Muhammad ﷺ of *isharat* and knowledges are infinite, but do you comprehend what Prophet ﷺ knows? Allah ﷻ saying, 'You comprehend nothing.'

Lightning and Thunder Are Signs of Allah's ﷻ Speech

You don't know what Prophet's ﷺ soul hears and how he hears Allah ﷻ. With what might? With what majesty? Allah ﷻ gives example in Holy Qur'an that, 'When I send lightning,' lightning is the sign of Allah's ﷻ Speech. Anyone wants to know what Allah ﷻ sounds like, go outside on a storm and Allah ﷻ gave the parable that disbelievers, they're frightened of lightning. That it shakes them when they hear the thunder, it's roaring.

And then the lightning cracking and it sends a fear into *insan* (human being) that, 'What kind of noise is this?' It's a shout from the heavens. That only for *insan* to even get a drop of the understanding. When Allah's ﷻ Might and Majesty speak, what type of lightning, what type of thunder is shaking? You can't even see it. The clouds are just merely, the angel, there's an angel the size of a thumb called *Habib*. He come with little thing 'ting' and the whole earth is 'agh' (thunder noise). The buildings are shaking and then 'woow,' the lightning hits. Allah ﷻ says, 'This is like an example of my speech. Imagine if I spoke, mankind would be dust out of fear and the energy that would hit to them.'

God's Voice is Like Thunder
Power of Qalam (Pen) – Writing Knowledge

Soul of Sayyidina Muhammad ﷺ is Ever Vigilant and Always in Authority

So, with what sound, what power, what might is Sayyidina Muhammad's ﷺ soul taking the knowledges of Allah ﷻ, the commands of Allah ﷻ? Allah ﷻ is saying, 'Of it, nothing you can comprehend.' What you comprehend is only the *isharat* (sign) coming to yourself, to your being, and to your heart. And the vastness of its knowledge, not understood.

What his soul sees, you don't understand. What his soul speaks, you don't understand. But know that his soul is in the position of authority. And that he's ever vigilant over this kingdom given to him by Allah ﷻ. *La ilaha illahu.* And Allah's ﷻ not within the ocean of *Hayyu Al-Qayyum* (ever-living and self-sustaining). As soon as *Hayyu Al-Qayyum* is mentioned, Allah ﷻ is before that. Allah ﷻ is not alive. Anything alive has death. Allah ﷻ is outside the understanding of life and death.

Seek Najat in the Presence of Sultanan Naseera

This means then these are the *azimah* and the greatness of what Allah ﷻ has dressed. And it's importance in knowing is because you have to know that, *'Ya Rabbi,* when I'm sick and when I'm not well and when I'm feeling scared and when I feel worried, I'm running into the presence of my king, who is my sovereign and whom has power over me and that he owns me and I

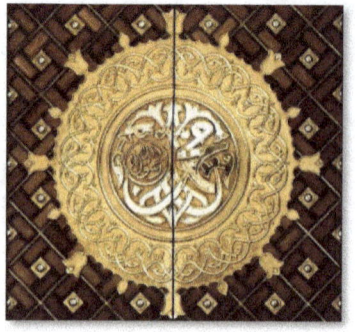

don't own myself. And in the presence of my liege lord, who is my king, I throw myself at his mercy. *Ya Sultanan Naseera* (the Authorized King), save me and help me, that you make the *du'a* (supplication) to Allah ﷻ to grant me a *najat* (salvation).'

It means we see ourself entering into the presence of the Authorized King. We asked to enter from the gate of truthfulness. And after we asked the King to leave through the gate of truthfulness, *Maka'as Siddiq* (Gate of Truth).

وَقُل رَّبِّ أَدْخِلْنِي مُدْخَلَ صِدْقٍ وَأَخْرِجْنِي مُخْرَجَ صِدْقٍ وَاجْعَل لِّي مِن لَّدُنكَ سُلْطَانًا نَّصِيرًا ﴿٨٠﴾

17:80 – *"Wa qul Rabbi adkhelni mudkhala Sidqin wa akhrejni mukhraja Sidqin waj'al li min ladunka Sultanan Naseera."*
(Surat Al-Isra)

"Say: O my Lord! Let my entry be by the Gate of Truth and Honour, and likewise my exit by the Gate of Truth and Honour; and grant me from Your Presence a Victorious King to aid (me)."
(The Night Journey, 17:80)

Enter and Leave Through Maka'as Siddiq

It means this *Maka'as Siddiq* are these *turuq* (spiritual paths). That did you sit with the people of *zikr* and be taught how to be truthful in your character and in your deeds? Then you entered into their gate. And you're asking that, 'When I leave his world, I want to leave through that gate. I don't want to enter back into the people of lies and deceit. Let me to live and die in their association.'

God's Voice is Like Thunder
Power of Qalam (Pen) – Writing Knowledge

If I'm in their gate, I'm asking always *Sultanan Naseera*, the one whom is the Authorized King of Allah ﷻ. The authorized one of Allah ﷻ, that grant me a *najat* (salvation). *Laa hawla wa la quwwata illa billahil 'Aliyyil 'Azheem.* That this power and might that coming through your hands let it to reach to me and take away my difficulties, take away my sicknesses.

وَلاَ حَوْلَ وَلاَ قُوَّةَ اِلاَّ بِاللهِ الْعَلِيّ الْعَظِيْم

"*Wa laa hawla wa la quwwata illa billahil 'Aliyyil 'Azheem.*"

"And there is no Support/ strength, nor power except by Allah, The Sublimely Exalted, The Magnificent."

Visualize Yourself At the Threshold of Sayyidina Muhammad ﷺ

If you don't know who to face and you don't understand the reality, then you don't know who you're talking to. It has less power. So, the way of

ma'rifah (gnosticism) is they come to teach us. When you're in difficulty and you have concerns and you have sicknesses, then visualize yourself at *Madinatul Munawwara*. Visualize ourselves at *Rauza Sharif*. Visualize ourselves at the threshold of Sayyidina Muhammad ﷺ. *Ya Rabbi*, I'm coming.' "*Jaooka fastaghfaro Allaha wastaghfara lahumur Rasul.*"

وَلَوْ أَنَّهُمْ إِذ ظَّلَمُوا أَنفُسَهُمْ جَاءُوكَ فَاسْتَغْفَرُوا اللَّهَ وَاسْتَغْفَرَ لَهُمُ الرَّسُولُ لَوَجَدُوا اللَّهَ تَوَّابًا رَّحِيمًا ﴿٦٤﴾

4:64 – *"Wa law annahum idh zhalamoo anfusahum jaooka fastaghfaro Allaha wastaghfara lahumur Rasulu lawajado Allaha tawwaban raheema." (Surat An-Nisa)*

"And if, when they had wronged themselves, they had but come to you and asked forgiveness of Allah, and asked forgiveness of the messenger, they would have found Allah Forgiving, Merciful." (The Women, 4:64)

That I'm coming to the presence of Sayyidina Muhammad ﷺ and 'I'm asking your forgiveness. I'm asking a *najat* (salvation), *ya Sayyidi, ya Rasul-e-Kareem*, from what Allah ﷻ has given  to you, reach to me and pray upon me. The Power and Might that Allah ﷻ has dressed to you, dress upon me.' Do you think that with that love and that request, *shaitan* (satan) can get near you? And difficulty will be able to attach to you? We pray that Allah ﷻ give us more and more understanding, more and more love, more and more of a heart to understand to move into that reality for the safety of ourselves, our family and our community, *inshaAllah*.

Subhana rabbika rabbal 'izzati 'amma yasifoon, wa salaamun 'alal mursaleen, walhamdulillahi rabbil 'aalameen. Bi hurmati Muhammad al-Mustafa wa bi siri Surat al-Fatiha

NOON WAL QALAM – OUR LIFE IS IN SEARCH OF THESE DIVINE LIGHTS

Sayyidatina Fatima Zahra ؏ Represents the Highest Station of Purity

That Sayyidatina Fatima ؏ represents *al-Batul*, 'The Purified Lights of Holy Qur'an.' Say, *"Ya Hamidu bi haqqi Muhammad (s), ya Aliyyu bi haqqi Ali ؏, ya Allahu al Khaliq bi haqqi Fatima Zahra ؏. Ya Rahman bi haqqi Imam al Hassan ؏, ya Raheem bi haqqi al Imam Hussain ؏."* That Allah ﷻ gave to these *Ahlul Bayt* ؏ (family of Prophet ﷺ) a tremendous reality and a tremendous secret.

يَا حَمِيدُ بِحَقِّ مُحَمَّدٍ ﷺ، يَا عَلِيُّ بِحَقِّ عَلِي (عَلَيْهِ السَّلَامُ)، يَا خَالِقُ بِحَقِّ فَاطِمَةَ الزَّهْرَاءِ (عَلَيْهِ السَّلَامُ)، يَا رَحْمَنُ بِحَقِّ حَسَنْ (عَلَيْهِ السَّلَامُ) ، يَا رَحِيمُ بِحَقِّ حُسَّيْنٍ (عَلَيْهِ السَّلَامُ)

"Ya Hamidu bi Haqqi Muhammad ﷺ, Ya 'Aliyu bi Haqqi 'Ali ؏, Ya Khaliqu bi Haqqi Fatimatuz Zahra ؏, Ya Rahmanu bi Haqqi Hassan ؏, Ya Raheemu bi Haqqi Hussain ؏."

"O' Most praised one for the sake of Prophet Muhammad (pbuh), O' the Most High for the sake of Imam 'Ali (as), O' the Creator for the sake of

Fatima Zahra (as), O the Most Compassionate for the sake of Imam Hassan (as), O' the Most Merciful for the sake of Imam Hussain (as). O the Most Merciful, for the sake of Imam Hussain (as)."

The Womb is the Immense Secret of Creation

The secret of the *rahem* and the womb, the secret of creation, that every creation is coming by means from Allah's ﷻ Secrets. And the understanding of *ar-Rahman*, the understanding of light, the understanding of a *rahem*, the womb, that these realities of light in which we are seeking the reality of light. And they come to teach us that everything is coming through a womb and that womb was given a secret. And all knowledges and all secrets are given to Sayyidina Muhammad ﷺ.

This is the Muhammadan Way of *haqqaiqs* (realities) and Prophet ﷺ gave and dressed that honour. Because of the name *al-Batul*, which is 'The Purified Lights of Holy Qur'an', that wanted this reality and this creation to be dressed by the highest of its realities, and that secret was given to Sayyidatina Fatima az-Zahra ؑ.

RAHMAN
NOON (LIGHT)   RAHEM (WOMB)

So, she holds the secret of creation, that Allah ﷻ when every time going to create through a secret through the womb, through a means in which this creation begins to appear. From Allah's ﷻ Divinely Will comes an *amr*, an order, and Allah's ﷻ Will will begin to manifest. So, from unseen oceans it enters into the order; as soon as the order is conveyed, that creation begins to manifest. So, they ask us to look then to *sifat ar-Rahman*. *Alif, lam, ra, ha, meem, noon*. If you don't understand don't worry, just meditate. It will all come later.

Allah ﷻ Can Only Be Known Through Sayyidina Muhammad ﷺ

Alif: Izzatullah (Allah's ﷻ Might and Magnificence). *Lam: Lisanul Haq* (the Tongue of Truth). Any time we are seeing *"al"* it denotes the highest authority, the highest understanding of that Attribute of Allah ﷻ. To know Allah ﷻ is impossible, but this Attribute of Allah ﷻ to the highest level of perfection will be known through Sayyidina Muhammad ﷺ. He is the Divine Mirror. When Allah ﷻ wants to appear, it appears through the mirror of the prophetic reality.

Nothing Can Carry Nor Contain Allah ﷻ

The *alif* is *Izzatullah* that connects to nothing. And the *alif* shows that the *lam* and the tongue is the *kursi*; the *lam* is a chair, it has the seat. Allah ﷻ shows that 'My king is upon the chair and I am the *Izzah* and the Power of that king. I sit upon the Throne of the king.' Allah ﷻ is not sitting on a chair, impossible. Otherwise the chair would be stronger because this chair has to hold my weight. Nothing can carry Allah ﷻ, nothing can contain Allah ﷻ. But that's why Allah ﷻ clarified that, *"Qalb al mumin baytullah."*

قَلْبَ الْمُؤْمِنْ بَيْثُ الرَّبْ

"Qalb al mu'min baytur rabb."

"The heart of the believer is the House of the Lord." (Hadith Qudsi)

'Nothing can contain Me in Heavens or on Earth except the heart of My believer.'

مَا وَسِعَنِيْ لَا سَمَائِيْ ولا أَرْضِيْ وَلَكِنْ وَسِعَنِيْ قَلْبِ عَبْدِيْ اَلْمُؤْمِنْ

"Maa wasi'anee laa Samayee, wa la ardee, laakin wasi'anee qalbi 'Abdee al Mu'min."

"Neither My Heavens nor My Earth can contain Me, but the heart of my Believing Servant."
(Hadith Qudsi conveyed by Prophet Muhammad (pbuh))

Allah's Izzah is Upon the Tongue of the Reality of Prophet

It is about the secret of creation that Allah is describing. That, 'I created this Muhammadan Light and I sit upon its throne. I am the *Izzah* and Power of this reality of tongue.' "*Wa alamahu fa shadeedul quwwa.*"

وَمَا يَنْطِقُ عَنِ الْهَوَىٰ ﴿٣﴾ إِنْ هُوَ إِلَّا وَحْيٌ يُوحَىٰ ﴿٤﴾ عَلَّمَهُ شَدِيدُ الْقُوَىٰ ﴿٥﴾

53:3-5 – "*Wa ma yantiqu 'anil hawa. (3) In huwa illa wahyun yooha. (4) 'Allamahu shadeedul Quwa. (5)*" (Surat An-Najm)

"Nor does he (Prophet Muhammad (s) speak from [his own] desire. (3) He is not but a revelation revealed. (4) He was taught by one Mighty in Power. (5)" (The Star, 53:3-5)

In Surat an-Najm because the *najm* and the stars, they denote the world of light. There is no form in a star. There is no form. It is *malakut* (heavenly realm) and light. And light is eternal, the stars are eternal. So, when Allah describes, 'He has been taught by *shadeed al quwwa*. The power of My *Izzah* is upon the tongue of the reality of Prophet ﷺ.' Then the *ra, ha, meem*; the *ra* to understand the *rahem* (womb) means then they come from the *meem*. And that is a Muhammadan *haqqaiq* (reality) that Allah ﷻ wants, 'You want to reach to this reality, come through in *dunya* (material world), *Muhammadun RasulAllah* ﷺ. In *akhirah* (the hereafter) in *malakut*, Sayyidina Mahmud ﷺ.'

That is why you pray *Salat al Tahajjud* so that Sayyidina Mahmud ﷺ, that the nearness of that reality comes. So, the *meem* is a rope that comes down to the believer, that you want to enter into this reality because the *rahem* (womb) means yet it has not fully manifested.

The Secret of Allah's ﷻ Will is Ever-Living

So that Muhammadan *haqqaiq*, they begin to enter only through the reality of Prophet ﷺ, that their whole path will take them to this *ha* of *hayat* (ever-living). This is the secret of Allah's ﷻ Will, when it wants to manifest it becomes the ever-living. These are oceans of *hayat*. If Allah ﷻ doesn't give something *hayat*, it does not manifest. So, this *rahem* in *malakut* that is the source of everything manifesting, Allah ﷻ is giving it its *ha* for *hayat* that these are the Oceans of Eternity. 'When I destined something to appear, I'm giving it life. I'm giving it an eternal reality.'

Rabbaniyoon Are From the Oceans of Hayat

And that *ha* takes them to the *rabb*; these are the lordly souls in which they learned the book and taught the book. And Allah ﷻ says 'Be *Rabbaniyoon*' (lordly souls) because through the reality of the book of what they learned and the life of teaching and giving *da'wah*, Allah ﷻ elevated their status to lordly souls.

Noon Wal Qalam – Our Life is in Search of These Divine Lights

...وَلَٰكِن كُونُوا رَبَّانِيِّينَ بِمَا كُنتُمْ تُعَلِّمُونَ الْكِتَابَ وَبِمَا كُنتُمْ تَدْرُسُونَ ﴿٧٩﴾

3:79 – "...Wa lakin kono rabbaniyena bima kuntum tu'allimoonal kitaba wabima kuntum tadrusoon." (Surat Ali-Imran)

"...Be Lordly Souls/faithful servants/worshippers of Him, Because (of what) you have taught the Book and you have studied it earnestly." (Family of Imran, 3:79)

These are lordly souls, the knowledge of lordly souls, because they are from the Oceans of *al-Hayat*. They have entered into that *meem* and they are *Muhammadiyun*.

Our Entire Life is in Pursuit of the Light

So, this tremendous secret of the *rahem* and our whole life is about finding out about the light, the *nur*. So, the *rahem* that carries this secret, when Allah ﷻ wants that secret to appear, it gives it a *noon* and becomes *Rahman*. So, the attribute of Allah ﷻ that governs the entire manifested world is *sifat ar-Rahman*. "ArRahmanu 'alal 'arshi istawa."

RAHMAN
NOON (LIGHT)   RAHEM (WOMB)

الرَّحْمَٰنُ عَلَى الْعَرْشِ اسْتَوَىٰ ﴿٥﴾

20:5 – "ArRahmanu 'alal 'arshi istawa." (Surat Taha)

"The Most Merciful [who is] above the Throne established." (Taha, 20:5)

That *Rahman, ar-Rahman*, it is the attribute of Allah ﷻ that controls all the manifested creation. Because it comes from the *rahem* (womb), the reality of Allah's ﷻ Will and Oceans of *Hayat* that come through Prophet ﷺ. As soon as Allah ﷻ gives it its *noon*, it has been granted *nur* (light) and an existence; no *nur*, no existence.

So, our whole life is about understanding the light, in pursuit of the light, how to reach to the light, how to be dressed by the light. That reality of the *noon* is that how to be dressed by that reality. So, when they show in their drawing of *ar-Rahman*, this *ra*, the *ha* is an Ocean of *Hayat*. The *meem* is all encompassing, *Bahrul Muheet* (All Encompassing Ocean), that everything is inside that *meem* and then it loops out of the *meem* with the *noon*.

Strive Towards the Noon of Insan

Because what is manifesting in these oceans of life is a *noon* of *nur*. So, as soon as Allah ﷻ gives it a *noon*, it manifests with a light. So, our life is how to reach to that *noon*. Then *awliyaullah* (saints) come and teach, Allah ﷻ gave us codes. Say, '*Ya Rabbi*, I want to now understand this whole manifestation is a light You gave me, the *nur* You gave me, the *noon* You gave me. What am I supposed to do with this *noon*?'

Even in *insan* (human being), there are two *noons*. *Al Insan* has two *noons* and a secret in the middle, but my life is about how to get to that *noon*. Then Allah ﷻ gives us a code in Holy Qur'an, *"Noon wal qalam."*

﴿ ن ۚ وَالْقَلَمِ وَمَا يَسْطُرُونَ ﴿١﴾

68:1 – *"Noon. wal Qalami wa ma yasTuroon."* (Surat Al-Qalam)

"Noon. By the pen and what they inscribe." (The Pen, 68:1)

Elevate Your Light Though "Noon wal Qalam"

"Noon wal qalam." Awliyaullah then direct us that Allah is teaching us, 'You want to understand how to elevate your light.' Because elevating light is not so easy. Making your light to be brighter is not easy. It is not only by your *amal* (actions); it is not only by you praying, by your fasting, by your giving *zakat* (charity) by you doing all these actions, because you may be going five steps forward and ten steps back. So, elevation of light by ourselves is virtually impossible unless Allah gives a special grant.

We are talking about the rule and not the exception. Those whom are trying to reach to Allah is different than when Allah grants. Not all creation is given a grant, a special gift. Those are *murad* whom Allah gave them a gift and they elevate how Allah wants them to elevate. The rule for *insan* is how to elevate my light, perfect my light, raise my light? Then *awliyaullah* teach 'Go to the understanding of the *qalam* (pen).' So, *"Noon wal qalam."* Allah swears by this light, has to do with this *qalam*. That the reality of this *noon* which is *nur* has to be brought out by the secret of this *qalam*.

Allah Teaches Ancient Knowledges Through His Qalam

And what was the first thing revealed to Prophet in Surat al-Iqra? 'That 'I am going to teach you *allam bil qalam* I am going to teach you *allam bil qalam*.' This is not about Allah teaching you accounting and math. This *allam* is Allah's ﷻ ancient *ayn*, Allah's ﷻ Ancient Knowledges He wants to convey through His *Qalam*.

اقْرَأْ وَرَبُّكَ الْأَكْرَمُ ﴿٣﴾ الَّذِي عَلَّمَ بِالْقَلَمِ ﴿٤﴾ عَلَّمَ الْإِنسَانَ مَا لَمْ يَعْلَمْ ﴿٥﴾

96:3-5 – *"Iqra, wa rabbukal akram (3). Alladhee 'allama bil Qalam (4). 'Allamal insana ma lam ya'lam. (5)"* (Surat Al-Alaq)

"Recite, and your Lord is the most Generous. (3) Who taught by the pen. (4) Taught man that which he knew not. (5)" (The Clot, 96:3-5)

This ancient knowledge always has to move through this *lisanul haq wa lisanul Siddiq al 'Aliya*, has to be through purified tongues.

وَوَهَبْنَا لَهُم مِّن رَّحْمَتِنَا وَجَعَلْنَا لَهُمْ لِسَانَ صِدْقٍ عَلِيًّا ﴿٥٠﴾

19:50 – *"Wa wahabna lahum min rahmatina wa ja'alna lahum lisana Sidqin 'Aliya."* (Surat Maryam)

"And We bestowed of Our Mercy on them, and We granted them lofty honour from/on the tongue of truth." (Maryam, 19:50)

Awliyaullah Have Been Granted Ancient Gifts

Allam because these are all *meem* and Muhammadan realities. Every *huroof* (Arabic letters) Allah ﷻ has encoded. Say, 'I am going to teach you, I am going to give you My ancient knowledges through My ancient tongues. I have created their souls in an ancient ocean.' *Awliyaullah* are not made on here (Earth). You don't pick

up two oranges and choose a banana and you became a *wali* (saint) by your cleverness. Right?

It is an ancient gift, anciently written. Allah ﷻ wrote those souls to be dressed by that reality and granted them that reality so that they are ancient *lams*. When they appear on Earth, Allah ﷻ has given them the *ayn*. They have been dressed with ancient knowledges and that *ayn* is the *ayn* that Allah ﷻ taught. That Arabic language is the language of Paradise, not the Arabic language you speak with your tongue. There is no tongue in heaven.

Rabbaniyoon Are Dressed by the Bahrul Qudra

There is no tongue up there, nobody walking around with a tongue up there. It's the world of light. So, they say, 'Oh, I thought Arabic is the language of Paradise.' Not the Arabic you think. It is the *ayn, ra, ba*.

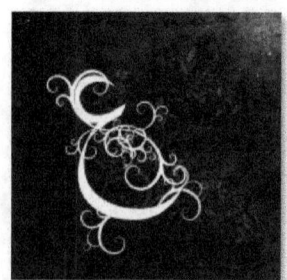

Those whom Allah ﷻ gave them *ayn*, 'ancient knowledges.' That they are *rabbaniyoon* (lordly souls). They are the *arbaab* (companions), and *ba* is that they have been dressed by the Oceans of *Bahrul Qudra* (oceans of power). All of Holy Qur'an is in that *ba*. So, When Allah ﷻ is talking about Arabic is the language of Paradise it means the language of Paradise that Allah ﷻ wants are the souls that have been dressed by ancient knowledges.

Heavenly Kingdom Consists of Lofty Souls Reaching Towards Realities

That everything is a knowledge and a light being conveyed throughout the oceans of the *malakut*. There are no people walking around speaking with tongues, but a light and energy being conveyed; where in every moment there is a new *tajalli* (manifestation), a new  knowledge, a new reality being dressed upon their souls. And Allah ﷻ is clarifying, 'These knowledges are from My Ancient Realities and these are souls that carry this whole Ocean of Power and they are not from the House of Commons but from the House of Lords.'

And that is why it is called 'Heavenly Kingdom' not the Heavenly Turkish Bazaar. It is a kingdom in which lofty souls, lofty realities and that they are trying to reach towards that understanding, that is the *allam*. So, when they are talking *allam* they go deep into the *huroof* and Allah ﷻ makes each letter talk to their heart by *malaika* (angels). *"Allama bil Qalam"* (Holy Qur'an, 96:3-5).

What is the Qalam of Allah ﷻ?

So, then our life is to be taught by the *qalam*. I am going to be taught that which I knew not. I don't sit anywhere where someone wants to tell me what I already heard ten times. That's not a *qalam*. So, our life is to seek.

Then they come and they teach what is a *qalam*? Because Allah ﷻ has no pen in Heavens. Now this is the astonishing part of technology. In a time when Prophet ﷺ came, he has to give everybody an understanding that we are with chisel, pen, paper where they get the feather and they put the ink. But when Allah ﷻ revealed all this He knows what is coming in the end of technologies. He created it. So, if you think the Heavens is using old technology and you use new technology, something is wrong in that understanding.

So *malakut* comes to clarify, 'No, no. Prophet ﷺ is voice recognition.' As soon as Prophet ﷺ speaks it is written 'swish, swish, swish, swish'  [refers to writing]. Only now we would understand that. Try to explain that 300 years ago! 'What are you talking about, that somebody speaks, and it appears? Who, who appeared it? Somebody had to chisel it.' But the *malakut* now understands and is easily explained, 'No, no, there is no pen. There is no *qalam* and *qudra* (power) up there that somebody, 'ksh, ksh, ksh, ksh' [refers to writing sounds]. It is merely Prophet ﷺ speaking.

Nothing Manifests Outside of Holy Qur'an

As Prophet ﷺ speaks, everything is being written by the angels and at the same time manifesting. We said that *Qalam, qul; Qaf, lam, qalam.* This *qaf*, lam – "*Qaf, wal Quranil Majeed.*" "*Qaf, wal Quranil Majeed*" means that if anything exists, it is in the holy book of Qur'an. Small or big, there can be nothing manifesting outside of Holy Qur'an. Holy Qur'an is the power of everything manifesting. "*Qaf, wal Quranil Majeed.*"

ق ۚ وَالْقُرْآنِ الْمَجِيدِ ﴿١﴾

50:1 – "*Qaf, wal Quranil Majeed.*" (*Surat Qaf*)

"*Qaf. By the honored Qur'an.*" (*The Letter Qaf,* 50:1)

قلم	
Qalam	
م	قل
Meem	Qul
محمد ﷺ	قل
Muhammad ﷺ (Prophet Muhammad ﷺ)	Qul (Say)

*Note: Please read English from right to left to coincide with Arabic.

Only Prophet ﷺ Can Contain Allah's ﷻ "Qul"

This *qaf* has to manifest in *manzil e Qur'an*. In the heart of Prophet ﷺ is the only place that Holy Qur'an which is the power for the entire created universe manifests from Prophet ﷺ. So, from the holy heart of the soul of Prophet ﷺ this power is manifesting onto the *lam* and the tongue of all realities. That is the power of *qul*. Nothing can contain the *qul* except Prophet ﷺ. There is not an angel that can hear *qul*, not an angel and not a prophet. Nothing in creation can hear Allah's ﷻ Speech. Allah ﷻ says 'If I reveal My Qur'an to the mountain it will be like dust but I reveal to Prophet ﷺ, he is standing.

لَوْ أَنزَلْنَا هَٰذَا الْقُرْآنَ عَلَىٰ جَبَلٍ لَّرَأَيْتَهُ خَاشِعًا مُّتَصَدِّعًا مِّنْ خَشْيَةِ اللَّهِ وَتِلْكَ الْأَمْثَالُ نَضْرِبُهَا لِلنَّاسِ لَعَلَّهُمْ يَتَفَكَّرُونَ ﴿٢١﴾

59:21 – "Law anzalna hadha alQurana 'ala jabalin laraaytahu, khashi'an mutasaddi'an min khashyatillahi, wa tilkal amthalu nadribuha linnasi la'allahum yatafakkaroon." (Surat Al-Hashr)

"Had We sent down this Qur'an on a mountain, verily, you would have seen it obliterated to dust (from its power) And these examples We present to the people that perhaps they will Contemplate..."
(The Exile, 59:21)

No One Can Hear Allah ﷻ Except Sayyidina Muhammad ﷺ

So, it means the angels, they don't hear it. The prophets, they don't hear it. The only ancient soul is RasulAllah ﷺ. The only creation that can hold

the *qul* of Allah ﷻ is the reality of Sayyidina Muhammad ﷺ. That's why the *qul* then points us to the *meem* and teaches us that is the *Qalam* of Allah ﷻ. Allah's ﷻ Pen is His Might, His Power and His *Irada* and His Will is in the heart of Sayyidina YaSeen ﷺ. 'All My *Irada* and *Amr* is in this heart and merely I speak and *kun faya kun*, it appears.' It appears through who? Sayyidina Muhammad ﷺ.

$$ \text{إِنَّمَا أَمْرُهُ إِذَا أَرَادَ شَيْئًا أَن يَقُولَ لَهُ كُن فَيَكُونُ ﴿٨٢﴾} $$

36:82 – *"Innama AmruHu idha Arada shay an, an yaqola lahu kun faya koon."* (Surat YaSeen)

"His command is when He intends a thing, He says to it, "Be," and it is!" (YaSeen, 36:82)

Everything Manifests When Prophet ﷺ Speaks

So *qul* to the *meem* and the *meem* of Prophet ﷺ, he speaks. So, it means that this is tremendous advanced technology of Prophet ﷺ is teaching from that time. It means, 'I merely speak and everything begins to manifest.' Everything would appear the moment Prophet ﷺ is speaking because Surat YaSeen ﷺ is teaching that His Will, His *Amr* and His *Irada* is in the heart of Prophet ﷺ. That when Allah ﷻ wants something, it is in the heart of Prophet ﷺ. When He gives a command, 'Speak something,' the *amr* has appeared. The order has appeared. As soon as the order comes, it manifests automatically. There is no pen to write anything. Latest technology in the heavens, beyond technology.

Allah's ﷻ Qalam is Prophet's ﷺ Speech

So that *qalam* is the speech. That *qalam* is Prophet's ﷺ speech. So, when Allah ﷻ is testifying *"Noon wal qalam,"* the only way to raise your light because Allah ﷻ swears by the Holy Qur'an at the beginning of *muqatta'at*. *"Noon wal qalam,"* that if you are in search of the noon and you are in search of the light and these are the lights, *nurul anwar wa sirratal asrar* (light of every secret and secret of every light).

We are not talking about fluorescent lights. We are talking about the most purified lights of the soul, the most purified lights of the heavens, the most purified lights that Allah ﷻ has created. Allah ﷻ then coding for us, 'Go to the *qalam*. Go the *qalam* of My reality and that Prophet ﷺ must be speaking to you.'

Raise Your Light by Accompanying the Qalam

So, then these *awliyaullah*, they have been trained, that they are, and they have been destined as ancient tongues. Allah ﷻ wrote for them that you will be from the inheritors of the tongues of the *siddiq* (truthful).

قَالَ رَسُولُ اللهِ صَلَّى اللهُ عَلَيْهِ وَسَلَّمَ "عُلَمَاءِ وَرِثَةُ الْأَنْبِيَاءِ"

Qala RasulAllahi (saws) "'Ulama e warithatul anbiya."

Prophet Muhammad (pbuh) said, "My scholars are the inheritors of the prophets." (Ibn Majah and Tirmidhi)

That your entire *wujud* (existence) and your entire being is meant to  inherit that reality and that you speak on the tongue of Sayyidina Muhammad ﷺ. You speak on the tongue of the Companions ﷺ, the *Ahlul Bayt* ﷺ and all *awliyaullah* (saints) are inheriting from that reality. 313 of them have permission to speak. Those not from the 313, they have jobs to do, but they don't have permission to speak.

So, then our life is to find the *qalam*, to accompany these *qalam*. As soon as they speak, as soon as they (do) *zikr* (remembrance), as soon as anything's coming from them, it is from that reality of *qalam*. And that reality of *qalam*, it dresses and blesses the light. It's filled with lights. It hits the soul and dresses the soul with all of its realities and all of its blessings. So, every knowledge that it conveys goes directly onto the soul. As a result, that soul, its frequency will be raised. That is why this is so important to understand.

The Entire World of Manifestation is By a Sound

This world of form is all based on lights, the science of it. The form, it's only manifesting on the quality of its light. Its light is an energy and its energy 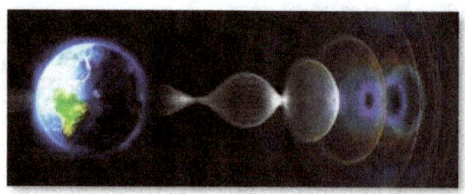 is a sound. So now what do they have? They have now coming, in wars that are coming, they have weapons of sound. Because they can, with a sound, they can completely bring down a form because every form has a sound vibration.

If the vibration moves, they counter the vibration and break the molecular structure of how that is resonating. And you will see buildings will collapse. You see glass shatter. You see people shatter. So *shaitan* (satan) knows, and *Rahman* knows better. Even they plan, Allah ﷻ plans better. Our whole life is about changing the form so then that sound is directly related to that *qalam*.

Sounds Emanating From Prophet's ﷺ Heart Have a Tremendous Energy

Qul ya Muhammad ﷺ. Everything is that I want to take from the reality of Sayyidina Muhammad ﷺ. I want to be in the company of those

Muhammadiyun that they take, and in their heart is that vibration of Prophet ﷺ teaching them, conveying to them of all these realities. As a result, they are continuously dressing and elevating. Even changing the form of people based on the sound vibration that is emanating with them, through the recitations, through the talks, through every channel available. The sound that they emanate from Prophet's ﷺ heart, it has a tremendous energy. *"Alamuhu fi shadeed al quwwa"* (Holy Qur'an, 53:3-5).

Not a regular energy, Allah ﷻ describing *shadeed al quwwa* when Allah ﷻ, *"Sayhatan wahidatan."*

إِن كَانَتْ إِلَّا صَيْحَةً وَاحِدَةً فَإِذَا هُمْ خَامِدُونَ ﴿٢٩﴾

36:29 – *"In kanat illa sayhatan wahidatan fa idha hum khamidoon."* (Surat YaSeen)

"It was not but one shout, and immediately they were extinguished/destroyed." (YaSeen, 36:29)

Sounds of Zikr and Praising Changes Your Energy

It is but one shout and Allah ﷻ says, 'You are destroyed,' and also another time, 'It is but one shout I will raise you again.'

إِن كَانَتْ إِلَّا صَيْحَةً وَاحِدَةً فَإِذَا هُمْ جَمِيعٌ لَّدَيْنَا مُحْضَرُونَ ﴿٥٣﴾

36:53 – *"In kanat illa sayhatan wahidatan fa idha hum jamee'un ladayna muhdaroon."* (Surat YaSeen)

"It will be no more than a single Blast/Shout, when at once, they will all be brought up before Us!" (YaSeen, 36:53)

Not only We can destroy you with the sound, they can raise you back up with the sound. These are all from Holy Qur'an. They can gather you with the sound.

Most important is by accompanying and doing the sound with them, the *zikr* (remembrance) with them, the *nasheed* (praisings) with them, learning from their knowledges. The simplest is that they are going to change your energy. You're going to find your energy heating up. You find you go home and you can't sleep; there's just too much. You have been connected to a live wire. That energy, if you keep it clean and keep your practices, they're changing the frequency of how you are manifesting.

The Angelic Reality Within the Water Reflects Your Energy

If you listen to bad things all day long you find your energy goes down and the color of your light actually changes. They now have experiments where they make sound on water. They say bad words and the water turns like mud because the angels can't carry the badness. And they

BEFORE PRAYER.........AFTER PRAYER

have an electron microscope on water and as soon as they say nice and pleasant and beatific words, the angelic reality of that water, it sparkles like crystals, like diamonds. And always at six points of different designs.

Your Reality Changes When You Accompany the Shaykh

This means there is a tremendous reality in all of what Allah ﷻ is sending around us. The sound, if I accompany them, my sound will begin to

change, my energy will begin to change. If my energy and I keep myself clean and do my practices, the actual light of how I am manifesting begins to change because they have the ability to raise the manifestation, from a low frequency to a high frequency. At the high frequency, even now their form begins to change.

The light, the look, the appearance, the characteristics of how that *insan* (human being) is manifesting and walking upon this earth completely changes. All our lives we have seen that. We have all seen that example. We came through the door one way and by the time we leave into the grave, *inshaAllah*, it is a completely different way, completely different look, completely different light, completely different character. From what? From these sounds, from these energies, from these realities.

Don't Waste Your Time Around Fake Fruits

If you sit with someone who doesn't have that, Mawlana ق describes it is like a fake fruit. You can sit for twenty years. That person did not change, and you didn't change because there is no frequency. There is no light, there is no energy emitting. Nothing changes in that association.

But those real *qalams*, the real ones whom they are, and you know by the realities in which they convey from the heart of Prophet ﷺ. The energy and the power in those associations, those *qalams* – that is why in that *Ni'mat-e-Ishq* (Farsi poem) that, 'What you are writing is changing my destiny. That *dastaye mubarak*, your hand is a blessed hand.' Because those *qalams*, everything that they are speaking and saying, it is changing your *kitab* (book), every knowledge they gave.

تو ولی نعمت عشقی ، از ملائک بهشتی
تو با دستای مبارک سرنوشتمو نوشتی

To vali nemate eshghi, az malaeke Beheshti
To ba dastaye mubarak, sarneveshtamo neveshti

You are the blessing of love. You are from the angels of paradise. With your blessed hands you wrote my destiny and guided me to the Divine's path.

Muhammadan Haqqaiqs Give Your Soul Honour in Divinely Presence

Tonight, what they conveyed to you completely changed your book because what is written on your book by the angels gives you honour in Divinely Presence. Every knowledge that is conveyed to you, your angels wrote it. If you write it, the angels write it even more. You have been dressed by a Muhammadan *haqqaiq* (reality). By the time you go home tonight, your soul, not you, you may not be clever enough, but the soul will say, 'My Lord, I heard something; I want to swim in that reality.' And the soul dives into that reality just by the *haqqaiq* and the soul will swim in it until it is full, until it has quenched its thirst which is infinite and can never be quenched.

That was the honour that was given that night. It means every secret has a name and every name has a secret. If you are not given the name, not given the secret, how can you be dressed by it? That is why then the *qalam* is so important in our life. As soon as we hear it, as soon as we accompany them, he is dressing us, blessing us, elevating us, changing us, and manifesting in a different form at every moment.

Subhana rabbika rabbal 'izzati 'amma yasifoon, wa salaamun 'alal mursaleen, walhamdulillahi rabbil 'aalameen. Bi hurmati Muhammad al-Mustafa wa bi siri Surat al-Fatiha

The Holy Face

AYAT AL KURSI ABOUT WAJHALLAH (FACE OF GOD)

To Be Nothing is the Door to Understanding Qur'an

When we mentioned last night, the mirror at the highest level of *ihsan* (moral excellence), at the highest level of realities is *la ilaha illAllah*, reflecting to the other mirror of *Muhammadun RasulAllah* ﷺ.

لَا إِلَهَ إِلاَّ اللهُ مُحَمَّدًا رَسُولُ الله

"La ilaha illAllahu Muhammadun RasulAllah."

"There is no deity but Allah, Prophet Muhammad is the messenger of Allah."

And the door for its understanding is that, 'I'm non-existent,' so that I'm not looking in between this *lam alif* and trying to appear. If I appear and I look at *la ilaha illAllah*, then everything is about searching myself. That's why when they read Qur'an, they think of everything about themselves, how Allah ﷻ is talking to them, how Allah ﷻ is guiding them. This is one level of understanding.

La Ilaha IllAllah Reflects to Muhammadun RasulAllah ﷺ

This level of *ma'rifah* (gnosticism), it's door is that you're non-existent. That *'Ya Rabbi*, I'm an oppressor to myself and I'm non-existent. I don't want to exist so I'm merely a spectator looking invisibly of this reality of *la ilaha illAllah*. If I'm not there then the *la ilaha illAllah* is reflecting *Muhammadun RasulAllah* ﷺ. And if I'm not there and I look at *Muhammadun RasulAllah* ﷺ, it's reflecting *la ilaha illAllah*.'

So, the problem is me. It's the 'me' in the middle that I'm trying to get rid of. And that's why then they teach us, 'Clean, clean, clean. As much as you can clean to make yourself and rid yourself of yourself, of bad character, bad desires, what I want, and everything of what I want is not important.' My character is to be good and I become clear and transparent, *inshaAllah*. And I begin to understand this mirror and its reflection and all its realities.

Like Allah ﷻ, Alif Has No Partner

And they begin to teach us that in every way of *ma'rifah* (gnosticism) is a higher level of knowing. When we say *IsmAllah*, "Allah," don't think that you know Allah ﷻ now because you're saying a name. In this way of *ma'rifah*, anything you draw near to with your heart and trying to seek its understanding and seek its knowledges, as soon as you move towards this *kalimah* (testimony) *alif, lam, lam, hey;* we say *hey* because we know it's not the *ha* of *hayat* (ever-living). It's of *hu*.

So, when we're moving towards this *hey*, they begin to teach that as soon as you move near this name *IsmAllah*, the *alif* is always separate; *alif* has no *sharik* (partner). It doesn't attach itself to anything. So, as soon as you want to know about Allah ﷻ, the *alif* moves and teaches you that you're not going to know about me, not that easy.

Lam Represents Mulk and Malakut

What's left is *lam, lam, hey*. *Lam* closest to the Allah ﷻ has to do with the tongue and the tongue is what speaks and brings that which is hidden to be known. That's why Mawlana Shaykh ق would teach that the *lam* is a *mulk* (earthly realm), is a creation. It brings creation. How? Because what's hidden from Allah's ﷻ Will, as soon as it manifests on the tongue of realities, it appears.

الله			
Allah ﷻ			
ه	ل	ل	ا
Hey	Lam of Dunya	Lam of Akhirah	Alif
هداية	مُلك	مَلكوت	عِزَّتُ الله
Hidayat (Guidance)	Mulk (Material World)	Malakut (Heavens)	'Izzatullah (Allah's ﷻ Might)

*Note: Please read English from right to left to coincide with Arabic.

So, this creation closest to the *alif* is the heavens, *malakut* (heavenly realm). The *meem* of *malakut*, the realities of *malakut*. Alif, lam, lam – that *lam* closest to the *alif* is the heavens. The *lam* closest to the *hey* is the *mulk* and the creation of all the world of form, what they call the *mulk*. The creation of *mulk* is everything that is visible. *Malakut*, that which you don't see but *"kulli shay."* It's the power of everything.

فَسُبْحَانَ الَّذِي بِيَدِهِ مَلَكُوتُ كُلِّ شَيْءٍ وَإِلَيْهِ تُرْجَعُونَ ﴿٨٣﴾

36:83 – *"Fasubhanal ladhee biyadihi Malakotu kulli shay in wa ilayhi turja'oon." (Surat YaSeen)*

"Therefore Glory be to Him in Whose hand is the [heavenly] dominion/kingdom of all things, and to Him you will be returned." (YaSeen, 36:83)

Allah ﷻ Has No Need of the Mulk

Like the atomic reality for us to understand in our sciences. Oh, I'm here but you didn't really see me. You just saw some guy with a beard and some clothes. But if you put me under a microscope, that's my reality. That's the reality that nobody feeds and nobody can deal and destroy that energy. That's my energy reality. That's *malakut* (heavenly realm), higher than that is then in the heavens, that which you don't understand and which we don't comprehend.

The *hey* is the guide, is the *hu*. This means that Allah ﷻ doesn't care for this creation of heavens and earth more than the wing of a mosquito, *hadith* (traditions of Prophet ﷺ) of Prophet ﷺ. Allah ﷻ doesn't care for creation for it is the wing of a mosquito. Allah's ﷻ not impressed by the heavens and He's not in need of the *mulk* (earthly realm). It's beyond anything that we can understand.

Awliyaullah Teach Us Not To Care For Dunya

So, then *tariqah* (spiritual path) comes to teach these two are like a *nuqt* (dot) because Allah ﷻ has no caring for it. So, they don't care for *dunya* (material world) and they're not hoping for a paradise reality like

Disneyland, 'I want to go to the most popular paradise. I want this and this paradise and I want rivers and streams and all of these things.' *Awliyaullah* (saints) come and teach us, 'Allah ﷻ doesn't care for them so you don't care for them.' They have like a *nuqt*, two *nuqts*.

Muhammadun RasulAllah ﷺ is the King of Mulk and Malakut

So, this *alif* is *Izzatullah* (Allah's ﷻ Might and Magnificence) but what Allah ﷻ does care for is that *hey* at the end. The *hey* at the end is the *huwa*, is the *hadi* (guide) and the guide of *hidayat* (guidance). To all these realities to go through the *lam* of *dunya* and *mulk*. Who is the king of

this entire world of form? *Muhammadun RasulAllah* ﷺ, *Sultan* (King). Who is the king of all *malakut*? When Sayyidina Muhammad ﷺ was teaching in *hadith al-Jabir*, 'I'm the first thing Allah ﷻ created before Adam ﷺ was between clay and water. Jabir, I am the *RasulAllah* ﷺ, eternal position of the soul of Sayyidina Muhammad ﷺ.'

قَالَ رَسُولَ اللهِ صَلَّى اللهُ عَلَيْهِ وَسَلَّمَ: "كُنْتُ نَبِيًّا وَآدَمُ بَيْنَ الْمَاءِ وَالطِّينِ"

Qala Rasulullahi ﷺ: "*Kuntu Nabiyan wa Adama baynal Maa e wat Teen.*"

"I was a Prophet and Adam was between water and clay." (Prophet Muhammad (pbuh))

Ayat al Kursi – About WajhAllah (Face of God)

All Will Perish Except the Divinely Face of Allah ﷻ

So, the two *lams* Allah ﷻ doesn't care for. We put two *nuqt*, two dots – the *alif* and the *hey*. So, the *alif* is sending all it's *tajallis* (manifestations) to that *hey*. Allah's ﷻ sending *Izzah* and Might to His *Hadi* (guide). So, then the Divinely Face that everything will perish, all these *lams* will perish except *"WajhAllah,"* the Divinely Face of Allah ﷻ. Everything perishes but His Holy Face.

$$...كُلُّ شَيْءٍ هَالِكٌ إِلَّا وَجْهَهُ...﴿٨٨﴾$$

28:88 – "...*kullu shayin halikun illa wajha*..." (Surat Al-Qasas)

"...Everything (that exists) will perish except His holy Face..." (The Stories, 28:88)

So, when they understood that everything will perish, they don't attach to *dunya* (material world). They're not asking for a *dunya* reality. And when they found that Allah ﷻ, everything will perish, the angels will perish, the heavens will perish, *Baitul Mamur* (the sacred house in heaven) – everything will perish except the Divinely Face. Then they ask, '*Ya Rabbi*, all we want is the Divinely Face. We want that which never perishes.'

The Throne is a Symbol of Authority and Power

And there are 7 essences that dress that *alif*, that is '*Arsh ar-Rahman* (the Throne of the Merciful). That is the reality of the Divinely Throne. That in *dunya* (material world), these 7 points, they're like a chair. The Face and the chair have the same attribute. The chair is a position of authority because your chair has four legs and two arms and the seat is like a tongue, like a 'L', like a *lam*. So, the Face is the chair of the Divinely Presence. There's no chair, but Allah (ﷻ) speaks in similitude, to give you an example because we don't know from that reality.

So, describes that in your world of form, you know kings and the authority of a king is his throne. So, the *Kursi*, the Throne is a symbol of authority and power. And its real reality is the Holy Face. That Holy Face has 7 openings – has two ears, two eyes, two nostrils and one tongue. That Divinely Face that has no Face but are attributes and essences that dress the soul of Sayyidina Muhammad (ﷺ). That is Allah's (ﷻ) *Kursi*. *"Wasi'a Kursiyyhu."*

... وَسِعَ كُرْسِيُّهُ السَّمَاوَاتِ وَالْأَرْضَ ۖ ... ﴿٢٥٥﴾

2:255 - *"...Wasi'a Kursiyyuhus samaawaati wal arda..."*
(*Surat Al-Baqarah*)

"...His Throne extends over the heavens and the earth..."
(*The Cow, 2:255*)

Ayat al Kursi – About WajhAllah (Face of God)

"Qul Hu" is Allah ﷻ Speaking to the Hu of Sayyidina Muhammad ﷺ

That is the Throne and the *'Arsh* (Throne) of *ar-Rahman* (the Merciful). It's the Divinely Face of Allah ﷻ that has no Face but are 7 holy attributes. They dress the world that has a Face which is the soul of Sayyidina Muhammad ﷺ.

And that's the *alif* shooting its 7 attributes to the *Hu* of Allah ﷻ because the two *lams*, they're *nuqt*. They're insignificant. Allah ﷻ reflects from His *Izzah* and His Might, reflecting to the *hu* and *hidayat* and guidance, that these 7 attributes are dressing your *hu*. From the unknown *Hu* of Allah ﷻ, it dresses the manifest known of the *hu* of Sayyidina Muhammad ﷺ and that's what Allah ﷻ meant by *"Qul hu."*

﴿قُلْ هُوَ اللَّـهُ أَحَدٌ ﴿١﴾

112:1 – *"Qul HuwAllahu Ahad."* (Surat Al-Ikhlas)

"Say, He is Allah, [who is] One." (The Sincerity, 112:1)

This is not about me and you. This is about Allah's ﷻ Ancient Speech; Allah ﷻ being the one speaking, *hu* being the one spoken to. There's two in this sentence, *"Qul hu."* Qul to who? The one speaking, *Izzah* and Might of Allah ﷻ, *Qul*. The one spoken to, *hu*. *Izzah* of Allah ﷻ dresses that *hu*.

The Reality of Hu Contains Immense Energy

From that power and that reality, Allah ﷻ, of these 7 essences of *hu*. The name "Allah" is an understanding of all the names and attributes. Above that reality is the reality of *hu*.

Beyond the understanding of names and attributes is a pure energy. And when they breathe and do the *zikr* (remembrance) of *hu*, they don't mention any other name that brings their energy to a lower level. So, a very high level of energy and reality. That *hu* is what's dressing and blessing that reality giving it its might and its power.

Insan Can Only Reflect to the Reality of Sayyidina Muhammad ﷺ

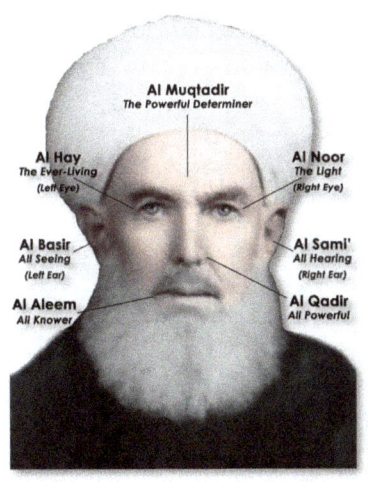

These essences dressing the *hu*. *Sami*, *Al-Basir*. *'Alim*, *Al-Qadir*. *Nur*, *Al-Hay* and *Al-Muqtadir*. These powers that dressing and essences, these are 7 divinely flames and essences that *insan* (human being) doesn't reach to but they reflect to the reality of Sayyidina Muhammad's ﷺ holy face. And that describes that reality, that neither sleep nor slumber overtakes Him.

﴿٢٥٥﴾ ... لَا تَأْخُذُهُ سِنَةٌ وَلَا نَوْمٌ ...

2:255 – "*...Laa taakhuzuhoo sinatunw wa laa nawm...*" (*Surat Al-Baqarah*)

"*...No slumber can seize him nor sleep...*" (The Cow, 2:255)

Who? Allah ﷻ describing the reality of the holy face and what Allah ﷻ dressed of Might and Majesty that this holy face and its power, its attributes and essences that's been given by Allah ﷻ.

Sayyidina YaSeen ﷺ Hears With Yaqeen

Sami, Al-Basir. It hears to the perfection of all creation and it's called *YaSeen* ﷺ because it hears complete with *yaqeen* (certainty). As a result, there is no prophet. The one whom hears the most speaks for the Divine because the *Sami* is at 100% perfection. Lesser perfection never speaks, the greater perfection speaks. *Sifat as-Sami* of Sayyidina YaSeen ﷺ, the one whom has *yaqeen* of the *seen.* That he ﷺ speaks for all of creation. Not a prophet and not an angel can reach to this *maqam* (station) of Sayyidina Muhammad ﷺ. All far below, not even anything comparable. *Al-Basir,* the one whom sees in complete perfection, his Lord at the station of *"Qaba Qawsayni aw Adna."*

فَكَانَ قَابَ قَوْسَيْنِ أَوْ أَدْنَىٰ ﴿٩﴾

53:9 – *"Fakana qaaba qawsayni aw adna."* (Surat An-Najm)

"And was at a distance of two bow lengths or nearer [to the Divine Presence]." (The Star, 53:9)

Nothing Comes Between La Ilaha IllAllah and Muhammadun RasulAllah ﷺ

Not from far but Allah ﷻ give an *ihtiram* and a respect that he's two bow-lengths or nearer. Nobody goes in the place of *"Aw adna."* Why Allah ﷻ put this *ihtiram* throughout Qur'an? Allah ﷻ put these immense, like a contract. When you read a contract and you find a clause that sort of locks the whole contract. That he's at

two bow lengths; if He didn't put *"Aw adna"* you would say, 'Well, then there's an angel in between them. So, he's not really that one.' And Allah ﷻ says, 'No, you're incorrect, *aw adna* or closer.' There is nothing that can come between the reality of *la ilaha illAllah* to *Muhammadun RasulAllah* ﷺ. Nothing!

Only Sayyidina Muhammad ﷺ Reaches "Qaba Qawsayni aw Adna"

There is no intercessor, there's no station. Anything outside of that becomes burnt and non-existent. That's why Sayyidina Jibreel عليه السلام said, 'I can't go to the *maqam* that you're going to. This audience that Allah ﷻ has called your physicality is only for you because this is your reality. If I go to that with you, I become non-existent. I cannot enter beyond the ocean of *Muhammadun RasulAllah* ﷺ to look at the reality of *la ilaha illAllah*.' Sayyidina Jibreel عليه السلام becomes non-existent at that point. *As-Sami, Al-Basir* means then nobody sees from *"Qaba Qawsayni aw adna"* (Holy Qur'an, 53:9) except Sayyidina Muhammad ﷺ.

That's why we don't have *wahdatul wujud* (oneness in existence). We have *wahdatul shahood* (oneness in witnessing). That you are allowed to enter with your soul into the soul and reality of Sayyidina Muhammad ﷺ. And from this *qalb* (heart) and its reality, it sees in *ayatul kareem, Ayatul Kursi* is describing what He sees.

Ayat al Kursi – About WajhAllah (Face of God)

Every Atom in Existence is Created From Muhammadun RasulAllah ﷺ

That what he sees, he sees in perfection and nobody sees like that. If he's seeing Allah ﷻ through *Izzah* and Might of Allah ﷻ, every creation is from his light. And that's why science understood that when you split the atom, the atom knows everything about every atom. But in this secret, Allah ﷻ says, 'The main atom knows every atom but those atoms encompass nothing of His knowledge'.

So, scientifically they could understand. But Allah ﷻ gave them also another clue. The originating atom, *"Man zal lazee yashfa'u,"* that nobody can intercede except and nobody has the knowledge of what he encompasses.

... مَن ذَا الَّذِي يَشْفَعُ عِندَهُ إِلَّا بِإِذْنِهِ ۚ ... ﴿٢٥٥﴾

2:255 - "...*Man zal lazee yashfa'u indahooo illaa bi-iznih...*"
(Surat Al-Baqarah)

"...Who is it that can intercede with Him except by His permission?..."
(The Cow, 2:255)

Nobody encompasses the knowledge of what he encompasses, that through his sight because of what he sees through Allah ﷻ, Allah's ﷻ *Izzah* and Might is giving all the power of everything coming from His light. It's all created from *Muhammadun RasulAllah* ﷺ.

Everything is From Prophet ﷺ and He Sees Through It All

Every particle in existence is in the light of Prophet ﷺ. It's not something our physicality can understand but it's because it is him, he sees through it all. And everything is from Him and He's in everything. *"Minni wa Minhum."* 'It's all from me and I see through it all.'

قَالَ رَسُولَ اللهِ صَلَّى اللهُ عَلَيْهِ وَسَلَّمَ: " أَنَا مِنَ اللهِ ، وَالْمُؤْمِنُونَ مِنِّي
(حديث مرفوع)

Qala Rasulullahi ﷺ: *"Anna minAllahi, wal muminoona minni."*

The Messenger of Allah, Prophet Muhammad (pbuh) said:" I am from Allah, and the believers are from me." (Hadith Marfo')

He sees through the atoms of your wall. He sees through the atom of your cup. He sees through the atom of every air and particle and breath. He sees everything. It's from him. How could something from somebody, and science knows it, and you not be understanding of it? And this is what Allah ﷻ meant. That he doesn't sleep. He doesn't pass out. These are the realities of the soul. And He's ever vigilant over everything that his light has been, everything made from his holy light. All made in truth.

All made from that reality and He's ever vigilant over it because it's all from *Muhammadun RasulAllah* ﷺ. And none encompass from it it's knowledge except what He allows. None can intercede for it without His permission. It's His light. How can you intercede or claim to have an intercession if Sayyidina Muhammad ﷺ is not permitting you?

Ayat al Kursi – About WajhAllah (Face of God)

7007 Naqshbandi Awliya Are Dressed From Wajhi hil Kareem

It means all of these realities they're teaching in just the simple *alif, lam, lam, hey*. *Izzatullah* is shining 7 attributes, 7 essences onto the *hey* and the *hu* of Sayyidina Muhammad ﷺ, the *hadi* (guide) and *hidayat* (guidance). Naqshbandiya, out of 124,000 *awliyaullah*, they have 7007 *awliya* that are always  under the authority of Mawlana Shah Naqshband ق. And that they're always present on earth and they don't even have to know each other or know themselves and some are from *jinn* (unseen beings) and *ins* (human beings), not all human. Many from the *jinn mureeds*.

Hey	Lam	Lam	Alif
7	0	0	7
7 Holy Openings of Face		7 Divinely Essences	

Note: Please read English from right to left to coincide with Arabic.

And 7007 because they're dressed from the realities of these seven. They're dressed from *Wajhi hil Kareem*, the holy face of Sayyidina Muhammad ﷺ dressing to their face. Because at 1001, one of Allah ﷻ, two *nuqt* (dot) for the two creations mean nothing, reflects to the oneness of His *Hadi*. This is the highest one. That reality reflects to the 7007 because they're no longer 1, they're 7. They carry the power of the

7 attributes of Prophet's ﷺ holy face and those 7 attributes are being dressed upon their *hidayat* and their guidance. And their 7 holy openings are dressed by the openings of Sayyidina Muhammad ﷺ.

Write Muhammadan Haqqaiqs to Burn Them Into Your Heart

This means we pray in these holy months that Allah give us a dress, give us an understanding to reach towards these realities. These realities have to be written and not recorded. We already record everything. You have to write with your hand and your finger. Not recorded, it doesn't do anything for you.  We spent 25 years in this path; those whom recorded, they gained absolutely nothing from its understanding.

Those who wrote, they became custodians of the reality because what they write, it will be burned into their heart as the holy scribes of the *Muhammadan haqqaiqs* (realities). What they write will be burned into their heart and written upon their *kitab* (book), not written upon Apple. You're not trying to glorify your iPhone. But if you don't have an *ihtiram* (respect) and don't care for the reality, you're not a scribe.

When You Write These Realities, It Will Be Written in Your Kitab

You can think you understand it all. It doesn't make a difference for them. But this way is to understand that these *haqqaiqs* and reality of Sayyidina Muhammad ﷺ are never to drop to the floor. These are realities that are unimaginable in the power to the soul. What they take from it, they grab.

Ayat al Kursi – About WajhAllah (Face of God)

As soon as they write it, it'll be written into their *kitab* (book). So, that  the angels that actually had to write what they wrote, their stations change because an angel who only writes your bad deeds, that's a small level angel. But the angel that's writing all the *haqqaiqs* of Sayyidina Muhammad ﷺ, the angels know its weight. *"Alam bil Qalam."* The angel knows what type of weight those realities have and that's what Allah ﷻ, *"Alam bil Qalam,"* that, 'I taught them by the reality of that pen.' The angel is changing; the angel is becoming dressed by its realities.

اقْرَأْ وَرَبُّكَ الْأَكْرَمُ ﴿٣﴾ الَّذِي عَلَّمَ بِالْقَلَمِ ﴿٤﴾ عَلَّمَ الْإِنسَانَ مَا لَمْ يَعْلَمْ ﴿٥﴾

96:3-5 – *"Iqra, wa rabbukal akram (3). Alladhee 'allama bil Qalam (4). 'Allamal insana ma lam ya'lam. (5)"* (Surat Al-Alaq)

"Recite, and your Lord is the most Generous. (3) Who taught by the pen. (4) Taught man that which he knew not. (5)" (The Clot, 96:3-5)

The soul is being dressed by its realities. As a result, it's a paradise soul walking on this earth. As a result, all their food, all their sustenance, all their *rizq* (sustenance), everything is under heavenly command, not *dunya*. This one whom from paradise and the *sultanates* (kingdoms) of paradise is walking the earth. And every food and drink and sustenance and reality is flowing to them through the *sultanate* (kingdom) of Sayyidina Muhammad ﷺ.

Have Ihtiram For Anything From the King

So, *tashreef* (honour) and *ihtiram* (respect) that they would show us in all their movies that if the seal of the king – remember we taught this 10 years ago – if the seal of the king would enter into a city, they would all be bowed down because this seal of the kingdom was walking and moving into the area. They would show  respect and these movies used to teach people how to respect. Why? Because they respected the king. You didn't need the presence of the king. You needed to just have an *ihtiram*, just for anything from the king.

Anything from the kingdom, they were incomplete. Just the seal of the kingdom would move through the city and everybody was in complete obedience. Imagine if the King comes. So, it means then these teachings are to prepare us for that reality. If a reality is coming from the kingdom of Sayyidina Muhammad ﷺ and it came and went through your ear with absolutely no benefit, then pity upon you for you did nothing with it.

Recording Knowledges is Not the Same As Writing Them

 And we have friends that were doing 25 years of Shaykh Nazim's ق *suhbahs* (discourses) on cassette recorders. Where is that now? Did you ever think cassette recorders were going to finish? Cassettes and cassettes and cassettes, cassettes and cassettes and I said, 'If we want to remember one thing, how are we going to find it in all these 50 cassettes you have?' Because they were coming and trying to teach us *tariqah* (spiritual path) at the beginning. 'Oh! I have all these

cassettes from London, Shaykh Nazim ق talked on this (topic).' You can spend hours trying to find which talk on this cassette was what he said.

But no, we were trained differently: have a book, write. Because you know in each book this was this year, this was Ramadan, this was this and this was that reality. I can pull my book, flip through it and say, 'This is what Mawlana Shaykh ق was teaching.' And because I wrote it, Allah ﷻ burned it into the heart. And if I heard it on my iPhone that has nothing to do, Allah didn't say, "*Alam bil iPhone*" into your ear.

We pray Allah ﷻ give us more and more opening and understanding. Especially these subjects, nobody's going to remember this: *alif, lam,* and *lam* and say, 'What was the *hey?* What was the *hu?* What's the *lam?* Who's the *lam?* Where's the *lam?*' And every *lam* has a *lam, alif, meem.* How many times we said that, but did you contemplate? Astonishing! Every tongue, it opens because *lam* opens. *Lam, alif, meem.* Again, you see Sayyidina Muhammad ﷺ there. You see the *lisan* (tongue) of realities and Allah ﷻ and His Muhammad ﷺ. And infinite, infinite, infinite. It means for every

creation, the reality of *la ilaha illAllah, Muhammadun RasulAllah* must be there. That is the formula bringing creation into existence. *La ilaha illAllah* sends the *Izzah* and a Might and hit and becomes a creation.

Subhana rabbika rabbal 'izzati 'amma yasifoon, wa salaamun 'alal mursaleen, walhamdulillahi rabbil 'aalameen. Bi hurmati Muhammad al-Mustafa wa bi siri Surat al-Fatiha

THE SECRET BOOK OF HU PERFECTION OF THE HOLY FACE

﴿٨٨﴾ كُلُّ شَيْءٍ هَالِكٌ إِلَّا وَجْهَهُ

28:88 – "...*kullu shayin halikun illa wajha.*" (Surat Al-Qasas)

"...*Everything (that exists) will perish except His holy Face*..." (The Stories, 28:88)

Awliya, Like Treasure Maps, Take Us to Divinely Treasures in Our Heart

The most Distinguished Naqshbandi Sufi Way takes its name from one of the biggest Sufi saints, our Master Muhammad Baha'uddin Shah Naqshband ق, who said, 'Our way is association and goodness is with the gathering.' In the presence of an authorized master, the hearts of seekers are slowly attuned to the Divine Presence. As much as the seeker can maintain the presence of their master, whether physically or spiritually through meditation, that master can affect a change in the condition of the seeker's heart. God says, 'I cannot be found in Heaven or on earth, but I can be found in the heart of a person who believes in Me.'

The Secret Book of Hu, Perfection of The Holy Face

مَا وَسِعَنِيْ لَا سَمَائِيْ ولا اَرْضِيْ وَلَكِنْ وَسِعَنِيْ قَلْبِ عَبْدِيْ اَلْمُؤْمِنْ

"Maa wasi'anee laa Samayee, wa la ardee, laakin wasi'anee qalbi 'Abdee al Mu'min."

"Neither My Heavens nor My Earth can contain Me, but the heart of my Believing Servant." (Hadith Qudsi conveyed by Prophet Muhammad (pbuh))

The purpose of a spiritual guide is that they are able to change the condition of your heart so that it becomes a source of Divine blessings. The heart of every person is like a treasure chest filled with precious jewels. We all have equal access to the treasure, but most people do not seek a means to open that chest. Every result requires a means – you need a way to achieve that result.

Watch any movie about a lost treasure, and you will find the treasure hunters seeking something that others have heard about but have abandoned hope of finding. It is the same in Sufism. Many people have heard of these realities, but they don't seek them out. Then the treasure hunters seek out a means to find that treasure. And in every movie, they find a treasure map. The map is symbolic of the lives of the saints who have already walked the spiritual path and received their spiritual trusts. When we read about their lives and study their teachings, we are following a map towards heavenly treasure.

'Self-help' is an Illusion – We Need a Guide to Diagnose and Treat Our Bad Characteristics

Therefore, the entire spiritual path is focused upon perfecting the light that is contained within the heart, and its foundation is the relationship between the student and a perfected spiritual guide who can mentor that student to perfection. This is a particularly important point in the era of the 'self-help' mentality. They take that knowledge from the Sufis because Sufism is an organic form of psychology. But when they brought this knowledge to the West, they took out the concept of a perfected guide and called it 'self-help.' Mawlana is teaching us that all of that is a false illusion with no spiritual fruits because it requires the individual to be truthful with him/herself, and the reality is that no one is truthful with themselves.

Generally, when someone is asked what their character defects are, they say, 'Well, I have a bit of a short temper sometimes, but other than that I'm a great person.' No one will say, 'I am a terrible person filled with bad characteristics' because the ego hides our defects so that we won't work on ourselves. The wisdom of following a spiritual guide is that they have walked the path and purified themselves of these defects. They know all of the defects and they know how to treat those defects. Just like a doctor knows how to diagnose and treat a patient, a Sufi master is able to diagnose and treat negative characteristics that you may not be aware of, but which are preventing you from reaching the Divine Presence.

We Are No Different From HellBoy

When we enter Mawlana's presence for the first time, we are like the character from the movie 'Hellboy.' Hellboy was a huge red-coloured demon with two horns that he filed down so as to not look so grotesque, and we do exactly the same thing! As Hellboy tries to hide his horns, we try to hide our bad character from others. We perfume ourselves and beautify the outside to mask the fact that our inner core is rotten. But in reality, true and lasting beauty comes from connecting the soul to its Divine source. That is why saints have a beautiful appearance and a beautiful and loving character. They have achieved a station of everlasting beauty by purifying their hearts from material desires.

وَنَفْسٍ وَمَا سَوَّاهَا ﴿٧﴾ فَأَلْهَمَهَا فُجُورَهَا وَتَقْوَاهَا ﴿٨﴾ قَدْ أَفْلَحَ مَن زَكَّاهَا ﴿٩﴾ وَقَدْ خَابَ مَن دَسَّاهَا ﴿١٠﴾

91:7-10 – *"Wa nafsinw wa maa sawwaahaa. (7) Fa-alhamahaa fujoorahaa wa taqwaahaa. (8) Qad aflaha man zakkaahaa. (9) Wa qad khaaba man dassaahaa. (10)" (Surat Ash-Shams)*

"By the soul and the proportion and order given to it, and its inspiration as to its wrong and its right; Truly he succeeds who purifies it, and he fails that corrupts it." (The Sun, 91:7-10)

When we enter the way, however, we are not purified. We are filled with anger and bad character that is making us to be very fiery, like Hellboy. The goal of the spiritual path is to move from that negativity which is represented by Hellboy, towards the perfected image that the Divine created us in, which is represented by the saints, because they are inheriting from the reality of the Prophet Adam ﷺ when God said, *"Wa laqad karramna bani adam"* (And We have certainly honored the children of Adam.) What was that honour? We are created in God's image.

وَلَقَدْ كَرَّمْنَا بَنِي آدَمَ... ﴿٧٠﴾

17:70 – *"Wa laqad karramna bani adama..."* (Surat Al-Isra)

"And We have certainly honored the children of Adam..."
(The Night Journey, 17:70)

Guides Help Us Move From a 'Hellboy State' to Our Divine Reality

In reality however, God does not have an image because He has no form, only an emanation of power which is called *Hu*. That emanation is reflecting from the Divine essence of *'Hu'* to the face of Prophet ﷺ, and from Prophet ﷺ to creation, but in reality, it reflects to the saints because we have not yet reached that nobility

of purpose that is our Divine inheritance. Therefore, we must seek to follow the guidance of saints. In following that guidance, they will gradually purify us and dress us with a Heavenly dress, so that we move from Hellboy towards our Divine reality.

Be in the Image of Prophets

It means that they will be dressing us from the reality of their holy face, because as God says in the Holy Qur'an, 'Everything will perish except the holy face.'

...كُلُّ شَيْءٍ هَالِكٌ إِلَّا وَجْهَهُ ۚ ... ﴿٨٨﴾

28:88 – "...*kullu shayin halikun illa wajha*..." (*Surat Al-Qasas*)

"*...Everything (that exists) will perish except His holy Face...*"
(*The Stories, 28:88*)

There is a deep secret to this verse that saints are able to understand through their heart. Because when that spiritual connection is established, inspirations come to the heart and provide insights that normal people would never think of. Mawlana Shaykh is teaching us that for every letter in the Holy Qur'an, there are 12,000 oceans of understanding, so there must be a secret here.

If the Divine is saying that, 'Everything will perish except My face' (Qur'an, 28:88), it is hinting to us that we must be in that image. To be in that image means to be in the image of the prophets, because God doesn't have an image. The Creator is outside of creation. God is the Essence which is powering creation, but He does not manifest as something created.

Secret of the Numbers 1 (Ahad) and 2 (Wahid) With a Waw of Love

This is the secret of the numbers 1 and 2, or to use Roman numerals, I and II. The number I is *Ahad*, meaning 'one and only' because there is nothing like the Creator. God has no partner, *la sharika la*.

Then the number II is a reflection of I, like a mirror (I + I = II). The II stands for *Wahid*, meaning 'unique.' *Wahid* has the Arabic *waw* attached to its *Ahad*. That *waw* is for *Wadud* meaning that it is in love with the *Ahad*. And that love for the Divine is the power behind its manifestation.

There is Only One Source of Power

The number II is the light of the Prophet ﷺ. It means that the first act of creation was the creation of the light of Sayyidina Muhammad ﷺ, as evidenced by the phrase *la ilaha illAllahu Muhammadun RasulAllah*.

لَا إِلَهَ إِلاَّ اللهُ مُحَمَّدًا رَسُولُ الله

"La ilaha illAllahu Muhammadun RasulAllah."

"There is no diety but Allah, Prophet Muhammad is the messenger of Allah."

The first part, *la ilaha illAllah*, is a negation: 'there is no god but God.' It means that there can only be one source of power. In that negation, all that exists is the Creator, there is nothing else. There cannot be two

The Secret Book of Hu, Perfection of The Holy Face

creators in that ocean of negation. Because all that exists is the essence of power and that essence is one.

How is the Divine Known?

But the Divine says, 'I was a hidden treasure wanting to be known'.

كُنْت كَنْزاً مخفيا فَأحْبَبْت أنْ أعْرَفَ؛ فَخَلَقْت خَلْقاً فَعَرَّفْتهمْ بي فَعَرَفُونِي

"Kuntu kanzan makhfiyya, fa ahbabtu an a'rafa, fa khalaqtu khalqan, fa 'arraftahum bi fa 'arafonee."

Allah (AJ) said, "I was a hidden Treasure then I desired to be known, so I created a creation to which I made Myself known; then they knew Me." (Hadith Qudsi)

It has to manifest, and that manifestation occurs through *Muhammadun RasulAllah* ﷺ. So, from one (I) and the Divine's Ocean of Oneness, comes a reflection of that oneness making two (II) which is now witnessing that oneness. It means that the Divine is known through the creation of the light of Sayyidina Muhammad ﷺ. That is why Prophet ﷺ said to Sayyidina Jabir ؓ, 'Verily, before your Lord made any other thing, He created from His own Light the light of your Prophet ﷺ, and that Light rested where God willed it to rest. And at that time there existed aught else-not the Preserved Tablets, not the Pen, not Heaven nor Hell, not the Angelic Host, not the heavens nor the earth; there was no sun, no moon, no star, no *jinn* nor man, nor angel – none was as yet creation, only this Light.'

عَنْ جَابِرٍ ، قَالَ : قُلْتُ : يَا رَسُولَ اللَّهِ صَلَّى اللَّهُ عَلَيْهِ وَسَلَّمَ ، " بِأَبِي أَنْتَ وَأُمِّي ، أَخْبِرْنِي عَنْ أَوَّلَ شَيْءٍ خَلَقَهُ اللَّهُ قَبْلَ الأَشْيَاءِ؟

قَالَ رَسُولَ اللهِ صَلَّى اللهُ عَلَيْهِ وَسَلَّمَ: يَا جَابِرُ ، إِنَّ اللهَ خَلَقَ قَبْلَ الْأَشْيَاءِ نُورُ نَبِيِّكَ مِنْ نُورِهِ ، فَجَعَلَ ذَلِكَ النُّورَ يَدُورُ بِالْقُدْرَةِ حَيْثُ شَاءَ اللهُ ، وَلَمْ يَكُنْ فِي ذَلِكَ الْوَقْتِ لَوْحٌ وَلَا قَلَمٌ، وَلَا جَنَّةٌ وَلَانَارٌ، وَلَا مُلْكٌ، وِلاسَمَاءٌ وَلَا أَرْضٌ، وَلَاشَمْسٌ وَلَا قَمَرٌ، وَلِاإِنْسٌ وَلَا جِنٌّ. فَلَمَّا أَرَادَ اللهُ تَعَالَى أَنْ يَخْلُقَ الْخَلْقَ قَسَّمَ ذَلِكَ النُّورَ أَرْبَعَةَ أَجْزَاءٍ: فَخَلَقَ مِنَ الْجُزْءِ الْأَوَّلِ الْقَلَمَ، وَمِنَ الثَّانِي اللَّوْحَ، وَمِنَ الثَّالِثِ الْعَرْشَ،...(وَمِنِ الاربعة كُلَّ شيءٍ.")

[رِوَايَةِ عَبْدِ الرَّزَّاقِ فِي مُصَنَّفَةٍ]

'An Jabir (ra) Qala: Qultu: Ya RasulAllah (saws), "Bi Abi anta wa Ummi, Akhberni 'an awwala shayin Khalqahu Allahu qablal ashyayi?"

Qala Rasulullah (saws): "Ya Jabir, in Allah khalaqa qablal Ashiya e Nooru Nabiyika min Noorehi. Faj'ala dhalikan Noore yadoro bil Qudrati haithu sha Allahu, wa lam yakun fi dhalikal waqti lawhun wa la qalamun, wa la Jannatun wa la Narun, wa la Mulkun, wa la samaun wa la ardun, wa la Shamsun wa la Qamarun, wa la insun wa la jinnun.

Falama arada Allahu ta'ala an yakhluqal Khalqi qasama dhalikan Nooru arba'a ajza: a: fakhalaqa minal juzil awwalu al Qalamu, wa minath thaniul Lawhu, wa minath thalithul 'Arshu, [minal Arba'ahu kuli shayin]"

Jabir ibn 'Abdallah (ra) said to the Prophet (pbuh): "O Messenger of Allah, may my father and mother be sacrificed for you, tell me of the first thing Allah created before all things."

He (Prophet Muhammad (pbuh) said: "O Jabir, the first thing Allah created was the light of your Prophet from His (Allah's) light, and that light remained (lit/ "turned") in the midst of His Power for as long as He wished, and at that time, there was no Tablet and no Pen, and no Paradise and no Fire, and

no angel, and no heaven and no earth, and no Sun and no Moon, and No Human being and no jinn.

And when Allah wished to create creation, he divided that Light into four parts and from the first made the Pen, from the second the Tablet, from the third the Throne, [and from the fourth everything else].

Two Distinct Oceans – Allah's ﷻ Essence and Nur Muhammad ﷺ
La Ilaha IllAllah, Muhammad RasulAllah ﷺ

There are two distinct oceans we are speaking about – the ocean of God's essence, which is *la ilaha illAllah*, and the ocean of manifestation  known as *Nur Muhammad* or the 'Muhammadan Reality.' When we speak of the light of Sayyidina Muhammad ﷺ, we are speaking about all of the prophets because each prophet was carrying that light until the physical arrival of Prophet ﷺ. So, all prophets are represented by the number II, which is the prophetic reality. Prophet ﷺ was created from God's Essence, and we are created from the light of Prophet ﷺ. We are all drops from the ocean of Prophet's ﷺ light. So, the Divine is saying, 'I have created you in My image', which is the image of the holy face.

(حديث مرفوع) حَدِيثٌ : " أَنَا مِنَ اللَّهِ، وَالْمُؤْمِنُونَ مِنِّي"

"Anna minallahi wal muminoona minni."

The Prophet (pbuh) said: "I am from Allah, and the believers are from me." (Hadith Marfo')

and

عَنْ أَبِي هُرَيْرَةَ، قَالَ: عَنِ النَّبِيّ صَلَّى اللهُ عَلَيْهِ وَسَلَّمَ قَالَ: "خَلَقَ اللهُ عَزَّ وَجَلَّ آدَمَ عَلى صُورَتِهِ طُولُهُ سِتُّونَ ذِرَاعاً،"...

[أخرج البخاري ومسلم]

'An Abi Hurairah (ra) 'an anNabi (saws) Qala: "Khalaqa Allahu Adama 'ala suratihi toluhu settona zera'an..."

Abu Hurairah narrated that the Prophet (pbuh) said: *"Allah (AJ) created Adam in His image, and he was sixty cubits tall..."* (Al-Bukhaari (6227) and Muslim (2841))

We Must Seek Those Who Seek the Holy Face of the Divine

But due to the circumstances of our existence in this material world, we are pulled towards evilness and bad desires which sicken the physicality and damage the soul, so that our image begins to reflect the excessive materialism of this world, rather than the Heavenly image of our Divine origin. Spiritually, we have assumed the appearance and characteristics of Hellboy.

That is why we must seek out true inheritors of the Prophetic way; those who have left the material world and material desires behind, and who only seek the Holy Face of the Divine.

وَاصْبِرْ نَفْسَكَ مَعَ الَّذِينَ يَدْعُونَ رَبَّهُم بِالْغَدَاةِ وَالْعَشِيِّ يُرِيدُونَ وَجْهَهُ ۖ وَلَا تَعْدُ عَيْنَاكَ عَنْهُمْ تُرِيدُ زِينَةَ الْحَيَاةِ الدُّنْيَا ۖ ﴿٢٨﴾

18:28 – "Wasbir nafsaka ma'al ladheena yad'ona Rabbahum bilghadati wal'ashiyi yureedona Wajhahu, wa la ta'du 'aynaka 'anhum tureedu zeenatal hayatid dunya..." (Surat Al-Kahf)

The Secret Book of Hu, Perfection of The Holy Face

"And keep yourself patient [by being] with those who call upon their Lord in the morning and the evening, seeking His Face. And let not your eyes pass beyond them, desiring adornments/glitter of the worldly life…" (The Cave, 18:28)

All Prophets Practiced Similar Sunnah/Ways

The Prophetic way is based upon the Prophetic *sunnah*, which refers to the actions, practices and manners of the prophets of God. All of the prophets had strikingly similar *sunnahs*/ways. For example, all of the

prophets had a beard and wore a turban, and most of them carried a walking stick. Furthermore, none of the prophets wore expensive clothes that were symbolic of worldliness. They were ascetics who saw through the illusion of this world and wanted nothing to do with it, and they reflected this state-of-being by wearing loose fitting garments which placed no emphasis on physical beauty or sexual attraction. So, when you turn on the TV and you see someone with a Versace suit and a gold watch, you must know that he is not representing the character of Prophet Jesus ﷺ, who cast-out the money lenders and who was so humble that he washed the feet of common people.

The Beautiful Character of Prophet Muhammad ﷺ

Many of the companions of Prophet Muhammad ﷺ described him as the gentlest, the most tolerant and the most merciful of human beings. God Himself called him 'kindest and most merciful.'

لَقَدْ جَاءَكُمْ رَسُولٌ مِّنْ أَنفُسِكُمْ عَزِيزٌ عَلَيْهِ مَا عَنِتُّمْ حَرِيصٌ عَلَيْكُم بِالْمُؤْمِنِينَ رَءُوفٌ رَّحِيمٌ ﴿١٢٨﴾

9:128 – *"Laqad jaa akum rasulum min anfusikum 'azizun 'alayhi maa 'anittum harisun 'alaykum bilmuminina raufun rahim."*
(Surat At-Tawbah)

"There has certainly come to you a Messenger from amongst/Within yourselves; it grieves him that you should perish; [he is] concerned over you, and to the believers he is most kind and merciful."
(The Repentance, 9:128)

He never kept one dinar or dirham in his house, always making sure that everything he had was given to the poor. So, when you see someone abusing women or blowing themselves up and killing innocent people, *astaghfirullah* (may God forgive us), that person is not representing the character of Sayyidina Muhammad ﷺ!

Awliya Are the Perfect Reflection of Prophet Muhammad ﷺ

We are living in a world that is filled with falsehood. That falsehood exists in each of us. But the saints of God are truthful servants of their Lord – there is no falsehood in them, nor is there any deficiency in their worship or their character.

They have been purified and perfected in the light of Prophet ﷺ, which means that they follow every Prophetic *sunnah* so that when you look at them you are seeing a perfected reflection of the image of Sayyidina Muhammad ﷺ. They dress like him, they talk like him, and they act like him. And when you are around them, you begin to feel a tremendous love developing in your heart for them because they have been authorized to carry the light of Sayyidina Prophet ﷺ.

You Can Complete Your Faith Through Awliya

Through them *(awliya)* you are able to complete your faith. When we say, 'I bear witness that there is no God but God, and I bear witness that Muhammad is the Messenger of God', it means that you must witness Sayyidina Muhammad ﷺ.

أَشْهَدُ أَنْ لَا إِلَهَ إِلاَّ الله وَأَشْهَدُ أَنَّ مُحَمَّدًا عَبْدُهُ وَرَسُولُهُ

"Ashhadu an la ilaha illAllah, wa ashhadu anna Muhammadan 'abduhu wa Rasulu."

"I bear witness that there is no god but Allah, and I bear witness that Muhammad is the messenger of Allah."

Is anyone witnessing him? No. We cannot see him, so that means that we are not even fulfilling the first requirement of the Spiritual way. But for sure the saints can see him, and through them you are developing a tremendous love for Sayyidina Muhammad ﷺ and all of the prophets, because you are witnessing someone who has been authorized to carry that Prophetic light.

Reality of Hu wa Hu – Divinely Light Reflecting to Prophetic Light

That is why God says, 'Obey God, obey the Prophet ﷺ and obey those charged with authority over you.'

...أَطِيعُواللهَ وَأَطِيعُواٱلرَّسُولَ وَأُوْلِي الْأَمْرِ مِنْكُمْ... ﴿٥٩﴾

4:59 – *"...Atiullaha wa atiur Rasula wa Ulil amre minkum..."* (Surat An-Nisa)

"... Obey Allah, Obey the Messenger, and those in authority among you..." (The Women, 4:59)

Seek out those spiritual teachers who have been given authority from Prophet ﷺ. Seek out those who have reached the station of annihilation in the Divine Presence. Those who have reached annihilation will no longer possess the appearance and manners of an ordinary person. Instead, they will possess the perfected reflection of the Prophetic reality.

This is 'Spiritual 101' – the reality of *HuwaHu*; the *Hu* which is the emanation of the ocean of *la ilaha illAllah* and is reflecting to the holy face of Sayyidina Muhammad ﷺ, *Muhammadun RasulAllah* ﷺ. From *Muhammadun RasulAllah* ﷺ, that light is reflecting to the heart of the 124,000 living saints, and the saints reflect that light towards their followers.

Allah ﷻ Sends His Message in Ways That We Could Hear

At that level of understanding, you begin to see the deep truths contained in movies like 'Lord of the Rings', 'Matrix', even 'Hellboy'! Because the Divine doesn't leave anyone out, everyone must hear the message. If we are not going to hear the message in church or in a religious gathering, the Divine is

going to reach us through something that we enjoy, like the story of Moses ؑ and the burning bush. Moses ؑ was seeking his Lord and he was cold, so God showed himself as a burning bush. Of course, God is not a burning bush, but it is something that we can understand and, more importantly, it made Moses ؑ to approach because he was in need of warmth.

إِذْ رَأَىٰ نَارًا فَقَالَ لِأَهْلِهِ امْكُثُوا إِنِّي آنَسْتُ نَارًا لَّعَلِّي آتِيكُم مِّنْهَا بِقَبَسٍ أَوْ أَجِدُ عَلَى النَّارِ هُدًى ﴿١٠﴾

20:10 – *"Iz ra aa naaran faqaala li ahlihim kusooo inneee aanastu naaral la'alleee aateekum minhaa biqabasin aw ajidu 'alan naari hudaa" (Surah Taha)*

'When he saw a fire and said to his family, "Stay here; indeed, I have perceived a fire; perhaps I can bring you a torch or find at the fire some guidance." (Taha, 20:10)

It is the same with modern technology and movies. So, when you watch a movie like Matrix, you see that in reality there are only two characters, Neo and the Agent, and they clone themselves. It means that we all approach looking like clones of Hellboy, and that frequency of light is very negative.

Saints Guide Us to Match and Reflect Our Real Image in Paradise

But as the saints begin to clean us and purify us, they pull from the secret of the ocean of *"Rabbana 'atmim lanaa Nuuranaa waghfir lanaa: innaka 'alla kulli shay'in Qadir."*

...رَبَّنَا أَتْمِمْ لَنَا نُورَنَا وَاغْفِرْ لَنَا ۖ إِنَّكَ عَلَىٰ كُلِّ شَيْءٍ قَدِيرٌ ﴿٨﴾

66:8 – "*...rabbanaaa atmim lanaa nooranaa waghfir lana innaka 'alaa kulli shai'in qadeer" (Surat At-Tahrim)*

"…*Our Lord! Perfect our Light for us, and grant us Forgiveness: for Thou hast power over all things." (The Prohibition, 66:8)*

Under the manifestations of that verse, saints are able to perfect our light so that we begin to walk in the Kingdom of Heaven. It means that we will all be matching our real image in paradise, like a mirror.

The Heart of the Seeker is a Kingdom That Belongs to Allah ﷻ

At that time, we will be dressed with the inner meaning of the Quranic verse, 'To whom belongs the Kingdom on this day? To God, the One, the Irresistible'.

يَوْمَ هُم بَارِزُونَ ۖ لَا يَخْفَىٰ عَلَى اللَّهِ مِنْهُمْ شَيْءٌ ۚ لِّمَنِ الْمُلْكُ الْيَوْمَ ۖ لِلَّهِ الْوَاحِدِ الْقَهَّارِ ﴿١٦﴾

40:16 – *"Yawma hum baarizoona, laa yakhfaa 'alal laahi minhum shai; limanil mulkul Yawma, lillaahil Waahidil Qahaar"*
(Surat Al-Mu'min)

"The Day whereon they will (all) come forth: not a single thing concerning them is hidden from Allah. Whose will be the Kingdom/dominion that Day?" That of Allah, The One, The Subduer!" (The Believer, 40:16)

According to the teachings of the famous gnostic, Shaykh Ubayd Allah al-Ahrar ق, 20th Grandshaykh of the Naqshbandi Spiritual Order, this verse requires us to understand that the 'kingdom' referred to is the heart of the seeker. If God looks at the heart of the seeker with the light of His vision, then He erases the existence of everything except God in his heart. In that state the heart is speaking, the heart from which God has erased everything but Himself.'

God says, 'I cannot be found on Heavens or earth, but I can be found in the heart of the believer.'

مَا وَسِعَنِيْ لَا سَمَائِيْ ولا أَرْضِيْ وَلَكِنْ وَسِعَنِيْ قَلْبِ عَبْدِيْ ٱلْمُؤْمِنْ

"Maa wasi'anee laa Samayee, wa la ardee, laakin wasi'anee qalbi 'Abdee al Mu'min."

"Neither My Heavens nor My Earth can contain Me, but the heart of my Believing Servant."
(Hadith Qudsi conveyed by Prophet Muhammad (pbuh))

7 Openings of the Holy Face

However, before we can open the heart, the crown of creation must be in submission. The example of a messenger is in the crown, the head. It means we must ask Mawlana Shaykh to take us towards the reality of *HuwaHu* and how to perfect the 7 openings of the Holy Face, so that we begin to reflect the face of God and the face of the prophets.

...كُلُّ شَيْءٍ هَالِكٌ إِلَّا وَجْهَهُ... ﴿٨٨﴾

28:88 – *"...kullu shayin halikun illa wajha..."* (Surat Al-Qasas)

"...Everything (that exists) will perish except His holy Face..."
(The Stories, 28:88)

So, when we first come to a spiritual path, we are like Hellboy, filled with bad characteristics, especially anger. That anger made Hellboy to have a red color, very fiery, and like a volcano he could explode at any time. Anger is a very bad character trait because it destroys faith. Those who have attained real faith never get angry. Why? Because they understand in their heart that God is the Originator of all events. But most people are filled with anger, and that anger symbolizes that we are struggling with our faith in the Divine.

So, when the student enters the doors of a Spiritual order, the first thing the Master does is to spark the light of faith in his or her heart. When that light has been sparked, the student can now begin to move towards understanding and opening the levels of the heart, which are five levels. These five levels of the heart are representing five big prophets of the Divine: Adam ﷺ, Noah ﷺ, Abraham ﷺ, Jesus ﷺ (peace and blessings be upon them all) and Sayyidina Muhammad ﷺ.

The Battle of Taming Our Ego to Free Our Soul

We are trying to align our reality with the Divine reality and align our will with God's will. The more that we are able to align ourselves with that reality, the more we can receive that Heavenly light, which frees the soul from its imprisonment in the physical body. The body is a horse which allows the soul to experience, but for most of us, it is a wild horse which needs to be tamed.

In the first stages of spiritual development, that horse is partnered with the ego and is battling hard against the soul. While the soul is desiring spiritual nourishment and to attend spiritual associations, the ego is making the body to go to Las Vegas and engage in activities that are of no lasting benefit to the soul. So, the first step is to start

attending spiritual associations; to sit, to meditate and contemplate and feel the energy of the association, but that takes a tremendous amount of willpower because the ego is going to fight you every step of the way. It doesn't want to go to those associations.

Body, Mind, Soul – Seek to Tame the Body Before the Mind

That is the reason for the concept of the 'body, mind, and soul' meditation that a lot of holistic movements talk about. However, many of them use the formula, 'mind, body and soul' where they first go after the mind. Spirituality takes a different approach. It seeks to first go after the body and discipline the body. Because we understand that if this physicality doesn't submit and go onto a spiritual path, then how is it going to benefit the mind and the soul? So then the reality is that if you just take your mind into meditation, but your body is free to do whatever it likes, then that is just a level of illusion where we're meditating only through the mind and the mind can go in any direction, but has no restriction on the physicality. So, then you see many of them can meditate and do anything with their bodies.

Spirituality comes to teach us energy and a holistic way, that if you discipline the physicality and place some restrictions on the physicality – bring down the power of the ego, and all of these desires instead of being a wild horse, your body becomes a tamed horse that you can use to take you to the Divine Presence. That is one understanding of the story of when Prophet ﷺ rode the *buraq*, which was a Heavenly horse, on a journey through the seven Heavens and came within 'two bow lengths or nearer to the Divine'. Your body is your *buraq*, but first it needs to be tamed.

$$\text{فَكَانَ قَابَ قَوْسَيْنِ أَوْ أَدْنَىٰ ﴿9﴾}$$

53:9 – "Fakana qaaba qawsayni aw adna." (Surat An-Najm)

"And was at a distance of two bow lengths or nearer [to the Divine Presence]." (The Star, 53:9)

We Must Discipline Our Physicality to Bring Down the Ego

Anyone who has watched how they tame wild horses; you know that a wild horse is not going to easily be ridden. It is not going to allow the rider onto a wild horse because it's not used to letting anything ride it. So, then the concept of breaking in the horse, which is the wild ego that has never been told and never been disciplined. It means they take these bags on the saddle, fill them with bricks and put this weight onto that wild horse, which makes the horse to buck and kick. Because it is extremely upset at that concept of being weighed down when it was once free to roam as it liked. It means that the horse has to be weighed down.

These disciplines are teaching us that I have to weigh down the physicality. That I have to contemplate on how much to eat and how much to drink and how much to play and how much to give to this physicality. When I start to put these weights onto the physicality and restrict the physicality, it starts to become more tamed and the mind becomes clearer. The bodily desires are no longer controlling the mind, and it is now able to think clearly and understand these realities. Then after the horse has been tamed, the mind is able to gain greater insight into the secrets behind our physical creation and what this body really is. Because the reality is that we are not created for the purpose of endless physical pleasures. 'Who knows himself will know his Lord.'

The Secret Book of Hu, Perfection of The Holy Face

مَنْ عَرَفَ نَفْسَهُ فَقَدْ عَرَفَ رَبَّهُ

"Man 'arafa nafsahu faqad 'arafa Rabbahu"

"Who knows himself, knows his Lord." Prophet Muhammad (pbuh)

Our Nobility as Human Beings is Having Access to Heavenly Knowledge

The reality behind this saying is the framework for the entire path of Sufism, where God says, 'We have honoured the children of Adam.'

وَلَقَدْ كَرَّمْنَا بَنِي آدَمَ... ﴿٧٠﴾

17:70 – "Wa laqad karramna bani adama..." (Surat Al-Isra)

"And We have certainly honored the children of Adam..."
(The Night Journey, 17:70)

Therefore, all of this knowledge is at the first level of the heart, which is the *qalb*, under the authority of the Prophet Adam ﷺ, because the Prophet Adam ﷺ is teaching us about ourselves – who we are and why we were created. The nobility of our creation is that we have access to heavenly knowledge.

And the first step in unlocking that knowledge is to understand our physical creation and what it means to be created in the image of the Divine. It means that we must understand the reality of the holy face, and perfect the 7 openings of the face because it is the crown of our creation; it symbolizes that nobility.

The 7 Openings of the Face Must Be Perfected Before the Heart Opens

The Divine said, 'I have created you in my image', which means that our face is a reflection of the holy face; 'Everything will perish except His own Face.'

$$...كُلُّ شَيْءٍ هَالِكٌ إِلَّا وَجْهَهُ ۚ... ﴿٨٨﴾$$

28:88 – "...*kullu shayin halikun illa wajha...*" (*Surat Al-Qasas*)

"...*Everything (that exists) will perish except His holy Face...*"
(*The Stories, 28:88*)

Therefore, the face and the 7 openings of the face, which are the 2 ears, 2 eyes, 2 nostrils and 1 tongue, must be perfected to begin the opening of the heart and the greater perfection of the self. That greater perfection opens the reality of the holy face because all of our five senses have a physical and a spiritual reality. It means that we can hear, see, smell, taste, and touch from the level of the soul. And that is an eternal gift from the Divine, as mentioned in the *Hadith Qudsi*, 'My servant continues to draw near to Me with supererogatory works so that I shall love him. When I love him, I am his hearing with which he hears, his seeing with which he sees, his hand with which he strikes and his foot with which he walks. Were he to ask [something] of Me, I would surely give it to him.'

The Secret Book of Hu, Perfection of The Holy Face

...وَلَا يَزَالُ عَبْدِي يَتَقَرَّبُ إِلَيَّ بِالنَّوَافِلِ حَتَّى أُحِبَّهُ، فَإِذَا أَحْبَبْتُهُ كُنْتُ سَمْعَهُ الَّذِي يَسْمَعُ بِهِ، وَبَصَرَهُ الَّذِي يُبْصِرُ بِهِ، وَيَدَهُ الَّتِي يَبْطِشُ بِهَا، وَرِجْلَهُ الَّتِي يَمْشِي بِهَا، وَلَئِنْ سَأَلَنِي لَأُعْطِيَنَّهُ،." [رَوَاهُ الْبُخَارِيُّ.]

"..., wa la yazaalu 'Abdi yataqarrabu ilayya bin nawafile hatta ahebahu, fa idha ahhabtuhu kunta Sam'ahul ladhi yasma'u behi, wa Basarahul ladhi yubsiru behi, wa Yadahul lati yabTeshu beha, wa Rejlahul lati yamshi beha, wa la in sa alani la a'Teyannahu, ..."

"...My servant continues to draw near to Me with voluntary acts of worship so that I shall love him. When I love him, I am his hearing with which he hears, his seeing with which he sees, his hand with which he strikes and his foot with which he walks. Were he to ask [something] of Me, I would surely give it to him..."
Hadith Qudsi (Sahih al-Bukhari, 81:38:2)

We Must Strive to Keep Company of the Saints

That is why 'the saints don't pray for Paradise, and don't fear Hell, but ask only to see the holy face.' And God tells us to find them and frequent their company' (Holy Qur'an, 9:119) 'And keep yourself content with those who call on their Lord in the morning and the evening, seeking His face, and let not thine eyes pass beyond them, seeking the pomp and glitter of this life.'

يَا أَيُّهَا الَّذِينَ آمَنُوا اتَّقُوا اللَّهَ وَكُونُوا مَعَ الصَّادِقِينَ ﴿١١٩﴾

9:119 – "Ya ayyuhal ladheena amanoo ittaqollaha wa kono ma'as sadiqeen." (Surat At-Tawbah)

"O you who have believed, have consciousness of Allah and be with those who are truthful/ Pious / sincere (in words and deed)."
(The Repentance, 9:119)

وَاصْبِرْ نَفْسَكَ مَعَ الَّذِينَ يَدْعُونَ رَبَّهُم بِالْغَدَاةِ وَالْعَشِيِّ يُرِيدُونَ وَجْهَهُ ۖ وَلَا تَعْدُ عَيْنَاكَ عَنْهُمْ تُرِيدُ زِينَةَ الْحَيَاةِ الدُّنْيَا ۖ ﴿٢٨﴾

18:28 – *"Wasbir nafsaka ma'al ladheena yad'ona Rabbahum bilghadati wal'ashiyi yureedona Wajhahu, wa la ta'du 'aynaka 'anhum tureedu zeenatal hayatid dunya..." (Surat Al-Kahf)*

"And keep yourself patient [by being] with those who call upon their Lord in the morning and the evening, seeking His Face;. And let not your eyes pass beyond them, desiring adornments/glitter of the worldly life..." (The Cave, 18:28)

First Level of the Heart is Knowledge Under Authority of Adam ﷺ

When we want to open the heart, the first thing we must do is unlock the crown of creation, which is the head. The first level of the heart, the *qalb*, under the authority of the Prophet Adam ﷺ, is showing us that there is a nobility in this creation and that I have been created by the two hands of the Divine. It means that our heart is connected to the Prophetic heart, which reaches to the Divine Presence.

The nobility in our creation is that we have access to Heavenly knowledge. The angel in charge of this station is Gabriel ﷺ, because he is in charge of conveying that knowledge.

Two Ears: Doorway to the Soul

The first step in trying to unlock that knowledge is, 'Do you hear the message?'

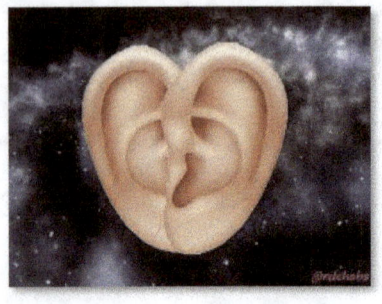

سَمِعْنَا وَأَطَعْنَا غُفْرَانَكَ رَبَّنَا وَاِلَيْكَ الْمَصِيْرُ ﴿٢٨٥﴾

2:285 – "Sam'ina wa ata'na, ghufranaka Rabbana wa ilaykal masir." (Surat Al-Baqarah)

"...We hear, and we obey: (We seek) Thy forgiveness, our Lord, and to Thee is the end of all journeys." (The Cow, 2:285)

The highest level of submission is the perfection of hearing. That is what makes a messenger to be a Messenger – their ears are entirely for the Divine. Their faculty of hearing is in complete submission waiting for the Divine order. It means that you have to open the two ears and the power of the two ears because the ears are the door to the soul.

What You Hear Affects Your Soul

As you begin to open the heart to the Divine Presence, the Divine is showing you that your ears are going to be the door to your soul. What you hear is going to affect your soul. If what you hear is good, it's going to nourish your soul. If what you hear is bad, it's going to crush the soul. So, the secret to open the soul is going to be found in what we hear and what we do with the ears. In the washing 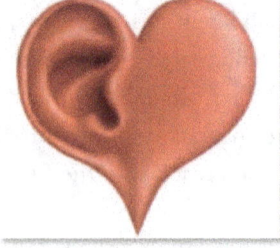 of the ears and the fasting of the ears is a tremendous Prophetic secret. You wash the ears to wash away negative energy. And you fast with the ears to abstain from negative sounds because those sounds will negatively impact your heart.

Angel Gabriel ﷺ Sends His Light and Inspirations to Our Hearts

Then, are you hearing the message? Are you seeking Heavenly knowledge? That Heavenly knowledge is going to nourish your soul. It is as if the Angel Gabriel ﷺ is going to establish like an agency office in your heart; he's going to establish his light in your heart. Why? Because then he can send from his Heavenly station to your physical station. He's going to start sending inspiration. As soon as you clean this body and say, 'I'm going to develop this temple, this Heavenly being,' Angel Gabriel ﷺ starts to send his light and, like grafting, his light starts to nourish your light.

Then they stand back and watch you to see what you do with what you have been given, because everything in this way is based on trust. Can you be trusted with this knowledge to do the right thing and serve creation?

As that light increases in you then you feel that inspiration becoming very strong because that presence is now very powerful in your heart. And he is able to instantaneously bring information in and dispense that light throughout the kingdom of your soul. Then we realize that there is a tremendous importance in my ears. What I hear is going to affect me when I'm breathing and meditating and contemplating. So, the ears must hear the message.

Even the Prophets Struggled With Obedience to the Divine

Then, the more difficult station is the station of obedience. Even the Prophets struggled in their obedience to the Divine. So, we have to know that this is going to be a major battleground. To obey something other than ourselves 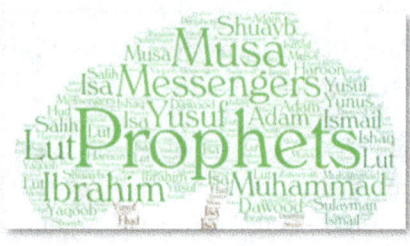 comes against the selfishness of the ego, and the ego is very upset by this. Because it means that you are saying, 'O my ego! Your opinion is useless to me.'

That is why very few people are able to seek out spiritual guidance and follow that guidance. It requires a certain level of humility and submission to the Divine. That submission is the ultimate goal of the Spiritual path; that I understood that I must give my will back to God. That free will was the test for me, and the greatest act of love and the greatest gift I can give is to offer it back. As Jesus ﷺ taught us in the Lord's Prayer, 'Thy will be done on earth as it is in Heaven.'

*"Your kingdom come, your will be done, on earth as it is in heaven…
And lead us not into temptation but deliver us from evil."
(The Lord's Prayer)*

3 Levels of Obedience – To God, to Prophet ﷺ, and to Saints

Then that opens the reality of the verse, 'Obey God, obey the Prophet and obey those charged with authority over you.'

﴿٥٩﴾ ...أَطِيعُواْ ٱللَّهَ وَأَطِيعُواْ ٱلرَّسُولَ وَأُوْلِي ٱلْأَمْرِ مِنكُمْ...

4:59 – "…Atiullaha wa 'atiur Rasula wa Ulil amre minkum…" (Surat An-Nisa)

"... Obey Allah, Obey the Messenger, and those in authority among you..." (The Women, 4:59)

To obey God is impossible. If we were in obedience to God, we wouldn't sin and we wouldn't do anything wrong. God knows that to obey Him is extremely difficult, which is why He gives three levels of obedience. The second level is to obey the Prophet ﷺ, but since Prophet ﷺ is not with us we must obey those charged with authority over us – those who are carrying that Prophetic authority. That verse is referring to the saints of God who are inheriting from the authority of Sayyidina Muhammad ﷺ.

Saints Show Us We Are Servants to Our Ego Like Fir'aun

The saints will train us on obedience and in doing so they will test us to show how much we are still servants of our ego. The ego is like Pharaoh saying, 'I am the Lord Most High!'

فَقَالَ أَنَا رَبُّكُمُ الْأَعْلَىٰ ﴿٢٤﴾

79:24 – *"Faqala ana rabbukumu al 'Aala." (Surat An-Nazi'at)*

"And Fir'aun (Pharoah) said, I am your Lord All-Highest!" (Those Who Drag Forth, 79:24)

Beware of Submitting to Your Desires

The ego makes it almost impossible to obey anyone because it sees itself as Lord over you. That is why Mawlana points out that when we say, 'Who knows themselves will know their Lord', we must recognize which Lord we are speaking about? Because there are degrees of lordship. The term 'lord' implies authority and obedience to that authority.

The Secret Book of Hu, Perfection of The Holy Face

مَنْ عَرَفَ نَفْسَهُ فَقَدْ عَرَفَ رَبَّهُ

"Man 'arafa nafsahu faqad 'arafa Rabbahu"

"Who knows himself, knows his Lord." Prophet Muhammad (pbuh)

And the saints are inspiring us towards the realization that the physical desires of our ego are the first lords over all of us – not God. It means that we are only obedient to our ego. That is why God asks in the Holy Qur'an, 'Do you see such a one as takes for his god his own passion (or impulse)?' (Holy Qur'an, 25:43) and 'Then do you see such a person as takes as his god his own vain desire? God has, knowing (him as such), left him astray, and sealed his hearing and his heart and put a veil over his eyes' (Holy Qur'an, 45:23).

أَرَأَيْتَ مَنِ اتَّخَذَ إِلَـهَهُ هَوَاهُ أَفَأَنتَ تَكُونُ عَلَيْهِ وَكِيلًا ﴿٤٣﴾

25:43 – "Ara'aita manit takhaza ilaahahoo hawaahu afa anta takoonu 'alaihi wakeelaa." (Surat Al-Furqan)

"Have you seen the one who takes as his god his own desire?" (The Criterian, 25:43)

and

أَفَرَأَيْتَ مَنِ اتَّخَذَ إِلَـهَهُ هَوَاهُ وَأَضَلَّهُ اللَّـهُ عَلَىٰ عِلْمٍ وَخَتَمَ عَلَىٰ سَمْعِهِ وَقَلْبِهِ وَجَعَلَ عَلَىٰ بَصَرِهِ غِشَاوَةً فَمَن يَهْدِيهِ مِن بَعْدِ اللَّـهِ ۚ أَفَلَا تَذَكَّرُونَ ﴿٢٣﴾

45:23 – "Afara ayta manit takhadha ilaha hu hawahu wa adallahu Allahu 'ala 'Ilmin wa khatama 'ala sam'ihi wa qalbihi, wa ja'ala 'ala basarihi ghishawatan faman yahdeehi min ba'di Allahi, afala tadhakkaron." (Surat Al-Jathiyah)

"Have you seen he who has taken as his god his [own] desire? And Allah has sent him astray due to knowing (him as such) and has sealed his hearing and his heart and put veil on his vision. So then who will guide him after Allah (has withdrawn Guidance)? Then will you not remember/mention?" (The Crouching, 45:23)

Following Our Desires Empowers the Ego and Blocks Our Spiritual Connection

When we follow our physical desires instead of God's will, we empower the ego and give it lordship over us, and that blocks the spiritual connection with the Divine Presence. The heart is like a satellite dish that is trying to establish a connection with the Heavenly reality, but the ego is like  a cloud which disrupts the transmission. That is why God uses the phrase 'sealed his hearing' rather than 'sealed his ears', because we are trying to open the spiritual faculty of hearing from the face of the Divine, but so long as we are following the ego, that reality cannot appear in us.

So, the job of a spiritual guide is to train us and to guide us towards that obedience. It means that they will give advice and then watch to see how much you are able to follow. Most of us, especially at the beginning, will struggle to follow even the simplest advice from Mawlana Shaykh. And that shows us the true nature of the spiritual battle that is taking place within us.

3 Tests of Naqshbandiya – Broken Shovel, Bucket, Go Towards Sustenance

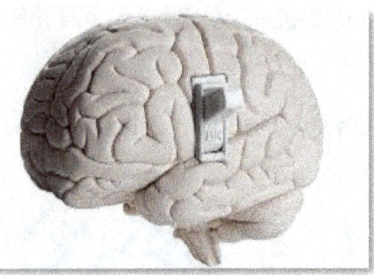

From Mawlana's teachings and Grandshaykh's teachings, they say that we should put three nails in our head. These three nails are fundamental to progressing within the Naqshbandi Order. The first nail is that if the teacher gives you a broken shovel and asks you to dig, you dig. The second nail is that if the teacher hands you a bucket and tells you to empty the ocean, you start trying to empty the ocean. The third nail is that if the teacher tells you that your sustenance is in the west and you are in the east, you start walking towards the west.

These examples are trying to emphasize the importance of the faculty of hearing, *samina wa atana* – 'we heard and we obeyed' (Holy Qur'an, 2:285).

Don't Use the Mind With Saints' Advice – Nothing is Impossible

Hear the advice and obey it. Don't try to use your mind. It is not the mind that is their focus, but the heart. So, you must know that their advice is unlikely to make sense to your mind, but still you must try and obey. We are speaking only on advice that is within the Divine Law and is not harmful. We are not talking about something crazy. So, when the teacher tells you to empty the ocean with a bucket, the first thing that goes through your mind is, 'This is impossible.' Why is it impossible?! If you have faith in your teacher and in God, then it is not impossible.

Quality of Your Hearing Determines Your Ability to Walk This Path

But faith does not come from the mind, it emanates from the heart of the believer. All that the teacher wants to see is whether we will listen and obey, listen and obey, and struggle in that obedience until Divine support comes. Then you see just how important these two ears are in enabling you to walk the spiritual path.

Glory be to God, the Divine shows us physically this spiritual reality because when someone gets vertigo, what happens? There is a problem with the inner ear, and suddenly you have trouble walking or even standing. The Divine is showing you that the quality of your hearing is going to determine your ability to walk this path.

Two Eyes: Window to the Soul

Then we move on to the importance of the two eyes, which are the window to the soul. Once you've heard that call of the Divine, then the next step in perfecting the face – are these eyes interested in the material world, or are they interested in the Divine Presence? The eyes of the Prophets were always closed to the material world. It means that they had no interest in it; they were not distracted by material concerns because their heart was only for the Divine. And they understood that what their physical eyes saw was not the truth.

This Material World is an Illusion and a Magic Show

The material world is built on falsehood. That is why you turn on the TV and one day they're telling you it's black, the next day telling you it's white. So, the truth of this material world is that it's like a big magic act – everything in it is an illusion and you will be lost by the magician. That is why Sayyidina Isa ﷺ (Jesus) described that in this world it is the blind leading the blind – people are not seeing with the spiritual vision that God has granted to them, they are only seeing with their physical eyes.

We Are in the Matrix

A perfect example is the movie 'Matrix.' What we see and experience is not the reality. When Neo reaches a certain station, he begins to see the world of the Matrix in binary code – he sees the  reality of the world through his spiritual vision. The Divine says that we are veiled from the truth so that we cannot see it.

خَتَمَ اللَّـهُ عَلَىٰ قُلُوبِهِمْ وَعَلَىٰ سَمْعِهِمْ ۖ وَعَلَىٰ أَبْصَارِهِمْ غِشَاوَةٌ ۖ ...﴿٧﴾

2:7 – "Khatama Allahu 'ala qulobihim, wa 'ala sam'ihim wa 'ala absarihim ghishawatun…" (Surat Al-Baqarah)

"Allah has set a seal upon their hearts and upon their hearing, and over their vision is a veil…" (The Cow, 2:7)

Our Vision is Like a Computer Screen

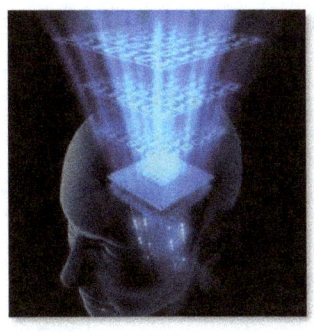

What is vision? These two pieces of flesh are connected to the brain, which is like a computer screen. If you are looking at a bird, for example, photons of light from that bird are transmitted to the retina in the eye, which then sends an electrical signal to the brain. The brain, already having the image of a bird in its 'files,' recognizes the pattern and immediately, an image of a bird pops-up on the screen. However, if the brain is not familiar with something, we often fail to see things that are right in front of us.

There is a famous story that when European ships appeared off the Atlantic coast of North America for the first time, the Native Americans did not notice them for many days or weeks because they had never seen ships like them before. The brain had no frame of reference to draw a picture from, and so the conscious mind was completely unaware, or 'in the dark.'

Control Your Vision – It Might Crush the Hard Drive of Your Heart

The Divine is showing us that, 'Don't place too much emphasis on what you see with these eyes. Try to open the vision of your heart instead.' This world is dirty and deceptive, and that dirtiness contaminates the heart. God shows us through technology because the heart is like a hard drive, and our eyes are like a digital camera that constantly capturing images all day long. If you allow your computer to capture negative images such as violence, pornography, horror and other

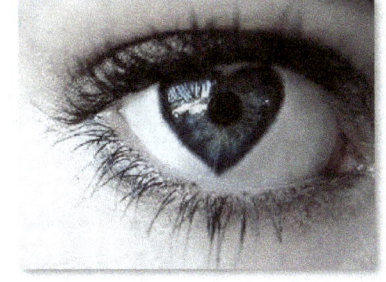

vulgar images you are going to crash the hard drive. Those images are saved – once we've downloaded them, it is very difficult to forget them. Then you have to format the hard drive with *zikr* and meditation.

So, when we want to perfect the eyes and open the spiritual vision of the heart, we must close the eyes to this world and spend more time in meditation and contemplation. This is the reason that one of the main principles of the Naqshbandi Order is to watch your steps *(nazar bar qadam)*. It means that the seeker should keep their eyes on their feet because the images of the material world veil the heart.

Nostrils: Unlocking the Divine Breath and Gift of Life

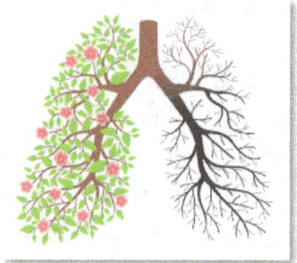

Lungs are the 'Tree of Life.' Then, we must become conscious of the breath because every breath is a pocket of life. So, are you breathing in remembrance of the Divine? And Mawlana Shaykh is teaching that the Naqshbandi way is built on the breath.

That breath is our gift of life, and when put in that context you realize that everything else in life is irrelevant if you can't take a breath. Your money, your spouse, your children, your house, your cars; all of it means nothing if you have no breath. So then go and look at children who are suffering with asthma and every breath they take it is as if they're dying, and that fear of suffocating is an absolutely horrible feeling. It means the breath is the single most important mercy from God. That is why we call it the *Nafas ar Rahmah* – 'breath of Mercy.'

Why? Because we are asking so many things in this room; each person upset with the Divine because they didn't get what they want. But we have to want what we have before we ask for other things. And the biggest and the greatest gift we have is the gift of life. If God at some time becomes upset with us, in one instant, He can make that breath become very difficult to get. And instead of arguing and complaining about all the things we want, we find ourselves just trying to take a single breath without difficulty. God forbid that happen to anyone! May He forgive us and keep such difficulties away from us!

We Must Be Thankful For Every Breath Given

So that is the breath of the Most Merciful. 'O! My Lord! I am praising You and thanking You for this breath!' It means that we begin to breathe consciously with remembrance. So, the Shaykhs are teaching that if we are thankful for that mercy, every other mercy opens because we appreciated the gift of life.

﴿لَئِن شَكَرْتُمْ لَأَزِيدَنَّكُمْ ۖ ٧﴾

14:7 – "...*La in shakartum la azeedanakum...*" (*Surah Ibrahim*)

"...*If you are grateful and thank Me, I will give you more (favours)...*" (*Abraham, 14:7*)

Then that answers many questions for us. We do not put all these things into the body that are going to contaminate that breath, that are going to poison that breath, that are going to put difficulty onto that breath. We are actually trying to purify the breath, not throw all sorts of pollutants into the breath. We are trying to purify that breath with remembrance, closing our eyes in meditation and breathing in with the *zikr* of '*Huuuuu*' from the Divine Essence, and breathing out with '*Huuuu.*'

Saints are Dressed From the Tongue of Truth

So, it means that the Prophets are showing us the importance of the ears, the eyes, and then the most important – the breath. When the ears are submitting, the eyes are submitting, and the breath is submitting, then we begin to open the power of the tongue, which is what makes a messenger to be a Messenger for the Divine. It means the opening of the 'tongue of truth.' That tongue of truth is flowing from Sayyidina Muhammad ﷺ to the saints because the saints speak the truth. At that time, when the holy face is in submission, then the Divine can work through that servant.

Subhana rabbika rabbal 'izzati 'amma yasifoon, wa salaamun 'alal mursaleen, walhamdulillahi rabbil 'aalameen. Bi hurmati Muhammad al-Mustafa wa bi siri Surat al-Fatiha.

INSAN AL KAMIL - BOOK OF REALITIES

Secrets of the Letters of Insan – Noon, Alif, Seen, Noon, Alif

There Must Always Be a Muhammadan Representative

Alhamdulillah, from the greatness of the Holy Qur'an and the greatness of what Allah is dressing the reality of Sayyidina Muhammad. From what Sayyidina Muhammad is granting to his *awliyaullah* (saints) who are his representatives on earth and carrying his reality throughout time. There must always be a Muhammadan representative, for all the creation in this universe, representing the realities of Prophet.

Muhammadan Awliya Are Inheritors of Prophets of Bani Israel

Throughout the Holy Qur'an, Allah (swt) gives us understanding of the prophets, and there are many holy *ahadith* (narrations of Prophet Muhammad ﷺ). Prophet Muhammad ﷺ said: *"Ulama e warithatul anbiya."* Throughout Holy Qur'an, Allah (swt) gives us understandings of the prophets and many different *ahadith*. That in the story of all the prophets, the highest of the completion of prophecy is from Nabi Musa (Moses) (as). It means that the Jewish prophets, they completed prophecy to the highest levels. Sayyidina Isa (as) came as a Jewish prophet – from *Bani Israel,* he came as a rabbi representing *Bani Israel* so it  means the completion of prophecy. From the next level is then the prophecy of Sayyidina Muhammad ﷺ. *Awliyaullah* of *ummah* (nation of) Muhammad ﷺ are inheritors of the understanding of prophets under *Bani Israel.*

قَالَ رَسُولُ اللهِ صَلَّى اللهُ عَلَيْهِ وَسَلَّمَ "عُلَمَاءِ وَرِثَةُ الْأَنْبِيَاءِ

Qala Rasulullahi (saws) "'Ulama e warithatul anbiya."

Prophet Muhammad (pbuh) said, "My scholars are the inheritors of the prophets." (Ibn Majah and Tirmidhi)

At every level of prophecy, *awliyaullah* (saints) are inheriting from that level of understanding. Not inheriting the title because Prophet ﷺ is a gift from Allah (swt) and that title can't be understood. But from its level of knowledge and understanding, Prophet ﷺ is giving to *awliyaullah.*

Prophets Can't Reach Their Reality Without Ma'rifah of Sayyidina Muhammad ﷺ

That sets an understanding framework for us that when we hear about the prophets of Allah ﷻ that nobody can reach their *ma'rifah* (gnosticism) without first the *ma'rifah* of Sayyidina Muhammad ﷺ. So, then each prophet comes to their understanding of themselves, but they cannot complete the reality of themselves. They can't go on their *mi'raj* (ascension) until the *mi'raj* of Sayyidina Muhammad ﷺ.

There are people who are *nurani* (luminous) but they don't have the secrets. All the prophets didn't have the secrets which show *'Azamate Nabi* (greatness of Muhammad ﷺ). Therefore, Allah ﷻ wants the prophets to come and get the secrets from Sayyidina Muhammad ﷺ. Therefore, throughout the Qur'an, you see the prophets asking for something more.

Prophet Yunus ؏ Jumped Into the Ocean of Ma'rifah For More Light

For us in the holy month of light (Rajab), Sayyidina Yunus ؏ is important, Jonah ؏. Sayyidina Yunus ؏ is given a community to deal with and the light in which he is teaching and the light and actions in which he is giving out, is not enough. It means the people were not adhering to that understanding and that teaching. The *nur* (light) alone was not enough to reach to his people. Then he became fed up with his nation and left them. Then the story is that he goes to a ship to leave town. Immediately there is a storm. Then the ship captain says, 'There's somebody here with a problem because we now have this weather.' He recognized himself and jumped into the ocean. He jumped into the oceans of *ma'rifah* (gnosticism). It means jumping into the oceans of *Allahu Akbar* (God is Great). It means that the knowledge that at that point that he has is not enough

to convey what needs to be conveyed to the souls of the people – they're hungry. And the *nur* (light) that is emanating is not enough of a *nur* to penetrate their reality and he knows that I must go back into the oceans of *ma'rifah*. And he jumps into that ocean of *ma'rifah* (gnosticism) and Allah describes that a whale came and took him.

وَإِنَّ يُونُسَ لَمِنَ الْمُرْسَلِينَ ﴿١٣٩﴾ إِذْ أَبَقَ إِلَى الْفُلْكِ الْمَشْحُونِ ﴿١٤٠﴾ فَسَاهَمَ فَكَانَ مِنَ الْمُدْحَضِينَ ﴿١٤١﴾ فَالْتَقَمَهُ الْحُوتُ وَهُوَ مُلِيمٌ ﴿١٤٢﴾

37:139-142 – *"Wa inna Yoonusa laminal mursaleen. (139) Iz abaqa ilal fulkil mash hoon. (140) Fasaahama fakaana minal mudhadeen. (141) Faltaqamahul hootu wa huwa muleem. (142)" (Surat As-Saffat)*

"So also was Jonah among those sent (by Us). (139) When he ran away (like a slave from captivity) to the ship (fully) laden. (140), He (agreed to) cast lots, and he was condemned: (141) Then the big Fish did swallow him, and he had done acts worthy of blame. (142)"
(Those Who Set the Ranks, 37:139-142)

Mawlana Shah Naqshband ق Represents the Whale

For us the ocean of realities, what swims within the ocean of realities, are the souls. And the souls based on their strength and what Allah ﷻ has given to them is then the importance of that ocean. So, one of the big whales of oceans of *ma'rifah* (gnosticism) is the reality and soul of Mawlana Shah Naqshband ق. It means that Mawlana Shah Naqshband ق came and took his reality and put him within himself to teach the knowledges and the reality that Sayyidina Yunus عليه السلام wanted of these realities. That I want from that reality.

Sayyidina Yunus عليه السلام Was Also Known As ZunNun, Owner of Two Lights

Sayyidina Yunus عليه السلام was also known as *ZunNun* (two *noons*) which means two lights. Sayyidina Yunus عليه السلام realized that he needs two lights to guide his people. The first light was from his prophecy. He wanted the second light from the essence of the soul which was the pearls under the guidance of Shah Naqshband ق. Therefore, that whale was to be dispatched to eat him when he was thrown to the ocean of *ma'rifah* (gnosticism).

وَذَا النُّونِ إِذ ذَّهَبَ مُغَاضِبًا فَظَنَّ أَن لَّن نَّقْدِرَ عَلَيْهِ فَنَادَىٰ فِي الظُّلُمَاتِ أَن لَّا إِلَٰهَ إِلَّا أَنتَ سُبْحَانَكَ إِنِّي كُنتُ مِنَ الظَّالِمِينَ ﴿٨٧﴾ فَاسْتَجَبْنَا لَهُ وَنَجَّيْنَاهُ مِنَ الْغَمِّ ۚ وَكَذَٰلِكَ نُنجِي الْمُؤْمِنِينَ ﴿٨٨﴾

21:87-88 – *"Wa Zan Nooni idh dhahaba mughadiban fazhanna al lan naqdira 'alayhi fanada fizh zhulumati an la ilaha illa anta Subhanaka, innee kuntu minazh zhalimeen. (87) Fastajabna lahu wa najjayna hu minal ghammi, wa kadhalika nunjee almumineen. (88)"*
(Surat Al-Anbiya)

Insan al Kamil – Book of Realities

"And [mention] Zulnun [Yunus (Jonah) (as)], when he went off in anger and thought that We had no power/decree over him! But he cried out through the depths of darkness, "There is no god/diety except You; Glory to you: Indeed I have been of the wrongdoers/Oppressor to Myself!" (87) So We responded to him and saved him from the distress. And thus do We save the believers. (88)" (The Prophets, 21:87-88)

Prophet Muhammad ﷺ is the Insan al Kamil

This with the arrival of Sayyidina Muhammad ﷺ in *dunya* (earthly realm), He brought perfection to humanity. Before Prophet's ﷺ arrival people had to seek perfection. When other prophets wanted something, they had to request and ask to go into the ocean of *ma'rifah* (gnosticism). When *khatam al anbiya* (seal of prophets), Muhammad ﷺ came, he ﷺ came with all the secrets. He is the *Insan al Kamil* (perfected being). Other prophets came through the first *noon* of *insan* which represents *nur* (light). They had certain *nur* (light) of prophecy but they wanted the light of perfection, the second *noon* of *insan* – *diya* (Divinely Fire).

When Allah's ﷻ Izzah Emanates in a Heart, Divinely Knowledge is Its By-product

So then in the Naqshbandiya *tariqah* (spiritual path) and in the *silsila* (chain) of the *tariqah* of Tayfur Abu Yazid Bistami ق wanted that same reality of Mawlana Shah Naqshband ق and he dove into the ocean of *ma'rifah* (gnosticism), just like Sayyidina Yunus ؑ. Because they know that knowledge that you have is what people would be feeding from. If the knowledge is not strong enough, it means the power and *Izzah* (Might) of Allah ﷻ is not emanating strong enough. When Allah's ﷻ

Izzah is emanating through your heart, the knowledge is a by product of that energy.

And when that energy is not enough, it means *"Alimal Qadir"* (All Knowing, All Powerful) – go back into the ocean. Achieve what you need of Allah's ﷻ *Qudra* (power). Allah's ﷻ *Qudra* will emanate from Allah's ﷻ ancient knowledges. Those ancient knowledges were 'Umar ؓ, 'Uthman ؓ, 'Ali ؓ. They carry the secret of that *ayn*. It means these ancient knowledges - they are the custodians and they hold it for the reality of Prophet ﷺ.

Dive Into the Ocean of Realities to Find Pearls Like Abu Yazid Bistami ق

It means then they have to dive back into that ocean to achieve more of that reality. Then they begin to teach that Sayyidina Yunus ؑ dove into that ocean to achieve these realities and to open more of the power of his soul. And Mawlana Shah Naqshband ق is the whale of that reality that brings you in. So Abu Yazid Bistami ق went into that ocean and dove and dove and dove deeper until he reached the point of hearing the *zikr 'Hu.'* And the emanation of *'Hu'* and then seeing Mawlana Shah Naqshband ق making a *zikr* over the pearls of the souls. It's from *"Lulu wal marjan"* which means the treasures of the ocean.

يَخْرُجُ مِنْهُمَا اللُّؤْلُؤُ وَالْمَرْجَانُ ﴿٢٢﴾ فَبِأَيِّ آلَاءِ رَبِّكُمَا تُكَذِّبَانِ ﴿٢٣﴾

55:22-23 - *"Yakhruju minhumal lu 'lu u wal marjaan (22) Fabi ayyi aalaaa'i Rabbikumaa tukazzibaan (23)"* (Surat Ar-Rahman)

"Out of them come Pearls and Coral: (22) Then which of the favours of your Lord will ye deny?" (The Beneficient, 55:22-23)

You Have to Crack Into Your Reality to Find the Pearl of Your Soul

In Surat ar-Rahman, Allah (swt) is not talking about the physical ocean. It means everything in the way of *ma'rifah* (gnosticism), Allah (swt) doesn't care about the physicality. But He's talking and teaching us that dive into the ocean and only in diving in the ocean of realities, you will find its treasures, its pearls, its corals and its pearls.

And the pearl, the concept of the pearl, is that it's hidden within the oyster. It means its hidden reality that you have to crack the oyster open to take the pearl. It means you have to crack your reality. You have to efface and smash your physicality, so that only your soul can dive into that ocean of reality. And then they begin to teach that as you dive with your soul into that ocean, into that light, only by diving deeper and deeper, you can get into that reality.

Decoding The Word 'Insan' (Human Being)

Everyone Seeks the Last Alif – Izzatullah (Allah's Might and Magnificence)

Then they begin to teach us. So, then *insan* (human being) in this month that we're asking, '*Ya Rabbi*, open for us light and open for us the reality of light.' They're teaching that what makes Prophet ﷺ to be *kamil*, to be perfected, what makes *awliyaullah* (saints) to be *kamil* because these are Sultanul Awliya, the *shaykh al kamil*. The completed shaykh of realities, what makes them to be *kamil* (perfected), is in the understanding of the letters of *insan*. It means everybody in the *ma'rifah* (gnosticism), we want the *alif* (last *alif* from left). Everybody wants to reach *Izzatullah* (Allah's Might and Magnificence). The only way to get to the power is to reach Allah's *Izzah*.

Izzatullah Flows to Izzat Rasul and Then to Izzat Mumineen (Ulul Amr)

And Allah is saying, 'My *Izzah* is *izzatullahi wa Rasuli wal mumineen*.' It means its power is in three.

﴿... وَلِلَّهِ الْعِزَّةُ وَلِرَسُولِهِ وَلِلْمُؤْمِنِينَ ...﴿٨﴾

63:8 – "...Wa Lillahil 'izzatu wa li Rasuli hi wa lil Mumineen..." (Surat Al-Munafiqoon)

Insan al Kamil – Book of Realities

"...And to Allah belongs [all] honor, and to His messenger, and to the believers…" (The Hypocrites, 63:8)

That *izzah* is that we're trying to reach, that Allah ﷻ says if you want to reach, *"Atiullah wa atiur Rasul wa ulil amre minkum."* So the *ulul amr* (saints), they're holding the *izzat al mumineen* (honour of believers). They carry the Divinely Power that's emanating from Sayyidina Muhammad ﷺ and Sayyidina Muhammad ﷺ is emanating from Allah ﷻ.

يَاأَيُّهَا الَّذِينَ آمَنُوا أَطِيعُواللهَ وَأَطِيعُواْلرَّسُولَ وَأُوْلِي الأَمْرِ مِنْكُمْ...﴿٥٩﴾

4:59 – *"Ya ayyu hal latheena amanoo Atiullaha wa atiur Rasula wa Ulil amre minkum…"* (Surat An-Nisa)

"O You who have believed, Obey Allah, Obey the Messenger, and those in authority among you…" (The Women, 4:59)

First Noon is Nur (Light)

First Alif – Represents Izzat Mumineen
Having a Light is Different Than Being From the Reality of Light

So, then all of the *ummahs* (nations) and many of the *tariqahs* (spiritual paths), they have *nur*, because they have the *izzah* of the *mumineen* (believers) and they emanate a light. But having a light and being from the reality of light is completely different. *Nur* is like sunbathing. You can go to the beach and you can sit in the *nur* (light) and enjoy the *nur*, but it doesn't

mean that you're from the source of that light. It means you can sit and enjoy the beach.

But there are souls, they are like suns that wherever they go, they tan and cook everyone from the light that's emanating from their soul. They're not merely reflecting and you look at them and say, '*MashAllah*, he's very *Nurani*.' No, they're not only *nurani* (luminous), but they're a source of power and emanating through them and cooking everybody, tanning everybody from those lights. So, then they begin to teach us in the way of *ma'rifah* (gnosticism) that this first *noon* which was dressed by that *alif* (first *alif* in *insan* from left). Those are *mumin* (believer).

Real Mumineen Live for Alif of Izzatullah, and To Be of Service to Prophet ﷺ

Mawlana Shaykh gave a *suhbah* (discourse), to give an understanding for us. That don't think that we're *mumin* (believer) or *mukhlis* (sincere) because we pray. You ask some people and say, 'Are you *mukhlis*?' and they say, 'Yes, I'm *mukhlis* because I do all my praying. I do all my fasting. I do everything.' You say, 'Yeah, but that was ordered

upon you.' Doing what you're ordered is no big reward. You can't approach Allah ﷻ saying, 'Ok, now grant me this because I prayed.' He'll say, 'But you were supposed to pray.'

They begin to teach us that these *awliyaullah* (saints), not because they just pray and fast, but because Allah ﷻ recognized a reality within them that they begin to live not for themselves. They live for the sake of that *alif (Izzatullah)* (last *alif* from the left). They live for the sake of that *alif* and recognize their whole existence is for this *noon* (the second *noon* from left). As a result, they are *mukhlis* (sincere). Far beyond praying and fasting, they live, eat, drink, and breathe to be of service to

Allah's Creation. And the highest of servants is to serve Sayyidina Muhammad as Sayyidina Muhammad is serving Allah.

Decoding 'Nur' (Light) = Noon, Waw, Ra

The Nur is From the Waw, the Oceans of Wadud (Love)

Then they begin to teach that *nur* (light), the *noon* (first *noon* from left)  that they give to you is from the oceans of *wadud*, the *waw*. Because they want you to understand when you're talking light, they're not giving you a fluorescent lightbulb. The light that's coming is from the oceans of *wadud* (love). The *waw* of *Ahad* (the One) now becomes *wahid* (the Unique); because *ahad* – *la sharik* – there's nothing like Allah. But Allah reflects that love to Sayyidina Muhammad. And all the *ashiqeen*, the lovers of Prophet, are emanating from the oceans of love. So, then they dress us with that *waw* for love.

Ra of Nur Symbolizes Rabbaniyoon (Lordly Souls)

Then Mawlana Shaykh Nazim ق says, 'Be *rabbaniyoon*.' Holy Qur'an says, 'Be *rabbaniyoon*' (lordly souls).

… وَلَٰكِن كُونُوا رَبَّانِيِّينَ بِمَا كُنتُمْ تُعَلِّمُونَ الْكِتَابَ وَبِمَا كُنتُمْ تَدْرُسُونَ ﴿٧٩﴾

3:79 – "…*wa lakin kono rabbaniyena bima kuntum tu'allimoonal kitaba wabima kuntum tadrusoon.*" (Surat Ali-Imran)

"...Be Lordly Souls/faithful servants/worshippers of Him, Because (of what) you have taught the Book and you have studied it earnestly." (Family of Imran, 3:79)

Those who give knowledge and receive knowledge. They pursued knowledges as their whole existence and they give that knowledge out. It means their life is only for attaining Divinely Pleasures, Divinely Knowledge. As a result, they've been dressed by Allah's ﷻ *Qudra* (power). These are *rabbaniyoon* (lordly souls).

So the *nur* (light) that they're giving means they're giving their *nur*; it's made from the ocean of *wadud*, of love and they're dressing everybody to be *rabbaniyoon*. And those *rabbaniyoon*, they begin to teach you to leave your desires, leave all of the things that are attaching to the heart. Like Mawlana Shaykh says, 'You can't completely walk away from *dunya* (material world), but you do it without any attachment to the heart.' And your heart is attached to the love of Prophet ﷺ, love of Sayyidina Isa (Jesus) عليه السلام, love of Nabi Musa (Moses) عليه السلام, love of Divine realities. You do what you do for the sake of serving Prophet ﷺ. It means the heart is no longer attached and begins to attach to them, begins to attach to the reality.

First Alif – Izzat Mumineen – Awliya Dress Us From Their Nur and Izzah

They begin to teach us they take us into this *noon* (first *noon* from left) and begin to dress us from that reality of *nur*, dress us from that *alif* (first *alif* from left), dress us from their dress. It means if you accompany that *wali* (saint), he'll dress you from his dress, he'll dress you from his *mi'raj* (ascension), he'll dress you from his sustenance. And then Allah ﷻ describes, 'They feed you from their food and they love their food.' It's not something that they give away because it's cheap or rotten. They feed you from their food and they love their food, but they give to the *miskeen* (poor). They give to the *yateem* (orphan) and the *asiran*, the captive. It means our three categories of who we are to eat with them. Not the physical food only, but the spiritual food.

وَيُطْعِمُونَ الطَّعَامَ عَلَىٰ حُبِّهِ مِسْكِينًا وَيَتِيمًا وَأَسِيرًا ﴿٨﴾

76:8 – *"Wa yu ta'imo nat Ta'ama 'ala hubbihi miskeenan wa yateeman wa aseera." (Surah Al-Insaan)*

"And they feed, in spite of love for it, to the needy/indigent, the orphan, and the captive." (The Human, 76:8)

It means whatever Prophet's ﷺ dressing their souls, they are merely reflecting it out. It means if you accompany a *Qutub*, you'll be dressed by the characteristics of that *Qutub*. If you're dressed from the *Budala, Nujaba, Nuqaba, Awtad, wal Akhyar* – any of the categories of their sainthood – they will dress you from the lights of their sainthood. Because Allah ﷻ is merely teaching them reflect out. It's not to be held in. As much as they receive, as much as they're reflecting.

Awliya Inherit From Prophets of Bani Israel Who Had Nur and Izzat Mumineen

Then they teach you that now come into that ocean and understand what makes *insan* so noble. That all the prophets realized their light is not enough, they are merely *mumin* (believer), *mukhlis* (sincere) (referring to first *alif* and *noon*). Then Prophet ﷺ says, 'The *mukhlis* of my *ummah*, they inherited the station of all the

prophets of *Bani Israel*.' It means they stopped right there (the first *alif* and *noon* – at *Nur* and *Izzat Mumineen*).

عُلَمَاءِ وَرِثَةُ الْأَنْبِيَاءِ

"*'Ulama e warithatul anbiya.*"

Prophet Muhammad (pbuh) said, *"My scholars are the inheritors of the prophets."*

So, then the prophets of *Bani Israel*, what did they want? They wanted the reality. Who did they need? A Muhammadan representative because Prophet ﷺ was not yet physically in *dunya* (material world), not yet made his *mi'raj* (ascension). He ﷺ didn't complete what he needed to complete. At that time, everybody after that completes. Prophet ﷺ goes first. So then dispatched a *Muhammadiyun* to take them to the secret.

Seen is the Sir (Secret)

The Sir (Secret) is Understood Through Oceans of Certainties

So, the secret is the *sir*, oceans of the secret, ocean of the soul; it's the secret of Sayyidina Muhammad ﷺ. So, they dress you from that *nur*  (light) to take us to the secret, the *sir*. And the *sir* (secret) can only be understood with *ilm ul-yaqeen* (knowledge of certainty), *ayn ul-yaqeen* (vision of certainty) and *haqq ul-yaqeen* (certainty of truth). It's from the knowledge of certainties. So, they say what is the *sir*? What is the *sir*? The *sir* is the secret and that secret can only be understood with *ilm ul-yaqeen*, *ayn ul-yaqeen* and *haqq ul-yaqeen*.

Ilm ul-Yaqeen – Knowledge of Certainty Requires Obedience

It means these divinely knowledges begin to dress the soul. If that knowledge is dressing the soul and the soul is in *itibah*, in obedience, because if it's not in obedience, it's not accepting the knowledge. So, they understand that when you're not obedient and we're not interested in listening, we're not interested in following. Then the *ilm* (knowledge) has not reached its *yaqeen* (certainty). It's not certain because you say, 'I don't really believe what you're saying so therefore I'm not following.' If I'm not following, then that knowledge no way is certain.

﴿كَلَّا لَوْ تَعْلَمُونَ عِلْمَ الْيَقِينِ ٥﴾

102:5 – *"Kal la law t'alamoona 'ilm al yaqeen." (Surat At-Takathur)*

"No! If you only knew with knowledge of certainty."
(The Rivalry in World Increase, 102:5)

Ayn ul-Yaqeen – Vision of Certainty

If that knowledge is not of certainty, then there's no way that the *ayn ul-yaqeen* (vision of certainty) opens. So, then the *itibah* and obedience is that knowledge with certainty, I believe in it and I follow. As I follow, they begin to open your heart to see, because they're transmitting that signal. We're not talking about the Sultanul Awliya (king of saints); it's far beyond this. We're talking about the transmitter. The transmitter that is transmitting that reality. They're transmitting that reality so that you can get to the secret.

When you get to the secret, *ilm ul-yaqeen*, the knowledges convey. Are you believing? Are you following and moving on them? If you are following and moving on them, then you should begin with the heart opening with *ayn ul-yaqeen* (vision of certainty). It's not you that opened anything – they opened it. They can close it in an instant. But the light and emanation of that *izzah* is dressing, hits the heart and begins to unveil the heart so that it can see.

$$ ثُمَّ لَتَرَوُنَّهَا عَيْنَ الْيَقِينِ ﴿٧﴾ $$

102:7 – *"Thum ma la tara wun naha 'ayn al yaqeen."*
(*Surat At-Takathur*)

"Then you will surely see it with the eye/vision of certainty."
(*The Rivalry in World Increase, 102:7*)

Ilm ul-Yaqeen and Ayn ul-Yaqeen Lead to Haqq ul-Yaqeen

If they're hearing with certainty, they begin to see with certainty. If they hear and see with certainty, they are now in *haqq ul-yaqeen* (certainty of truth). Because everything you begin to witness through your heart, it's a brick of *haq* (truth), brick of *haq*, brick of *haq*, brick of *haq*, until so many bricks of *haq* that your faith is certain. Like you know your hand, you know your belief and that certainty opens that reality.

$$ إِنَّ هَذَا لَهُوَ حَقُّ الْيَقِينِ ﴿٩٥﴾ $$

56:95 – *"Inna hadha la huwa haq qul yaqeen."* (*Surat Al-Waqi'ah*)

"Indeed, this is the true certainty." (*The Inevitable, 56:95*)

Second Noon - Naar (Divinely Fire)

Second Noon – Opens the Reality of Naar (Divinely Fire)

Then they're teaching that once they've been dressed, these are the shaykhs teaching the *ma'rifah* (gnosticism) of the self. Once they've been

dressed by that secret, they carry the secret. And as a result, they're taken to this *noon* (second *noon* of *insan*) of Sayyidina Muhammad ﷺ. That *noon* of Sayyidina Muhammad ﷺ then comes and opens the reality of *naar* (divinely fire).

What makes the *naar* different than the *nur* (light) is that the *naar* carries the *izzah* because the *alif* is in there. There must be a fire for you to enjoy the light. It means we live and all our life is based on the sun. If no sun, no breath. You can't breathe, the plants don't produce oxygen. You can't eat. With no sun, you can't see. It means our existence is based on that *naar*. So, the *naar* is the source of fire. It burns, it consumes and as it consumes, it burns and with its burning is so intense, it produces light. So, you cannot have that *nur* without that *naar*. Otherwise, you're merely a reflection.

Prophet ﷺ Teaches to Open Your Heart to Be a Source of Fire, Like the Sun

So, then Prophet ﷺ is teaching that when I take you towards *kamil*, to be perfected, that I open within your heart to be a source of fire, to be a source like a sun that you're moving on this *dunya* (material world) with that energy and that power emanating within your heart. So then that *noon*  (second *noon* in *insan*) is different than the first *noon*.

So, Sayyidina Yunus (as) had this *noon* (first *noon* in *insan*) and that *noon* wasn't enough to reach his people. So, he became ZunNun. He jumped into the ocean of *ma'rifah* (gnosticism), dressed from the realities, the Muhammadan reality. And Allah (swt) said, 'Now you are of the two *noons*, ZunNun.' He said you have been dressed from that reality.

وَذَا النُّونِ إِذ ذَّهَبَ مُغَاضِبًا فَظَنَّ أَن لَّن نَّقْدِرَ عَلَيْهِ فَنَادَىٰ فِي الظُّلُمَاتِ أَن لَّا إِلَـٰهَ إِلَّا أَنتَ سُبْحَانَكَ إِنِّي كُنتُ مِنَ الظَّالِمِينَ ﴿٨٧﴾ فَاسْتَجَبْنَا لَهُ وَنَجَّيْنَاهُ مِنَ الْغَمِّ ۚ وَكَذَٰلِكَ نُنجِي الْمُؤْمِنِينَ ﴿٨٨﴾

21:87-88 – "Wa Zan Nooni idh dhahaba mughadiban fazhanna al lan naqdira 'alayhi fanada fizh zhulumati an la ilaha illa anta Subhanaka, innee kuntu minazh zhalimeen. (87) Fastajabna lahu wa najjayna hu minal ghammi, wa kadhalika nunjee almumineen. (88)"
(Surat Al-Anbiya)

"And [mention] Zulnun [Yunus (Jonah) (as)], when he went off in anger and thought that We had no power/decree over him! But he cried out through the depths of darkness, "There is no god/diety except You; Glory to you: Indeed I have been of the wrongdoers/Oppressor to Myself!" (87) So We responded to him and saved him from the distress. And thus do We save the believers. (88)" (The Prophets, 21:87-88)

Second Alif – Izzat ar Rasul is Hidden in the Alif of Naar

And *tariqah* (spiritual path) coming and teaching that *alhamdulillah*, Naqshbandiya til 'Aliyya – this is from the reality of the Naqshbandi shaykhs. That Mawlana Shah Naqshband ق is teaching that, 'Come our way. Come into that *ma'rifah*. Come into that secret and we dress you from that fire. That your heart will be like a lit sun and you become a source of light.' And they dress you from not only *izzat mumineen* (honour of believers) (first *alif* in *insan* from left), but *izzat ar Rasul* (honour of Prophet ﷺ). *Izzat ar Rasul* is the *alif* hidden within the *naar*.

That Allah ﷻ describes in Surat al-Nur, 'He's a very blessed tree, neither of the east or the west but he produces a light upon his own light.'

اللَّـهُ نُورُ السَّمَاوَاتِ وَالْأَرْضِ ۚ مَثَلُ نُورِهِ كَمِشْكَاةٍ فِيهَا مِصْبَاحٌ ۖ الْمِصْبَاحُ فِي زُجَاجَةٍ ۖ الزُّجَاجَةُ كَأَنَّهَا كَوْكَبٌ دُرِّيٌّ يُوقَدُ مِن شَجَرَةٍ مُّبَارَكَةٍ زَيْتُونَةٍ لَّا شَرْقِيَّةٍ وَلَا غَرْبِيَّةٍ يَكَادُ زَيْتُهَا يُضِيءُ وَلَوْ لَمْ تَمْسَسْهُ نَارٌ ۚ نُّورٌ عَلَىٰ نُورٍ ۗ يَهْدِي اللَّـهُ لِنُورِهِ مَن يَشَاءُ ۚ وَيَضْرِبُ اللَّـهُ الْأَمْثَالَ لِلنَّاسِ ۗ وَاللَّـهُ بِكُلِّ شَيْءٍ عَلِيمٌ ﴿٣٥﴾

24:35 – "Allahu noorus samawati wal ardi. mathalu noorehi kamishkatin feeha misbahun, almisbahu fee zujajatin, azzujajatu kaannaha kawkabun durriyyun yoqadu min shajaratim mubarakatin zaytoonatil la sharqiyyatin wa la gharbiyyatin yakadu zaytuha yudeo wa law lam tamsashu narun. noorun 'ala noorin. yahdellahu linoorihi man yashao. Wa yadribullah ul amthala linnasi, wallahu bikulli shayin 'Aleem." (Surat An-Nur)

"Allah is the Light of the heavens and the earth. The Parable of His Light is as if there were a Niche and within it a Lamp: the Lamp enclosed in Glass: the glass as it were a brilliant star: Lit from a blessed Tree an Olive, neither of the east nor of the west, whose oil is well-nigh luminous, though fire scarce touched it: Light upon Light! Allah guides whom He will to His Light: Allah present examples for the people: and Allah knows all things." (The Light, 24:35)

Allah ﷻ Empowers the Reality of Prophet Muhammad ﷺ

Because when you look at the sun, you think it's a self-contained power because of what? Fusion. Fusing together with Allah ﷻ; this is the reality of *Qaba qawsayni aw adna*. When Allah ﷻ merely brings His *Qudra* (power) and the reality of Prophet ﷺ approaches, it begins to produce an energy. That is eternal energy and never diminishes because what Allah ﷻ gives it can never be diminished.

فَكَانَ قَابَ قَوْسَيْنِ أَوْ أَدْنَىٰ ﴿٩﴾

53:9 – *"Fakana qaaba qawsayni aw adna."* (Surat An-Najm)

"And was at a distance of two bow lengths or nearer [to the Divine Presence]." (The Star, 53:9)

The Three Alifs in Insan
Izzatullah, Izzat ar-Rasul, Izzat al Mumineen

Izzat Rasul Takes Us to the Presence of Izzatullah – From Hidden Alif of Naar to Last Alif

So, then they're teaching us that when we'll be dressed by that *sir* (secret) (*seen*), then they'll take us to that second *noon* and to be a source of light. At that time, you are in the presence of the *alif* (last *alif* in *insan*). They take you all the way to the presence of that *alif* and that is *Izzatullah* (Allah's ﷻ Might and Magnificence). And then this hidden *alif*

(hidden *alif* in *naar*), *izzat ar-Rasul* and *izzat al mumineen* (the first *alif* from left in *insan*). Those three *alifs* are in *insan*.

وَلِلَّهِ الْعِزَّةُ وَلِرَسُولِهِ وَلِلْمُؤْمِنِينَ... ﴿٨﴾

63:8 – "...Wa Lillahil 'izzatu wa li Rasuli hi wa lil Mumineen..." (Surat Al-Munafiqoon)

"...And to Allah belongs [all] honor, and to His messenger, and to the believers..." (The Hypocrites, 63:8)

انسان				
Insan (Human Being)				
ن	ا	س	ن	ا
Noon	*Alif*	*Seen*	*Noon*	*Alif*
نور		سر	نار / ضيا = ن ا ر	
Nur (Light)		*Sir* (Secret)	*Naar/Diya* Noon, Alif, Ra (Divinely Fire)	
عزة المؤمنين			عزة الرسول	عزة الله
'Izzatul Mumineen (Honour of the Believers)			*Izzatur Rasul* is in the Hidden *Alif* of the *Naar* (Honour of Prophet Muhammad ﷺ)	*Izzatullah* (Might of Allah ﷻ)

*Note: Please read English from right to left to coincide with Arabic.

Three Alifs Represent the Three Holy Months

Atiullaha wa atiur Rasula wa Ulil amre minkum is also in the word of *insan*.

...يَاأَيُّهَا الَّذِينَ آمَنُوا أَطِيعُوا اللَّهَ وَأَطِيعُوا الرَّسُولَ وَأُولِي الْأَمْرِ مِنْكُمْ...﴿٥٩﴾

4:59 – *"...Ya ayyu hal latheena amanoo Atiullaha wa atiur Rasula wa Ulil amre minkum..." (Surat An-Nisa)*

"O You who have believed, Obey Allah, Obey the Messenger, and those in authority among you..." (The Women, 4:59)

The first *alif* of *insan* (from right), is *Atiullah* which is the holy month of Rajab (Allah's month). The second *alif* is hidden in the *naar* of the second *noon* and that means *atiur Rasul*, which is the holy month of Sha'ban. The third *alif* which sometimes it's written as *fatha* in Arabic is the *ulul amre minkum*, which is the month of Ramadan.

Then follow *ulul amr* (those in authority), and *Husn ur Rafiqa* (those who follow the *ulul amr*). Then when you sit in *Lailatul Qadr* (Night of Power) in Ramadan, you will be dressed by these lights. The light described for that night of power is from these realities of Rajab and Sha'ban. From the *barakah* (blessing) of *tariqah* (spiritual path), *awliya* (saints) are always dressed by these realities of *Lailatul Qadr*.

We pray that in this holy month of Rajab, Allah opens for us from *Izzatullah*, in Sha'ban, *izzat ar-Rasul* and in Ramadan, *izzat al mumineen*. And to be dressed by that, and that's why *Lailatul Qadr* (Night of Power). *"Lailatul Qadr min alfe shahr."*

لَيْلَةُ الْقَدْرِ خَيْرٌ مِّنْ أَلْفِ شَهْرٍ ﴿٣﴾

97:3 – "Laylatul Qadre khairum min alfe shahr." (Surat Al-Qadr)

"The Night of Decree is better than a thousand months."
(The Power, 97:3)

Allah ﷻ says, 'If you can reach that reality and We dress you from that secret and We dress you from that light, then you've been dressed from the best of gifts.' Why 1,000 months? Because that's 83 years which means it's better than your entire lifetime if you can achieve that light. We pray that Allah ﷻ opens these lights and realities for us.

Subhana rabbika rabbal 'izzati 'amma yasifoon, wa salaamun 'alal mursaleen, walhamdulillahi rabbil 'aalameen. Bi hurmati Muhammad al-Mustafa wa bi siri Surat al-Fatiha.

REALITIES OF THE FACE, PRESENCE, ESSENCE

Everything Perishes But the Holy Face – It's Eternal

The Holy Face, the holy presence and the essence within that presence. And Allah reminding that, "...*kullu shayin halikun illa wajha,*" 'That everything perishes but, the Holy Face.'

...كُلُّ شَيْءٍ هَالِكٌ إِلَّا وَجْهَهُ ﴿٨٨﴾

28:88 – "...*kullu shayin halikun illa wajha*" (Surat Al-Qasas)

"*...Everything (that exists) will perish except His Holy Face...*" (The Stories, 28:88)

From Mawlana Shaykh's teaching for contemplating and *tafakkur* and to go into the reality is that everything is perishing. Don't focus on that

which perishes but focus on that which is eternal. If you meditate and focus on a tree or focus on a tomato or focus on something from the material world, it's perishing. So, then Divine reminding that why focus on that which perishes and is perishable?

And by its nature, everything perishable is false. And that which is eternal is only to be worshipped. And that which is eternal is and should be our entire focus.

$$\text{وَ قُلْ جَآءَالْحَقُّ وَزَهَقَ الْبَطِلُ، إِنَّ الْبَطِلَ كَانَ زَهُوقًا ﴿٨١﴾}$$

17:81 – *"Wa qul jaa alhaqqu wa zahaqal baatil, innal batila kana zahoqa." (Surat Al-Isra)*

"And say, Truth has come, and falsehood has perished. Indeed falsehood, [by its nature], is ever perishing/ bound to perish."
(The Night Journey, 17:81)

The Face, Presence, and Divinely Essence Reflected in Three Holy Months

And Divine teaching, *"Atiullaha wa atiur Rasula wa Ulil amre minkum."*

$$\text{يَاأَيُّهَا الَّذِينَ آمَنُوا أَطِيعُواالله وَأَطِيعُواالرَّسُولَ وَأُولِي الْأَمْرِ مِنْكُمْ... ﴿٥٩﴾}$$

4:59 – *"Ya ayyu hal latheena amanoo Atiullaha wa atiur Rasula wa Ulil amre minkum…" (Surat An-Nisa)*

"O You who have believed, Obey Allah, Obey the Messenger, and those in authority among you…" (The Women, 4:59)

And all of Rajab, and middle of Sha'ban, and Mawlana Shaykh teaching for us, from here is the reality of *insan*. That to reach to that Divinely *Izzah*, the Divinely Essence which is the secret of Rajab. Hidden within the presence of Sha'ban which is the reality of the prophetic reality, the prophetic reality of Sayyidina Muhammad ﷺ and all the prophets. And the secret of Ramadan being the face. This means that everything we're approaching has a face. From its face, it has a presence. From its presence, within that presence, there must be a secret. Those that are clever enough to move within the ocean with that presence, they dive towards its secret.

رَجَبٌ شَهْرُ اللَّهِ ، وَشَعْبَانُ شَهْرِي ، وَرَمَضَانُ شَهْرُ أُمَّتِي

Rajabu shahr ullahi, wa Sha'banu shahryi, wa ramadanu shahru Ummati

Rajab is the month of Allah, Sha'ban is my month, and Ramadan is the month of my followers.

رجب	شعبان	رمضان
Rajab	Sha'ban	Ramadan
Divinely Essence	Presence (Prophetic Reality)	Face (Saints)

Holy Qur'an Has a Surah (Face), Ayah (Sign), and a Secret Within Each Sign

Another analogy would be a door. That you have to move through the door. From the door, it opens a room. And the quest is not stopping in the room but moving towards the secret within the room.

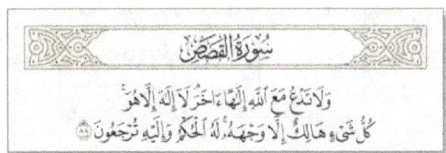

And that's why Holy Qur'an has a *surah* (chapter/face), has a face. It has an *ayah* (verse/sign) which is the presence, a sign. Within the secret of every *ayah* is its reality. This means then for us, the contemplation and the ocean of contemplation, every formula that we are doing, it carries through in every act of worshipness.

1. *Surah* = Face
2. *Ayah* = Sign – Presence
3. Secret in each *Ayah* = Heavenly Reality

Realities of the Face, Presence, Essence

Enter Through the Door to Have Access to Divinely Essence in the Room

It means that as soon as you *tafakkur* and contemplate, then the Divine says that 'Contemplate on My Divinely Presence. My Divinely Presence is not known to you yet.' Then keep yourself as if in the presence of the prophets *(alayhi salatu salaam)*, that that is the room. Within the heart of the prophets is the Divinely Essence. What beats within their heart is the Divinely Presence. The *ulul amre minkum* are then carrying the holy face of the prophetic reality.

Face	→	Presence	→	Essence
Door	→	Room	→	Secret in the Room
Ulul Amr (Saints)		RasulAllah ﷺ (Prophetic Reality)		Allah (Divinely Essence)

Ulul Amr (Awliya) Are the Face That Take Us to Prophetic Reality

So, as soon as we meditate in *tariqah* (spiritual path), you focus upon the face. From the face and trying to keep their face, saying that, 'My lord, let me to be from those whom you are pleased with. Let me to focus on their association, and be with them, to be present with them.' Their holy face merely grabs us and brings us into their presence. And their presence is the prophetic presence. This is the power of *ulul amr*.

يَاأَيُّهَا الَّذِينَ آمَنُوا أَطِيعُواللَّه وَأَطِيعُواْ الرَّسُولَ وَأُوْلِي الْأَمْرِ مِنْكُمْ...﴿٥٩﴾

4:59 – *"Ya ayyu hal latheena amanoo Atiullaha wa atiur Rasola wa Ulil amre minkum..." (Surat An-Nisa)*

"O You who have believed, Obey Allah, Obey the Messenger, and those in authority among you..." *(The Women, 4:59)*

The *ulul amr*, why Allah ﷻ says to obey them? To follow them? Because the real *ulul amr*, they are from the realities of what we were talking about, Mawlana Shaykh's teaching of *insan kamil* (perfected human being).  Their *nur* (light) is shining to bring us into that secret. By focusing on their face, closing our eyes, and asking my lord, like a GPS, 'I want to be with them. I'm trying to keep the memory of them, the image of them, their holy face.' Everything else will perish. But the light that shines from their face is the reality of what's within their heart. And what's within their heart is the love of the prophetic presence, and love of the Divinely Presence. So that face draws us into the presence. Then you begin to elevate your ability to contemplate where the face brings you immediately into the presence. And in the presence, you feel the prophetic presence. And from the prophetic presence, it's a chute into the Divinely Oceans and the Divinely Essence.

Contemplate On the Face and Keep the Holy Presence

We pray that in this holy month of Sha'ban, a tremendous reality of that reality is *Lailatul Nisf e Sha'ban* (15th of 8th lunar month). That all of these holy nights, that Mawlana Shaykh is teaching for us to safeguard and to cherish is to merely be dressed by them. If we don't feel anything, it doesn't matter. But to sit and wait and to copy their way, to be dressed and dressed and dressed until the dress is enough upon the soul that the eye of the heart, the eye of the soul, can begin to move. It has its *qudra*,

Realities of the Face, Presence, Essence

it has its power, it has its cleanliness, in which the eye of the heart opens and begins to witness their holy face. And from their holy face begins to witness their holy presence. And to know that we're in that holy presence. And from there, it's like a spark into the Divine Essence.

For those that can keep their (*awliya's*) face, keep the face. To move into the presence, from the presence asking always, '*Ya Rabbi*, dress me from the essence.' If you are not able to keep their face, then keep the face of holy Ka'bah. And see ourselves at the presence and the image of holy Ka'bah within the heart and then asking to move within the presence of the holy Ka'bah and for the light of the essence to dress us. If not that, then the presence and the holy presence of light and asking to see ourselves in that light. Then to move into the presence of that light and then to be dressed by the essence of that light, *inshaAllah*.

Subhana rabbika rabbal 'izzati 'amma yasifoon, wa salaamun 'alal mursaleen, walhamdulillahi rabbil 'aalameen. Bi hurmati Muhammad al-Mustafa wa bi siri Surat al-Fatiha.

REALITIES OF INSAN (PERFECT HUMAN) THE SUN AND THE MOON

INSAN

Decoding the Word 'Insan' (Human Being)

The eternity of these teachings, that Allah's ﷻ prophets, they come to

perfect our reality and to give from their understanding. From Sayyidina Yunus ﷺ that ZunNun ﷺ. And that from the understanding of *Rashidin al-Mahdiyeen wal kamilin*, that these are states in which the spiritual guides are to be taken and to be dressed and blessed, so they are of benefit to *ummat al-Muhammad* ﷺ (nation of Muhammad ﷺ).

Realities of Insan – Perfect Human – The Sun and the Moon

انسان				
Insan (Human Being)				
ن	ا	س	ن	ا
Noon	Alif	Seen	Noon	Alif
نور		سر	نار / ضيا = ن ا ر	
Nur (Light)		Sir (Secret)	Naar/Diya Noon, Alif, Ra (Divinely Fire)	
عزة المؤمنين			عزة الرسول	عزة الله
'Izzatul Mumineen (Honour of the Believers)			Izzatur Rasul is in the Hidden Alif of the Naar (Honour of Prophet Muhammad ﷺ)	Izzatullah (Might of Allah ﷻ)

*Note: Please read English from right to left to coincide with Arabic.

In the last days, there are many who walk around talking about their shaykh is *kamil* (perfected). And for us an understanding from that teaching so that before people say somebody is *kamil*, they have to have the reality of this understanding. That from just the word *insan* (human being), Allah ﷻ puts all its coding for us to understand. And every reality has to be from the left side moving to the right side especially for Arabic. That the goal is this *alif* (first letter of *insan* in Arabic) is to reach Allah's ﷻ Divinely Presence, *izzatullah, izzat Rasul wa izzat al-mumineen*, is hidden within this reality of *insan*. This *noon* (the first *noon* from left) is a *nur* (light) and a moon, this *noon* (the second *noon* from left of *insan*) is a *diya*, is a *naar*, is a fire and is a star. There's a sun (pointing to the second *noon*) and there's a moon (pointing to the first *noon*) in this. These are the two lights of *insan*.

...وَلِلَّهِ الْعِزَّةُ وَلِرَسُولِهِ وَلِلْمُؤْمِنِينَ وَلَٰكِنَّ الْمُنَافِقِينَ لَا يَعْلَمُونَ ﴿٨﴾

63:8 – "...Wa Lillahil 'izzatu wa li Rasuli hi wa lil Mumineena wa lakinnal munafiqeena la y'alamoon." (Surat Al-Munafiqoon)

"...And to Allah belongs [all] honor, and to His messenger, and to the believers, but the hypocrites do not know." (The Hypocrites, 63:8)

Sayyidina ZunNun ﷺ Was Thrown into the Mercy Ocean to Perfect His Lights

When Sayyidina Yunus, ZunNun ﷺ, didn't have the light that was necessary for his guidance, he had one of these lights of a *nur*. But that *nur* was not enough of a reflection to guide his people to the reality in which he was needing to guide that community. He took himself upon a ship and went into the ocean. The storm of the ocean means there's always a reality for eternity.

This is Allah's ﷻ Ocean of *Rahmah* (mercy), Allah ﷻ took him, threw him into that ocean of *rahmah* that you are not yet complete and *kamil* (perfected). And in that ocean, a big whale from *awliyaullah* (saints) came from *ummat Muhammad* ﷺ, *houti* (fish). One of the *Ahlul Hu* (people of *Hu*) showed up as a whale and took his soul into their reality, into their soul, and perfected his lights, perfected his reality, and threw him back up onto the shore of *dunya* (material world) for guidance. Now go and guide your people. *"La ilaha illa anta Subhanaka, innee kuntu minazh zhalimeen. Fastajabna lahu wa najjayna hu minal ghammi, wa kadhalika nunjee almumineen."* This means this way is based on negating ourselves. I'm nothing, *ya Rabbi*, and glory be to You and that I am an oppressor to myself and Allah's ﷻ reply is correct. You are definitely an oppressor to yourself, but I give a *najat* (salvation) to those who believe. Allah ﷻ wants the door of humility.

Realities of Insan – Perfect Human – The Sun and the Moon

وَذَا النُّونِ إِذ ذَهَبَ مُغَاضِبًا فَظَنَّ أَن لَّن نَّقْدِرَ عَلَيْهِ فَنَادَىٰ فِي الظُّلُمَاتِ أَن لَّا إِلَٰهَ إِلَّا أَنتَ سُبْحَانَكَ إِنِّي كُنتُ مِنَ الظَّالِمِينَ ﴿٨٧﴾ فَاسْتَجَبْنَا لَهُ وَنَجَّيْنَاهُ مِنَ الْغَمِّ ۚ وَكَذَٰلِكَ نُنجِي الْمُؤْمِنِينَ ﴿٨٨﴾

21:87-88 – *"Wa dhan Nooni idh dhahaba mughadiban fazhanna al lan naqdira 'alayhi fanada fizh zhulumati an la ilaha illa anta Subhanaka, innee kuntu minazh zhalimeen. (87) Fastajabna lahu wa najjayna hu minal ghammi, wa kadhalika nunjee almumineen. (88)"*
(Surat Al-Anbiya)

"And [mention] Zulnun [Yunus (Jonah) (as)], when he went off in anger and thought that We had no power/decree over him! But he cried out through the depths of darkness, "There is no god/deity except You; Glory to you: Indeed I have been of the wrongdoers/Oppressor to Myself!" (87) So We responded to him and saved him from the distress. And thus do We save the believers. (88)" (The Prophets, 21:87-88)

The Noon Carries the Nur of Qamarun

Then they begin to teach us this letter, this word of *insan* (human being), is our way of reality. That we're trying to open the reality of this *noon* which is a moon. It's a *nur* and a *nur*, *"shamsi diya wal qamaru nuran"* (the sun a shining glory and the moon to be a light).

هُوَ الَّذِي جَعَلَ الشَّمْسَ ضِيَاءً وَالْقَمَرَ نُورًا وَقَدَّرَهُ مَنَازِلَ... ﴿٥﴾

10:5 – *"Huwal ladhee ja'alash shamsa Diya an wal qamara Nooran wa qaddarahu manazila…"* (Surat Yunus)

"It is He who made the sun a shining glory/splendor and the moon to be a light (of beauty) and measured out stages for her…" (Jonah, 10:5)

So, the *qamar* (moon) is a reflection. When we say *qamarun, qamarun,* it's a lower level. Prophet ﷺ is *shamsun.* Lower level is to say *qamarun,* we don't even feel comfortable saying that. *Qamarun* are *awliya* (saints).

They are the moons of this nation. It means they begin to teach that a moon is merely a reflection of light. It means they have to be given and through their training, *rashidin,* that Allah ﷻ gave that they are the people of *irshad* (guidance) and *ar-Rashid* is dressing them that you've been given the way of guidance. This means they cannot become *rashidin* unless Allah ﷻ says you're now going to be destined to be a moon. As a moon you'll be taught, 'You don't have any light. It's not about you. It's about you being nothing.' Right?

Beware of Those Who Speak of Allah ﷻ But Forget Their Imam, RasulAllah ﷺ

So, Pharaoh said, *"Ana Rabi al-ala."* Pharaonic teaching on this earth from *shaitan* is that you are everything, you have everything. Everything contained within you, so that build myself thinking I'm something.

$$﴿٢٤﴾ فَقَالَ أَنَا رَبُّكُمُ الْأَعْلَىٰ$$

79:24 – *"Faqala ana rabbukumu al 'Aala." (Surat An-Nazi'at)*

"And Fir'aun (Pharaoh) said, I am your Lord All-Highest!"
(Those Who Drag Forth, 79:24)

Allah's ﷻ door is different; it's no, no admit that you have nothing. So, then the moon comes as a symbol. Because somebody asked that I went somewhere, and the person was speaking very nice and was talking very eloquently. The first thing we ask is did they praise Sayyidina

Muhammad ﷺ excessively? And every word of their talking, was it about the *haqqiqat al-Muhammadiya* ﷺ? If not, it's not from these people. If someone talks too much about Allah ﷻ, they don't know their name, they don't know the realities of Sayyidina Muhammad ﷺ. Why they're talking about Allah ﷻ? As if they forgot the *imam* (leader); you forgot the one who's in front of you. You forgot the one leading your way. You forgot that everything is based on Sayyidina Muhammad ﷺ. It's a different level of a teacher. When somebody is a scholar and they talk excessively in one way, but they don't mention anything from the reality of Sayyidina Muhammad ﷺ, they are not a moon.

The Moon Focuses Only on the Sun of Prophet Muhammad ﷺ

The moon doesn't talk about Venus, it doesn't talk about Pluto, it doesn't talk about anything other than the *shams* (sun). The moon, its *nazar* (gaze) is completely on the reality of the *shams* (sun). As a result of how strong their *firasah* (spiritual vision) and their *qadam* (footstep), their path is and their

istiqam, the firmness of their path, is going to be how much light and power they're able to reflect from the presence of the sun.

Sun is a Star and Has Diya (Fire/Shining Glory)

That's why Prophet ﷺ described, 'My companions are all stars.' Why? Because Prophet ﷺ is hinting I am the star maker.

أَصْحَابِيْ كَالنُّجُومْ بِأَيِّهِمْ اَقْتَدَيْتِمْ اَهْتَدَيْتِمْ

"Ashabi kan Nujoom, bi ayyihim aqta daytum ahta daytum."

"My companions are like stars. Follow any one of them and you will be guided." (Prophet Muhammad (pbuh))

If all my companions are stars, then you better believe I'm the one who makes stars. This is the reality in which he brings this creation into becoming *shams*. *Shams* (sun) is a *diya* (fire). When Nabi Musa ﷺ wanted to reach to the fire, the word in the Qur'an is a *diya*. *Diya* is a fire, is a divine light that must be struck. So, it means the reality of fire and *diya* is a sun, is a star. Prophet ﷺ was teaching at that time that stars and planets are different. A star is a fire, it's gaseous. It lost all its mass and it's an eternal flame, burning, burning, burning. So, there must be a star lit in the believer. For this *insan* (human being) to work, the heart must be lit. He must be following these real *insan al kamil* (perfected being) whom dress them, bless them and lifted them up.

Take Your Testing and Remain Silent Like the Moon

Then they begin to teach your life has to be the outer *noon*, that you have to take a path in which to achieve *nur* and that *nur* can only be achieved like the moon. Take your beating, take your testing, take everything that they throw at you and remain silent and calm, patient and calm. Every difficulty in life, the moon is looking  at you. That's why when they want to make *du'a* (supplication), they can ask for the intercession of the moon. As soon as you see the moon, they say recite *Fatiha*. The moon is a *maqam* – not to the moon itself, the *maqam* (station) in it which it represents. The first reflection of that month, as soon as they see it, they recite Surat al-Fatiha that, *ya Rabbi*, grant me the intercession of that *maqam*.

Mountains Represent Awliya on This Earth

Everything here stands for something, *"Wal jibalan awtadun."*

وَالْجِبَالَ أَوْتَادًا ﴿٧﴾

78:7 – *"Wal jibala awtadan."* (Surat An-Naba)

"And Mountains like Pegs." (The Tidings, 78:7)

The mountains are representing the *awtads* (pegs) of this earth, the *awliya* (saints) that keep everything firm. *"Wa laqad karama bani Adam."* Allah ﷻ said, 'I gave the honour to the *Bani Adam*, not to the mountains.' The mountain merely represents there is an *awliya* in that area that's holding everything to be firm upon this earth and that's his station.

وَلَقَدْ كَرَّمْنَا بَنِي آدَمَ...﴿٧٠﴾

17:70 – *"Wa laqad karramna bani adama..."* (Surat Al-Isra)

"And We have certainly honored the children of Adam..." (The Night Journey, 17:70)

The Moon Represents the Spiritual Station of Maqam al-Fardani

Now think about the moon and the station of the moon – *maqam al-fardani*. So, then there's an *awliya* from *maqam al-fardani* that represents that reality. As soon as they witnessed the moon, they ask for its intercession, they ask for the *Fatiha* to be dressed by that reality. So, we took a path of being this *noon*.

Take a path of being the moon; you take, you take, you take every type of difficulty so that this *nur* (light) can begin to reflect upon you. As they're moving on this *noon*, this is *rashidin*. If they pass all of this testing, and this test is coming from *izzatullah*, *izzat ar-Rasul* and then dress from *izzatul-mumineen* is coming. This *izzat of mumineen*, they're *qamarun*. They can make moons. It means if you follow them, they teach you on how to take the difficulty, take the difficulty and have the best of character.

$$ \text{وَلِلَّهِ الْعِزَّةُ وَلِرَسُولِهِ وَلِلْمُؤْمِنِينَ... ﴿٨﴾} $$

63:8 – "…Wa Lillahil 'izzatu wa li Rasuli hi wa lil Mumineen…"
(Surat Al-Munafiqoon)

"…And to Allah belongs [all] honor, and to His messenger, and to the believers…" (The Hypocrites, 63:8)

Tariqah Teaches Not to Complain to Others About Anything

That's why in *tariqah* (spiritual path), you don't complain to anyone. You don't sit with another student and begin to complain to them. People's ears are not for your problems. Your problem is only for yourself, not even to complain to the shaykh because Allah ﷻ put you in that condition and Allah ﷻ won't relieve you from that condition until He finds what He wants of satisfaction.

$$ \text{...إِنَّ اللَّـهَ لَا يُغَيِّرُ مَا بِقَوْمٍ حَتَّىٰ يُغَيِّرُوا مَا بِأَنفُسِهِمْ ﴿١١﴾} $$

13:11 – "…Inna Allaha la yughayyiru ma bi qawmin hatta yughayyiro ma bi anfusihim…" (Surat Ar-Ra'd)

"Indeed Allah will not change the condition of a people until they change what is in themselves." (The Thunder, 13:11)

Can you imagine if every time you put your ear for somebody, every *shaitan* will come and begin to throw from your heart now every type of complaining? If you feel that you have an audience for complaining, the complaining never stops. You'll think now of everyone; I want to complain about him, I want to complain about him, I want to complain about him, I want to complain about everybody, I want to complain about the building. I want to complain about the landlord. I want to complain about everyone. So, *tariqah* (spiritual path) comes and says don't complain about anyone, don't talk!

The Souls of the Ahbab Are With Sayyidina Muhammad

Take every type of difficulty – they're going to make you into a moon. This has to be that *rashidin*, they have to be with somebody that is *kamilin* (perfected) and that everything they talk about is from where they are. So, if one of these beings, they're lost in the ocean of *Muhammadun RasulAllah*, their soul is swimming in the *qalb* (heart). They are *ahbab* (lovers) – you'll be with whom you love.

قَالَ رَسُولُ اللَّهِ صلى الله عليه و سلم: الْمَرْءُ مَعَ مَنْ أَحَبَّ

Qala RasulAllah (saws): "Almar o, ma'a man ahab."

Prophet Muhammad (pbuh) said: "One is with those whom he loves."

Not physically with Prophet, spiritually. Their soul is with the soul of Prophet, in the heart of Sayyidina Muhammad. Everything they talk about is the horizon of what they see. They don't talk from out there. So, when they're lost in the *ishq*, they're lost in the love, every *qalam*, every word, every *ruhaniyat* (spirituality) comes out is the love of Prophet. That's why *qalam al-awliya* (words of saints) are these *naats* (praisings); why were they singing these *naats*? Because they are lost in this love of what Allah ﷻ threw them in the ocean of *Muhammadun RasulAllah* ﷺ.

لَا إِلَهَ إِلاَّ اللهُ مُحَمَّدًا رَسُولُ الله

"La ilaha illAllahu Muhammadun RasulAllah."

"There is no deity but Allah, Prophet Muhammad is the messenger of Allah."

Hadith Uwais al-Qarani ؓ: Prophet Muhammad ﷺ is Insan al Kamil and Everything Exists in Him

If you're not following that and the scholar talks too much, he talks about everything else. But if his knowledge seems to be interesting for you, the test is that it must be *Muhammadiyun*, it must be the *ishq* and the love of Prophet ﷺ. If so, he's one of these *insan* reaching to be *kamil*? There is no one *kamil* (perfected) but Prophet ﷺ. *Insan al Kamil* is that everything exists within the reality of Prophet ﷺ and that was the *hadith* of Sayyidina Uwais al-Qarani ؓ and Imam 'Ali ؓ.

Uwais al-Qarani ؓ, who received the *jubbah* (robe) of Prophet ﷺ, asked the two *Sahabi* (Companions), 'Have you ever seen Sayyidina Muhammad ﷺ?' And Sayyidina 'Umar ؓ wanted to give it to him. He said, 'Do you know who we are? We spent all our life in every battle with him.' And Imam 'Ali ؓ said, 'I think he's asking us a different question.' And out of *adab* (manners), Imam 'Ali ؓ said, 'I saw him once ﷺ. That we were fixing the *khiswah* (cover) of the Ka'bah and I lifted Prophet ﷺ. As soon as I lifted, the whole universes appeared to me. That Prophet ﷺ vanished and all the galaxies and all of Allah's ﷻ creation existed within the being of Sayyidina Muhammad ﷺ. I saw and I looked, and I looked all the way up to the neck of Prophet ﷺ, above that *'Arsh-e-Rahman,'* and he stopped talking. And Sayyidina Uwais al-Qarani said, 'Yes, you have seen him.' It means they wanted to bring the *haqqaiq* (reality) of *insan al kamil* out. That everything is in *Muhammadun RasulAllah* ﷺ and Allah is *la ilaha illAllah* (there is no deity but Allah). By virtue of the *la ilaha illAllah*, means nothing is with it.

'"We went to that place and we saw in the distance a man sitting with his back to us. We approached. When we came near, without turning around, he said, 'O 'Ali, O 'Umar, give me my trust.' Immediately we handed him the robe of the Prophet ﷺ. He stood up, kissed the robe, put it on his head, then put it to his heart and said, 'I accept, I accept, I accept.'

'We wondered why he was kissing the robe and saying these words, because he had never seen the Prophet (s) in all his life. But we were hesitant to ask.'

'Then he turned to Sayyidina 'Umar and said to him, 'Ya 'Umar, how many times have you seen the Prophet ﷺ?' 'Umar was astonished at this question. He said, 'That is a strange question. I spent my whole life in the company of the Prophet.' Sayyidina Uwais said, 'I am asking for a reason. How many times did you actually see him?' Sayyidina 'Umar said, 'How do you mean? I was with him all the time!' Sayyidina Uwais al-Qarani said, 'Describe him to me.' Sayyidina 'Umar began to describe the Prophet, his eyes, his features, his appearance. Then Sayyidina Uwais said, 'Ya 'Umar, this description is known to everyone, including those who disbelieved in him.'

'Then he looked at me and said, 'Ya 'Ali, how many times did you see the Prophet ﷺ?' I knew what he meant, and I said, 'Ya Uwais, in my life I only saw the Prophet ﷺ one time.' Sayyidina 'Umar was looking at me in amazement. I said, "I saw him one time."' I said, "I saw him one time. The Prophet ﷺ called me and told me, 'Look at me from my navel and above.' I looked and I saw that the Prophet ﷺ from his navel up filled the universes and the Seven Heavens. From his neck and up, I was unable to see, but it was above the Sidratul Muntaha (Furthermost Limit). Then he told me, 'Look from my navel and down.' I looked and I saw all these universes, all these worlds, stars and planets had disappeared and all that I saw was the Prophet ﷺ from his waist to his knees filling up that entire space. And from his knees down to his feet I was unable to see. Then he ﷺ said, 'Look at all of me, from top to bottom.' I looked at him, and the Sidratul Muntaha and all these universes disappeared, and all I saw was Muhammad ﷺ, everywhere. At that time I knew that Muhammad ﷺ is the Heart of the Divine Presence (al-Haqqiqat al-Muhammadiyya)."

(Hadith of Sayyidina Uwais al-Qarani ؓ and Sayyidina 'Ali ؓ)

Everything is Created From the Light of Prophet Muhammad ﷺ

There is no partner with Allah ﷻ. Allah's ﷻ *Izzah* and Might is the power of *Muhammadun RasulAllah* ﷺ So, it means everything is existing within the soul of Prophet ﷺ. Everything from the light of Prophet ﷺ came into existence. And that's the *hadith al-Jabir* that he asked, what was the first thing created, Ya Sayyidi, Ya RasulAllah, he said, 'the light of your Prophet.'

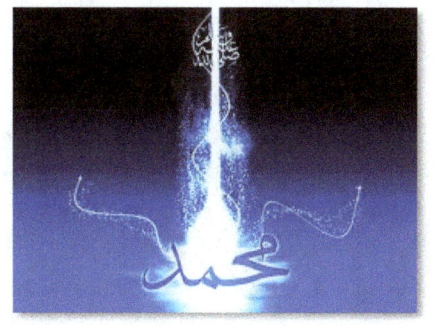

عَنْ جَابِرٍ ، قَالَ : قُلْتُ : يَا رَسُولَ اللَّهِ صَلَّى اللَّهُ عَلَيْهِ وَسَلَّمَ ، "بِأَبِي أَنْتَ وَأُمِّي ، أَخْبِرْنِي عَنْ أَوَّلَ شَيْءٍ خَلَقَهُ اللَّهُ قَبْلَ الْأَشْيَاءِ؟

قَالَ رَسُولَ اللَّهِ صَلَّى اللَّهُ عَلَيْهِ وَسَلَّمَ: يَا جَابِرُ ، إِنَّ اللَّهَ خَلَقَ قَبْلَ الْأَشْيَاءِ نُورَ نَبِيِّكَ مِنْ نُورِهِ ، فَجَعَلَ ذَلِكَ النُّورُ يَدُورُ بِالْقُدْرَةِ حَيْثُ شَاءَ اللَّهُ ، وَلَمْ يَكُنْ فِي ذَلِكَ الْوَقْتِ لَوْحٌ وَلَا قَلَمٌ، وَلَا جَنَّةٌ وَلَانَارٌ ، وَلَا مَلَكٌ، ولاسَمَاءٌ وَلَا أَرْضٌ، وَلَاشَمْسٌ وَلَا قَمَرٌ، وَلَاإِنْسٌ وَلَا جِنٌّ. فَلَمَّا أَرَادَ اللَّهُ تَعَالَى أَنْ يَخْلُقَ الْخَلْقَ قَسَّمَ ذَلِكَ النُّورَ أَرْبَعَةَ أَجْزَاءٍ:

Realities of Insan – Perfect Human – The Sun and the Moon

فَخَلَقَ مِنَ الْجُزْءِ الْأَوَّلِ الْقَلَمَ، وَمِنِ الثَّانِي اللَّوْحَ، وَمِنِ الثَّالِثِ الْعَرْشَ، ... (وَمِنِ الاربعة كُلَّ شِيءٍ.") [رِوَايَةِ عَبْدِ الرَّزَّاقِ فِي مُصَنَّفَةٍ]

'An Jabir (ra) Qala: Qultu: Ya RasulAllah (saws), "Bi Abi anta wa Ummi, Akhberni 'an awwala shayin Khalqahu Allahu qablal ashyayi?"

Qala Rasulullah (saws): "Ya Jabir, in Allah khalaqa qablal Ashiya e Nooru Nabiyika min Noorehi. Faj'ala dhalikan Noore yadoro bil Qudrati haithu sha Allahu, wa lam yakun fi dhalikal waqti lawhun wa la qalamun, wa la Jannatun wa la Narun, wa la Mulkun, wa la samaun wa la ardun, wa la Shamsun wa la Qamarun, wa la insun wa la jinnun. Falama arada Allahu ta'ala an yakhluqal Khalqi qasama dhalikan Nooru arba'a ajza: a: fakhalaqa minal juzil awwalu al Qalamu, wa minath thaniul Lawhu, wa minath thalithul 'Arshu, [minal Arba'ahu kuli shayin]"

Jabir ibn 'Abdallah (ra) said to the Prophet (pbuh): "O Messenger of Allah, may my father and mother be sacrificed for you, tell me of the first thing Allah created before all things."

He (Prophet Muhammad (pbuh)) said: "O Jabir, the first thing Allah created was the light of your Prophet from His (Allah's) light, and that light remained (lit / "turned") in the midst of His Power for as long as He wished, and at that time, there was no Tablet and no Pen, and no Paradise and no Fire, and no angel, and no heaven and no earth, and no Sun and no Moon, and No Human being and no jinn.

And when Allah wished to create creation, he divided that Light into four parts and from the first made the Pen, from the second the Tablet, from the third the Throne, [and from the fourth everything else].

Durood Sharif is Allah's ﷻ Zikr

This light of the messenger that there was no throne, there was no Ka'bah, there was no *Baitul Mamur*, there was no angel, without the light of *Muhammadun RasulAllah* ﷺ and Allah's ﷻ *Izzah* and Might and *Zikr* is the power of it. That's why *Allahumma Sali ala Sayyidina Muhammad wa ala Ali Sayyidina Muhammad*. Even the *salawat* on Prophet ﷺ is Allah's ﷻ *Zikr* and Might upon everything.

اللَّهُمَّ صَلِّ عَلَى سَيِّدِنَا مُحَمَّدٍ، وَعَلَى آلِ سَيِّدِنَا مُحَمَّدٍ وَ سَلِّمْ

"Allahumma salli 'ala Sayyidina Muhammadin wa 'ala aali Sayyidina Muhammadin wa Sallim."

"O Allah! Send Peace and blessings upon our master Prophet Muhammad (pbuh) and upon the Family of our master Prophet Muhammad (pbuh)."

Rashidin Take the Path of the Moon and Inherit Khuluq Azeem of Prophet ﷺ

So, it means then these people must be taking a path. If they're going to be *rashidin*, and rightly guided and give an *irshad* (guidance), Allah ﷻ going to take them on a path of the moon. They're going to be crushed and crushed and given *khuluqul azeem*, the best of character to inherit from Prophet ﷺ.

وَإِنَّكَ لَعَلَىٰ خُلُقٍ عَظِيمٍ ﴿٤﴾

68:4 – *"Wa innaka la'ala khuluqin 'azheem."* (Surat Al-Qalam)

Realities of Insan – Perfect Human – The Sun and the Moon

"Truly, You (O Muhammad!) are of a magnificent character."
(The Pen, 68:4)

"Adabanee Rabbi fa ahsana ta'deebee." Prophet's ﷺ only claim is that *"Adabanee Rabbi fa ahsana ta'deebee,"* that Allah ﷻ has given me the best of character, perfected my character and that's my only claim for my nation.

أَدَّبَنِي رَبِّي فَأَحْسَنَ تَأْدِيبِي

"Addabanee Rabbi fa ahsana ta'deebee."

"My Lord taught me good manners and He taught me in the most excellent way" (Prophet Muhammad (pbuh))

Seen: Sir (Secret) Inside Insan – Mahdiyeen are Dressed From Nurul Anwar Wa Sirratul Asrar

So, it means this is the stage of receiving this *noon*. Then these *mahdiyeen*, that same shaykh has to be dressed from *mahdiyeen* in which he has to dress the student from this *sir* (pointing towards the *seen*), from this secret. This secret that is the center of *insan* and that he has *nurul anwar wa sirratul asrar* (light of every secret and secret of every light) because the *malakut* (heavenly realm) is everything. The one whom has access to *malakut* is owner of the *mulk* (earthly realm). Power from the inside controls the outside. Your form has no power, you get a nail or a back pain or a cold you find how *dayeef* and how weak you are. But the one whom Allah ﷻ gives the power and command for *malakut*, means his power is within the atoms and the lights. From that power Allah ﷻ is dressing.

Seen is From Secret of YaSeen: Ilm ul-Yaqeen, Ayn ul-Yaqeen and Haqq ul-Yaqeen

So, this *sir* and the secret – the shaykh has to take the student towards that secret. That is the secret of YaSeen ﷺ. Every knowledge, every reality, *nurul anwar wa sirratul asrar*, the light of every secret and the secret of every light. That *seen* has to be from *ilm ul-yaqeen* (knowledge of certainty), *ayn ul-yaqeen* (vision of certainty), *haqq ul-yaqeen* (truth of certainty). The secret in which he is going to bestow upon the student are the heavenly knowledges. It cannot be found in books. At least not translated and especially not by *ummi shaykh* who doesn't speak Arabic. That's a *daleel* (proof) for you that he's not from reading because the *ummi shaykh* has no reading, he doesn't even understand the language. He's taught by one who is powerful. So, this *'seen'* – *ilm ul-yaqeen, ayn ul-yaqeen, haqq ul-yaqeen*.

So, their life is on their path. When people want to say should I go here, should I go there, should I go? I don't know wherever you want to go, go. Are you in training to be a moon? Are you taking a lot of testing in your life and are you being continuously fed *ilm ul-yaqeen, ayn ul-yaqeen, haqq ul-yaqeen*? These are the knowledges of certainty, not the knowledge that is in every single book or on a YouTube page unless it's a page from that reality.

1. Practice Tafakkur to Open Your Ayn ul-Yaqeen

Ayn ul-yaqeen; have you been in training with them to close your eyes and take a path of *tafakkur* (contemplation)? Close your eyes. Because this world is but an illusion and begin to train yourself on how to open your heart. How to contemplate and how to see the guides in the world of light. How to receive their connection in the world of light, where every *faiz* (downpouring) begin to dress upon you. The reality of their *tawajju* (focusing), the reality of their vision to be dressed upon you. Their reality of *tawassul* (conveyance) to be dressed upon you. If you can see them and feel them, everything you ask from them will be conveyed like a heavenly internet.

All of these realities have to be opened, but in *tafakkur* (contemplation). It's not by asking the shaykh continuously to his face that I want this, I want this, I want this. This is not of any value but to take a path in which you train to be nothing. Connect your heart. As soon as you connect your heart, you make a connection with them that send your *faiz* to me, the emanations, the *barakah* and the blessing that dresses everything and everywhere around them.

2. Establish Your Connection to Open Your Ilm ul-Yaqeen

As a result, then you're making your *tawajju* (focusing), that you're making a connection with their holy face. They see your face; you see their face and you can make your *tawassul* (conveyance). You can begin to ask that connection, that please I'm in need of this. When they pray, they pray with their connection, right? They close, they see whom they're seeing, and they begin to convey what's necessary to convey. Then, of course, Allah ﷻ open their *juzba* (attraction) and their realities and *haqqiqat al-irshad*.

3. Ilm ul-Yaqeen and Ayn ul-Yaqeen Becomes Haqq ul-Yaqeen

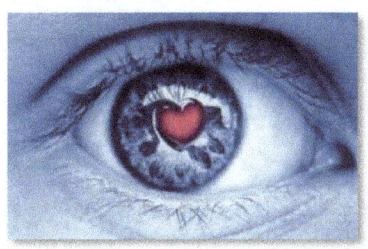

Allah ﷻ says, 'You are now dressed from the reality of guidance; We've given you *ilm ul-yaqeen*. We gave you *ayn ul-yaqeen*.' Everything of your knowledge and your vision, it became a *haq* and a truth for you because you saw it. You saw it with the eyes of your heart. You cannot deny it later, they saw what Allah ﷻ wanted them to see.

كَلَّا لَوْ تَعْلَمُونَ عِلْمَ الْيَقِينِ ﴿٥﴾

102:5 – *"Kal la law t'alamoona 'ilmal yaqeen."* (Surat At-Takathur)

"No! If you only knew with knowledge of certainty."
(The Rivalry in World Increase, 102:5)

ثُمَّ لَتَرَوُنَّهَا عَيْنَ الْيَقِينِ ﴿٧﴾

102:7 – *"Thum ma la tara wun naha 'aynal yaqeen."*
(Surat At-Takathur)

"Then you will surely see it with the eye/vision of certainty."
(The Rivalry in World Increase, 102:7)

إِنَّ هَذَا لَهُوَ حَقُّ الْيَقِينِ ﴿٩٥﴾

56:95 – *"Inna hadha la huwa haqqul yaqeen."* (Surat Al-Waqi'ah)

"Indeed, this is the true certainty." (The Inevitable, 56:95)

Realities of Insan – Perfect Human – The Sun and the Moon

This means when they speak of a *haqqaiq*, it's real and true for them. You're not allowed to speak somebody's *haqqaiq* (reality) and speak about it. It's not true for you. So, you're actually a liar when you're talking to people. The way of *haqqaiq* is so truthful that Allah ﷻ says, 'Are you trained in this knowledge?' Yes. 'Did you close your eyes to witness that knowledge?' They say yes. Now that you witnessed it, it's a *haq* (truth) for you. This means now you are understanding this *sir* (secret) and this *seen* that you've been dressed with.

Second Noon of Insan is Diya (Divinely Fire)

As a result, Allah ﷻ brings them to that reality (pointing to the second *noon* from the left); that reality of the *diya* (fire), the *diya* what Nabi Musa ؑ said, he saw a fire in a distance and he told his wife, 'I'm going to go to the fire.' She said, 'why do you want to go to the fire for?' 'To get some warmth or maybe some guidance.' Warmth and guidance – big difference.

فَلَمَّا قَضَىٰ مُوسَى الْأَجَلَ وَسَارَ بِأَهْلِهِ آنَسَ مِن جَانِبِ الطُّورِ نَارًا قَالَ لِأَهْلِهِ امْكُثُوا إِنِّي آنَسْتُ نَارًا لَّعَلِّي آتِيكُم مِّنْهَا بِخَبَرٍ أَوْ جَذْوَةٍ مِّنَ النَّارِ لَعَلَّكُمْ تَصْطَلُونَ ﴿٢٩﴾

28:29 – "*Falammmaa qadaa Moosal ajala wa saara bi ahliheee aanasa min jaanibit Toori naaran qaala li ahlihim kusooo ineee aanastu naaral la 'alleee aateekum minhaa bikhabarin aw jazwatim minan naari la 'allakum tastaloon*" (Surat Al-Qasas)

"And when Moses had completed the term and was traveling with his family, he perceived from the direction of the mount a fire. He said to his family, 'Stay here; indeed, I have perceived a fire. Perhaps I will bring you from there [some]

news/information or burning wood from the fire that you may warm yourselves.'" (The Stories, 28:29)

Like Nabi Musa ﷺ, Our Hearts Must Be Lit to Seek Heavenly Realities

Allah ﷻ appears to the servant in the condition that you're in. Allah's ﷻ not a fire but He'll make you cold so that you can seek out that reality.

When you seek out that reality, it means that the fire has to be lit within the heart of the student. They were trained to be a moon, trained to be a moon. They had a discipline; they never left their discipline. They kept their way, kept their way, until Allah ﷻ says, now we're going to light your heart. And your heart is going to become like a sun on earth. As soon as that heart is lit, their heart is lit like a fire. They're an eternal fire. They carry the reality of this sun, greater than that sun they carried onto earth.

Awliya Hearts Are the Sun and Their Faces Are the Moon

As a result of Allah ﷻ lighting their heart like a *shams* (sun), they are able to consume the badness because every sun has a fuel source. It burns the badness of people and in exchange gives back out *nur* (light). So, the *insan* (human being) whom is open and is *kamil* (perfected) or on a path of being *kamil*, not that anyone is perfect. Prophet ﷺ is perfect. But on the path of that reality, Allah ﷻ begin to make their face a *qamar*, a moon. Their heart been lit because *baytullah*.

قَلْبَ الْمُؤْمِنْ بَيْتُ الرَّبْ

"Qalb al mu'min baytur rabb."

"The heart of the believer is the House of the Lord." (Hadith Qudsi)

Realities of Insan – Perfect Human – The Sun and the Moon

When Allah ﷻ lights the heart with that light like a fire, their heart like a sun, they heat up. As a result of the sun, they take the burdens and the  badness of people as a fuel for their sun. Their sun burns the fuel and as a result gives out *nur* (light) back to people. And that becomes the reality of what *insan*, what Allah ﷻ, *"Wa la qad karramna bani Adam."*

وَلَقَدْ كَرَّمْنَا بَنِي آدَمَ وَحَمَلْنَاهُمْ فِي الْبَرِّ وَالْبَحْرِ وَرَزَقْنَاهُم مِّنَ الطَّيِّبَاتِ وَفَضَّلْنَاهُمْ عَلَىٰ كَثِيرٍ مِّمَّنْ خَلَقْنَا تَفْضِيلًا ﴿٧٠﴾

17:70 – *"Wa laqad karramna banee adama, wa hamalna hum filbarri wal bahri wa razaqnahum minat tayyibati wa faddalnahum 'ala katheerin mimman khalaqna tafdeela. (Surat Al-Isra)*

"And We have certainly honored the children of Adam and carried them on the land and sea and provided good and pure sustenance and bestow upon them favours, and preferred them over much of what We have created, with [definite] preference." (The Night Journey, 17:70)

It's what he wanted for *insan* (human being), the nobility of *insan* is to be of service to the Divine. This means to take a path in which to reach towards these realities.

Subhana rabbika rabbal 'izzati 'amma yasifoon, wa salaamun 'alal mursaleen, walhamdulillahi rabbil 'aalameen. Bi hurmati Muhammad al-Mustafa wa bi siri Surat al-Fatiha.

The Holy Chest

ALLAH WANTED TO BE KNOWN, HE CREATED NUR MUHAMMAD (MISBAH)

Mi'raj (Ascension) of Sayyidina Muhammad Was to La Ilaha IllAllah

For hearts to understand where we came from and know where we're going. We said many times, and repeat for myself to get a better understanding, always for myself. That *la ilaha illAllah* (There is no diety but Allah) means don't look here. There's no *sharik*, no partner with Allah . That we are from the ocean of *Muhammadun RasulAllah* . That in *Muhammadun RasulAllah* , the *mi'raj* (ascension) of Sayyidina Muhammad was to the reality of *la ilaha illAllah*.

*Allah 🕮 Wanted to Be Known,
He Created Nur Muhammad ﷺ (Misbah)*

لَا إِلَهَ إِلَّا اللهُ مُحَمَّدًا رَسُولُ الله

"La ilaha illAllahu Muhammadun RasulAllah."

"There is no diety but Allah, Prophet Muhammad ﷺ is the messenger of Allah."

Allah 🕮 Described This Creation is in a Misbah (Lamp)

The Parable of His Light Is as if there were a Niche and within it a Lamp; the Lamp enclosed in Glass: the glass as it were a brilliant star

When Allah 🕮 wants to disclose his reality to His Beloved creation. So, we said before, this *misbah*, Allah 🕮 describes in Surat an-Nur, that this creation is in a *misbah*, in a candle holder. And Allah 🕮 is a force and power outside of creation. Allah 🕮 is not inside creation. Allah 🕮 is outside of creation. *La ilaha illAllah* is outside.

اللَّهُ نُورُ السَّمَاوَاتِ وَالْأَرْضِ ۚ مَثَلُ نُورِهِ كَمِشْكَاةٍ فِيهَا مِصْبَاحٌ ۖ الْمِصْبَاحُ فِي زُجَاجَةٍ ۖ الزُّجَاجَةُ كَأَنَّهَا كَوْكَبٌ دُرِّيٌّ ... يَكَادُ زَيْتُهَا يُضِيءُ وَلَوْ لَمْ تَمْسَسْهُ نَارٌ ۚ نُورٌ عَلَىٰ نُورٍ ... ﴿٣٥﴾

24:35 – *"Allahu noorus samawati wal ardi. mathalu noorehi kamishkatin feeha misbahun, almisbahu fee zujajatin, azzujajatu kaannaha kawkabun durriyyun ... yakadu zaytuha yudeeo wa law lam tamsashu naarun. noorun 'ala noorin..." (Surat An-Nur)*

"Allah is the Light of the heavens and the earth. The Parable of His Light is as if there were a Niche and within it a Lamp: the Lamp enclosed in Glass: the glass as it were a brilliant star: ... though fire scarce touched it: Light upon Light!..." (The Light, 24:35)

When Allah 🕮 wanted to be known, He made creation. The whole ocean of creation is called *Muhammadun RasulAllah* ﷺ, *Nurul Muhammad* ﷺ, *nurul anwar wa sirratal asrar* – the light of every secret and the secret of every light. When we understand where we came from, because *arifeen* (knowers), why Allah ﷻ calls them *arifeen*? Because Allah ﷻ showed them. They're not blind people on this Earth. Allah ﷻ took, opened their heart, and showed them their reality. That you're not from Me. You're nowhere close to any of that reality. Your reality and your *arwah* (soul) is with *Abu Arwah*, the father of souls, Sayyidina Muhammad ﷺ. If you don't know, don't worry. Be patient, Allah ﷻ will one day disclose to you.

That, that reality of my light, it cannot be *sharik* with Allah ﷻ. My light doesn't go back to be one with Allah ﷻ. We don't have *Wahdatul Wujud* (Oneness in Existence), *Wahdatul Shuhood* (Oneness in Witnessing) and Allah ﷻ will let you to see His realities, but you never become one with Allah ﷻ , *astaghfirullah*! That our light is from Muhammadun RasulAllah ﷺ.

Sadiqeen's Mi'raj is to the Reality of Sayyidina Muhammad ﷺ

This means when we know where we came, very easy to go for our *mi'raj*. That if you're sitting and waiting for a *mi'raj* to Allah ﷻ, you wait ten thousand years and that won't come. That's why those who don't understand, they wait, nothing comes. *Arifeen* (knowers), why Allah ﷻ says, *"Ittaqollaha wa kono ma'as sadiqeen?"*

يَا أَيُّهَا الَّذِينَ آمَنُوا اتَّقُوا اللَّهَ وَكُونُوا مَعَ الصَّادِقِينَ ﴿١١٩﴾

9:119 – "Ya ayyuhal ladheena amanoo ittaqollaha wa kono ma'as sadiqeen." (Surat At-Tawbah)

"O you who have believed, have consciousness of Allah and be with those who are truthful/ Pious / sincere (in words and deed)." (The Repentance, 9:119)

*Allah Wanted to Be Known,
He Created Nur Muhammad (Misbah)*

That they had consciousness and accompanied the *sadiq* (truthful). Those whom their character, their action in their deed is truthful. Because Allah opened for them, Allah brought them back onto Earth, said you don't have to die, you're *mawt qablil mawt* (death of desires before physical death). You reached what we wanted you to reach of these oceans of light. We sent you back to humanity – guide them, teach them. That when you realize that our *mi'raj* is to the reality of Sayyidina Muhammad .

If you're from this light, your *mi'raj* is not out here (outside of the lamp) to find Allah . Because Allah said *"Qalb al mu'min baytullah."* Where are you looking? 'Not in heaven, not on earth, but I'm in the heart of my believer, Allah's only believer, real belief, is Sayyidina Muhammad .

قَلْبَ الْمُؤْمِنْ بَيْتُ الرَّبّ

"Qalb al mu'min baytur rabb."

"The heart of the believer is the House of the Lord." Hadith Qudsi

مَا وَسِعَنِيْ لَا سَمَائِيْ ولا أَرْضِيْ وَلَكِنْ وَسِعَنِيْ قَلْبِ عَبْدِيْ ٱلْمُؤْمِنْ

"Maa wasi'anee laa Samayee, wa la ardee, laakin wasi'anee qalbi 'Abdee al Mu'min."

"Neither My Heavens nor My Earth can contain Me, but the heart of my Believing Servant."
(Hadith Qudsi conveyed by Prophet Muhammad (pbuh))

Our Iman is to Love Sayyidina Muhammad ﷺ More Than Anyone

So, then Prophet ﷺ, all these *ahadith* and Qur'an where Prophet ﷺ is teaching, you be with whom you love.

قَالَ رَسُولُ اللَّهِ صلى الله عليه و سلم: الْمَرْءُ مَعَ مَنْ أَحَبَّ

Qala Rasulullah (saws): "Almar o, ma'a man ahab."

Prophet Muhammad (pbuh) said: "One is with those whom he loves."

And if you love me, you have *iman* (faith). If you love me more than yourself, more than your father, and your brother, and your children, and your mother. Love me more than you love all of those. You're from the people of *iman* (faith). So, it means that you be with whom you love.

لاَ يُؤْمِنُ أَحَدُكُمْ حَتَّى أَكُونَ أَحَبَّ إِلَيْهِ مِنْ وَالِدِهِ وَوَلَدِهِ وَالنَّاسِ أَجْمَعِينَ

"La yuminu ahadukum hatta akona ahabba ilayhi min walidihi wa waladihi wan Nasi ajma'yeen."

"None of you will have faith till he loves me more than his father, his children and all mankind." (Prophet Muhammad (pbuh))

*Allah Wanted to Be Known,
He Created Nur Muhammad (Misbah)*

Look Within, Purify Your Heart and Make it the House of Allah

So, Prophet was teaching us, you don't have to look out. You actually have to look in. What are you looking on the out for? What, what is out there? House with stones? Allah is not in there. Allah say, 'I gave you the greatest gift I can give, *Qalb al mu'min baytullah*. I gave you My house. If you clean it, you wash it, and you purify it.'

...أَن طَهِّرَا بَيْتِيَ لِلطَّائِفِينَ وَالْعَاكِفِينَ وَالرُّكَّعِ السُّجُودِ ﴿١٢٥﴾

2:125 – "...*An Tahhir baytee liTayifeena, wal 'Aakifeena, wa ruka'is sujood.*" (Surat Al-Baqarah)

"...*Purify/Sanctify My House for those who perform Tawaf (circumambulation) and those who seclude themselves for devotion and bow and prostrate [in prayer]*." (The Cow, 2;125)

So, every house, every heart is a house of Allah. And what Allah wants from this *Isra wal Mi'raj* is make your house the *haramain*, make your house where there is no *haram* (forbidden). When you cut the *haram* and cut what's incorrect, Allah will make His house upon your heart.

So, they teach very simple. The *mi'raj* is very powerful. But *awliyaullah*

(saints), they understood that our *mi'raj* is to our reality. I'm not looking out. I'm trying to go into what is this *nurul anwar*? What is this *sirratal asrar*? Why did Prophet call all his companions a star? 'That all of them became stars, I am the star maker.' Come back into that light and realize the secret of that light.

أَصْحَابِيْ كَالنُّجُومْ بِأَيِّهِمْ اَقْتَدَيْتُمْ اَهْتَدَيْتُمْ

"Ashabi kan Nujoom, bi ayyihim aqta daytum ahta daytum."

"My companions are like stars. Follow any one of them and you will be guided." (Prophet Muhammad (pbuh))

Awliya's Miraj is to the Soul of Prophet Muhammad ﷺ

When these *awliyaullah* (saints), their *mi'raj* and their movement was with their soul and their body to fall in love with Prophet ﷺ, it became a Divinely Companionship. That they made their body and their soul to accompany Sayyidina Muhammad ﷺ by following the *sunnah*, the way,

and the *muhabbat*, the character, the *akhlaq* of Sayyidina Muhammad ﷺ. Where Allah ﷻ says, *Qul inni kuntum tuhibbon Allaha fattabi'oni, wa yuhbibkumullahu?* They followed that way; they followed the order of Allah ﷻ. As a result, they became dressed – you will be with whom you love – they became dressed with *Nurul Muhammadi* ﷺ.

قُلْ إِنْ كُنْتُمْ تُحِبُّونَ اللَّهَ فَاتَّبِعُونِيْ يُحْبِبْكُمُ اللَّهُ وَيَغْفِرْ لَكُمْ ذُنُوْبَكُمْ ۗ وَاللَّهُ غَفُورٌ رَحِيمٌ ﴿٣١﴾

3:31 – "*Qul in kuntum tuhibbon Allaha fattabi'oni, yuhbibkumullahu wa yaghfir lakum dhunobakum wallahu Ghaforur Raheem.*" (Surat Ali-Imran)

"Say, [O Muhammad], "If you should love Allah, then follow me, [so] Allah will love you and forgive you your sins. And Allah is Forgiving and Merciful." (Family of Imran, 3:31)

Allah ﷻ Wanted to Be Known,
He Created Nur Muhammad ﷺ (Misbah)

Nurul Iman – When Your Light Loves Prophet ﷺ More Than You

Then Allah ﷻ described, *Feekum*, that Prophet ﷺ is amongst you. Many different deep realities in that. But if you draw so near to Prophet ﷺ with all your love and all your *ishq*, and that light begins to graft upon you, that *Nurul Muhammadi* ﷺ begins to overtake all your light.

كَمَا أَرْسَلْنَا فِيكُمْ رَسُولًا مِّنكُمْ يَتْلُو عَلَيْكُمْ آيَاتِنَا وَيُزَكِّيكُمْ وَيُعَلِّمُكُمُ الْكِتَابَ وَالْحِكْمَةَ وَيُعَلِّمُكُم مَّا لَمْ تَكُونُوا تَعْلَمُونَ ﴿١٥١﴾

2:151 – *"Kama arsalna feekum Rasulan minkum yatlo 'Alaykum ayatina wa yuzakkeekum wa yu'Allimukumul kitaba walhikmata wa yu'Allimukum ma lam takono ta'Alamon."* (Surat Al-Baqarah)

"Just as We have sent among (within) you a messenger of your own, reciting to you Our Signs, and purifying you, and teaching you the Book/Scripture (Quran) and Wisdom, and teaching you New Knowledge, that which you did not know." (The Cow, 2:151)

Because *iman* (faith) is not body. *Iman* is *nur* (light). *Islam* is your body. *Maqamul Iman* (station of Faith) has nothing to do with your body. *Maqamul Iman* has to do with *nur*, it's *nurul iman* (light of faith). It means when your light loves Prophet ﷺ more than it loves you. You surrender your light and your *wujud* (existence), '*Ya Rabbi*, I'm nothing, I'm nothing. I'm tired of loving myself, and I love myself, and it got nowhere.' Love that which is eternal.

Love of Prophet ﷺ Turns Our Temporary Candle into an Eternal Sun

So, when the candle moves towards the sun, it reaches eternity. Everybody's life on this earth is a temporary candle. Don't think you made it just because you're born. The light of your candle is still temporary. It didn't reach its eternal reality. It didn't become *daim* (eternal). Allah ﷻ gave us all a life; don't waste it. This candle is about to burn out. If it goes, it's finished.

So, they (saints) use this *dunya* (material world) to reach their *daim*, to reach their eternal reality. When they fell in love and move towards the love, the love of Prophet ﷺ overtook their light. Say I'm going to make your temporary light to be a permanent light, and that is the reality of the intercession of Sayyidina Muhammad ﷺ.

Feekum – Prophet ﷺ is Amongst Us Through Awliyaullah (Saints)

When Prophet ﷺ intercedes, it's not by *lisan* (tongue), and it's not by *badan* (physicality), but it's by the light of Prophet ﷺ. When Prophet ﷺ intercedes for your light, it means his light will move into your light, overtake your light, and become *Nurul Muhammadi* ﷺ. These *awliyaullah* (saints), they're dressed by the light of Prophet ﷺ. Wherever they go, it's *Nurul Muhammad* ﷺ spreading.

*Allah Wanted to Be Known,
He Created Nur Muhammad (Misbah)*

And that's why Allah describes, *Feekum*, they're amongst you (Holy Qur'an, 2:151). 124,000 *awliyaullah* are always on this earth and they are the light of Prophet . They are the reflections of those light. They are the walking realities of those light. Holy Qur'an is reflecting through their soul. Holy *hadith* reflecting through their soul.

Our Miraj is to the Presence of Prophet Through Awliyaullah – Find One of 124,000 Saints

If the *mi'raj* is to the presence of Sayyidina Muhammad , then our life is to find one of these 124,000 *awliyaullah* (saints). It's enough for you just to sit with them, eat with them, pray with them. As soon as you sit in their association or you look at them, the light that's reflecting from Prophet begin to reflect upon the people.

Light! When that light begins to hit upon your light, and this is from the *hadith* that you'll be with whom you love. It creates that love and that energy and it pulls your light back to their reality. Their reality pulls to the shaykh, to the shaykh, to the shaykh, all the way to presence of Sayyidina Muhammad . This means they're in a continuous *mi'raj*.

قَالَ رَسُولُ اللَّهِ صلى الله عليه و سلم: الْمَرْءُ مَعَ مَنْ أَحَبَّ

Qala RasulAllah (saws): "Almar o, ma'a man ahab."

Prophet Muhammad (pbuh) said: "One is with those whom he loves."

These holidays (*Lailatul Isra wal Miraj* – Night of Ascension), are for the nation to stop one day and recognize what they're doing. But the *mi'raj* of the believer is at every moment. Every *salah* (prayer) is a *mi'raj*. Every *zikr* (remembrance) is a *mi'raj*. Every association is a *mi'raj* because their soul immediately goes back into the presence of Sayyidina

Muhammad ﷺ. And the fastest way is by praising upon Prophet Muhammad ﷺ. As soon as you praise upon whom Allah (swt) loves, praise upon Sayyidina Muhammad ﷺ, upon *Ahlul Bayt (as)*, upon *Ashab an Nabi* ﷺ. Give the story and the *qisa* of *awliyaullah fis Samyi wa fil Ardi* (saints in the heavens and on earth).

Ashiqeen Are in a Continuous Mi'raj to the Presence of Sayyidina Muhammad ﷺ

Your soul immediately moves to be present with them and is in a continuous *mi'raj* at all moments as it's ascending into the heavens. So, it means that every moment is a *mi'raj*, not once a year. Once a year because the nation, 99% of the nation, is so busy that Prophet ﷺ said, 'At least one day stop and remember what I accomplished.' Just by you stopping and doing that day, Prophet ﷺ will dress you from the realities.

But for those whom are seeking the reality, every moment of their life is a *mi'raj*. Every moment of their life, Prophet ﷺ is continuously

ascending to *"qaba qawsayni aw adna"* (two bows or nearer, Holy Qur'an, 53:9) which means that wherever Allah's (swt) creation is expanding, Prophet ﷺ is right there. As much as Allah (swt) expands the universe, as much as *Nurul Muhammadi* ﷺ is moving. So, it means that Prophet ﷺ is continuously in expansion and movement. And those whom are *ashiqeen* (lovers), their souls are continuously moving in

*Allah Wanted to Be Known,
He Created Nur Muhammad (Misbah)*

---

that reality. Just by coming to the associations of love, immediately they dress and bless all the souls.

فَكَانَ قَابَ قَوْسَيْنِ أَوْ أَدْنَىٰ ﴿٩﴾

53:9 – *"Fakana qaaba qawsayni aw adna."* (Surat An-Najm)

"And was at a distance of two bow lengths or nearer [to the Divine Presence]." (The Star, 53:9)

Real Taqwa (Consciousness) is to Use Your Senses for Allah

So, the *mi'raj* is not something difficult to achieve. That's why Allah, be conscious, *ittaqullah*. Use all of your *taqwa*, consciousness.

يَا أَيُّهَا الَّذِينَ آمَنُوا اتَّقُوا اللَّهَ وَكُونُوا مَعَ الصَّادِقِينَ ﴿١١٩﴾

9:119 – *"Ya ayyuhal ladheena amanoo ittaqollaha wa kono ma'as sadiqeen."*
(Surat At-Tawbah)

"O you who have believed, have consciousness of Allah and be with those who are truthful/ Pious / sincere (in words and deed)."
(The Repentance, 9:119)

You sit with them, but you don't see them. You hear them, but you don't hear them. You know them, but you don't know them. So, you didn't reach *taqwa*. Had you reached *taqwa* (consciousness), you would've heard something different when you sat with them. And you would've seen many astonishing things, had you really seen them.

It means that these senses are not being used the way Allah wants. *Taqwa* means that these senses are all being used for Allah. They're not being used for the deceit of *dunya* (material world), 'Oh, I have eyes

Shaykh, I see.' No, you see MTV, you see YouTube, not see them. Because the real sight is in the heart.

Allah ﷻ Dresses Sayyidina Muhammad and He ﷺ Dresses Awliya With Lights

You hear, but you don't really hear. It means you didn't open the hearing of the heart in which it hears realities. As the Shaykh is speaking, the heart can hear many realities from the heavens. This means when all those senses are opening, then Allah ﷻ says, now you understand, why, who are the *sadiqeen*. When you accompany the *sadiq*, they dress you from all the lights that Allah ﷻ has dressed upon them. From *Ati ullah ati ar Rasul wa ulil amri minkum*, that whatever Allah ﷻ dressed upon Prophet ﷺ, Prophet ﷺ dressed upon his *awliyaullah* (saints).

...أَطِيعُوا اللَّهَ وَأَطِيعُوا الرَّسُولَ وَأُولِي الْأَمْرِ مِنكُمْ... ﴿٥٩﴾

4:59 – "...*Atiullaha wa atiur Rasula wa Ulil amre minkum...*" (Surat An-Nisa)

"... Obey Allah, Obey the Messenger, and those in authority among you..." (The Women, 4:59)

Awliyaullah Are the Qamarun (Moons) and the Face of this Nation

Awliyaullah and those whom love Prophet ﷺ, they are the face of this nation and they're *qamarun*. As soon as you look at their face, their *nazar*

*Allah ﷻ Wanted to Be Known,
He Created Nur Muhammad ﷺ (Misbah)*

(gaze), and that's why Allah ﷻ says, 'Everything perishes, but the Holy Face.'

وَلَا تَدْعُ مَعَ اللَّـهِ إِلَـٰهًا آخَرَ ۘ لَا إِلَـٰهَ إِلَّا هُوَ ۚ كُلُّ شَيْءٍ هَالِكٌ إِلَّا وَجْهَهُ ۚ لَهُ الْحُكْمُ وَإِلَيْهِ تُرْجَعُونَ ﴿٨٨﴾

28:88 – *"Wala tad'uo ma'Allahi ilahan aakhara la ilaha illa huwa kullu shayin halikun illa wajha hu la hul hukmu wa ilayhi turja'oon." (Surat Al-Qasas)*

"…Everything (that exists) will perish except His holy Face. To Him belongs the Command, and to Him you will be returned." (The Stories, 28:88)

This means don't distract your life with everything else in life. Find one of these 124,000. It's enough for you to look at their face. Their face has enough power through their two ears, their two eyes, their nostril, and their tongue to grab your soul and bring you into the presence. From *Ati ullah ati ar Rasul wa ulil amri minkum* (Holy Qur'an, 4:59). This *ulul amr*, they're the face of the nation, *qamarun* (moons).

Awliya's Face is a Door to the Room of Reality

By looking at them, their *nazar* (gaze), that Allah ﷻ gave for 7 *sifats*, 7 essences to dress them, dresses their holy openings. As a result, when they look at you, they pull your soul into that reality. So, for us to understand is as if they pull you into the reality. The reality is like a room, their face is like the door. How can you get into the room if you don't go through the door? You can't break through a window. So, Allah ﷻ said, 'Enter the house through the correct door.'

...وَلَيْسَ الْبِرُّ بِأَن تَأْتُوا الْبُيُوتَ مِن ظُهُورِهَا وَلَٰكِنَّ الْبِرَّ مَنِ اتَّقَىٰ ۗ وَأْتُوا الْبُيُوتَ مِنْ أَبْوَابِهَا ۚ وَاتَّقُوا اللَّـهَ لَعَلَّكُمْ تُفْلِحُونَ ﴿١٨٩﴾

2:189 – "...Wa laysal birru bi-an tatol buyoota min zuhooriha wa lakinnal birra manit taqa, wa' tol buyoota min abwabiha, wat taqollaha la'allakum tuflihoon." (Surat Al-Baqarah)

"...And it is not righteousness to enter houses from the back, but righteousness is [in] one who fears Allah. And enter houses from their doors. And be Conscious of Allah that you may succeed."
(The Cow, 2:189)

Don't Say Shaykh Listen to Me, But Ask For His Nazar

This means go to my 124,000 faces. If you're under their *nazar* (gaze), that's why you don't say, 'Listen to me, Shaykh, listen to me.' As in Allah ﷻ corrected the nation, 'Don't tell Prophet ﷺ to listen to you.' He's *"samina wa atana"* (we hear and we obey, Holy Qur'an, 24:51). This is the nation of, we hear and we obey. We never tell Prophet ﷺ to listen to us, but *unzur halana wa ishfalana* (Holy Qur'an, 2:104). That put your holy *nazar* upon me, *Ya Sayiddi, Ya Rasul Kareem, Ya Habibul Azeem*; if your *nazar* comes upon me, immediately you'll be taking me into the Divinely Presence because the *nazar* has power. It's not empty. It's filled with power.

إِنَّمَا كَانَ قَوْلَ الْمُؤْمِنِينَ إِذَا دُعُوا إِلَى اللَّـهِ وَرَسُولِهِ لِيَحْكُمَ بَيْنَهُمْ أَن يَقُولُوا سَمِعْنَا وَأَطَعْنَا ۚ وَأُولَٰئِكَ هُمُ الْمُفْلِحُونَ ﴿٥١﴾

24:51 – "Innama kana qawlal mumineena idha du'ao ilAllahi wa Rasulihi liyahkuma baynahum an yaqolo samina wa atana, wa olaika humul muflihoon." (Surat An-Nur)

"The only statement of the [true] believers when they are called to Allah and His Messenger to judge between them is that they say, "We hear and we obey." And those are the successful." (The Light, 24:51)

Allah Wanted to Be Known, He Created Nur Muhammad (Misbah)

and

يَا أَيُّهَا الَّذِينَ آمَنُوا لَا تَقُولُوا رَاعِنَا وَقُولُوا انظُرْنَا وَاسْمَعُوا ... ﴿١٠٤﴾

2:104 – *"Yaa ayyuhal ladheena aamano, laa taqolo ra'yina wa qolu unzurna wasma'o…" (Surat Al-Baqarah)*

"O you who believe! Do not say (to Prophet Muhammad (pbuh)) Raina, listen to us, and say Unzurna (gaze upon us) and you listen (to him (pbuh))…" (The Cow, 2:104)

Holy Faces of Awliyaullah Bring You to Their Heart, Their Room of Reality

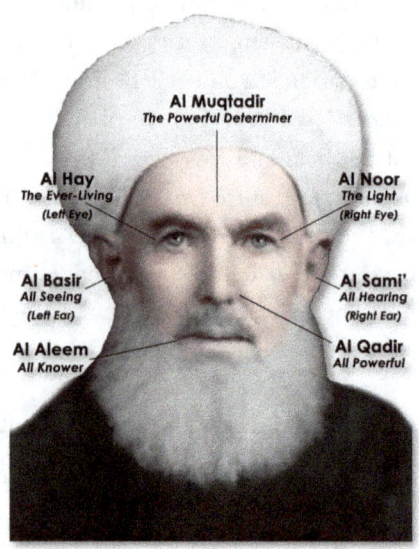

These 7 essences that dress the one (right ear), two (left ear), three (right eye), four (left eye), five (right nostril), six (left nostril), seven (mouth), *lisanul haq*. That face grabs your soul, brings you into the presence. If you cannot reach the face of Prophet ﷺ, then the *ulul amr* (saints) – they are the faces of the nation. They're *qamarun*. They're shining moons that reflect the reality of Prophet ﷺ. So, when you look at them, they are like a door, immediately bring your soul into their heart, into their room.

Who's in their room? What Allah ﷻ described of the house of Allah ﷻ? *Nabiyeen, Siddiqeen, Shuhadahi wa Saliheen.*

وَمَن يُطِعِ اللَّهَ وَالرَّسُولَ فَأُولَٰئِكَ مَعَ الَّذِينَ أَنْعَمَ اللَّهُ عَلَيْهِم مِّنَ النَّبِيِّينَ وَالصِّدِّيقِينَ وَالشُّهَدَاءِ وَالصَّالِحِينَ ۚ وَحَسُنَ أُولَٰئِكَ رَفِيقًا ﴿٦٩﴾

4:69 – *"Wa man yuti' Allaha war Rasula faolayeka ma'al ladheena an'ama Allahu 'alayhim minan Nabiyeena, was Siddiqeena, wash Shuhadai, was Saliheena wa hasuna olayeka rafeeqan."*
(Surat An-Nisa)

"And whoever obeys Allah and the Messenger (pbuh) are in the company of those on whom Allah has bestowed His Favours/Blessings – of the prophets, the sincere Truthful, the witnesses (who testify), and the Righteous, and excellent are those as companions." (The Women, 4:69)

And with Allah ﷻ because we said, *Qalb al mu'min baytullah.* So, their house became *baytullah,* and who's in their house? *Nabiyeen, Siddiqeen, Shuhadayi wa Saliheen.* And Allah ﷻ says this is the best of company, if you keep that. Their face brings you into their heart. That's why your interaction with them, if you gain a sense of love and respect and  character, it's enough for their *nazar* to be upon you and bring you into their heart.

Allah ﷻ Wanted to Be Known, He Created Nur Muhammad ﷺ (Misbah)

$$\text{قَلْبَ الْمُؤْمِنْ بَيْتُ الرَّبْ}$$

"Qalb al mu'min baytur rabb."

"The heart of the believer is the House of the Lord." (Hadith Qudsi)

The Presence and Nurul Muhammadi ﷺ is in the Hearts of Awliyaullah

From in their heart, the face, it takes you into the presence. Because who is in the presence of their heart? It's Sayyidina Muhmmad ﷺ. That *Nurul Muhammad* ﷺ is in their heart; the presence of Prophet ﷺ is inside their heart. As soon as you look and they look at you, they bring your light and your *ishq* into their heart, and they present you to the presence of Sayyidina Muhammad ﷺ.

Prophet Muhammad ﷺ Takes You to the Divinely Essence in His Holy Heart

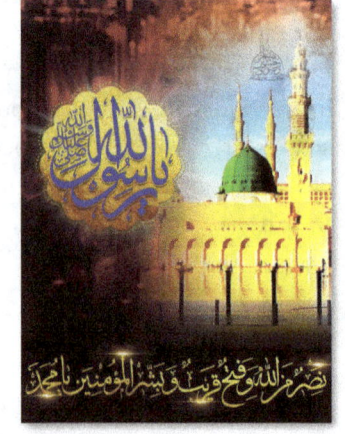

If Prophet ﷺ grabs you and begins to love you, then Prophet ﷺ takes you to his essence. Who's in the heart of Sayyidina Muhammad ﷺ? So, it's like a telescope, that's why, *"Innal ladhina yubayyonaka inama yubayion Allah."* They can't reach me, but *ati ullah*, they want to reach My Essence? *Wa Ati ur Rasul*, then let them obey you. And if they want to follow you, then you have to have *ulil amr minkum* for Prophet ﷺ.

إِنَّ الَّذِينَ يُبَايِعُونَكَ إِنَّمَا يُبَايِعُونَ اللَّـهَ يَدُ اللَّـهِ فَوْقَ أَيْدِيهِمْ ۚ فَمَن نَّكَثَ فَإِنَّمَا يَنكُثُ عَلَىٰ نَفْسِهِ ۖ وَمَنْ أَوْفَىٰ بِمَا عَاهَدَ عَلَيْهُ اللَّـهَ فَسَيُؤْتِيهِ أَجْرًا عَظِيمًا ﴿١٠﴾

48:10 – *"Innal ladheena yubayi'oonaka innama yubayi'on Allaha yadullahi fawqa aydeehim, faman nakatha fa innama yankuthu 'ala nafsihi, wa man awfa bima 'ahada 'alayhu Allaha fasayu teehi ajran 'azheema." (Surat Al-Fath)*

"Indeed, those who give Bayah (pledge allegiance) to you, [O Muhammad] – they are actually giving Bayah (pledge allegiance) to Allah. The hand of Allah is over their hands. So, he whoever breaks his pledge/oath, only breaks it to the detriment/Harm/loss of himself. And whoever fulfills their covenant (Bayah) that which he has promised Allah (AJ) – He will grant him a great reward." (The Victory, 48:10)

It's like a rope coming from Divine Essence. That I want to bring them into My Essence. Only rope that can reach to My Essence is *Muhammadun RasulAllah* ﷺ. And then Prophet ﷺ brings as a *rahmah* (mercy), my *ulul amr* (saints). They're *qamarun*, they're those full moons. Those whom are *ashiqeen* (lovers), not the ones who are only teaching the outside, but they don't teach anything of their good character inside.

No, no. These *Ahbab un Nabi* ﷺ, they're sweet. When squeezed, when released, with everything. Their *khuluq* (character) is as if the *khuluq* of Prophet ﷺ (Holy Qur'an, 68:4).

They don't lie. They don't deceive. They don't yell and scream. It's all based on love. It's all based on *ishq*, all based on *rahmah* and mercy. As a result, they bring to the love and the presence of Prophet ﷺ those *arwah* (souls). And in the presence of Prophet Muhammad ﷺ, dress them, bless them, perfect them, and take them to the reality of Allah ﷻ.

Allah ﷻ Wanted to Be Known,
He Created Nur Muhammad ﷺ (Misbah)

We Cannot Be Tabioni (Followers) Without Following Ulul Amr

In which Allah's ﷻ Divinely presence, *Qul inni kuntum tuhibbunallah, fattabiuni,* Allah ﷻ dress them, *yuhbibkumullahu.*

قُلْ إِنْ كُنْتُمْ تُحِبُّونَ اللَّهَ فَاتَّبِعُونِي يُحْبِبْكُمُ اللَّهُ وَيَغْفِرْ لَكُمْ ذُنُوبَكُمْ ۗ وَاللَّهُ غَفُورٌ رَحِيمٌ ﴿٣١﴾

3:31 – *"Qul in kuntum tuhibbon Allaha fattabi'oni, yuhbibkumullahu wa yaghfir lakum dhunobakum wallahu Ghaforur Raheem." (Surat Ali-Imran)*

"Say, [O Muhammad], "If you should love Allah, then follow me, [so] Allah will love you and forgive you your sins. And Allah is Forgiving and Merciful." (Family of Imran, 3:31)

There is no way to be *tabioni* (following) without the *tabi'een* (followers). There's no way to be *tabioni* if you're not following *ulul amr* (people of the Divinely Command/saints). So, the whole system of this reality of Qur'an is all pointing always to the same direction. Whatever you do, find them. If you find them, love them, have good character. They'll bring you in through their *nazar* (gaze). They bring you in, they perfect your character.

Awliya's Entire Existence is Based on Praising Sayyidina Muhammad ﷺ

If their heart has the presence of Sayyidina Muhammad ﷺ, this is a *daleel* (proof). If you say that you're with Sayyidina Muhammad ﷺ, well you should be lost in the love and the praising of Prophet ﷺ. Could you imagine somebody who says they're with Sayyidina Muhammad ﷺ, but they're never doing *durood*? They are never doing the *mehfil* (gatherings), they are never doing the *salawat* (praising), they are never doing the *ishq* (love). What Prophet ﷺ is in there with no sound, no noise, no love?

If you're saying *Qalb al Muhammadiya* ﷺ, shouldn't you be like amazing explosions of the love of Prophet ﷺ? Everything about you should be *Hub e Rasul*. Everything about you should be about the praise of *tazim* (honour). Of the most magnificent and munificent character of Allah ﷻ, creation of Allah ﷻ, is *Tazimun Nabi* ﷺ,

because the heart is filled with the love of Prophet ﷺ. How are they going to give the *tazim* (honor) of that love that's in their heart? It has to be continuous, continuous praisings upon Prophet ﷺ. Then we know, oh those are *ashiqeen* (lovers). Their entire *wujud* (existence), their entire reality is about that.

We pray that Allah ﷻ dress us and bless us. Easiest way to that are these *nasheeds*, *salawats*, and *naat shareef*. As soon as we recite, we feel the love and our soul begins to move into that presence.

Subhana rabbika rabbal 'izzati 'amma yasifoon, wa salaamun 'alal mursaleen, walhamdulillahi rabbil 'aalameen. Bi hurmati Muhammad al-Mustafa wa bi siri Surat al-Fatiha.

MALIK AL HAYAT, MALIK AL DUNYA – MEEM, HA, MEEM, DAAL
All Creation Within Muhammad RasulAllah ﷺ

MEEM, HA, MEEM, DAAL

﴿٥٩﴾ ...أَطِيعُوا ٱللَّهَ وَأَطِيعُوا ٱلرَّسُولَ وَأُوْلِي ٱلْأَمْرِ مِنكُمْ...

4:59 – "...Atiullaha wa atiur Rasula wa Ulil amre minkum..." (Surat An-Nisa)

"... Obey Allah, Obey the Messenger, and those in authority among you..." (The Women, 4:59)

In this holy month of Rabbiul Awwal, Allah ﷻ granted us a tremendous gift to see this holy month, a life in which to see these nights open and the *tajallis* (manifestations) open. The reality of *"Meem Ha, Meem Daal,"* Nabi Muhammad ﷺ, is not something that its reality opened per chance onto this *dunya* (material world). But the reality of Sayyidina Muhammad ﷺ, and every reality of Allah ﷻ, is an ancient reality that was already written from *qadim* (ancient). When Allah ﷻ wrote is beyond comprehension.

The Decoration Upon the Pot is Not Important

Awliya (saints) come into our lives and there are many different ways of teaching the same thing. One is from Sayyidina Jalaludin Rumi ق, teaching that this *dunya* is like a pot for a flower. And that the *insan* (human being) and the person is like a vase or pot that holds a flower. That no matter how much the vase is ornate and how much decoration the pot has upon it, it's not important. The importance of the decoration upon the pot is of no importance. But that the pot took an understanding of emptiness.

"When everyone is trying to be something, be nothing. Range with emptiness. Humans should be like a pot. As the pot is held by its emptiness inside, human is held by the awareness of its nothingness."
– Shams Tabriz

"It is not the decorations outside but the emptiness inside that holds us straight." – Shams Tabriz

It means that you never know in which way *awliya* (saints) are teaching that may all of sudden enter into the heart of someone. They say it's not the vase that makes this to be important. If it's all so beautifully ornate but it doesn't understand that, it has to be empty.

Empty Yourself Like a Pot and Allah ﷻ Will Plant Realities

When it understood its reality that I am just a pot. No matter how much you beautify me, I still have to take a path in which to be nothing. Because the pot being filled with itself and love of itself is of no value. It's just a pot loving itself. So, they came and began to teach, 'No, the reality of that pot is that

it should be nothing.' It should take a path in which to enter its nothingness so that Allah (AJ) can begin to plant what Allah (AJ) wants to plant within that reality. In its nothingness, its reality appears, and the firmness of its reality will begin to appear. If the pot understood to be nothing, Allah (AJ) will not grow yourself into it, but Allah's (AJ) realities and *haqqaiqs*. Like the roses, they begin to grow only when this vase understands that it's nothing. Then the beatific reality begins to appear. Once the beatific reality appears, then no matter how much you make it ornate and how much you make it beautiful, it doesn't matter. At least it understood in its nothingness for Allah's (AJ) flowers and beauties to appear. Material world, they're stuck on themselves. They're stuck on the beauty of their pot and what they think they know; what they think they achieve and yet never took a path in which to train to be nothing.

Secrets of the Name of Muhammad ﷺ
Meem Ha, Meem Daal – Malik al Hayat, Malik al Dunya

محمد ﷺ	
Muhammad ﷺ - MHMD	
مد	مح
Meem Daal	Meem Ha
مَالِكُ الدُّنْيَا	مَالِكُ الْحَيَاة
Malik al Dunya (King of Manifested Worlds)	Malik al Hayat (King of Oceans of Eternity)

Note: Please read English from right to left to coincide with Arabic.

Then Allah (AJ) inspired all His creation and Sayyidina Muhammad ﷺ, being the cream of that reality, the pinnacle of that reality, just in the *huroof* of his holy name, *Malik al Hayat wa Malik al Dunya. Meem, Ha – Malik al Hayat. Meem, Daal – Malik al Dunya*, the king of this *dunya* (material world). That Allah (AJ) inspired all creation, no matter what I gave to you, come back to the pot. Whatever I gave to you of title, whatever I gave to you of position, whether I gave you to be a Prophet,

Malik al Hayat, Malik al Dunya – Meem, Ha, Meem, Daal

---

whether I gave you to be a king, whether I gave you to be a merchant, whether I gave you to be nothing, these are just the decor of your pot. Be nothing.

This means then they approached that reality through the *daal*. The *meem ha, meem daal* – the *meem* to the right is the Divinely Presence, the closest towards the heavens. So, you approach from the left going to the right. They know *meem, ha, meem, daal* – it's easy. This is the easy one, *inshaAllah*.

Malik al Dunya – King of Manifested Worlds
Daal Represents the Dalail al Khayrat, the Best of Guides

So, *meem, ha, meem, daal*. You approach from this *daal*. It means that the reality of that *daal* is the *Dalail al Khayrat*. He's the best of guides.

When Allah ﷻ wants all creation that come to this *sultanate* (kingdom), come to this reality. That come to this *daal*; he is the guide for all creation. So, we recite *Dalail al Khayrat* as a part of our *awrad*. That it has the best of guidance and it's an ancient reality from Allah ﷻ, so you have to come to the guide of Allah ﷻ. That guidance of Allah ﷻ, when they begin to say, *ya Rabbi*, I want to be guided in this *dunya* (material world), Allah ﷻ begins to reveal to them the king and the *sultanate* of this *dunya*. And that everything is under that *sultanate* of Sayyidina Muhammad ﷺ. That, that *malik* and the king of all of this *mulk* that is appearing, everything of the world of form. The king of that is Sayyidina Muhammad ﷺ. It means then at that point, in their *ma'rifah* (Gnosticism), they understood that there must be a king; there must be a representative on this earth and there must be *khalifa*. And Allah ﷻ reveals to all His holy books, there is a *khalifa* (deputy).

وَإِذْ قَالَ رَبُّكَ لِلْمَلَائِكَةِ إِنِّي جَاعِلٌ فِي الْأَرْضِ خَلِيفَةً... ﴿٣٠﴾

2:30 – *"Wa idh qala rabbuka lil Malayikati innee ja'ilun fil ardi khaleefatan,…"* (Surat Al-Baqarah)

"And [mention, O Muhammad], when your Lord said to the angels, "Indeed, I will make upon the earth a Deputy/Representative…" (The Cow, 2:30)

All Prophets Are Representatives of One Khalifa

There is only one *khalifa* (deputy) and many agents and representatives for that *khalifa*. So, then we take from the example of the prophets of Allah ﷻ whom were given the highest reality, which means they were given the highest and the greatest honour. When Nabi Musa ﷺ reached

to that door. Because they were given the reality of *dunya* (material world), not the reality of their *akhirah* (afterlife) yet. Everyone is on this road of *ma'rifah*. When a *nabi* (prophet) of Allah ﷻ, he's a guide and through guiding his people and Allah ﷻ guiding himself (Musa ﷺ) to his own *ma'rifah* (gnosticism). Comes now the pot, that no matter what I gave to you because they are the highest example so that everyone lower can understand, lower yourself, be nothing. If a *nabi* (prophet) of Allah ﷻ is saying, 'I'm speaking to Allah ﷻ, *ya Rabbi*, let me to see you. I want to see who I'm talking to.' And Allah ﷻ says, 'There is no way for you to see Me, I'll show you My glory.' As soon as Nabi Musa ﷺ went to go see that glory, to recognize that reality, Allah ﷻ revealed His glory upon the mountain and Nabi Musa ﷺ was out like death, like passed out.

وَلَمَّا جَاءَ مُوسَىٰ لِمِيقَاتِنَا وَكَلَّمَهُ رَبُّهُ قَالَ رَبِّ أَرِنِي أَنظُرْ إِلَيْكَ ۚ قَالَ لَن تَرَانِي وَلَٰكِنِ انظُرْ إِلَى الْجَبَلِ فَإِنِ اسْتَقَرَّ مَكَانَهُ فَسَوْفَ تَرَانِي ۚ فَلَمَّا تَجَلَّىٰ رَبُّهُ لِلْجَبَلِ جَعَلَهُ دَكًّا وَخَرَّ مُوسَىٰ صَعِقًا ۚ فَلَمَّا أَفَاقَ قَالَ سُبْحَانَكَ تُبْتُ إِلَيْكَ وَأَنَا أَوَّلُ الْمُؤْمِنِينَ ﴿١٤٣﴾

Malik al Hayat, Malik al Dunya – Meem, Ha, Meem, Daal

7:143 – *"Wa lamma jaa Musa limeeqatina wa kallamahu Rabbuhu, qala rabbi arinee anzhur ilayka, Qala lan taranee wa lakini onzhur ilal jabali fa inistaqarra makanahu, fasawfa taranee, falamma tajalla Rabbuhu lil jabali ja'alahu, dakkan wa kharra Musa sa'iqan, falamma afaqa qala subhanaka tubtu ilayka wa ana awwalul Mumineen."*
(Surat Al-A'raf)

"And when Moses arrived at Our appointed time and his Lord spoke to him, he said, "My Lord, show me [Yourself] that I may look at You." [Allah] said, "you will not see Me, but look at the mountain; if it should remain in its place, then you will see Me." But when his Lord manifested His glory on the mountain, He made it as dust, and Moses fell unconscious. And when he awoke/recovered his senses, he said, "Glory be to You! to You I turn in repentance, and I am the first of the believers." (The Heights. 7:143)

Nabi Musa (Moses) ﷺ Witnessed Nurul Muhammadi ﷺ

The *tajalli* (manifestation) of what was seen and the reality of what was seen obliterated every aspect of the character and the *nafs* (ego). Completely obliterated, at that time, Nabi Musa ﷺ witnessed what Allah ﷻ wanted His prophet to witness. He witnessed the reality of Sayyidina Muhammad ﷺ, *Nurul Muhammad* ﷺ. From witnessing that reality, came back to say that,

'My life, my death, everything, *Anna awal ul Muslimeen.*' It means he took the *shahada* (testimony of faith) and the understanding that I am the first of the Muslims. I'm first of those who submit myself of what I saw of this reality.

قُلْ إِنَّ صَلَاتِي وَنُسُكِي وَمَحْيَايَ وَمَمَاتِي لِلَّهِ رَبِّ الْعَالَمِينَ ﴿١٦٢﴾ لَا شَرِيكَ لَهُ ۖ وَبِذَٰلِكَ أُمِرْتُ وَأَنَا أَوَّلُ الْمُسْلِمِينَ ﴿١٦٣﴾

6:162-3 – "Qul inna salati wa nusuki wa mahyaya wa mamati lillahi Rabbil 'Aalamin. (162) La sharika lahu wa bidhalika omirtu wa ana awalul Muslimin." (163) (Surat Al-An'am)

Say, "Indeed, my prayer, my services of sacrifice, my living and my dying are for Allah, Lord of the worlds. No partner has He; and this I have been commanded, and I am the first of those who submit."
(The Cattle, 6:162-163)

Nabi Musa ﷺ Sought Where the Two Rivers of Kalima Meet La Ilaha IllAllaHu Muhammadan RasulAllah ﷺ

Nabi Musa ﷺ witnessed the reality and the light of Sayyidina Muhammad ﷺ. At that time, moving and teaching that from what I witnessed in my soul of the king of this *sultanate* (kingdom), the king of the heavens, *ya Rabbi*, I won't stop until where these two rivers meet.

وَإِذْ قَالَ مُوسَىٰ لِفَتَاهُ لَا أَبْرَحُ حَتَّىٰ أَبْلُغَ مَجْمَعَ الْبَحْرَيْنِ أَوْ أَمْضِيَ حُقُبًا ﴿٦٠﴾

18:60 – "Wa idh qala Musa lefatahu laa abrahu hatta ablugha majma'a albahrayni aw amdiya huquba." (Surat Al-Kahf)

"Behold, Moses said to his attendant, I will not give up until I reach the junction of the two seas or (until) I spend years and years in travel."
(The Cave, 18:60)

The two rivers, *awliyaullah* (saints) come and teach is *la ilaha illAllah Muhammadun RasulAllah* ﷺ. I will not stop until these two rivers where they meet, means where *la ilaha illAllah – hey, waw* points to *meem* of the Muhammad ﷺ. It means from the *Hu* of Allah ﷻ, directs itself to *Muhammadun RasulAllah* ﷺ. It's enough for us to understand that it directed, the *Hu* directed itself to the *meem*. The *kalimah* was showing Sayyidina Musa عليه السلام that if you want where these two *haqqaiqs* are meeting, its door is *Muhammadun RasulAllah* ﷺ.

لَا إِلَهَ إِلاَّ اللهُ مُحَمَّدًا رَسُولُ الله

"*La ilaha illAllahu Muhammadun RasulAllah*"

"*There is no deity but Allah, Prophet Muhammad is the messenger of Allah.*"

Prophet Muhammad ﷺ is Malik al Hayat – the King of Oceans of Eternity

That *Hu* is the reality of the *Ha* of this *meem ha*. Because now from the *daal* of guidance, he came to the *haqqaiq* of the *meem* of Sayyidina Muhammad ﷺ. That lost everything of himself, emptied his pot. It

means no matter what title I have, what birthright I have, whoever I think I am, you are nothing in the presence of Prophet ﷺ. Be nothing, take a path of nothingness. They have to be trained in that path of nothingness. At that time, Prophet ﷺ will open now come to the *hayat* (eternal life). Come to my *ha* because I'm *Malik al Hayat*, I am the king of everything that is given a life. Every ocean of *hayat* exists within this reality. Everything that's given a life is existing within that and Prophet ﷺ is the king and the owner of that reality.

So, it means if we want to reach towards that reality, this love of Prophet ﷺ is essential for everything. That they're entering into that reality. They are understanding the *sultanate* of Prophet ﷺ. Then Allah عز وجل begins to inspire that this ocean of eternal life, this ocean of the reality of *hayat*, you have to enter into that *hayat* (eternal life). You have to enter into where the two rivers meet. The sign for Nabi Musa عليه السلام was where the dead fish came to life and jumped into the spring.

قَالَ أَرَأَيْتَ إِذْ أَوَيْنَا إِلَى الصَّخْرَةِ فَإِنِّي نَسِيتُ الْحُوتَ وَمَا أَنْسَانِيهُ إِلَّا الشَّيْطَانُ أَنْ أَذْكُرَهُ ۚ وَاتَّخَذَ سَبِيلَهُ فِي الْبَحْرِ عَجَبًا ﴿٦٣﴾

18:63 – "Qala araayta idh awayna ilas sakhrati fa-innee naseetu alhoota wa ma ansaneehu illash shaytanu an adhkurahu, wat takhadha sabeela hu fee al bahri 'ajaba." (Surat Al-Kahf)

"He said, Did you see when we retired to the rock? Indeed, I forgot [there] the fish. And none made me forget it except Satan – that I should mention it. And it took its course into the sea amazingly." (The Cave, 18:63)

Sayyidina Isa ﷺ Was Kept Alive to Witness Sayyidina Muhammad ﷺ

It was same for Sayyidina Isa (Jesus) ﷺ. All the Prophets of Allah ﷻ, they relinquished their title for the greater reality. And Sayyidina Isa ﷺ said from what you gave to me of realities, don't let me to die without taking my *shahada* (testimony of faith) from Sayyidina Muhammad ﷺ. Allah ﷻ accepted the *du'a* (supplication) of Sayyidina Isa ﷺ and kept him alive to witness Prophet ﷺ. To witness that reality, to be under *ummat Muhammad* ﷺ. That I don't want that title for myself, the greatest title is to be under the flag of Sayyidina Muhammad ﷺ. It means then they were taken to the oceans of *al-Hayat*.

Board the Ship of Awliya, They Take You to Oceans of Al-Hay Al-Qayyum

That these *khatm* and these *zikrs* that *awliyaullah* (saints) are authorizing these associations, they are like we described before when we were talking to some people. They're like a tram, a shuttle, that from there's one seat here and through a wire, it goes all the way into the *malakut*

(heavenly realm). Everybody boards that tram. As soon as the *zikr* starts, these *awliyaullah* (saints) who are in charge of these oceans of *al-Hayat*. Everything that's being recited in the *zikr* is a dress upon the soul. Your body may be sitting here, don't understand why it's sitting here, maybe it's hungry for dinner. They don't care. This is a reality of the soul. As soon as they begin the *zikr*, the soul entered their tram, entered their ship. And this ship now is moving. As it's moving, it's moving towards the presence of *Malik al Hayat*.

When they're making the *zikr* of '*Hu*', when they're making the *zikr* of '*Hay*', when they make the *zikr* of '*Qayyum*'; all of these are dress upon the soul. As soon as they say *Hay, Hay*, the souls are being dumped into the oceans of *hayat*. Being washed into the oceans of *hayat*. As soon as they say *Qayyum*, takes it out and puts it into the oceans of eternity. The *haq* of Allah ﷻ is *Hayyu al Qayyum*. Ha of *al-Hayat*, qaf of *Qayyum*, the *haq* of Allah ﷻ is the reality of the soul. Dresses it from the *Hay*, dresses it from the *Qayyum*; every *zikr* that's being made by their authority is a dress upon the souls. These are like trams that are taking people into the *malakut* (heavenly realm). These are not for entertainment purposes. These *awliyaullah* (saints) are guiding through the soul of these realities.

They begin to teach on this tram. This is the way of *ma'rifah* (gnosticism), that don't for a moment think that you are moving now into the presence of Allah ﷻ. Allah ﷻ is far beyond anything that can be imagined. This ocean of realities of *hayat*, it's not Allah ﷻ. Allah ﷻ is beyond *Hay*. Because Allah ﷻ described we created '*Hay*' and '*mayt*.' We created life and death to test you. Allah ﷻ is not *Hay*, is not *Mayt*. Allah's ﷻ not death and not life. Life and death are for us that we are from creation.

الَّذِي خَلَقَ الْمَوْتَ وَالْحَيَاةَ لِيَبْلُوَكُمْ أَيُّكُمْ أَحْسَنُ عَمَلًا ۚ وَهُوَ الْعَزِيزُ الْغَفُورُ ﴿٢﴾

67:2 – "Alladhee khalaqal Mawta wal Hayata liyabluwakum ayyukum ahsanu 'amalan, wa huwal 'Azizu ul Ghafoor." (Surat Al-Mulk)

"He Who created Death and Life, to test you [as to] which of you is best in deed – and He is the Exalted in Might, the Forgiving."
(The Sovereignty, 67:2)

The Second Meem of Muhammad (s) is Bahrul Muheet (All Encompassing Ocean of Realities)

So, this *Malik al Hayat*, is a reality and a soul that Allah ﷻ created. And they're taking us on these *zikrs* and on this way of *ma'rifah* to dress us from that ocean of *al-Hayat*. And when they reach the *meem* of Sayyidina

Muhammad ﷺ, *Bahrul Muheet* (All-Encompassing Ocean of Realities), that that *meem* of *malakut* (heavenly realm) of *mulk* (earthly realm), all of them. Allah ﷻ encoded for us to understand. Why it's called *malakut*? It's Prophet ﷺ. Why is it called *mulk*? It's Prophet ﷺ. Everything has a *meem*. Every reality of that reality has a *meem*.

At that time, when they were dressed in the oceans of *al-Hayat* (eternal life), they were blessed from the oceans of *al-Hayat*, Allah ﷻ then begins to open for him this reality of malakut, this *Bahrul Muheet*. This last

Malik al Hayat, Malik al Dunya – Meem, Ha, Meem, Daal

---

meem is an all-encompassing *meem* of *Muhammadun RasulAllah* ﷺ. That every creation exists within that *meem*. Outside of that *meem* is not for us, that's *la ilaha illAllah*. Everything is existing in this *meem* of *Muhammadun RasulAllah* ﷺ (the *Meem* connected to *ha*). Out here (outside the meem) *la ilaha illAllah* means don't look here, this is not your place. You're from creation, we're from creation. This *Bahrul Muheet*, that everything exists within this *meem* is creation. Everything else is Allah's ﷻ realities that have nothing to do with us. Everything is in this *meem*. Everything must be found within this meem. Outside is *la ilaha illAllah*. Allah ﷻ says don't look to here, this is not your reality.

Allah ﷻ Sits Upon the Heart of the King of Both Worlds, Sayyidina Muhammad ﷺ

Don't contemplate the Creator but contemplate the creation. And the best of creation is *Muhammadun RasulAllah* ﷺ.

عَنْ أَبِي جَعْفَرٍ عَلَيْهِ السَّلَامُ قَالَ: إِيَّاكُمْ وَالتَّفَكُّرَ فِي اللهِ وَلَكِنْ إِذَا أَرَدْتُمْ أَنْ تَنْظُرُوا إِلَى عَظَمَتِهِ فَانْظُرُوا إِلَى عَظِيمِ خَلْقِهِ.

'An Abi Ja'far (as) qala: "Iyakum wat tafakkaru fillahi wa lakin idha aradtum an tunzaro ila 'azamatihi fanzaro ila 'azimi khalqihi."

Abu Ja'far (A) said, "Beware of *tafakkur* in God. But if you wish to view His grandeur, observe the great of His creations."

So, the *sultan* and the soul that encompasses every reality is *Muhammadun RasulAllah* ﷺ. Allah ﷻ described that is the king and I sit upon his throne. I sit upon his heart. This means *izzatullah* (Allah's ﷻ Might and Magnificence) and the might of Allah ﷻ sits upon the heart and the soul of Prophet ﷺ. That's why those *ahadith*. When Allah ﷻ

talking about *'qalabil mumin baytullah'*, He's not talking about us, although we'd like to think that.

$$\text{قَلْبَ الْمُؤْمِنْ بَيْتُ الرَّبّ}$$

"Qalb al mu'min baytur rabb."

"The heart of the believer is the House of the Lord." (Hadith Qudsi)

Sayyidina Muhammad ﷺ is the Insan al Kamil and His Heart is Manzil al Qur'an

In the *haqqaiq*, in the highest part of the reality, and Allah ﷻ says, 'I'm not on heavens and I'm not anywhere on earth, I'm only on the heart of my believer.' The only believer for Allah ﷻ that contains every reality is *Muhammadun RasulAllah* ﷺ.

$$\text{مَا وَسِعَنِيْ لَا سَمَائِيْ ولا اَرْضِيْ وَلَكِنْ وَسِعَنِيْ قَلْبِ عَبْدِيْ اَلْمُؤْمِنْ}$$

"Maa wasi'anee laa Samayee, wa la ardee, laakin wasi'anee qalbi 'Abdee al Mu'min."

"Neither My Heavens nor My Earth can contain Me, but the heart of my Believing Servant."
(Hadith Qudsi conveyed by Prophet Muhammad (pbuh))

So, this big reality, this soul that *awliyaullah* (saints) describe is a soul, *Insan al Kamil*, that everything is within that soul, in that reality. The power of that *qalb* (heart) because we can't understand other than our physical. The power of that reality is Allah ﷻ. The power of that reality is Allah ﷻ and that's why the heart of that reality, *Manzil al Qur'an*. Manzil

al Qur'an is coming out from the heart of that reality. Every reality is flowing from the heart of that reality.

So then imagine the power of *Mawlid an Nabi* ﷺ. When we don't understand the greatness of our Messenger ﷺ, we don't have any understanding of the greatness of the reality. So *awliyaullah* come say first thing to do is establish the *Mawlid* (celebration of Prophet's ﷺ birth) so that Allah ﷻ will begin to open all of these realities. That everything within that ocean and that Allah's ﷻ Might and Majesty sit upon the heart of that reality. And that everything emanating from that reality.

Inside the All-Encompassing Meem, Remains Hamd and the Power of Creation

Then we begin to understand, Nabi Ahmad ﷺ. That reality of the soul of Sayyidina Muhammad ﷺ, that *meem* that everything is within that, now begin to contemplate the *huroof*. If the *meem* is all-encompassing, what remains inside is a *hamd*. If the *meem* is all-encompassing, what remains inside is a *hamd*. So, then what's the power of this creation? *Hamd* (praise). *'Yusabi hu wa bihamdi.'*

تُسَبِّحُ لَهُ السَّمَاوَاتُ السَّبْعُ وَالْأَرْضُ وَمَن فِيهِنَّ ۚ وَإِن مِّن شَيْءٍ إِلَّا يُسَبِّحُ بِحَمْدِهِ وَلَٰكِن لَّا تَفْقَهُونَ تَسْبِيحَهُمْ ۗ إِنَّهُ كَانَ حَلِيمًا غَفُورًا ﴿٤٤﴾

17:44 – "*Tusabbihu lahus samawatus sab'u wal ardu wa man fee hinna wa in min shayin illa yusabbihu bihamdihi wa lakin la tafqahoona tasbeehahum innahu kana haleeman ghafoora.*" (Surat Al-Isra)

"The seven heavens and the earth and whatever is in them exalt [praises] Him. And there is not a thing except that it exalts [Allah] by His praise, but you do not understand their [way of] exalting/praising."

Indeed, He is ever Forbearing and Forgiving."
(The Night Journey 17:44)

Creation Will Be Annihilated if Allah's ﷻ Zikr Comes onto Them

'Bihamdi.' *Awliyaullah* (saints) come and tell that if you think Allah's ﷻ praise is empowering this creation, Allah ﷻ clarifies, 'If I praise and release My Qur'an onto a mountain, it will be *khashi'a*. It will be dust.'

لَوْ أَنزَلْنَا هَٰذَا الْقُرْآنَ عَلَىٰ جَبَلٍ لَّرَأَيْتَهُ خَاشِعًا مُّتَصَدِّعًا مِّنْ خَشْيَةِ اللَّهِ... ﴿٢١﴾

59:21 – "Law anzalna hadha alQurana 'ala jabalin laraaytahu, khashi'an mutasaddi'an min khashyatillahi..." (Surat Al-Hashr)

"Had We sent down this Qur'an on a mountain, verily, you would have seen it obliterated to dust (from its power)..." (The Exile, 59:21)

If you think Allah's ﷻ *zikr* is keeping the flowers? It would have annihilated all creation. If Allah's ﷻ *zikr* came onto the moon, it would have annihilated the moon. If Allah's ﷻ *zikr* came upon the earth, it would have annihilated the earth. Nothing can contain the *zikr* of Allah ﷻ.

Malik al Hayat, Malik al Dunya – Meem, Ha, Meem, Daal

Power of Allah's ﷻ Praise Sustains Prophet ﷺ

The *'Qul'* of Allah ﷻ, nothing can contain it, except the *qalb* (heart) of Sayyidina Muhammad ﷺ. Because that *'Qul'* is only to the *'Ba'* and the reality of Prophet ﷺ, who contains the secret of *Bismillahir Rahmanir Raheem*. That only one who can contain  and hold what Allah's ﷻ orders and *zikr* and *hamd* is the reality of Prophet ﷺ. Then, the *MuHamd* begins to praise and all creation is in that reality. The power of Prophet's ﷺ praising is sustaining. The power of Allah's ﷻ praise sustains Prophet ﷺ. And the *hamd* (praise) of Prophet ﷺ sustains creation.

Subhana rabbika rabbal 'izzati 'amma yasifoon, wa salaamun 'alal mursaleen, walhamdulillahi rabbil 'aalameen. Bi hurmati Muhammad al-Mustafa wa bi siri Surat al-Fatiha.

The All-Encompassing Ocean
Bahrul Muheet

MA'RIFAH OF ALLAH ﷻ
ENTER HEY, LAM, LAM, ALIF

The Hand of the Malakut Encompasses Everything

Asking always to be nothing and enter Allah's ﷻ Oceans of *Rahmah* (Mercy), and *alhamdulillah*, from Mawlana Shaykh's teachings, from *ilm ul huroof* (knowledge of Arabic letters) and the understandings of *huroof*, and these are the knowledges of *malakut* (heavenly realm). And Allah ﷻ, from the heart of Surat YaSeen, from the heart of Sayyidina Muhammad ﷺ describes that, 'The hand of the *malakut* encompasses everything.'

فَسُبْحَانَ الَّذِي بِيَدِهِ مَلَكُوتُ كُلِّ شَيْءٍ وَإِلَيْهِ تُرْجَعُونَ ﴿٨٣﴾

36:83 – "Fasubhanal ladhee biyadihi Malakotu kulli shay in wa ilayhi turja'oon." (Surat YaSeen)

"Therefore Glory be to Him in Whose hand is the dominion/kingdom over everything in heavens, and to Him you will be returned." (YaSeen, 36:83)

That if we begin to contemplate that from heavenly realm because if we say in our associations 'the world of light', then the Muslims don't understand what you're talking about of world of light, means from *malakut* (heavenly realm). And the knowledges of the *malakut*, Allah ﷻ describes in Surat YaSeen that, that knowledge and the hands that have that knowledge, that knowledge encompasses everything.

Malakut is the Power That Allows the Form to Appear

The *malakut* (heavenly realm) encompasses everything means we know now that the world of light encompasses the world of form, because the world of form is hollow. What's inside the world of form are the atoms and the molecules and the *qudra* and the power. That the *malakut* is the power and the source of what's making that form, allowing that form to appear.

The Subtle World Controls the Physical World

So it's not only the subtle world, but that subtle world controls even the physical world. It means that the *malaika* (angels), the energies, the power and the reality exist within every form. Every form is moving by that energy and from *ilm ul huroof* (knowledge of Arabic letters) will begin to teach us to step towards the horizon which means elevate the understanding and the way of *ma'rifah* (gnosticism) is to know.

And the first thing they begin to teach is that everything from a distance has a certain colour. As you approach, the concept of *ma'rifah* is as you're approaching that reality, it begins to immensely expand. So, they describe like a mountain from a distance; mountain looks dark, black, but there's no mountain dark. As soon as you enter and begin to approach a mountain, you see it's huge: colours, rivers, streams. It means so many realities but at a distance it has a certain appearance. As soon as you begin to move and become from *arifeen* (knowers), those who are seeking to know, Allah ﷻ begins to expand infinite capacity of realities.

Nothing Can Contain Allah ﷻ

On one understanding of the *kalimah*, *alif, lam, lam, hey* – Allah ﷻ. That they begin to teach us that nothing can encompass Allah ﷻ. Nothing can truly understand Allah ﷻ, nothing can contain Allah ﷻ, especially the *huroof* (Arabic letters). This means we have only an understanding when we say *"Allah"*, not that you know Allah ﷻ but merely Allah ﷻ gave us a way in which to approach that reality. And from *ilm ul huroof*, Mawlana Shaykh begins to teach that the *huroof* will begin to teach us that nothing can contain Allah ﷻ. There's no name that can contain Allah ﷻ. There's nothing written on anything manifested that can contain Allah ﷻ. There are merely signs directing us towards Allah ﷻ, and that everything must be based on *La ilaha illAllah Muhammadun RasulAllah* ﷺ.

لَا إِلَهَ إِلاَّ اللهُ مُحَمَّدًا رَسُولُ الله

"La ilaha illAllahu Muhammadun RasulAllah"

"There is no deity but Allah, Prophet Muhammad is the messenger of Allah."

Every Reality Contains Sayyidina Muhammad ﷺ

This means every *haqqaiq* and every reality that Allah ﷻ wants us to  move into, it must contain Sayyidina Muhammad ﷺ. There's nothing for us beyond that. It means every reality must have an *adab* (manner), must have a way. That way is within the ocean of *Muhammadun RasulAllah* ﷺ.

We said last night that if not by the understanding of *A'udhu Billahi Minash Shaitanir Rajeem*, every knowledge from *Bismillahir Rahmanir Raheem* is going to have a variation of reality. If we know the *A'udhu Billah*, its reality is 'seek refuge.' What we're reciting on the *Qasidah Burdah*? It means that we're saying that, 'Who can I seek refuge in, other than you, Sayyidi, ya RasulAllah ﷺ, through every calamity and every difficulty.'

Because Allah ﷻ said, 'The heart of My believer is My House. I'm not on heaven and I'm not on earth but I'm on the heart of My believer.'

مَا وَسِعَنِيْ لَا سَمَائِيْ ولا اَرْضِيْ وَلَكِنْ وَسِعَنِيْ قَلْبِ عَبْدِيْ اَلْمُؤْمِنْ

"Maa wasi'anee laa Samayee, wa la ardee, laakin wasi'anee qalbi 'Abdee al Mu'min."

"Neither My Heavens nor My Earth can contain Me, but the heart of my Believing Servant."
(Hadith Qudsi conveyed by Prophet Muhammad (pbuh))

It means Allah's ﷻ telling us, 'If you want to seek refuge in Me, you'll find Me in the heart of Sayyidina Muhammad ﷺ.' So, it means be then with Prophet ﷺ. Love Sayyidina Muhammad ﷺ.

Enter Through the Door of Allah ﷻ

The *huroof* begins to teach us that you cannot approach to understand the *alif*; you have to go through the door of the *hey*. When you're trying to understand a reality, you can't go from its apex. You have to enter through the door. Allah ﷻ says, 'Everything has a door, enter every house through its door."

*Note: Please read English from right to left to coincide with Arabic.

...وَلَيْسَ الْبِرُّ بِأَن تَأْتُوا الْبُيُوتَ مِن ظُهُورِهَا وَلَٰكِنَّ الْبِرَّ مَنِ اتَّقَىٰ ۗ وَأْتُوا الْبُيُوتَ مِنْ أَبْوَابِهَا ۚ وَاتَّقُوا اللَّهَ لَعَلَّكُمْ تُفْلِحُونَ ﴿١٨٩﴾

2:189 – "...Wa laysal birru bi-an tatol buyoota min zuhooriha wa lakinnal birra manit taqa, wa' tol buyoota min abwabiha, wat taqollaha la'allakum tuflihoon." (Surat Al-Baqarah)

"...And it is not righteousness to enter houses from the back, but righteousness is [in] one who fears Allah. And enter houses from their doors. And be Conscious of Allah that you may succeed."
(The Cow, 2:189)

Come to Hidayat Through Your Five Senses

They begin to teach us in just the *huroof* of Allah ﷻ, *hey* it stands for *hidayat* and guidance. That Allah ﷻ beginning to teach, 'You want to come to Me, you want to come to My realities, then come to that *hey*, come to that *hidayat* and that guidance.'

And in the *abjad* realities, that *hey* has a value of five, because Allah ﷻ is describing, 'These are your senses.' How you going to use *hidayat* to reach Allah ﷻ? That *hidayat* has to be through the senses: to hear, to see, to feel, to smell, and to taste. That is what makes us and gives us the honour of our creation, that use your senses to reach towards your reality.

Tune Into Your Spiritual Senses to Open the World of Light

And since this is not the level of *mulk* (earthly realm), but from *malakut* (heavenly realm) and the world of light, they're teaching you have also your spiritual senses. Don't be so stuck on only what you hear from these ears because Allah ﷻ throughout Qur'an, 'They have ears but they don't really hear.' What does that mean? 'They have eyes but they don't really see.' They're lost in the illusion.

...لَهُمْ قُلُوبٌ لَا يَفْقَهُونَ بِهَا وَلَهُمْ أَعْيُنٌ لَا يُبْصِرُونَ بِهَا وَلَهُمْ آذَانٌ لَا يَسْمَعُونَ بِهَا ۚ أُولَٰئِكَ كَالْأَنْعَامِ بَلْ هُمْ أَضَلُّ ۚ أُولَٰئِكَ هُمُ الْغَافِلُونَ ﴿١٧٩﴾

7:179 – "...*Lahum quloobul laa yafqahoona bihaa wa lahum a'yunul laa yubisiroona bihaa wa lahum aazaanul laa yasma'oona bihaa; ulaaa'ika kal an'aami bal hum adall; ulaaa'ika humul ghaafiloon.*" *(Surat Al-Ar'af)*

"*...They have hearts wherewith they understand not, eyes wherewith they see not, and ears wherewith they hear not. They are like cattle, nay more misguided: for they are heedless (of warning).*" *(The Heights, 7:179)*

The *malakut* and the world of subtlety, the atomic reality, reality of energy and light, means that hearing must be a hearing through the soul.

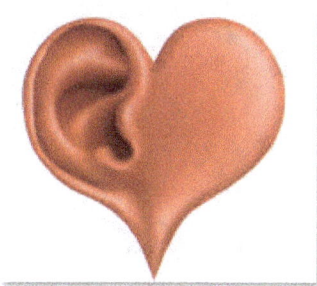

You have a hearing through your ears and you have a hearing through your soul. You can hear with your ears and begin to discipline your ears. That's why the highest level of fasting is to fast with all the senses because the fasting of all the senses begins to open up the realm of the world of light. It means just through the *hey* begins to teach us, come through *hidayat*, come through guidance and who's Allah's *Hadi* (guide)? It's Sayyidina Muhammad ﷺ.

Our Spiritual Senses Are Activated Through the Soul

That guide to the *alif* starts right here. The guide towards that reality is teaching us that come with your senses because you're going to use your physical sense. Did you hear this message and did you accept? Because many

people hear it but they're not truly accepting it in their soul. Are you seeing with your eyes its reality? Are you sensing and feeling? Are you smelling it and are you tasting it?

Ma'rifah of Allah – Enter Hey, Lam, Lam, Alif

And then they begin through every sense that must be activated through the soul. You must begin to hear with your soul. And that's what Allah ﷻ describes, 'When you approach Me through voluntary worship and through love, I will become the hearing in which you hear, the seeing in which you see, the hands in which you feel, the tongue in which you speak, the breath that which you breathe'; the whole *Hadith Qudsi*.

[وَلَا يَزَالُ عَبْدِي يَتَقَرَّبُ إِلَيَّ بِالنَّوَافِلِ حَتَّى أُحِبَّهُ، فَإِذَا أَحْبَبْتُهُ كُنْت سَمْعَهُ الَّذِي يَسْمَعُ بِهِ، وَبَصَرَهُ الَّذِي يُبْصِرُ بِهِ، وَيَدَهُ الَّتِي يَبْطِشُ بِهَا، وَرِجْلَهُ الَّتِي يَمْشِي بِهَا، وَلَئِنْ سَأَلَنِي لَأُعْطِيَنَّهُ،." [رَوَاهُ الْبُخَارِيُّ ...

"...Wa la yazaalu 'Abdi yataqarrabu ilayya bin nawafile hatta ahebahu, fa idha ahbabtuhu kunta Sam'ahul ladhi yasma'u behi, wa Basarahul ladhi yubsiru behi, wa Yadahul lati yabTeshu beha, wa Rejlahul lati yamshi beha, wa la in sa alani la a'Teyannahu..."

"...My servant continues to draw near to Me with voluntary acts of worship so that I shall love him. When I love him, I am his hearing with which he hears, his seeing with which he sees, his hand with which he strikes and his foot with which he walks. Were he to ask [something] of Me, I would surely give it to him..."
Hadith Qudsi (Sahih al-Bukhari, 81:38:2)

Contemplate With Eyes Closed To Open the Khashf

This means then there must be a soul hearing where you discipline yourself, stop listening to badness, stop listening to bad advice, stop and begin to fast with your ears that, 'I don't need to hear everything and everyone. If it's not from *malakut* (heavenly realm), it has no value on my soul. It's a waste of time.' Begin to see with your eyes, not with these eyes - see of the *bazaar* and the market and the streets - but begin to close your physical eyes and train the eyes of the soul to begin to open.

And that's only with *tafakkur* and contemplation that when you isolate yourself and begin to play Qur'an and play *salawat* (praisings) and lock yourself into a room. And begin to breathe and say, '*Ya Rabbi*, what these eyes are seeing are of no value. Let me to enter into a state of nothingness and train the eyes of my heart to begin to see.'

Follow Prophet ﷺ and Train to Open Your Spiritual Senses

The more you can keep your eyes to be closed and train yourself through contemplation and *tafakkur*, the more the eyes of the soul will begin to open - what they call the *khashf* (spiritual vision). Allah ﷻ begins to send images, begins to send a  consciousness and awareness where you begin to see what people don't see. As you're controlling your hearing, you begin to hear what people don't hear. You hear the greater reality within your soul that Allah's ﷻ dressing it.

Ma'rifah of Allah – Enter Hey, Lam, Lam, Alif

From the heavenly kingdom, Allah's ﷻ dressing the soul with all of its realities, *"Allamal Qur'an. Khalaqal Insaan."*

$$\text{عَلَّمَ الْقُرْآنَ ﴿٢﴾ خَلَقَ الْإِنسَانَ ﴿٣﴾}$$

55:2-3 – *"Allamal Qur'an (2). Khalaqal Insaan (3)."*
(Surat Ar-Rahman)

"It is He Who has taught the Qur'an. (2) He has created Mankind. (3)" (The Beneficent, 55: 2-3)

Reaching back to what Allah ﷻ taught us of realities, that *hidayat* (guidance) they're teaching us; come to reality of *Hadi* of Allah ﷻ and the Guide of Allah ﷻ. That the way of Prophet ﷺ is going to teach us, that you begin to train to how you're going to hear, how you're going to see spiritually, how you're going to open up your sense of feeling. Not just the feeling of physicality, but the sense of your subtle being, how to feel with your soul.

Believers Pay Attention to the Subtleties of Their Being

If you are a believer you know that many times you go somewhere, and you know in your soul that's not the place for you. You feel a sense of panic that maybe you have entered into an area or somewhere or something is dangerous. This is a subtlety. Or if your heart is subtle, you feel the *tajallis* (manifestations) and begin to cry. You feel the emanation and the presence of the Prophetic light. This is a subtlety. This is the sense of feeling with the soul, hearing with the soul, seeing with the soul, feeling with the soul. The feel and the touch that the whole being is activated. If those are all activated, now the rising of the *malakut* (heavenly realm) is to begin to smell with the soul. Seek that which smells nice and pleasurable. What they call aromatherapy is angelic reality.

Shaykhs Can Smell the Dirt People Put Upon Their Souls

If you are rising with the reality of your soul, your soul cannot take bad fragrance. Your soul cannot take bad smells. Your reality can't take. They say the shaykhs, they can smell the dirt that people put upon their souls and it smells worse than the worst sewage plant. It's a waste. It's like a

like a smell worse than death of a rotting carcass because the bad actions are causing a state of death upon the being and release a tremendous and horrific smell. This is from now the rising of the *malakut* and the angelic realm.

All within the *hey* of *hidayat* is teaching that you begin to train; fake it until you make it. You begin to fragrance everywhere so that you like good fragrances. You begin to fragrance yourself knowing that these angelic beings, they don't like to come to bad smells. They don't like an environment of bad smells. They won't come and if they don't come, their support will be cut. So, you live your life off of your soul's reality.

Shaykhs Walk Within Their Oceans of Certainty

They're not living off of their physical reality. They depend upon what their soul can hear. They depend upon what their soul is witnessing because they are from the people of *haqqaiq* (reality). They have reached *ilm ul-yaqeen* (knowledge of certainty); they have been granted in *darajats* (levels), *ayn ul-yaqeen* (vision of certainty). If this *ilm ul-yaqeen* and *ayn ul-yaqeen* means they are walking in *haqq ul-yaqeen* (certainty of truth). They are walking within the oceans of their certainty. As a result, their sense, they live by that smell, by what they see, what they begin to smell. Their breath is the power of their *zikr* (remembrance). Their *zikr* is through their soul and the energy that's dressing their soul. Their sense of touch, and then the highest of that *hidayat* (guidance) is their sense of taste.

So, then those who came from paradise most recently, all you see them do is put everything into their mouth – little babies. You see them always hold their thumb for their energy and put everything into their mouth. Because they came from the realm of reality; they came from the people of taste and they entered into the dead zone. The earth is the zombie, walking - what do they call the show? 'Walking Dead', it was an analogy of *dunya*. *Awliyaullah* (saints), they see this *dunya* (material world), they are walking dead. They are smelling corpses and all they pursue is that which is evil and nasty.

Fasting With All Your Senses Opens Immense Realities

And they begin to teach your highest reality, *zawq*, is taste. That's why Allah wanted so much for us Ramadan, and the focus of the mouth and the focus of abstinence. The focus of fasting was not just the fasting of one thirty-day period but was an entire life of fasting. Fast with your ears as much as you can, especially more rewards in this busy *dunya* (material world). If they would have  made us to live in Mecca and Madina, *alhamdulillah*, it would have been great. Allah put us in the candy shop and said, 'There's more reward for you because every temptation is around your senses.' Abstain and fast. Fast with your ears, fast with your eyes, fast with your breath so that

Allah ﷻ can open the reality of tasting these realities. That is under the control of Sayyidina Muhammad ﷺ.

Like Allah ﷻ, the Alif Connects to Nothing But Supports Everything

The *alif, lam, lam, hey* is a direction towards the Divinely Kingdom but in no way should we think it is a description of Allah ﷻ. Allah ﷻ, *la sharik* (no partner), *la shabi*. Merely direct yourself to the kingdom. The *alif* begins to teach us that, 'I'm not connected to anything, but I can support everything.' They're all separate. When Allah ﷻ wants to show His support, they merely write this *alif* upon that *lam*; the *alif* hits the *lam* like that.

This *alif* is always by itself because you're pursuing Allah ﷻ and Allah ﷻ is a mystery, always keeping that, 'No partner with Me, but when I want to show My support, I merely begin to write it like that. That My *Alif* is supporting, My *Izzah* is supporting.' Begin to teach now this is the way of *ma'rifah* (gnosticism). You're on a journey towards realities. You start with *hidayat* and guidance.

Prophet ﷺ Perfects Our Hidayat to Move Towards Our Soul

So, Prophet ﷺ comes to perfect your *hidayat*, that Allah ﷻ gave you senses, use these senses to reach your reality. Use your God-given gifts that make you to be different than a baboon and reach your guidance and reach the *malakut* (heavenly realm). Don't be stuck on just the physical

world guidance – how many times to make *wudu* (ablution)? How many times and percentage of your *zakat* (charity)? This, you need that, but move towards the heavenly realm and that which is eternal, which is the soul.

Lam is the Lisanul Haq, the Tongue of Truth

And they begin to take us with this *hidayat*, come to this *lam* [first *lam*

from left of Allah ﷻ]. And they begin to open the reality of the *lam* is *lisanul haq* (tongue of truth). So when we read Holy Qur'an, when you come across the *hey*, it has a reality within *hidayat* (guidance). Any word that has *hey* has some flavour of *hidayat* because *ilm ul huroof*. Allah ﷻ describing the word that you know from *mulk* (earthly realm) has maybe completely different understanding in *malakut* (heavenly realm). But the *huroof* of it is Allah's ﷻ ingredients. If you put a little bit of *hey* in every word that you read, it must have a flavour of *hidayat* in it.

The *lam* has to do with the reality of *lisanul haq*, the tongue of truth. We said for every manifestation to begin, for Allah ﷻ to grant an existence, for a universe to come into existence, it must be spoken. And Allah ﷻ speaks to no one but Sayyidina Muhammad ﷺ. That's why we're leaving Holy Qur'an to Prophet ﷺ and we're not talking physicality; we're talking about the world of light.

When Allah's ﷻ *Irada* and Allah's ﷻ Will wants to be known, it must be for us everything through *la ilaha illAllah Muhammadun RasulAllah* ﷺ and then Prophet ﷺ gives the order for all of creation.

لَا إِلَهَ إِلاَّ اللهُ مُحَمَّدًا رَسُولُ الله

"La ilaha illAllahu Muhammadun RasulAllah."

"There is no deity but Allah, Prophet Muhammad is the messenger of Allah."

Sayyidina Muhammad ﷺ Speaks With the Lisanul Haq

When Allah ﷻ wants to bring creation into existence, must go from the Will and begin to give the permission to manifest upon the tongue of truth known as Sayyidina Muhammad ﷺ. So every time we see a *lam*, has to do with a *mulk*, a creation coming into existence. It has to do with the secret of the tongue of Sayyidina Muhammad ﷺ because nothing comes into existence without Prophet ﷺ speaking it.

Allah ﷻ giving the order, *"Qul"* and Sayyidina Muhammad ﷺ, *"Kun faya kun." Kun faya kun* is inheritable. That's why the *Hadith Qudsi*, 'Come, I be your hearing, your seeing, all the way until you become *rabbaniyoon* and you have power of *kun faya kun*.'

...وَلَا يَزَالُ عَبْدِي يَتَقَرَّبُ إِلَيَّ بِالنَّوَافِلِ حَتَّى أُحِبَّهُ، فَإِذَا أَحْبَبْتُهُ كُنْتُ سَمْعَهُ الَّذِي يَسْمَعُ بِهِ، وَبَصَرَهُ الَّذِي يُبْصِرُ بِهِ، وَيَدَهُ الَّتِي يَبْطِشُ بِهَا، وَرِجْلَهُ الَّتِي يَمْشِي بِهَا، وَلَئِنْ سَأَلَنِي لَأُعْطِيَنَّهُ." [رَوَاهُ الْبُخَارِيُّ]

"..., wa la yazaalu 'Abdi yataqarrabu ilayya bin nawafile hatta ahebahu, fa idha ahbabtuhu kunta Sam'ahul ladhi yasma'u behi, wa Basarahul ladhi yubsiru behi, wa Yadahul lati yabTeshu beha, wa Rejlahul lati yamshi beha, wa la in sa alani la a'Teyannahu, ..."

"...My servant continues to draw near to Me with voluntary acts of worship so that I shall love him. When I love him, I am his hearing with which he hears, his seeing with which he sees, his hand with which he strikes and his foot with which he walks. Were he to ask [something] of Me, I would surely give it to him..."
Hadith Qudsi (Sahih al-Bukhari, 81:38:2)

Ma'rifah of Allah – Enter Hey, Lam, Lam, Alif

Submitting Your Will to Ulul Amr is to Submit to Prophet ﷺ and to Allah ﷻ

The more your will is submitting to the will of *ulul amr*, "Bismillahir rahmanir raheem, Atiullaha wa atiur Rasula wa Ulil amre minkum."

يَا أَيُّهَا الَّذِينَ آمَنُوا أَطِيعُوا اللَّهَ وَأَطِيعُوا الرَّسُولَ وَأُولِي الْأَمْرِ مِنْكُمْ... ﴿٥٩﴾

4:59 – "Ya ayyu hal latheena amanoo Atiullaha wa atiur Rasula wa Ulil amre minkum…" (Surat An-Nisa)

"O You who have believed, Obey Allah, Obey the Messenger, and those in authority among you…" (The Women, 4:59)

The more your will submits to the *ulul amr*, the more your will submits to Prophet ﷺ, the more your will has submitted to Allah ﷻ. So no doubt what comes into your heart begins to manifest.

Many *awliyaullah* (saints) merely want something within their heart. It's what Allah ﷻ wants, what Prophet ﷺ wants, what their *ulul amr* want that merely they put into their heart and it begins to manifest. And this is the world *of malakut* (heavenly realm). And they're teaching, *kun faya kun* is for Sayyidina Muhammad ﷺ. *Qul* is for Allah ﷻ and *qul* is teaching us that *Qaf wal Qur'anil Majeed* can only go to the *lam*.

قٓ وَالْقُرْآنِ الْمَجِيدِ ﴿١﴾

50:1 – "*Qaf, wal Quranil Majeed.*" (Surat Qaf)

"*Qaf. By the honored Qur'an.*" (The Letter Qaf, 50:1)

Ulul Amr Inherit From the Tongue of Sayyidina Muhammad ﷺ

And the only *lam* for Allah ﷻ is Sayyidina Muhammad ﷺ, *lisanul haq*. And the *ulul amr*, they are the tongues of truth. They inherit from the tongue of Sayyidina Muhammad ﷺ, *wa lisan as-siddiq*.

So then this *lam* (first *lam* from left) closest to *hidayat* (guidance) is representing the world of form, what they call the *mulk*. *Lam* closest to *hidayat* is the world of form. Why form? Because Prophet ﷺ is speaking it, everything in the material world that's manifesting because you're now moving from *mulk* to *malakut*. It means come through *hey* of *hidayat* to the *mulk* (earthly realm) of Allah ﷻ, the kingdom of Allah ﷻ that's manifesting. You can't go *malakut* first, you have to go *mulk wal malakut*.

الله			
Allah ﷻ			
ه	ل	ل	ا
Hey	Lam of Dunya	Lam of Akhirah	Alif
هداية	مُلك	مَلكوت	عزّت الله
Hidayat (Guidance)	Mulk (Material World)	Malakut (Heavens)	'Izzatullah (Allah's ﷻ Might)

*Note: Please read English from right to left to coincide with Arabic.

Ma'rifah of Allah – Enter Hey, Lam, Lam, Alif

Allah's ﷻ Power is Upon the Heart of His Believer, Sayyidina Muhammad ﷺ

That's why *awliyaullah* come in the *huroof* (Arabic letters) and they teach when you put this *alif*, you put it on the *lam* closest to the *hey* because Allah's ﷻ teaching, 'Come to My *Mulk*, come through My *Hadi*, and you'll find My Power and My *Qudra* upon his heart.' And that's why the *hadith*, 'I'm not on heaven, I'm not on earth but I'm on the heart of my believer.'

مَا وَسِعَنِيْ لَا سَمَائِيْ ولا اَرْضِيْ وَلَكِنْ وَسِعَنِيْ قَلْبِ عَبْدِيْ اَلْمُؤْمِنْ

"Maa wasi'anee laa Samayee, wa la ardee, laakin wasi'anee qalbi 'Abdee al Mu'min."

"Neither My Heavens nor My Earth can contain Me, but the heart of my Believing Servant."
(Hadith Qudsi conveyed by Prophet Muhammad (pbuh))

The believer of Allah ﷻ is Sayyidina Muhammad ﷺ. All of these are in *hadith*. That's why the *alif* is always moving and *qalb al-mu'min baytullah*. So, they move the *alif* onto that *lam* to teach that Allah's ﷻ *Izzah* is upon that reality.

قَلْبَ الْمُؤْمِنْ بَيْتُ الرَّبّ

"Qalb al mu'min baytur rabb."

"The heart of the believer is the House of the Lord." (Hadith Qudsi)

Sayyidina Muhammad ﷺ is Allah's ﷻ Only Representative

So then in *dunya* (material world), we have to come through *hidayat* and say *La ilaha illAllah Muhammadun RasulAllah* ﷺ and then you entered in now towards paradise realities. From there, Prophet ﷺ takes us to the second *lam*. And that is the kingdom of the heavens, where Prophet ﷺ described that, 'I was a *Rasul* before Adam was between clay and water.'

قَالَ رَسُولَ اللهِ صَلَّى اللهُ عَلَيْهِ وَسَلَّمَ: "كُنْتُ نَبِيًّا وَآدَمَ بَيْنَ الْمَاءِ وَالطِّينِ"

Qala Rasulullahi (saws) "Kuntu Nabiyan wa Adama baynal Maa e wat Teen."

"I was a Prophet and Adam was between water and clay."
(Prophet Muhammad (pbuh))

This means in *malakut*, 'I am *RasulAllah* ﷺ. I am *Habibullah (alaihis salaatus salaam)*.' It means Prophet's ﷺ *risalat* and messengership is eternal. In the world of light, the only one who represents Allah ﷻ is the soul of Sayyidina Muhammad ﷺ.

Ma'rifah of Allah – Enter Hey, Lam, Lam, Alif

Only Sayyidina Muhammad ﷺ Reaches the Divinely Presence

When you enter into the *nur* (light), the Divinely Presence of that *nur*, that is the reality of Sayyidina Muhammad ﷺ. And nobody can pass that reality to go towards Allah ﷻ. That's why *Isra wal Mi'raj* (Night of Ascension), that even Sayyidina Jibreel عليه السلام clarified that, 'I don't go beyond this limit because there's nobody between *Muhammadun RasulAllah* and *La ilaha illAllah*.' And that is *qaba qawsayni aw adna*. That there is no one in between, *bayna Ahad wa Ahmad* ﷺ, is only the *meem* of Muhammad ﷺ.

فَكَانَ قَابَ قَوْسَيْنِ أَوْ أَدْنَىٰ ﴿٩﴾

53:9 – *"Fakana qaaba qawsayni aw adna."* (Surat An-Najm)

"And was at a distance of two bow lengths or nearer [to the Divine Presence]." (The Star, 53:9)

Sayyidina Muhammad ﷺ is in the Lam, Lam, Hey of Allah ﷻ

They begin to teach us that the *lam, lam, hey*, everywhere in it is found

Muhammadun RasulAllah ﷺ. *Alif, Izzatullah*, is moving. Every time you see *lam, lam, hey*, Sayyidina Muhammad ﷺ is in there. So what they call that, from the Arabs, is *masiwa Allah* – all that's other than Allah ﷻ because Allah's ﷻ *Izzah* can only be found in the *alif*. When you see *lam, lam, hey*, there's a reality of Sayyidina Muhammad ﷺ in there.

So now when you're reading Holy Qur'an, they want us to understand that there's a reality of Prophet ﷺ. When the *alif* is moving, this is the way of *ma'rifah* (gnosticism). That Allah ﷻ merely puts *Izzah* on the *lam* and says, 'My *Izzah* upon this *lam* giving it its power.'

Within Each Lam Are Three More Realities: Lam, Alif and Meem

And beginning to teach, that when you open the *lam* – how they say that they can go into the *darajats* (levels) of knowledge of the *huroof*? They can take the one *huroof* and begin to open it. From the understanding of *lam*, they can open into three more levels of reality, that within every *lam* must be a *lam*, *alif* and a *meem*. Again, Allah ﷻ proving for us that, 'Even the *lam* has My *Izzah* and closest to you is the *meem* of Sayyidina Muhammad ﷺ.' It means that reality is containing that reality.

MEEM   ALIF   LAM

So when Mawlana Shaykh was teaching this is the reality of *ma'rifah* (gnosticism), that you must come to the guidance of Prophet ﷺ and begin to open the reality of the kingdom of form [first *lam* from left], the kingdom of the heavens [second *lam* from left], that subtle reality to reach towards *ma'rifah* of Allah ﷻ. And Allah ﷻ is always a hidden treasure wanting to be known, and will be known through the reality of Sayyidina Muhammad ﷺ.

كُنْتَ كَنْزاً مخفيا فَأَحْبَبْتُ أَنْ أُعْرَفَ؛ فَخَلَقْتُ خَلْقاً فَعَرَّفْتهُمْ بِي فَعَرَفُونِي

"Kuntu kanzan makhfiyya, fa ahbabtu an a'rafa, fa khalaqtu khalqan, fa 'arraftahum bi fa 'arafonee."

Allah (AJ) said, "I was a hidden Treasure then I desired to be known, so I created a creation to which I made Myself known; then they knew Me." (Hadith Qudsi)

Ma'rifah of Allah – Enter Hey, Lam, Lam, Alif

Alif – Lam – Meem Are the Keys to Enter Into the Holy Qur'an

So when they're teaching Holy Qur'an, Surat al-Baqarah starts with *alif, lam, meem*.

﴿الم ١﴾

2:1 - *"Alif-Lam-Meem"* (Surat Al-Baqarah)

"Alif, Lam, Meem." (The Cow, 2:1)

All of Holy Qur'an will be found in that understanding. *Izzatullah* through the *lam* and the tongue of truth will be known to you as *Muhammadun RasulAllah* ﷺ. So, when they say nobody knows those *huroof*, that's incorrect. They don't know what that *huroof* means, but Allah ﷻ has taught many that reality, and those are the keys in which they enter into the reality of Holy Qur'an. That is the key in which dresses their being and their soul. That from the *alif, lam, meem* is the whole story of creation, that always Allah's ﷻ *Izzah* is dressing the tongue of truth, and the only way towards that reality is through the Muhammadan reality.

The Meem is the Rope of Allah ﷻ

And that's why Allah ﷻ describes the *meem* like a *habl*, that hold tight to the rope of Allah ﷻ and don't separate.

﴿وَاعْتَصِمُوا بِحَبْلِ اللَّـهِ جَمِيعًا وَلَا تَفَرَّقُوا ١٠٣﴾

3:103 – *"Wa'tasimo bihab lillahi jamee'an wa la tafarraqo…"* (Surat Ali-Imran)

"And hold firmly to the rope of Allah all together and do not separate…" (Family of Imran, 3:103)

The rope of Allah ﷻ is the rope of that *meem*. When the *meem* is coming down, it's a rope towards humanity. That Prophet's ﷺ reality is a rope towards this understanding. And all reality is from that *alif*. And they begin to open the *alif*, and from within the *alif* you find *alif, lam, fa*. Just from *Izzatullah* that, that *alif, lam, meem* is a description that everything is contained in that reality. The whole story of creation from *Izzatullah* is coming to the *lisanul haq* and will be known to you as Sayyidina Muhammad ﷺ. What Allah ﷻ wants from us is reach *Maqamul Mahmud*. Come towards the reality of Prophet ﷺ, and the whole story of creation will be dressed upon you.

Alif – Lam – Fa Are the Opening of Al-Fatiha

If *awliyaullah* (saints) go into the *alif* and they begin to open the *alif*, the *alif* becomes *alif, lam, fa* which is a description of Allah's ﷻ opening of Al-Fatiha; and all Qur'an in seven verses of Fatiha. It means that's how they begin to show that story of creation can be unfolded with the reality of the *huroof*. And a deep understanding between this *lam* and *alif* is signified by *lam jalala*, that the way towards Allah ﷻ is based on *la*.

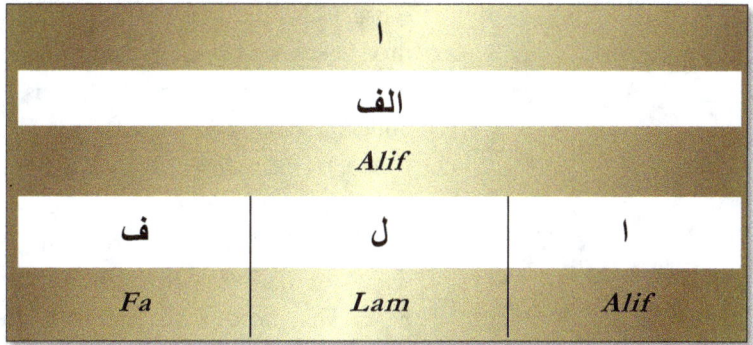

*Note: Please read English from right to left to coincide with Arabic.

So *la ilaha illAllah* – the *la* upon the head means don't use your head. *Lam alif* means no, *la*. But this is a deep meaning. This *lam* is for the tongue of truth known as *Muhammadun RasulAllah* ﷺ. The *alif* for *la ilaha illAllah*, when you combine them become *la* which means all the reality is based on that *la*.

Lam Alif Represents the Zulfiqar of Imam 'Ali

That *la* is the sword of Sayyidina 'Ali which we talked about when we talked about Sayyidina 'Ali. *Zulfiqar* is the *lam alif*. Given, it was the sword of Sayyidina Muhammad given to Sayyidina

'Ali, because he's *baabahu*. This is the city of knowledge. And the one who was holding Imam 'Ali was holding the secret of *lam alif* because these two *shak* (points) that are coming, these are the heads of the sword, that they come out to take the head off. That's why the first *zikr* for every *tariqah* (spiritual path) is *la ilaha illAllah*.

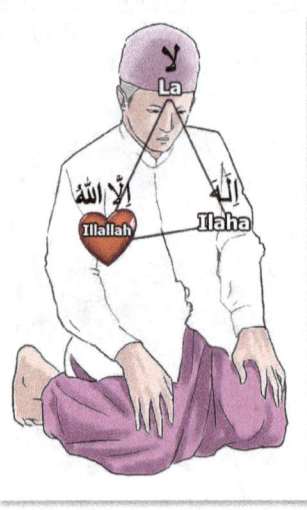

This means the way towards reality is not through the head where you sit and contemplate, 'That doesn't make sense.' The head has no capacity for that reality. It's based on the heart. And begin to teach every reality is in understanding *la, la, la,* that, '*Ya Rabbi*, let me to lose my head and open my heart.' So it's *la ilaha illAllah, illAllah, illAllah*, because that *nur* (light) of faith has to enter into the heart. That *nur* of faith enters the heart and begins to shut off the head.

Our Heart Must Be Like a Sun, Our Head Like A Moon

They want the head off and they want the heart to be like a sun. If the heart is a sun, *'Ash-shamsi wal qamar.'* Your head must be like a moon, not a sun. If your head is like a sun, it means it's constantly thinking and double-thinking and trying to contemplate what he's saying is wrong. But the sun, it just shines; the sun shines and the moon polishes. When the moon is polishing, polishing, polishing that,  'I don't know, I don't know, I don't know.' The reality of the sun can begin to shine upon the moon and become what they describe Prophet ﷺ was a full moon. It means every reality in that *lam alif.*

Subhana rabbika rabbal 'izzati 'amma yasifoon, wa salaamun 'alal mursaleen, walhamdulillahi rabbil 'aalameen. Bi hurmati Muhammad al-Mustafa wa bi siri Surat al-Fatiha.

REAL KA'BAH IN THE HEART OF MUHAMMAD ﷺ

Realities of Hu, Allah, Ahad

Allah ﷻ Directs Us to Sayyidina Muhammad ﷺ

Sayyidina Muhammad ﷺ from the oceans of Allah's ﷻ Divinely Lights. *"Bismillahir rahmanir raheem, ati ullah wa ati ar Rasul wa ulil amri minkum."*

...أَطِيعُوا اللَّهَ وَأَطِيعُوا الرَّسُولَ وَأُوْلِي الْأَمْرِ مِنكُمْ... ﴿٥٩﴾

4:59 – "...*Atiullaha wa atiur Rasula wa Ulil amre minkum...*" (Surat An-Nisa)

"... *Obey Allah, Obey the Messenger, and those in authority among you...*" (The Women, 4:59)

That we come to the love of Allah ﷻ and then Allah ﷻ directs us to Prophet ﷺ. That if you want to obey Me, then you follow the hand of Sayyidina Muhammad ﷺ. And by coming to the love of Sayyidina Muhammad ﷺ, Prophet ﷺ begins to inspire within our hearts, then look for my real *ulul amr* (saints).

Prophet ﷺ Inspires Us to Look For Ulul Amr

This means they are under Allah's ﷻ *Amr* (Command) and they have obeyed the commands within their heart. They have forbidden what is wrong within themselves, not the commanding to other people. But to command within themself what is not allowed and to follow what Allah ﷻ wants for that reality, so that the reality within the heart begins to open. They teach us by analogy and one understanding like the telescope. That it's coming out to us as a *rahmah* (mercy). That the obedience of Allah ﷻ, as soon as you want it, the rope extends that follow Sayyidina Muhammad ﷺ. And then look  for the way of Sayyidina Muhammad ﷺ. And then the rope from Prophet ﷺ extends and says, 'Look for my *ulul amr* (saints)'.

Real Ulul Amr Are Heavenly Ropes – 'Hold Tight and Don't Separate'

 These are the shaykhs of *tariqah* (spiritual path), the shaykhs of perfection, of *tazkiya* and cleaning and purification. So, now that rope has extended. And Allah ﷻ describes that holy rope in Qur'an, that, 'Hold tight to that rope and don't separate.'

وَاعْتَصِمُوا بِحَبْلِ اللَّهِ جَمِيعًا وَلَا تَفَرَّقُوا ۚ ﴿١٠٣﴾

3:103 – "Wa'tasimo bihab lillahi jamee'an wa la tafarraqo…" (Surat Ali-Imran)

"And hold firmly to the rope of Allah all together and do not separate..." (Family of Imran, 3:103)

Don't separate from the rope because that rope is a *najat* (salvation) in which to lift us back up into that reality. It's not just coming down, but it's lifting back up. It means that the *ulul amr* (saints) are the secret of *Hu*. And they are the real *huuu* men, *huuu*-man, *huuu*-man. We even have woman, but *hu*-man to be politically correct. But the reality of the *hu*-man – these are the *ulul amr*. They carry the secret of that *hu* within their heart. And they take us to the heart of Sayyidina Muhammad ﷺ.

The Ocean of Islam is the Ocean of Submission

And Sayyidina Muhammad ﷺ takes us to the Divinely *Haq* (truth). It means Allah ﷻ guides us in that direction. As soon as we hold tight, their duty is to take us back into that reality. And everything in that reality, everything from that ocean then is an understanding for us. That for the ocean of *Islam* is submission. It means that they bring us into the  ocean of submission. Ocean of *iman* (faith) is not the same as the ocean of *Islam*.

Islam is merely that you have accepted. These are the conditions; these are the rules – are you accepting in your life? And then we will be tested. As we become tested and proven, the light of *Islam* begins to open within the heart. And it's an experience, an overwhelming sense of light that comes into the heart and as if a whole recollection of your life is given to you. As if you've hit something and you reached a state of death and your whole life plays before you like a film. And then Allah ﷻ teaching that that is your life. Are you happy with it? And are you ready for that recording to be played in My Divinely Presence?

Islam and Iman Gives Us a Sense of Accountability

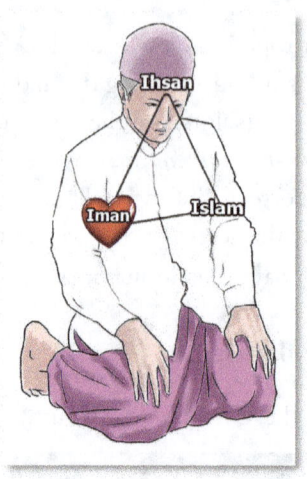

It means the light of *Islam*, once it begins, that light of *iman* (faith) begins to open within the heart. It begins to open the sense of reality that we are accountable. And we try to perfect ourselves to the best of our perfection, to the best of our ability, and live every moment in trying to clear that film, clear what has been taken as an account for us. That if there's something negative that can't be wiped off, '*Ya Rabbi*, let me at least to provide a positive in something good so that not to be ashamed when that film is played.'

Maqamul Ihsan is the Abode of Perfection

And then that *iman* now is opening *maqamul ihsan* (station of excellence). *Maqamul ihsan* is the abode of perfection. Because if you're constantly busy in trying to perfect ourselves, correct ourselves, clean ourselves, then we're reaching towards perfection and Allah has to grant that. That Allah grants *nasrullah*. That you keep struggling, you keep struggling, with everything I give you in life, you struggle.

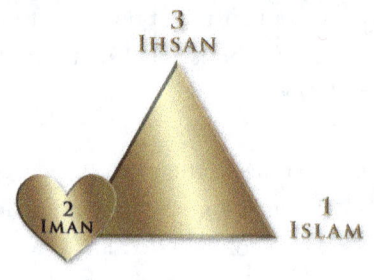

Regardless if anybody understands your struggle, cares for your struggle, you struggle for My purpose. And I grant you the satisfaction that when My *Nasrullah* comes, when My Oceans of Support comes, then at that time you'll understand what the abode of excellence is.

﴿إِذَا جَاءَ نَصْرُ اللَّهِ وَالْفَتْحُ ﴿١﴾﴾

110:1 – "Idha jaa a Nasrullahi wal Fath." (Surat An-Nasr)

"When there comes the Divine Support of Allah and the Victory." (The Divine Support, 110:1)

Prophet ﷺ is in the Heart of Ulul Amr

Then Mawlana Shaykh teaches this becomes the foundation of our belief. That Allah's ﷻ going to be found in the heart of Prophet ﷺ. Prophet ﷺ is going to be found only in the heart of the *ulul amr* (saints), the real *huuu-men*. That, and it is not a coincidence that most of their *zikrs* (remembrances) are *Allah Hu, Allah Hu, Allah Hu Haq,* because everything about them is from that reality. And they are an oasis of hope, bringing people back to the love of Sayyidina Muhammad ﷺ. Then it's Sayyidina Muhammad's ﷺ responsibility to bring them back to the love of Allah ﷻ. These are the oases of hope and the oases of *rahmah* (mercy).

Then, Mawlana Shaykh begins to teach in many different aspects of our life. One understanding is in the holy Ka'bah to put everything in its place and in its understanding. This means from *Qul huwa Allahu ahad.*

$$\text{قُلْ هُوَ اللَّـهُ أَحَدٌ ﴿١﴾}$$

112:1 – "Qul HuwAllahu Ahad." (Surat Al-Ikhlas)

"Say, He is Allah, [who is] One." (The Sincerity, 112:1)

The Ka'bah Directs Us to the Oneness of Allah ﷻ

It means we have *Hu, Allah, Ahad. Hu, Allah, Ahad* because it goes both directions. We go one direction understanding in the purpose of the holy Ka'bah is to bring people to the Oneness of Allah ﷻ. It's not to be worshipped. It's merely a direction. Ka'bah is not to be worshipped. Allah ﷻ is not within the holy Ka'bah.

This means the holy Ka'bah is a direction in which all mankind, because if the Earth was flat, it has to have its center in our life. But since it's round, same concept that it has a center, direct all of mankind to the *Ahad*, the unique Oneness of the Creator. That many things may be similar, but there is nothing like unto the Creator. That Allah ﷻ, many holy people, many great things, but there is nothing like the Creator of all creation, Allah ﷻ, Allah ﷻ, God Almighty, and Magnificent, and Munificent.

Sayyidina Muhammad ﷺ is the True Imam of the Ka'bah

So, then that Ka'bah symbolizes that for us. That from wherever you are, take off your identity. Take off what would identify you of your wealth, of your location, of who you are, what language you speak. And you put your white cloth and come almost as if you were born and they wrapped you in a blanket.

So, the *ahadiyya* reality is that Allah ﷻ saying then, 'Bring all creation towards that Ka'bah. Direct them towards My Oneness.' And that becomes now an understanding that everything must direct itself to the Oneness of Allah ﷻ.

Prophet ﷺ is the Owner of the Ka'bah

Then, as soon as we enter into the holy precincts, what happens there? This means at the time of Prophet ﷺ is most important for us. The *namaz* (prayer) at the Ka'bah is based on the *imam* of the Ka'bah. And the *imam* of the Ka'bah, not nowadays *imam*. *Imam*, the real *imam* of the holy Ka'bah is Sayyidina Muhammad ﷺ. What brings that honour, what brings *tashreef*, what brings nobility to the holy Ka'bah was the presence of Sayyidina Muhammad ﷺ. From its arrival in the time of Sayyidina Ibrahim ﷺ, Allah ﷻ brought that for the honour of Sayyidina Muhammad ﷺ. That when he arrives in this precinct, that he will be the owner of this house and that he will, *alayhis salatu salam*, will direct people towards My Oneness in the oceans of perfection.

Allah's ﷻ Reality is Within the Heart of Sayyidina Muhammad ﷺ

This means then it represents an opening that we are moving towards the oneness of Allah ﷻ. Allah ﷻ begins to clarify that I am not in that house. It's merely the direction of My Oneness. But I am in the heart of my believer.

It means then who is carrying the *Ahad* is coming towards the Ka'bah? From, from *ikhlas*, Allah ﷻ, *Qul hu Allahu ahad. Hu. Allah. Ahad.*

قُلْ هُوَ اللَّـهُ أَحَدٌ ﴿١﴾

112:1 – *"Qul HuwAllahu Ahad."* (Surat Al-Ikhlas)

"Say, He is Allah, [who is] One." (The Sincerity, 112:1)

Surat al-Ikhlas is About Sincerity

First *Ahad* is coming towards the oneness. Drop everything and lose your identity, lose your ego, lose your individuality and become one with that ocean. So, then *tariqah* (spiritual path) comes and specializes in that *tariqah*, in that reality. Lose your entire identity. Come into the  real ocean of oneness. As soon as you come into that ocean of oneness, then the next *maqam* (station) is the *Maqam* of Allah ﷻ because this is the ocean of purity.

Surat al-Ikhlas is *ikhlas*, is sincerity. So, Allah's ﷻ saying then, 'The people who are understanding *Ahad*, they come towards the Oneness.' So, then you see many people in this world only coming and calling everybody to oneness. But then to come towards the reality of Allah ﷻ is teaching then, 'My Reality is within the heart of the *imam*, within the heart of Sayyidina Muhammad ﷺ.'

Show Love of Prophet ﷺ By Following the Sunnah

This means then we're moving into that reality. We're coming towards holy Ka'bah, and then Allah ﷻ reminding us that if you're now looking for Allah ﷻ, it is within the heart of Sayyidina Muhammad ﷺ. And then we begin to direct ourselves to the love of Prophet ﷺ.

As soon as we direct ourselves to the love of Prophet ﷺ, it begins the opening of *sunnah* (way of Prophet ﷺ). That, when you love someone, you read about them and you emulate them. You copy them, you follow everything that Prophet ﷺ was doing – from how he was eating, how he was drinking, how he was interacting and loving people, teaching people.

The Heart of the Believer is the House of the Lord

It means everything you adorned yourself from that love, from that respect, from that *ihtiram*. And then Prophet ﷺ begins to open in his heart and towards that holy ocean of love. That in my heart is Allah's ﷻ Divinely Presence where Allah ﷻ is not in heavens, not on Earth, but in the heart of his believer and *qalb al mu'min baytullah*.

قَلْبَ الْمُؤْمِنْ بَيْتُ الرَّبّ

"*Qalb al mu'min baytur rabb.*"

"The heart of the believer is the House of the Lord." (Hadith Qudsi)

And then Allah ﷻ directing them, the real Ka'bah is within the heart of Prophet ﷺ. Direct yourself into the heart of Sayyidina Muhammad ﷺ and you should find the lights and the signs of Allah ﷻ within that holy heart.

Awliyaullah Are Lost Within the Ocean of Hu

As soon as we begin to direct ourself into that light and into that love, the reality of *Hu*, and the essence of Allah ﷻ from whatever Allah ﷻ wants to reveal because these are the *darajat* (levels) of *awliyaullah* (saints). What they are going through, it's unimaginable. But from whatever they're giving of an understanding for us, that they are lost within the ocean of *Hu*.

Go To Prophet ﷺ, Imam of Ka'bah, And Ask His Permission to Enter His Heart

And the *Hu*-ness which is the reflection of the Divine Essence and that reflection of *Hu* is always reflecting to the reflection of *Huwa* Muhammad ﷺ. And Prophet ﷺ reflecting and taking that reflection and giving it out to the lovers and the *ashiqeen* who are within his heart, who are  circumambulating within the heart of Prophet ﷺ and asking for Allah's ﷻ Divinely Presence. They are making the real *labayk Allahumma labayk* (Here I am, O Allah, here I am).

It means that, 'We came, *ya Rabbi,* to Your Ka'bah and we are coming to the door of Your *Imam* and asking for Your *Imam* to let us in within his heart so that we can really make our *tawaf* to Your Divinely Presence.'

Enter the Heart of Prophet ﷺ By Zikr Hu

Then beginning the lights of *Hu*; the lights of that reality begin to dress us. From the light of that reality, then beginning again into the oceans of reality. Now in that heart, in that presence only by *zikr Hu*, can the real – now goes back the other way. We came *Ahad* looking for Allah ﷻ because *Ahad* is Oneness. Stop all the *mushrikeen*. Stop everything that's false. Stop even putting association upon yourself as if you're important. You're an internal *mushrik* (idolator). Don't believe in technology, believe in Allah ﷻ.

So, this means *ahad, ahad, ahad, ahad* – looking for Allah ﷻ in the heart of Prophet ﷺ. Come within the heart of Prophet ﷺ. Only by *zikr Hu* is that reflection of the essence emanating within the heart of Prophet ﷺ. And all the souls trying to jump into that reality.

Sayyidina Bilal ؓ Was Tortured For His Love of Sayyidina Muhammad ﷺ

Only from that *zikr* (remembrance) of *Hu* then Allah ﷻ can open now, 'I open for you, Allah ﷻ.' From the reality of Allah ﷻ begins to open *Ahad, Ahad, Ahad*. It means the real uniqueness of *Ahad* where Sayyidina Bilal ؓ, the companion of Prophet ﷺ, when he was being crushed to death with the rock upon his chest. They say his *zikr* was *Ahad, Ahad, Ahad*.

It means the *maqamul ihsan* (station of excellence) that he had reached, unimaginable. He is a holy companion. But to struggle in accepting *Islam*, but that's not what got the rock on him. But it was his accepting of Sayyidina Muhammad ﷺ that put him through being tortured. They told him denounce the holy Prophet ﷺ.

Sayyidina Bilal ؓ Reached Perfection Through His Sincerity

So, this is now the understanding. You came to *Ahad*, you came to love of Allah ﷻ, *alhamdulillah*. But the companion is teaching us not only that, but they were telling him, 'Leave the Messenger of Allah ﷻ.' And he's teaching us the only way to that reality is in the service and the love of Sayyidina Muhammad ﷺ and, 'You're better off to kill me now.' And they put a rock to crush him. And as the state of dying is coming and the crushing is killing, the only *zikr* (remembrance) he is making now because he's now reached to that perfection.

And Prophet ﷺ described Sayyidina Bilal ؓ, 'As I hear his footsteps in paradise' while he was a companion in the presence of Prophet ﷺ, teaching from the highest levels of these realities. That at that time, after that love and struggling for the sake of Prophet ﷺ, reaching the *zikr Ahad, Ahad, Ahad*.

Our Love of Sayyidina Muhammad ﷺ Will Save Us From Difficulty

We pray that in these holy days, we understand these realities that Ka'bah is a place that directs us to that Oneness. But what's making holy Ka'bah to be Holy is the presence of Sayyidina Muhammad ﷺ. And that our love and *ashiqeen* (lovers), these are the people of *muhabbat* (love). The love of Sayyidina Muhammad ﷺ, and asking *ya Rasul Allah* ﷺ, *ya Habib Allah* ﷺ, *ya Nabi Allah* ﷺ means that the door of the *Nabi* (Prophet ﷺ) has to open and inside the heart is Allah ﷻ. The heart of that believer is emanating that light of the Divinely Presence.

We pray that in these holy nights they open for us more and more to go within that reality, to understand that reality and to keep their love. The love of Prophet ﷺ is everything for us. The love of Prophet ﷺ will save us. The love of Prophet ﷺ will lift us and take away difficulty from us. The love of Sayyidina Muhammad ﷺ will grant us *Islam*, will grant us *iman* (faith) and will grant us *maqamul ihsan* (station of excellence), *inshaAllah*.

Subhana rabbika rabbal 'izzati 'amma yasifoon, wa salaamun 'alal mursaleen, walhamdulillahi rabbil 'aalameen. Bi hurmati Muhammad al-Mustafa wa bi siri Surat al-Fatiha.

REALITY OF HU, FROM THE OCEAN OF LA ILAHA ILLALLAH, MUHAMMAD RASULALLAH ﷺ

Awliya Uplift Their Students to Teach Them About Themselves

Alhamdulillah, awliyaullah come into our life and lift us. When they lift us, they bring to life every holy *hadith* of Sayyidina Muhammad ﷺ and Prophet ﷺ taught that who knows himself, will know his Lord.

مَنْ عَرَفَ نَفْسَهُ فَقَدْ عَرَفَ رَبَّهُ

"Man 'arafa nafsahu faqad 'arafa Rabbahu"

"Who knows himself, knows his Lord." (Prophet Muhammad (pbuh))

One of the greatest gifts that Allah ﷻ can give by that uplifting is to have an understanding of yourself. What Allah ﷻ gives to you of a *sifat*, that attribute that governs your *wujud* (being). What Allah ﷻ created you from that *sifat*, from that attribute of Allah ﷻ. To know that reality is one of the greatest gifts. That's the power of that guide, the ability to uplift and take you into that presence and that that guide is teaching you about yourself. All of the *adab* (manners) of the *tariqah* (spiritual path) comes to show that be grateful. Be grateful for whatever Allah ﷻ reveals to the servant about themself.

Reality of Hu, From the Ocean of La Ilaha IllAllah, Muhammad RasulAllah ﷺ

Less Than 1% of People Might Truly Know Themselves

It's beyond imagination, with all the billions in creation, how none of them know anything about themself. And less than 1% of 1% of 1%, Allah ﷻ may reveal to them because of their struggle, their strive, their *muhabbat*, most important, their love. Their love will bring them to that reality and that is a tremendous gift. When Allah ﷻ says, 'Whom We bestowed wisdom upon has been given a tremendous gift.'

يُؤْتِي الْحِكْمَةَ مَن يَشَاءُ ۚ وَمَن يُؤْتَ الْحِكْمَةَ فَقَدْ أُوتِيَ خَيْرًا كَثِيرًا ۗ وَمَا يَذَّكَّرُ إِلَّا أُولُو الْأَلْبَابِ ﴿٢٦٩﴾

2:269 – *"Yu'til Hikmata mai yasha o; wa mai yutal Hikmata faqad otiya khairan kaseeraa; wa maa yazzakkaru illa ulul albaab." (Surat Al-Baqarah)*

"He gives wisdom to whom He wills, and whoever has been given wisdom has certainly been given abundant goodness. And none will remember except those of understanding." (The Cow, 2:269)

Our Character is Based on the Attribute That Allah ﷻ Bestowed Upon Us

A gift that keeps giving and a gift that shows the depth and the reality in Divinely Presence. And that's why the *turuq* (spiritual paths) come to

teach the *adab* (manners). That any time you don't show gratefulness, Allah ﷻ will be offended. This way is based on taking every reality and going deep, saying *subhanAllah*, that Allah ﷻ revealed about myself a reality. My responsibility is to write it, look at it, meditate upon it and go into it, the depth of which cannot be understood. And on the character of that individual, based on the attribute that Allah ﷻ made their soul. And they become a servant to that attribute. As a reality then they'll find that reality throughout its creation. If Allah ﷻ dressed you from *kareem* (the generous) and made you to be a generous servant, everything about your reality is based on generosity. You'll find the generosity in everything, if Allah ﷻ begin to open for it. It means then the character has to be based on good manners, good character.

Shaykhs of Ilm Kitab Take You to Divinely Presence

Understanding that these *awliyaullah* (saints) are shooting you like a rocket into that Divinely Presence, nothing from yourself. If for a moment you think it's you, then you're already like *Fir'aun* (Pharoah). *'Wa anna rabbil 'ala'*, Fir'aun told Nabi Musa ﷺ, 'I am the Lord most high', *astaghfirullah al-Azeem*.

فَقَالَ أَنَا رَبُّكُمُ الْأَعْلَىٰ ﴿٢٤﴾

79:24 – "Faqala ana rabbukumu al 'Aala." (Surat An-Nazi'at)

"And Fir'aun (Pharoah) said, I am your Lord All-Highest!" (Those Who Drag Forth, 79:24)

The path was based on negating yourself, I'm nothing, I'm nothing, I'm nothing. As soon as Allah ﷻ finds sincerity in that nothingness, give the *isharat* (sign) of the shaykh that lift. These shaykhs are from the people of *Ilm al-Kitab*, not the *jinn*. The *jinn* said, 'I'll lift but it's going to take some time.' One who has knowledge of the book, by the blink of your eye, you're already in that presence. Because they're swimming far beyond that. Whatever you think you're achieving, they're 1,000 *darajats* (stations) at least above. This is the greatness of this *deen* (religion).

Reality of Hu, From the Ocean of La Ilaha IllAllah, Muhammad RasulAllah ﷺ

قَالَ الَّذِي عِندَهُ عِلْمٌ مِّنَ الْكِتَابِ أَنَا آتِيكَ بِهِ قَبْلَ أَن يَرْتَدَّ إِلَيْكَ طَرْفُكَ ۚ فَلَمَّا رَآهُ مُسْتَقِرًّا عِندَهُ قَالَ هَٰذَا مِن فَضْلِ رَبِّي لِيَبْلُوَنِي أَأَشْكُرُ أَمْ أَكْفُرُ... ﴿٤٠﴾

27:40 – *"Qala alladhee 'indahu 'ilmun minal kitabi ana ateeka bihi qabla an yartadda ilayka Tarfuka, falamma raahu mustaqirran 'indahu qala hadha min fadli rabbi…"* (Surat An-Naml)

"Said one who had knowledge of the book: "I will bring it to you within the twinkling of an eye!" Then when (Solomon) saw it placed firmly before him, he said: "This is by the Grace of my Lord!…"
(The Ant, 27:40)

Reality of La Ilaha IllAllah – Allah ﷻ Wants to Be Known

What we wanted to talk about today in the *jummah*, in the celebration of the *Mawlid* of Sayyidina Muhammad ﷺ is the reality of *La ilaha illAllah Muhammadun RasulAllah* ﷺ.

لَا إِلَهَ إِلَّا اللهُ مُحَمَّدًا رَسُولُ الله

"La ilaha illAllahu Muhammadun RasulAllah."

"There is no deity but Allah, Prophet Muhammad is the messenger of Allah."

This is a secret of love and *muhabbat*. That when you write the *kalima*, *la ilaha illAllah*, alif-lam-lam-hey, there is a *waw*. The *hey* and the *waw* is the secret of *Hu*. So, everything about *la ilaha illAllah*, that there is nothing but Allah (عز وجل). In its reality, its magnificence, there is nothing but Allah (عز وجل) and everything is a temporary manifestation. Allah (عز وجل) is going to manifest this creation to be known. He's not manifesting because He likes tall buildings, not manifesting because He likes accounting. Not manifesting from anything of creation other than Allah (عز وجل) wants to be worshipped and wants to be known.

﴿وَمَا خَلَقْتُ الْجِنَّ وَالْإِنسَ إِلَّا لِيَعْبُدُونِ ٥٦﴾

51:56 – *"Wa ma khalaqtu aljinna wal insa illa liya'budoon."*
(*Surat Adh-Dhariyat*)

"I did not create jinn and humans Except to worship Me."
(*The Winnowing Winds, 51:56*)

Then you write the reality of *la ilaha illAllah*, that Allah (عز وجل) wants to be known. Allah (عز وجل) wants to be known by the *sifat* and the attribute that governs this entire reality, *sifat al-Wadud*. Through the *hey* and the *waw* of Allah (عز وجل), that *hey* is *hidayat*, means guided. That Allah (عز وجل) wants to be known so then whatever He creates from this point on has to be guided to *la ilaha illAllah*.

Reality of Hu, From the Ocean of La Ilaha IllAllah, Muhammad RasulAllah ﷺ

Allah ﷻ is the Power That Manifests Creation in Reality of Muhammadan RasulAllah ﷺ

The *Mawlid an-Nabi* ﷺ, for our understanding, only the 12th of Rabi' Al-Awwal is for the *dunya*. When did Allah ﷻ create that reality? Beyond understanding. When Allah ﷻ wanted to be known, it brings the *hey* of *hidayat* and through my *Hu*, My unknown 'He'. '*Hu*' is He. The 'He-ness' of Allah ﷻ, the unknown 'He-ness' of Allah ﷻ is about to bring the reality of Muhammadun RasulAllah ﷺ. Not only a physical personality, that's the smallest of understanding. But the light of Prophet ﷺ in which every light and every creation is going to be manifesting from that ocean. It's not manifesting from *la ilaha illAllah*. *La ilaha illAllah* is a power and a *qudra*. There is no *sharik* (partner), there is nothing like unto Allah ﷻ, there is no creation inside that reality. But Allah ﷻ is the power and the might that is going to make everything now manifest in the reality of *Muhammadun RasulAllah* ﷺ.

Allah ﷻ Makes Continuous Zikr of Hu to the Meem

By this power of *hey waw*, by the reality of *Hu*, Allah's ﷻ eternally making a *zikr* of *Hu*, *Hu* into that ocean that begins to manifest and appear as *Muhammadun RasulAllah* ﷺ. So, anything in this universe, it is in Bahrul Muheet, all existing within the *meem* of Muhammadun RasulAllah ﷺ.

Because the *Hu* is a continuous, eternal *zikr* to *meem*. The rest is going to be just an explanation of every reality. The *Hu* eternally is a *zikr* upon the *meem*.

إِنَّ اللَّهَ وَمَلَائِكَتَهُ يُصَلُّونَ عَلَى النَّبِيِّ يَا أَيُّهَا الَّذِينَ آمَنُوا صَلُّوا عَلَيْهِ وَسَلِّمُوا تَسْلِيماً ﴿٥٦﴾

33:56 – *"InnAllaha wa malaikatahu yusalluna 'alan Nabiyi yaa ayyuhal ladhina aamanu sallu 'alayhi wa sallimu taslima."*
(Surat Al-Ahzab)

"Allah and His angels send blessings upon the Prophet [Muhammad ﷺ]: O you that believe! Send your blessings upon him and salute him with all respect." (The Combined Forces, 33:56)

So *Muhammadiyun* and those whom Allah ﷻ raised in that reality, they understood. They go back all the way. Because the *usool* is *tawheed* (oneness). The first of the *usool* is *tawheed* (oneness). They become *Muhammadiyun* and Allah ﷻ makes them to have a heart of realities. They go back to that *meem* and they begin to make the *zikr* of *Hu*. 'Huuuuuuu.'

Mawlana Shah Naqshband ق is the Custodian of the Secret of Hu

Awliyaullah (saints) describe that Sultanul Awliya Mawlana Shah Naqshband ق is the custodian of that secret. That in that ocean of *Hu* when Sayyid Abu Yazid al-Bistami ق was diving and hearing the *zikr* of

Hu, entered into the realm in which he saw Mawlana Shah Naqshband ق making his spiritual *nazar* (gaze) upon infinite number of pearls. Because they describe – it's only for us to understand because we have no comprehension from what Allah ﷻ created of our brain. These are analogies for us to understand that in an ocean represents Allah's ﷻ infinite realities. Their soul swims into the ocean and they saw a pearl. Because the pearl symbolizes a reality that it takes something from this ocean and within it begins to create a jewel, something precious. And

Reality of Hu, From the Ocean of La Ilaha IllAllah, Muhammad RasulAllah ﷺ

Mawlana Shah Naqshband's ق *nazar* and secret from what Allah ﷻ dressed his soul of a Muhammadan *haqqaiq* (reality), his *nazar* (gaze) was *zikr* "*Hu*" upon this pearl.

Shaykhs Who Received Their Pearl From Shah Naqshband ق Have 12,000 Secrets

And *awliyaullah* (saints) who achieved this reality and can speak from that reality, they were given their pearl by Mawlana Shah Naqshband ق. These are not realities taught by somebody's book. This is not somebody copying and pasting from their shaykh. The shaykh is merely a rocket that takes him and throws him into his reality. And he speaks from what Allah ﷻ gave him of his reality in the Muhammadan *haqqaiq* (reality). He's not sharing anybody's reality. He's not stealing and plagiarizing from other people's reality.

Naqshbandiya *tariqah* (spiritual path), it's sign and it's miracle, Rifayi (*tariqah*) they put swords in their head. Naqshbandiya miracle is the *uloom* and the knowledges that are not on a book, not on a page, not on the internet unless they published it as a reality. But that pearl was given to them from Mawlana Shah Naqshband ق and put into their heart and into their chest and they witnessed and saw it. They witnessed the pearl enter into their chest and every reality and *"uloom ul-awaleen wa 'l-akhireen,"* (knowledges of the beginning and the end) begin to dress upon them. Then they were told by Mawlana Shah Naqshband ق that you'll have up to 12,000 secrets. Most of which, not even one can appear into *dunya*. Imagine 5, 6, 7, 8, of those *haqqaiqs* (realities) beginning to manifest into *dunya*. That is the reality of that *Hu*.

All Atoms in Creation Are Based on the Waw of Wadud and Love

When they talk of the *Hu*, this *hidayat* (guidance) that Allah (swt) not only the guides who bring basic people to Islam or take them to *Maqamul Iman* (Station of Faith) These are *kamil* (perfected), who they achieved *Maqamul Ihsan* (Station of Excellence). That they saw Allah (swt) in everything. Everything is Allah (swt); they feel Allah's (swt) presence in everything! And they begin to see Allah (swt) seeing in everything.

هو	
Hu	
و	ه
Waw	*Ha*
ودود	هداية
Wadud (The Most Loving)	*Hidayat* (Guidance)

*Note: Please read English from right to left to coincide with Arabic.

That ocean of *Hu* and *hidayat* and *waw*, that Allah (swt) link that *Hu* is now a description of the *meem*. And every reality of this *meem* of *Muhammadun RasulAllah* ﷺ. Everything is based on this *waw*. This whole entire manifestation, we said many times is based on *waw*, based on love. Not love that you say in the English language. That could mean many things, most of which are not right. Love and *wadud* means a deep, deep reality. The atom's world is based on *wadud* and *ishq* (love). Every movement, every manifestation, everything that's appearing as a hologram. All this creation is a hologram, infinite universes all a hologram. If Allah (swt) gives the order, stop and cut my love, pull *wadud*, everything stops spinning, everything stops moving, everything collapses into nothing.

Allah Wants This Creation to Manifest in Love

This whole of creation is based on *sifat al-Wadud*. Imagine then if Allah dresses the servant from *wadud* and divinely love, which they hold the secret of this manifestation. They hold the secret of *ishq* and love from the Divinely Presence. Then we begin to understand why these *Muhammadiyun*, why all these *awliyaullah* (saints) of the past. Not the ones who focus on business and money and taking people's money. The *awliyaullah* of the past who their only focus was on *wadud* and love. Because they witnessed that love in everything.

When they looked to the flower, they understand that the flower has a love and an *ishq* for the sun, because of the Muhammadan light that's emanating. And out of its love, it reciprocates. Out of its love, it wants to show the love of that Muhammadan light and begins to give a fragrance back. Because of the love affair between the sun and the flower, everybody benefits by its fragrance. Everything benefiting by the fragrance of  that reality, the perfume of that reality, the beatific reality of this *dunya* (material world) is its *ishq* and its love. Those lights and those realities are all *Muhammadiyun* because this is an ocean of *Muhammadun RasulAllah*. All of it is a manifestation of love that Allah wants this creation to manifest its love.

Sayyidina Muhammad ﷺ is in Need of Allah's ﷻ Love and Prophet's ﷺ Hamd is the Holy Qur'an

And what Allah ﷻ loves is this reality he created of *Muhammadun RasulAllah* ﷺ. When we understand this love then we understand this relationship. That Prophet ﷺ, the reality of *Muhammadun RasulAllah* ﷺ is in need, is in need for *la ilaha illAllah*, is in need for the love of Allah ﷻ. As soon as that love begins to hit Prophet ﷺ, emanates and dresses upon Sayyidina Muhammad ﷺ, begins to reveal the Holy Qur'an like a flower of immense realities. That Prophet ﷺ is like singing the praises of Allah ﷻ known to us as the Holy Qur'an because of the *ishq* and the love for Allah ﷻ.

When Allah ﷻ sends a love and *muhabbat* (love) upon the heart and the *wujud* and the soul of Sayyidina Muhammad ﷺ, this is the love relationship. Prophet ﷺ begins to make a *hamd* (praise). And Allah ﷻ saying he's *MuHamd*, my most praised. He's *Ahamd* above the *malakut* (heavenly realm) in his praise. The praise of Prophet ﷺ is the Holy Qur'an.

That Allah ﷻ is in want and love for Sayyidina Muhammad ﷺ, never in need. But Allah ﷻ wanted this creation to know Allah ﷻ. So, Allah ﷻ sends that love to Prophet ﷺ. As a result of that love, Prophet ﷺ begins to manifest all the *hamd* and all the praisings so that Allah ﷻ will be known. It takes two to tango, it takes two to dance. It takes the sun and the flower to show this *ishq* (love).

Reality of Hu, From the Ocean of La Ilaha IllAllah, Muhammad RasulAllah ﷺ

Allah ﷻ Wants to Be Known by the Best of Creation, Sayyidina Muhammad ﷺ

Allah ﷻ says, 'I want to be known.'

كُنْتُ كَنْزاً مخفيا فَأَحْبَبْتُ أَنْ أُعْرَفَ، فَخَلَقْتُ خَلْقاً فَعَرَّفْتهُمْ بِي فَعَرَفُونِي

"Kuntu kanzan makhfiyya, fa ahbabtu an a'rafa, fa khalaqtu khalqan, fa 'arraftahum bi fa 'arafonee."

Allah (AJ) said, "I was a hidden Treasure then I desired to be known, so I created a creation to which I made Myself known; then they knew Me." (Hadith Qudsi)

I'm going to send an immense love to this *Muhammadun RasulAllah* ﷺ. As a result, all this creation is manifesting from this love and this *hamd* (praise) that's emanating from the soul of Prophet ﷺ. And Prophet ﷺ is in need of that love from Allah ﷻ and Allah ﷻ is pleased by the manifestation of that love. Now I'll be known by *'khuluqul azeem'* (magnificent character).

وَإِنَّكَ لَعَلَىٰ خُلُقٍ عَظِيمٍ ﴿٤﴾

68:4 – *"Wa innaka la'ala khuluqin 'azheem."* (Surat Al-Qalam)

"Truly, You (O Muhammad!) are of a magnificent character."
(The Pen, 68:4)

I don't want to be known by anyone because all of their understanding is low. I want to be known by *Muhammadun RasulAllah* ﷺ. It means that the best of creation, *khuluqin azeem*, the best of character, the ambassador, my *khalifa* (deputy) that will show the best of example is how I want to be known to this creation. This is a love affair in which Allah ﷻ sends the love and we're all in need of manifesting that reality. We are all in need because we are carrying the Muhammadan light. We're in need, *ya Rabbi*, send for us the reality of *la ilaha illAllah*.

Seek the Love and Muhammadan Haqqaiq!

Ya Rabbi, send for us that reality of *muhabbat* and love that that *Hu*, that secret is in every atom, in every breath, in every molecule. As soon as we bring that love, we begin to manifest the Muhammadan *haqqaiqs* (realities). That sun begins to hit the flower and the flower begins to send its fragrance and its love. That is the reality of this relationship. The *awliyaullah* (saints)  are responsible in raising their Muhammadan students – that seek love, not characteristics of evilness and badness and jealousy and pride, egoistic desires of power, wealth. But seek the love! Seek the *muhabbat*, seek the reality in which Allah ﷻ is pleased with.

If you can seek that love, your life becomes like a hummingbird continuously in search of a nectar. And Allah ﷻ may send you a big nectar, a flower in which you can take an immense amount of love. As that love begins to nourish that reality of *la ilaha illAllah*, begin to enter into your Muhammadan RasulAllah ﷺ and your reality becomes powered.  But if by bad character, that *la ilaha illAllah* never enters into Muhammadun RasulAllah ﷺ because its secret is in the *waw* of *wadud*. This path is based on love, the characteristics are based on love, the actions are based on love. You have to tell yourself and ask yourself if

Reality of Hu, From the Ocean of La Ilaha IllAllah, Muhammad RasulAllah ﷺ

I'm a loving person, would I do that action? Would I take that action? Is that something that Prophet ﷺ would be pleased with? Let love govern your path. Let the love of the Divine govern the heart. Let the reality of *la ilaha illAllah* govern and nourish the reality of *Muhammadun RasulAllah* ﷺ. And then the reality of Prophet ﷺ begin to dress you even more and seeks more of that reality and that becomes the secret of fusion.

We pray that Allah ﷻ in these holy nights, coming tonight, tomorrow night, Sunday night, Monday night for the rest of this month, dress us from these lights, bless us from these lights *inshaAllah*. *Wa astaghfirullah Azeem.*

Subhana rabbika rabbal 'izzati 'amma yasifoon, wa salaamun 'alal mursaleen, walhamdulillahi rabbil 'aalameen. Bi hurmati Muhammad al-Mustafa wa bi siri Surat al-Fatiha.

19 LETTERS OF BISMILLAHIR RAHMANIR RAHEEM AND 19 LETTERS OF AHLUL BAYT ؏

The 19 Letters of Bismillah and Ahlul Bayt ؏ Hold Reality of Holy Qur'an

Asking from Mawlana Shaykh's teachings, from so many infinite oceans of *Bismillahir Rahmanir Raheem*. That many realities all are realities in *La ilaha illAllah Muhammadun RasulAllah* ﷺ. And from the oceans of creation, so many fountains flowing from *Bismillahir Rahmanir Raheem*. *Alhamdulillah*, we've talked before about Mawlana Shaykh's teaching from holy *hadith an-Nabi* ﷺ that all of Holy Qur'an in 30 *juz*. All 30 *juz*

(parts) like a laser in Surat Al-Fatiha. All of the reality of Surat Al-Fatiha that holding all of the reality of Holy Qur'an means it breaks from these 7. All of holy Fatiha is in the secret of *Bismillahir Rahmanir Raheem*. And *Bismillahir Rahmanir Raheem* is 19 letters. And 19 letters in Muhammad ﷺ, 'Ali, Fatima, Hassan, *wa* Hussain, *alayhis salatu wa salam* (peace and blessing be upon them).

19 Letters of Bismillahir Rahmanir Raheem and
19 Letters of Ahlul Bayt ﷺ

19 Letters of Bismillahir Rahmanir Raheem			
19, 18, 17, 16, 15, 14	13, 12, 11, 10, 9, 8	7, 6, 5, 4	3, 2, 1
الرحيم	الرحمن	الله	بسم
م ي ح ر ل ا	ن م ح ر ل ا	ا ل ل ه	ب س م
Al Raheem	Al Rahman	Allah	Bism
Ra, Lam, Alif Meem, Ya, Ha	Ra, Lam, Alif Noon, Meem, Ha	Lam, Alif, Hey, Lam	Meem, Seen, Ba

19 Letters of Ahlul Bayt ﷺ				
19, 18, 17, 16	15, 14, 13	12, 11, 10, 9, 8	7, 6, 5	4, 3, 2, 1
حسين	حسن	فاطمة	علي	محمد ﷺ
ن ي س ح	ن س ح	ة م ط ا ف	ي ل ع	د م ح م
Hussain ؑ	Hassan ؑ	Fatima ؑ	Ali ؑ	Muhammad ﷺ
Seen, Ha, Noon, Ya	Seen, Ha, Noon	Ta, Alif, Fa Ha, Meem	Lam, Ayn, Ya	Ha, Meem, Daal, Meem

Note: Please read English from right to left to coincide with Arabic.

All Creation is from Ocean of Muhammadun RasulAllah ﷺ

That everything that Allah ﷻ gave of the treasures of creation is in the

ocean of *Muhammadun RasulAllah* ﷺ. That's why we've said at the beginning that everything is in *La ilaha illAllah, la sharik* (no partner) with Allah ﷻ. When Allah ﷻ wants to be known, he creates *Muhammadun RasulAllah* ﷺ. It means that every creation is now blossoming from the ocean of *Muhammadun RasulAllah* ﷺ. So, the owner of *Bismillahir Rahmanir Raheem*, its reality is in *Muhammadun RasulAllah* ﷺ.

كُنْت كَنْزاً مخفيا فَأَحْبَبْت أَنْ أُعْرَفَ؛ فَخَلَقْت خَلْقاً فَعَرَّفْتهمْ بِي فَعَرَفُونِي

"Kuntu kanzan makhfiyya, fa ahbabtu an a'rafa, fa khalaqtu khalqan, fa 'arraftahum bi fa 'arafonee." Hadith Qudsi

Allah (AJ) said, "I was a hidden Treasure then I desired to be known, so I created a creation to which I made Myself known; then they knew Me."

Sayyidina Adam ؑ Saw the Realities of Ahlul Bayt ؑ in the Palace of Lights

When Sayyidina Adam ؑ was created and Sayyidina Jibreel ؑ, they put these different secrets together for us, for the seeker who is seeking realities. That Sayyidina Jibreel ؑ came and gave Sayyidina Adam ؑ a tour of paradise and went from one place to another place until he had come across the Palace of Lights. He said, unimaginable, unimaginable lights, and what are these lights, and who is this

seated upon the throne of lights? And many descriptions that we don't have written now in front of us, to perfectly quote its reality. But he saw the realities of Sayyidina Muhammad ﷺ, Sayyidatina Fatima ؑ, Sayyidina 'Ali ؑ, Sayyidina Hassan ؑ wa Sayyidina Hussain ؑ. And he saw their lights and he saw their magnificence and munificence.

*19 Letters of Bismillahir Rahmanir Raheem and
19 Letters of Ahlul Bayt ؑ*

Sayyidina Adam's ؑ Du'a of Repentance From Paradise

And he was taught certain words by Sayyidina Jibreel ؑ that, 'Remember these words, you'll need them,' knowing that Sayyidina Adam ؑ was soon going to fall from the paradise reality and be sent to this *dunya* (material world). And the words that he had told him was "Ya Hameed bi haqq e Muhammad ﷺ, sifat al Hameed bi haqq e Muhammad. Ya 'Ali bi haqq e 'Ali ؑ , Ya Khaliq bi haqq e Fatima ؑ, Ya Rahman bi haqq e Hassan ؑ, Ya Raheem bi haqq e Hussain ؑ."

بِسْمِ اللهِ الرَّحْمَنِ الرَّحِيمِ

بِسْمِ اللهِ الرَّحْمَنِ الرَّحِيمِ يَا حَمِيدُ بِحَقِّ مُحَمَّدٍ ﷺ ، يَا عَلِيُّ بِحَقِّ عَلِيٍ ؑ ، يَا خَالِقُ بِحَقِّ فَاطِمَةُ الزَّهْرَاءِ ؑ ، يَا رَحْمَنُ بِحَقِّ حَسَنٍ ؑ ، يَا رَحِيمُ بِحَقِّ حُسَّيْنٍ ؑ

Bismillahir Rahmanir Raheem

"Ya Hamidu bi Haqqi Muhammad ﷺ, Ya 'Aliyu be Haqqi 'Ali ؑ, Ya Khaliqu bi Haqqi Fatimatuz Zahra ؑ, Ya Rahmanu bi Haqqi Hassan ؑ, Ya Raheemu bi Haqqi Hussain ؑ."

In the name of Allah, the Most compassionate, the Most Merciful

O' the Praiseworthy for the sake of Prophet Muhammad (pbuh), O' the Most High for the sake of Imam 'Ali (as), O' the Creator for the sake of Fatima Zahra (as), O the Most Compassionate for the sake of Imam Hassan (as), O' the Most Merciful for the sake of Imam Hussain (as).

Ya Rabbi, from the blessings of their reality, forgive me, grant me your *maghfirah* and your forgiveness. He was taught these words and they called it the repentance of Sayyidina Adam ﷺ. That when he had landed on Earth, for 40 years of crying, and then a *khater* (thought) came into his heart and says, 'Remember, look up.' And when he looked up to the Divinely Throne, he immediately remembered, made that *du'a*, and Allah ﷻ says, 'If you had asked, anything with those words, I would have granted them instantly.'

The Four Rivers From Bismillahir Rahmanir Raheem: Water, Milk, Nectar & Honey

For us in the oceans of *ma'rifah* (gnosticism), it's teaching that everything has a dress from the family of Sayyidina Muhammad ﷺ. We've said before, *Bismillahir Rahmanir Raheem* – the *meem, ha, meem, meem - Muhamma*. It means just the *Bismillahir Rahmanir Raheem*, the *meem* of *Bismi*, *meem, ha, meem, meem - Muhamma*. It means the whole of *Bismillahir Rahmanir Raheem* is the *hamd* (praise) of Sayyidina Muhammad ﷺ. *Ya Hameed bi haqq e Muhammad* ﷺ, which means the whole umbrella of *Bismillahir Rahmanir Raheem* is Muhammad.

And those are the four fountains of paradise. The fountain coming from the *meem* of *Bismi* is the fountain of Water. From the Allah ﷻ, the *hey* of Allah ﷻ, *hidayat* (guidance), coming the fountain of Milk. From the *meem* of *Rahman*, the fountains of Nectar. And Prophet ﷺ had seen this on the *Mi'raj* (ascension) and saw before the bounty, the lote tree that he saw all of creation on the tree of *Bismillahir Rahmanir Raheem*. And saw the four rivers that are flowing beneath the tree of *Bismillahir Rahmanir Raheem* to the pond of the *Kawthar*. The *meem* of *Raheem* is the fountain

19 Letters of Bismillahir Rahmanir Raheem and
19 Letters of Ahlul Bayt ﷺ

of *asal*, Honey. So, you have the Water, Milk, Nectar, and Honey. From that reality, all of it is *Muhamma*, the spinning oceans of power.

Sayyidina Muhammad ﷺ is the Reflection of Every Divine Attribute

So, in the understanding and the unlocking of the keys of *Bismillahir Rahmanir Raheem*, that it's a question, that Allah ﷻ, and many secrets and fruits within that. That Allah ﷻ is asking in which name of *Rahmanir Raheem* do you open every reality? Because for every action, first is *Bismillahir Rahmanir Raheem*, and move into that reality, move into that action. So, for us the understanding is Sayyidina Muhammad ﷺ is the umbrella of all creation. That he is *Bismillahir Rahmanir Raheem*. "*Inna Huwa Sulayman, Wa inna Huwa Bismillahir Rahmanir Raheem.*" That is Allah's ﷻ *Rahman*. He is Allah's ﷻ *Raheem*. He is Allah's ﷻ every attribute, Prophet ﷺ is the reflection of that for creation to know.

إِنَّهُ مِن سُلَيْمَانَ وَإِنَّهُ بِسْمِ اللَّـهِ الرَّحْمَـٰنِ الرَّحِيمِ ﴿٣٠﴾

27:30 – "*Inna Hu min Sulaymana, Wa inna Hu Bismillahir Rahmanir Raheem.*" (*Surat An-Naml*)

"Indeed, it is from Solomon, and indeed, He/it is (as follows): 'In the name of Allah, the Most Beneficent, the Most Merciful.
(The Ant, 27:30)

The Ba of Bismi is the Reality of Imam 'Ali ﷺ – Baab e Hu (Door of Hu)

Then from the *Bismi*, they begin to teach us that the reality of the *ba* and all the power of *Bismillahir Rahmanir Raheem* is in the *ba*. And all the power of the *ba* is in the *nuqt*. And that reality is under Sayyidina 'Ali. And that *Ya 'Ali bi haqq e 'Ali* means Allah Most High. It means that *qudra* and that power, Allah Most High and by the reality that he's dressing Sayyidina 'Ali. And that's why Prophet said, *"Ana Madinatul, Madinatul Ilm, wa 'Ali, BaabHu."* Baab e Hu. Baab e Hu; he's the door of – because we take everything very simplistic, instead of making it complicated – he's the *Baab e Hu* (door of Hu).

قَالَ رَسُولُ اللَّهِ صَلَّى اللَّهُ عَلَيْهِ وَسَلَّمَ : "أَنَا مَدِينَةُ الْعِلْمِ وَعَلِيٌّ بَابُهَا، فَمَنْ أَرَادَ الْمَدِينَةَ فَلْيَأْتِ مِنْ بَابِهَا."

Qala RasulAllah (saws): "Ana Madinatul 'Ilmi wa "Ali yyun Babuha, Faman Aradal Madinata falya'ti min Babuha." (Hassan)

The Prophet (s) said: "I am the city of knowledge and Imam "Ali is its gate/gatekeeper, so whoever wants from the city must take from its gate/gatekeeper" [Sound hadith by Imam Tirmidhi in al-Awsat]

That Prophet is all of *Bismillahir Rahmanir Raheem* and the *baab*, the door of the *Hu*, the door of the reality is Sayyidina 'Ali. The *nuqt* of Sayyidina 'Ali then becomes the opening and the secret of how all this creation manifesting.

*19 Letters of Bismillahir Rahmanir Raheem and
19 Letters of Ahlul Bayt ؑ*

Allah ﷻ Completely Owns the Sifat Al Khaliq – The Creator

Next, in the family from *Bismi* under the *tajalli* (manifestation) of Sayyidina 'Ali ؑ, Allah ﷻ, what makes Allah ﷻ for us, is the uniqueness. And what makes Allah ﷻ unique is that only Allah ﷻ can create. So, *sifat al Khaliq*. So, from the *qudra* this is now how creation unfolds. From *qudra*, there must be a power. There must be from ancient knowledges, *"Khalaqal Insana min alaq."* There must be an ancient knowledge that begins to move. And through that knowledge, Allah ﷻ is going to manifest what Allah ﷻ wants to manifest.

$$\text{خَلَقَ الْإِنسَانَ مِنْ عَلَقٍ ﴿٢﴾}$$

96:2 – *"Khalaqal insana min 'alaq." (Surat Al-Alaq)*

"Created Human from a clinging substance." (The Clot, 96:2)

Sifat al-Khaliq is the secret of Allah ﷻ, the uniqueness of Allah ﷻ. You can be merciful and Allah ﷻ, Most Merciful. You can be compassionate and Allah ﷻ, Most Compassionate. But you cannot be Creator. Allah ﷻ owns that completely; unique that I am the Creator and nobody creates.

Secret of Creation Was Given to Sayyidatina Fatima az-Zahra ؏

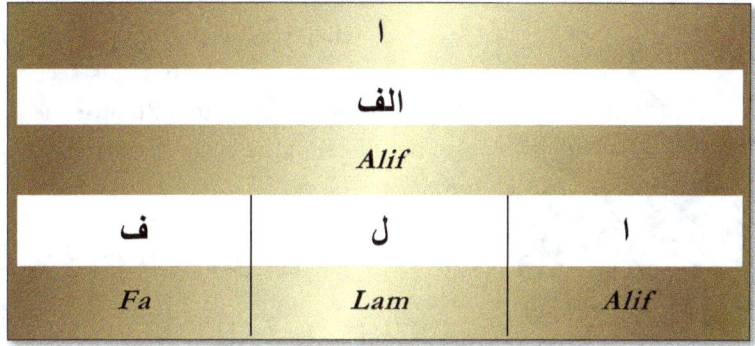

Note: Please read English from right to left to coincide with Arabic.

But, Allah ﷻ dresses *sifat al-Khaliq* on the secret and the reality of Fatima ؏, because she holds the secret of the *fa*. Fa, *al-Fatah* (the Opener/Reliever), *fa*, al-Fatiha (the Opener). This means from every opening has to come from the *fa*. The *fa* even hidden in that *'alif*. *'Alif, lam, fa* because *'alif* is written *'alif*. *'Alif*, once spoken, becomes *'alif, lam, fa*. That is Allah ﷻ, the beginning.

It means Sitna Fatima ؏ is dressed by this reality of Allah ﷻ because everything has to manifest through Prophet ﷺ. Every attribute doesn't come from Allah ﷻ directly to you. It must go through *tawheed* (oneness). It must move through *La ilaha illAllah Muhammadun RasulAllah* ﷺ and out through creation. So, *Khaliq*, its secret is given to Sayyidina Muhammad ﷺ. And Prophet ﷺ has given a secret of creation to Sayyidatina Fatima az-Zahra ؏, that everything coming into creation is that secret in her hands.

*19 Letters of Bismillahir Rahmanir Raheem and
19 Letters of Ahlul Bayt ﷺ*

Souls of Ahlul Kisa (Family of Prophet ﷺ) Are the Main Pillars of Creation

So, then when you begin to ponder when a woman gives birth, she has this secret of creation within her womb. Because the soul comes first, not the body. *"Allamal Quran, Khalaqal Insan."*

عَلَّمَ الْقُرْآنَ ﴿٢﴾ خَلَقَ الْإِنسَانَ ﴿٣﴾

55:2-3 – "Allamal Qur'an (2). Khalaqal Insaan (3)." (Surat Ar Rahman)

"It is He Who has taught the Qur'an. (2) He has created Mankind. (3)" (The Beneficent, 55: 2-3)

Allah's ﷻ Ancient Souls is the soul of Sayyidina Muhammad ﷺ and all these *Ahlul Bayt* ﷺ, especially the *ahlul kisa* (people of the cloak - 'Ali ﷺ, Fatima ﷺ, Hassan ﷺ, Hussain ﷺ), are the main pillars of creation. That those are ancient souls and the ancient reality dressed upon them. It is the fountain of all creation that's opening. So, Allah ﷻ giving the secret of creation to the light of Sayyidina Muhammad ﷺ, so that in our ocean of creation things are being born.

What Power Allah ﷻ Has Given to Women to Bear Children? Secret of 'Alaq

So in what power, a womb of a woman has power to bear children, must be a secret from knowledge. *"Khalaqal insana min alaq."* Allah's ﷻ Ancient Knowledge, *Al 'Alim, lam* through the *lisanul haq,* through the tongue of His truthful

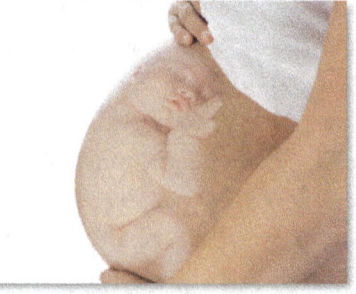

representative, *Qaf*, *"Qaf, wal Quranil Majeed"* (Holy Qur'an, 50:1). If they have the reality of Holy Qur'an within them, Allah ﷻ says they can revive the dead. They can bring creation to existence. Everything is by *Izzatullah* (Allah's ﷻ Might and Majesty) under the Holy Qur'an.

$$خَلَقَ الْإِنسَانَ مِنْ عَلَقٍ ﴿٢﴾$$

96:2 – *"Khalaqal insana min 'alaq. (Surat Al-Alaq)*

"Created Human from a clinging substance." (The Clot, 96:2)

This means the secret that's dressing how a woman has a child in her womb. It's from Allah ﷻ but she must have some sort of secret that this molds a child in a *rahem* (womb).

Secret of Rahem and the Unimaginable Nobility of Sayyidatina Fatima ؑ

This is *sifat ar-Rahman*. *Ar Rahem*, before the *noon* that that secret, once it's born is granted a *noon*. And comes into existence, but it must have an owner of that secret. So, *Ya Khaliq bi haqq e Fatima* ؑ, that for everything coming into existence, and everything coming out of the oceans of creation. That secret given to Sayyidina Muhammad ﷺ, Sayyidina Muhammad ﷺ dressing Sayyidatina Fatima az-Zahra ؑ from that reality. It means that majesty and the nobleness is unimaginable.

*19 Letters of Bismillahir Rahmanir Raheem and
19 Letters of Ahlul Bayt* ؏

With the water, (from the *Bismi* of *Bismillah*) it's coming to the reality of Sayyidatina Fatima az-Zahra ؏ (refers to Allah ﷻ in *Bismillah*). So, then the water and the reality of Sayyidina 'Ali ؏, an ancient soul of Allah's ﷻ reality, is destined to meet with the secret of Sayyidatina Fatima az-Zahra ؏. And what happens when *insan* meet, creation comes into existence. It means from the power and the *qudra*, that reality of Sayyidina 'Ali ؏ in the womb and the reality of Sayyidatina Fatima az-Zahra ؏ is the birth of Imam al Hassan ؏.

Sifat Ar-Rahman Dresses Imam Hassan ؏

From this tree of life, everything under *sifat ar-Rahman* is in the physical world. That everything that Allah ﷻ says, I am *Ar-Rahman* and I sit upon the throne, *'alal 'Arshi istawa*.

$$\text{الرَّحْمَٰنُ عَلَى الْعَرْشِ اسْتَوَىٰ ﴿٥﴾}$$

20:5 – "*ArRahmanu 'alal 'arshi istawa.*" (Surat Taha)

"*The Most Merciful [who is] above the Throne established.*"
(Ta-ha, 20:5)

This means that everything in the physical world is under *sifat ar-Rahman*. So, Ya ArRahman bi haqq e Imam al Hassan al Mujtaba. This means that from that reality of lights, Sayyidatina Fatima ؏ gave birth to *hasanat*, the goodness. And all the *sifat* of *Rahman* is dressing and blessing and coming through the soul of Imam Hassan ؏. And that everything in the physical world is being dressed by that reality.

From the Noon of Rahman is the Nur of Existence

Then they begin to tell us, look at the *huroof: ra, ha, meem – rahem*. *Rahem* is womb. That from the *rahem*, anything born, Allah ﷻ grants to it a *noon*, a *nur* (light). Once you have light, you have existence. So, from the *rahem* comes a *nur* and it's born. That *Rahman* and the secret of that *noon* and that ocean of *noon*, if you look at just the *ha, meem, noon*. That that light of *noon* is connected to the *meem* of Sayyidina Muhammad ﷺ. It means if you want the light of *Rahman*, you want that *nur*, you have to enter into that *noon* and that *noon* leads us to the *meem* of Sayyidina Muhammad ﷺ. It's *Bahrul Muheet*, that everything is within the ocean of *Muhammadun RasulAllah* ﷺ. Leads us to what? *Hay* from the oceans of *hayat* (ever-living). For us then because the *ahle haq* (people of truth), these are also the *ahle hub* (people of love).

رحمن			
Rahman			
ن	م	ح	ر
Noon	Meem	Ha	Ra
نور	محمداً ﷺ	حياة	ربوبية
Nur (Light)	Muhammadan ﷺ (Muhammadan Realities ﷺ)	Hayat (Ever-Living)	Rubbubiya (Lordship)

*Note: Please read English from right to left to coincide with Arabic.

19 Letters of Bismillahir Rahmanir Raheem and
19 Letters of Ahlul Bayt ؑ

Decoding the Name of Imam Hassan ؑ – Ha, Seen, Noon

It means we are asking to understand the attribute of *Rahman*. And the breakup for us that you want a light, then the light begins to show us, 'Go to the *meem* of Sayyidina Muhammad ﷺ,' and from the *meem* of Sayyidina Muhammad ﷺ take us to the oceans of *Al-Hayat*. And who is from the ocean of *Al-Hayat*? That Allah ﷻ granted him to be named *al-Hassan* because he is from the reality of the oceans of *hayat* (ever-living).

He has the *seen*. Hassan ؑ is the *seen* because he has the secret from Prophet ﷺ. He carries the *noon* which is the light of his reality. It is the inheritance of the *noon* of *Rahman*. For Allah's ﷻ attribute to be known, it must manifest through Prophet ﷺ, from Prophet ﷺ to his *Ahlul Bayt* ؑ to *Ashab an-Nabi* ﷺ. So, they're teaching us that the *ha*, the *ha* of Hassan ؑ is from the ocean of *hayat*. He carries the *sir* and the secret of Sayyidina Muhammad ﷺ which was the *Bismi*, the secret of his *jad* (grandfather). The *seen* was in the *Bismi*. He carries the secret of Prophet ﷺ, of Imam 'Ali ؑ, Sayyidatina Fatima az-Zahra ؑ. And he is the *noon* and the *nur*, emanating within *dunya* (material realm).

	حسن (عليه السلام)	
	Hassan (as)	
ن	س	ح
Noon	Seen	Ha
نور	سر	حياة
Nur (Light)	Sir (Secret)	Hayat (Ever-Living)

*Note: Please read English from right to left to coincide with Arabic.

The Best Hasanat (Goodness) is to Hold Fast to Holy Qur'an and Ahlul Bayt ﷺ

So, then Allah ﷻ tells us in Holy Qur'an, *"Fid dunya Hassanat, wa aakhira Hassanat, wa qinaa azaaban naar."* Attain the *hasanat* in *dunya* and the *hasanat* of *akhirah* and stay away from the fire.

وَمِنْهُم مَّن يَقُولُ رَبَّنَا آتِنَا فِي الدُّنْيَا حَسَنَةً وَفِي الْآخِرَةِ حَسَنَةً وَقِنَا عَذَابَ النَّارِ ﴿٢٠١﴾

2:201 – *"Wa minhum mai yaqoolu rabbanaaa aatina fid dunyaa Hassanatawn wa fil aakhirati Hassanatanw wa qinaa azaaban Naar."* (Surat Al-Baqarah)

"Our Lord, give us in this world [that which is] good and in the Hereafter [that which is] good and protect us from the punishment of the Fire." (The Cow, 2:201)

Hasanat for us is not good deeds. Because the best of deeds is to accompany the family of Prophet ﷺ. Not good deeds of reading a book and picking up change of the floor. The highest of *Hasanat* is Prophet's ﷺ *hadith*, 'I leave for you Qur'an, my *sunnah*, and my family.'

عَنْ جَابِرِ بْنِ عَبْدِ اللهِ رَضِيَ اللهُ عَنْهُ: عَنْ رَسُولِ اللَّهِ صَلَّى اللهُ عَلَيْهِ وَسَلَّمَ قَالَ: يَا أَيُّهَا النَّاسُ، إِنِّي تَرَكْتُ فِيكُمْ مَا إِنْ أَخَذْتُمْ بِهِ لَنْ تَضِلُّوا: كِتَابَ اللهِ وَعِتْرَتِيْ أَهْلَ بَيْتِيْ. اَلتِّرْمِذِيْ (٣٧٨٦)

'An Jabiri bin Abdullahi ﷺ: *"'An Rasulallahi* ﷺ *qala: 'Ya ayyuhan naasu, inni taraktu fikum ma`a in akhaztum bihi lan tadillo: Kitaballahi wa 'itrati ahla bayti.'"*

19 Letters of Bismillahir Rahmanir Raheem and
19 Letters of Ahlul Bayt ؑ

Narrated Jabir bin 'Abdullah (ra): "the Messenger of Allah said, 'O people! Indeed, I have left among you, that which if you hold fast to it, you shall not go astray: the Book of Allah (Quran) and my descendants from the people of my house (my family).'" [Al Tirmidhi (3786)]

Accompany Family of Prophet ﷺ in Dunya to be With Them in Akhirah

This means keep the company of my family. Eat with them in *dunya*, drink with them in *dunya*, pray with them in *dunya*, live and be happy and sad with them in *dunya* (material world), and you must know that you will be with them in *akhirah* (hereafter). You spend your *dunya* with the family of Sayyidina Muhammad ﷺ, asking, 'Ya Rabbi, grant me *Hasanat*. Grant me from the reality of Imam Hassan ؑ, that to live this *sifat ar-Rahman* with that light.' Then Allah ﷻ says, 'Then accompany that light, and they'll dress you from their secret.' Imam Hassan ؑ comes to dress us from that light, dress us from the *sir* (secret), and that *sir* opens into the oceans of *Al-Hayat* (ever-living).

When our *dunya* is with them and living with them, eating with them, drinking with them, praying with them. Loving Prophet ﷺ, loving *Ashab an-Nabi* ﷺ, loving *Ahlul Bayt an-Nabi* ﷺ, and that our whole life is for Sayyidina Muhammad ﷺ and *tashreef* (honour) and respect and *ihtiram*. This is the holy month of Sha'ban. And in the month of Rajab, Allah ﷻ showed, 'My Love for Prophet ﷺ, you can never do what I did for the love of Sayyidina Muhammad ﷺ. Whatever you do it still comes short. I brought all my creation to witness the greatness of Prophet ﷺ.' In the holy month of Sha'ban, then we're asking 'Ya Rabbi, grant us the real *Hasanat*.'

Sifat Ar-Raheem Dresses Imam Hussain ؏

So, then the next born from that reality is also Hassan, but he's younger and called Hussain ؏. Hussain means 'small Hassan.' If keeping the company of Imam Hassan ؏ and *Hasanat* of *Ahlul Bayt* ؏, and blessings of *Ahlul Bayt* ؏, and the love of Sayyidina Muhammad ﷺ, love of the way, and the Companions of Sayyidina Muhammad ﷺ, then Imam Hussain ؏ comes and begins to teach us that *'Ya Raheem bi haqq e Hussain ؏.'*

بِسْمِ اللهِ الرَّحْمَنِ الرَّحِيمِ

بِسْمِ اللهِ الرَّحْمَنِ الرَّحِيمِ يَا حَمِيدُ بِحَقِّ مُحَمَّدٍ ﷺ ، يَا عَلِيُّ بِحَقِّ عَلِي ؏ ، يَا خَالِقُ بِحَقِّ فَاطِمَةُ الزَّهْرَاءِ ؏ ، يَا رَحْمَنُ بِحَقِّ حَسَنٍ ؏ ، يَا رَحِيمُ بِحَقِّ حُسَّيْنٍ ؏

Bismillahir Rahmanir Raheem

Ya Hamidu bi Haqqi Muhammad ﷺ, *Ya 'Aliyu be Haqqi 'Ali* ؏, *Ya Khaliqu bi Haqqi Fatimatuz Zahra* ؏, *Ya Rahmanu bi Haqqi Hassan* ؏, *Ya Raheemu bi Haqqi Hussain* ؏."

In the name of Allah, the Most compassionate, the Most Merciful

O' Most praised one for the sake of Prophet Muhammad (pbuh), O' the Most High for the sake of Imam 'Ali (as), O' the Creator for the sake of Fatima Zahra (as), O the Most Compassionate for the sake of Imam Hassan (as), O' the Most Merciful for the sake of Imam Hussain (as).

19 Letters of Bismillahir Rahmanir Raheem and
19 Letters of Ahlul Bayt ﷺ

Every Secret is Coming from Prophet Muhammad ﷺ and His Ahlul Bayt ﷺ

Why *sifat ar-Raheem*? Because this is the *du'a*. It's not just that we're making a *du'a* and asking, 'Ya Rabbi, grant us just from the *du'a*.' Allah ﷻ says you have to live the *du'a*. Ya Hameed bi haqq e Muhammad ﷺ. That all my life is to be accompanying the love of Prophet ﷺ. And he  is *Hameed*, the Most Praised One and the One who praises Allah ﷻ the most – whom Allah ﷻ praises and whom he praises Allah ﷻ the most. So, then accompany that *Hamd*. Ya 'Ali bi haqq e 'Ali ﷺ. Then know that my greatness is with that family, my love is with that family. Ya Khaliq bi haqq e Fatima ﷺ. That Ya Rabbi, every secret is coming from that reality, that love and that respect. And then *sifat ar-Rahman* that in the physical world, seek them out. Be with them, eat with them, drink with them, and then Imam Hussain ﷺ comes to teach us.

Imam Hussain ﷺ is Sayyid e Shuhada: Master of Those Who See with Yaqeen

حسين (عليه السلام)			
Hussain (as)			
ن	ي	س	ح
Noon	Ya	Seen	Ha
نور	يقين	سر	حياة
Nur (Light)	Yaqeen (Certainty)	Sir (Secret)	Hayat (Ever-Living)

*Note: Please read English from right to left to coincide with Arabic.

That in my name is *ha*, from the ocean of *hayat*. *Seen* from the secret of Sayyidina Muhammad ﷺ, but I have the *ya* of *yaqeen* because I am *Sayyid e Shuhada*. That the light that I am going to give to you, and the light I am going to teach you is from your paradise reality. *Sayyid e Shuhada* means he is the master of those who see. There is no *awliyaullah* (saints) that their heart can be opened that is not seeing under the permission of Imam Hussain ؑ. Impossible!

All of them take from the hand of Imam 'Ali ؑ. All *wilayat* (sainthood) and all the fountain of *kawthar*, all *awliyaullah*, they take from the hand of Imam 'Ali ؑ. And this water pours through the family of Imam 'Ali ؑ and that reality pouring from that reality.

Imam Hussain ؑ is the Key With 72 Locks, Opened by Shuhada e Karbala to Intercede For Us

And Imam Hussain ؑ comes to teach us that the *yaqeen* that you want, and the certainty you want, Allah ﷻ has given that honour to me. That through 72 *shuhada* (martyrs) because 72 is the gate of paradise. Turn 72 locks that each *shaheed* from *Karbala* opened that lock. And the one key, the *miftah* (opener), *miftah ar-Rahmah*, the key of *Rahmah* was the reality of Imam Hussain ؑ. He's the key with 72 locks. Each one of

the *shaheed* and those who died in *Karbala* are intercessors for the nation of Sayyidina Muhammad ﷺ. That my nation will have 72 groups that went astray, but he's not throwing them in *jahannam* (hellfire). 72 groups that Sayyidina Muhammad ﷺ, "*Ummati, ummati, ummati,*" and the family stepped in. And *samina wa atana* that we should sacrifice ourself, that Allah ﷻ grant us to intercede for all those who went wrong. It means every number meticulously perfected by Allah ﷻ.

19 Letters of Bismillahir Rahmanir Raheem and
19 Letters of Ahlul Bayt ﷺ

عَنْ أَبِي هُرَيْرَةَ، أَنَّ رَسُولَ اللهِ ﷺ قَالَ :" تَفَرَّقَتِ الْيَهُودُ عَلَى إِحْدَى وَسَبْعِينَ أَوِ اثْنَتَيْنِ وَسَبْعِينَ فِرْقَةً وَالنَّصَارَى. مِثْلَ ذَلِكَ وَتَفْتَرِقُ أُمَّتِي عَلَى ثَلَاثٍ وَسَبْعِينَ فِرْقَةً. كُلُّهُمْ فِي النَّارِ إِلَّا وَاحِدَةً"، قَالُوا: مَنْ هِيَ يَا رَسُولَ اللهِ ؟ قَالَ:" مَا أَنَا عَلَيْهِ وَأَصْحَابِي"
[جامع الترمذي ٢٦٤٠]

'An Abi Huraira ؓ, anna RasulAllahi ﷺ qala: "tafarraqatil Yahudu 'ala ehda wa wasab'yina awe ethnatayni wa sab'yina ferqatan wan Nasara. Methla zalika wa taftarequ ummati 'ala thalathin wa sab'yina ferqatan. Kullahum fin nari illa wahidah."
Qalo: man hiya ya RasulAllahi?
Qala: "Ma ana 'alayhi wa ashabi."

Narrated by Abu Hurairah (ra) that the Messenger of Allah (pbuh) said:

"The Jews split into seventy-one sects, or seventy-two group/party, and the Christians. Similarly my Ummah will split into seventy-three groups/party. All of them are in fire, except one group/party." They said: "And which is it O Messenger of Allah?"
He said: "What I am upon and my Companions."
(Jami` at-Tirmidhi 2640)

The Kamil and Perfected Awliya Take From Sayyid e Shuhada

So, when we want from *sifat ar-Raheem* that *ya Rabbi*, not only *hasanat* in *dunya* (material world) and just being prosperous and wealthy and rich. Grant us *hasanat* of *akhirah* (hereafter) and open the reality of our heart. Then you open from the *kamil*, from the perfected ones who are the *awliyaullah*, Sultan al Awliya Mawlana Shaykh Muhammad Nazim Haqqani ق. But where are they taking from? From *Sayyid e Shuhada*. These titles are not small. I come as the master of those who see because my reality is the reality of Paradise. And that's why the *nasheeds* say, 'Do you want the owners of the two paradises? The owners of Qur'an? Everything is in this reality.'

أَسْيَادِي الْحَسَنْ وَالْحُسَيْنْ
إِلَى النَّبِيْ قُرَّةُ الْعَيْنْ
وَيَا شَبَابَ الْجَنَّتَيْنْ
جَدُّكُمْ صَاحِبُ الْقُرْآنَ

Asyadil Hassan wal Hussaini
Ilan Nabi qurrato 'aini
Ya shabaa bal janna'taini
Jaddukum Saahibul Qur'ana

Our Masters, Imam Hassan (as) and Imam Hussain (as),
They are the coolness of Prophet's (pbuh) eyes.
O the Youth of the Paradises, Your Grandfather (Prophet Muhammad
(pbuh)) is the owner of the Holy Qur'an.

Imam Hussain ﷺ Teaches Us to Sacrifice Our Bad Characters

So, Imam Hussain ﷺ comes to teach us that I have been granted the *yaqeen* (certainty). And I teach you how to sacrifice yourself, sacrifice your desires, sacrifice your bad character, sacrifice your want so that you have the best of character. And that Prophet ﷺ should be happy with our manners and our *adab*. And that we're the owners of the  Kawthar. Bismillahir Rahmanir Raheem, "Atayna kal kawthar, fasalli li rabbika wanhar."

19 Letters of Bismillahir Rahmanir Raheem and
19 Letters of Ahlul Bayt ﷺ

إِنَّا أَعْطَيْنَاكَ الْكَوْثَرَ ﴿١﴾ فَصَلِّ لِرَبِّكَ وَانْحَرْ ﴿٢﴾ إِنَّ شَانِئَكَ هُوَ الْأَبْتَرُ ﴿٣﴾

108:1-3 – *"Inna 'atayna kal kawthar. (1) Fasalli li rabbika wanhar. (2) Inna shani-aka huwal abtar. (3)" (Surat Al-Kawthar)*

"To thee (O Muhammad) we have granted the Fount (of Abundance). (1) So pray to your Lord and Sacrifice. (2) Indeed, your enemy is the one cut off. (3)" (The Abundance, 108:1-3)

Pray unto your Lord, *wanhar*, Imam Hussain ﷺ comes; I'm going to teach you how to pray, *fasalli li rabbika*. Who to direct yourself to pray and sacrifice yourself, and your want and your desire? So that it's only Allah's ﷻ Desire and the desire of Sayyidina Muhammad ﷺ. *Atiullah, Atiur Rasul, wa Ulul amre minkum.*" So that we can fulfill that request, so that we can fulfill that request. *"Wa shaniaka huwal abtar."* Allah ﷻ then says if you're able to fulfill that, I will cut off all your enemies. Because you become *mukhlis* (sincere). No more *shaitan* has anything to do with you.

...أَطِيعُوا اللَّهَ وَأَطِيعُوا الرَّسُولَ وَأُولِي الْأَمْرِ مِنْكُمْ... ﴿٥٩﴾

4:59 – *"...Atiullaha wa atiur Rasula wa Ulil amre minkum..." (Surat An-Nisa)*

"... Obey Allah, Obey the Messenger, and those in authority among you..." (The Women, 4:59)

It means that key and that *rahmah* and that ocean, then why *asal* and why honey? Because it's the healing for paradise and the paradise reality.

Praise the One Whom is Most Praised in the Divinely Presence

So, that when we're saying "*Ya Hameed bi haqq e Muhammad* ﷺ, *ya Rabbi*, keep us always in the praise of the one whom is most praised in Your Divinely Presence.

يَا حَمِيدُ بِحَقِّ مُحَمَّد ﷺ

Ya Hamidu bi Haqqi Muhammad ﷺ.

O' the Praiseworthy for the sake of Prophet Muhammad (pbuh).

So, begins to open; why then *awliyaullah* come into our lives and teach us, make *mawlid*, make *durood*, keep praising on Prophet ﷺ? Not because he needs it, but because you need it. I need it. You're not doing him a favour. Allah ﷻ doesn't care. It doesn't raise Prophet ﷺ up and doesn't bring Prophet ﷺ down. That *Ya Hameed bi haqq e Muhammad* ﷺ. *Ya Rabbi*, let me praise upon him because he is your Most Praised, and open that reality and open that dress upon the soul.

19 Letters of Bismillahir Rahmanir Raheem and
19 Letters of Ahlul Bayt ﷺ

Love Prophet ﷺ, Ahlul Bayt ﷺ, Ashab an Nabi ﷺ and Awliya

And the most high and most power that ocean of *qudra* (power) that dressing them, the secret of Creation that's blessing them. And what type of dress you have put into these *Ahlul Bayt* ﷺ? That let the love of them be more than the love of myself. The way of their example be more than the way of myself and find that

reality and that peace. And for us, it's all in the love of *Ashab an-Nabi* ﷺ, that following the Companions, following the greatness of Prophet ﷺ, the love of *Ahlul Bayt* ﷺ, love of *awliyaullah*. We pray that in this holy month, they open from these realities.

Subhana rabbika rabbal 'izzati 'amma yasifoon, wa salaamun 'alal mursaleen, walhamdulillahi rabbil 'aalameen. Bi hurmati Muhammad al-Mustafa wa bi siri Surat al-Fatiha.

HIDDEN THINGS WILL BE REVEALED DRINKING FROM KAWTHAR

Seek to Understand the World of Light

Bismillahir rahmanir raheem, that, *ati ullah ati ar rasul wa ulil amri minkum.* That they are teaching from the world of light to a people lost in the world of form.

...أَطِيعُوا اللَّهَ وَأَطِيعُوا الرَّسُولَ وَأُولِي الْأَمْرِ مِنكُمْ... ﴿٥٩﴾

4:59 – "...*Atiullaha wa atiur Rasula wa Ulil amre minkum...*"
(Surat An-Nisa)

"… Obey Allah, Obey the Messenger, and those in authority among you…" (The Women, 4:59)

And hard to have a reference of the world of light so everything people equate back to the world of form. That our way is based on this *malakut*, this world of light. And they try to guide us to the understanding of the world of light. In the world of light, everything is light. That when they describe the *Kawthar*, it's a light. When they describe the river, it's rivers of light. When they describe an ocean, they're oceans of light. On a body of light, it's not a physical water. It's a spiritual water. It's a *nur* (light) that flows like a river. What they ask of us is this Muhammadan reality.

Sayyidina Muhammad ﷺ Witnessed Four Streams From the Tree of Creation

In the articles that they've taught from is the reality of *Bismillahir Rahmanir Raheem*. When Sayyidina Muhammad ﷺ, now in the month of *Rajab*, *Subhana man huwal Khaliq anNur* (Glory to Him who is the Creator, the Light), went for *Isra wal Mi'raj* (Night of Ascension). And in that *mi'raj*, Sayyidina Jibreel ؑ showing this kingdom that Allah ﷻ has given to Sayyidina Muhammad ﷺ. Said, 'Look upon this *Bismillahir Rahmanir Raheem*, the tree of all creation. Everything created, emanating from this beautific *Bismillahir Rahmanir Raheem*.'

And from the *meem* of *bismi* a fountain and a stream was flowing. From the *hey* of Allah's ﷻ *Hidayat*, a stream was flowing. From *Rahman* and the *meem*, a stream was flowing. From *Raheem*, a stream was flowing. And Sayyidina Muhammad ﷺ, for us to have an understanding said, 'I looked upon and these 4 streams were flowing down, ended into an immense, immense, what they call fountain, and ocean', and asked that, 'What is this ocean?' Again for us, this is all from the light of Sayyidina Muhammad ﷺ. The dialogue was for later people who would come to pull and extract its realities.

And Sayyidina Jibreel ﷺ said, 'This is your *Kawthar, ya Rasulul Kareem.* That from this ocean of *Bismillahir Rahmanir Raheem* are 4 streams flowing down, and Allah ﷻ gave to you the *Kawthar. Inna 'atayna kal kawthar.'* That *kathiran,* more than *kathir* (abundant), that everything is emanating from it.

إِنَّا أَعْطَيْنَاكَ الْكَوْثَرَ ﴿١﴾

108:1 – *"Inna 'atayna kal kawthar."* (Surat Al-Kawthar)

"To thee (O Muhammad) we have granted the Fount (of Abundance)." (The Abundance, 108:1)

Ahlul Bayt ﷺ Are the Secret of Bismillahir Rahmanir Raheem

And from, *Bismillahir, Inna Hu Sulayman wa inna huwa bismillahir rahmanir raheem.*

إِنَّهُ مِن سُلَيْمَانَ وَإِنَّهُ بِسْمِ اللَّهِ الرَّحْمَٰنِ الرَّحِيمِ ﴿٣٠﴾

27:30 – *"Inna Hu min Sulaymana, Wa inna Hu Bismillahir Rahmanir Raheem."* (Surat An-Naml)

"Indeed, it is from Solomon, and indeed, He/it is (as follows): 'In the name of Allah, the Most Beneficent, the Most Merciful. (The Ant, 27:30)

And *awliyaullah* understood that actually *Bismillahir Rahmanir Raheem,* and its 19 letters is the secret of Muhammad ﷺ - *meem ha, meem daal.*

Hidden Things Will Be Revealed Drinking From Kawthar

Ali ؑ, Fatima ؑ, Hassan ؑ, and Hussain ؑ - that their names are holding that secret of *Bismillahir Rahmanir Raheem*.

And from the *bismi*, that stream of Imam 'Ali ؑ is flowing down. From *bey* of Allah ﷻ, a stream of Sayyidatina Fatima az-Zahra ؑ is flowing down. From *ar-Rahman*, Sayyidina Imam al-Hassan ؑ, a stream is flowing down. From *Raheem*, a stream from Sayyidina Imam al-Hussain ؑ is flowing down. When they witness, they witness the immensity of light. And from this light opens from that light, a stream from the light of Imam 'Ali ؑ begins to flow.

The Lights of Ahlul Bayt ؑ Originate From the Light of Prophet Muhammad ﷺ

So, it's not physical saying I am going to go somewhere where there is a pond. This *nurul Muhammadi* ﷺ, an immense light. From it, all of a sudden comes out from its light, a light of Imam 'Ali ؑ flowing down. From it comes out the light of Sitna Fatima az-Zahra ؑ comes flowing out. From it comes from that light of Prophet ﷺ, a light emerges for the light of Imam al-Hassan ؑ come flowing down. From it, the light of Imam al-Hussain ؑ comes flowing out.

And that's why these *awliyaullah* (saints), when they were sitting and seeing, they said, do you see these *chiraghs* (lights)? Their *ma'rifah* (gnosticism) was did you see these *chiraghs* and these lights? This *nurul Ahmad* ﷺ and how beautiful it is that I am seeing the lights of Imam 'Ali ؑ flowing, the lights of Imam al-Hassan ؑ, flowing, moving lights. Imam al-Hussain ؑ flowing. Out of *ihtiram* (respect), they didn't want to mention Sayyidatina Fatima az-Zahra ؑ. Out of a respect, they said Imam 'Ali's ؑ wife. But he's sitting at the fountain of the *Kawthar*. At a fountain of light and his *ma'rifah* (gnosticism), he's sitting and washing and drinking from these lights, and looking from its source, and how they're all coming out from the light of Sayyidina Muhammad ﷺ.

Nurul Ahmadi ﷺ Are the Life of the Fountain

This *nurul Ahmadi* ﷺ, immense beatific light. And from it, streaming out. From it, streaming out and making the *Kawthar*. They are the ocean of the light of *Kawthar*, above the *Bismillahir Rahmanir Raheem*. Ha, bi haqqi Muhammad ﷺ, wal hamd. All the *hamd* (praise), is the *hamd* of Sayyidina Muhammad ﷺ. So, it means the *Ahlul Kisa* (people of the cloak) above *Bismillahir Rahmanir Raheem* is the *meem ha, meem daal* of Sayyidina Muhammad ﷺ. I am *Liwal Hamd* (Flag of Praise). I am the praise. Below that is that reality. This means the immensity of that secret is coming, dressing, so this is a fountain of light.

Souls of Awliyaullah Are Immersed in the Fountain of Abundance

So, when these *awliyaullah* (saints), who are *kawthari*, they sit into this fountain with their light. If you're in a light being and you're in this fountain, you're drinking it. You're swimming in it. You have become it. So, when we're listening to those *nasheeds*, understand? Their journey was to that fountain. *Hasti o masti*, they passed all of that, to manifest and then to die. All they asked is, '*Ya*

Rabbi, let us to be at this fountain. Let my light to enter this light, and never to leave its light, to become from that light.'

The manifestation in the reality of that light is the secret that the shaykh is speaking. If the shaykh doesn't have a secret, he's not speaking from that *Kawthar*. He's not from that reality. But what's opening from his mouth is because his soul is in that *Kawthar*. As a result of his soul in that *Kawthar*, everything flowing down is from that reality. It's from the light of Sayyidina Muhammad ﷺ flowing down. It's from the light of Imam 'Ali ؑ flowing down. It's from the light of Sayyidatina Fatima az-Zahra ؑ flowing down. It's from the light of Sayyidina Imam al-Hassan ؑ wa Imam al-Hussain ؑ flowing.

Allah ﷻ Puts You With a Kawthari to Drink From its Reality

Because as his soul is in that *Kawthar*, every word that he speaks into this *dunya* (material world) is a *Kawthar* coming down. And they have *uloom ul awaleen wal akhireen* (knowledges of the beginning and the end). Depending upon what Allah ﷻ want them to speak from, they're speaking from the *Kawthar*. That speech, that light, that energy is the *Kawthar*. I don't know, some people are thinking they're going to go somewhere and find an actual river, and I'm going to drink from that river. It's not that. When Allah ﷻ wants you to drink from the *Kawthar*, He puts you with a *kawthari*. And then every word that *kawthari* says, you're drinking from its reality. They revive the dead based on that power.

Immediately, just the function of *Bismillahir Rahmanir Raheem*, their *insan*, their being, has been activated in that reality. And that reality is sending an *isharat* (sign) down upon this creation coming from *Izzatullah* (Allah's ﷻ Might and Magnificence), coming by permission of

Sayyidina Muhammad ﷺ, *wa izzat ar-Rasul* (honour of the Messenger), and then dressed from the beatific *Ahlul Bayt* ؑ (Family of Prophet ﷺ) and *ashab an-Nabi* ﷺ for *izzat al-mumineen* (honour of the believers). It's not coming empty.

﴾...وَلِلَّهِ الْعِزَّةُ وَلِرَسُولِهِ وَلِلْمُؤْمِنِينَ... ﴿٨﴾

63:8 – "...Wa Lillahil 'izzatu wa li Rasuli hi wa lil Mumineen..." (Surat Al-Munafiqoon)

"...And to Allah belongs [all] honor, and to His messenger, and to the believers..." (The Hypocrites, 63:8)

During Tafakkur Empty Yourself and Fill Your Heart

So, the concept of *tafakkur* (contemplation) is to empty yourself. That when he speaks, don't do anything. Just feel the speech and ask that,

'Dress me in your light and dress me from the *haqqaiq* (reality) that you are bringing into this Earth. Let my soul to feel it and to experience it.' Not the one whom speaking from his head about somebody else's heart, but the one whose heart itself is a *kawthar*. It's not the way of books. This reality, they sit in that ocean. They drink and bathe in that ocean. They are from that ocean and it moves and emanates upon this Earth. So, the one whom been granted a permission to hear them, Allah ﷻ granting you a dress of *kawthar*.

Awliyaullah Pull Your Soul Into the Ocean of Kawthar

And that's why Imam 'Ali ؑ – if you took one *alif* and understanding from them, you owe your life to them because you don't even

understand what you've been dressed with. This means then *tafakkur* is the way in which to contemplate, lock your heart. 'I'm nothing', and as soon as they speak, everything from the *kawthar* is flowing through. And their speech is strong enough to grab your soul and immediately pull you into that reality and put you and bathe you into that *kawthar*. It's not something small. It's not something difficult. It's a power and a *qudra* from their soul. When that soul is activated in this, blessing is coming down. That blessing grabs everyone's soul, and immediately pulls it back into that ocean. They don't need your permission. They don't need your ability.

Your *tafakkur* (contemplation) was to give you a sense of what's happening – what are you doing? What are you experiencing? So that you feel a shyness that, 'They're dressing me, blessing me, putting me and bathing me into realities that if I would have lived 1,500, 1,700 years on this Earth, I would have never got that with my *salah* (prayer). I wouldn't have gotten that with my Ramadan.' No *amal* (actions) anyone can do that or can achieve that. And that's why Allah ﷻ says, whom we gave the light, we gave the light. Whom we didn't give the light, they have no light. They don't have that reality. If Allah ﷻ gave the reality, it's a *ni'mat* and a gift from Allah ﷻ.

﴿...وَمَن لَّمْ يَجْعَلِ اللَّهُ لَهُ نُورًا فَمَا لَهُ مِن نُّورٍ ٤٠﴾

24:40 – *"... wa mal lam yaj'a lillahu lahu noora famaa lahu min noor."* (Surat An-Nur)

"...And he to whom Allah has not granted light – for him there is no light." (The Light, 24:40)

Become One Who Feeds Others From the Abundant Fountain

So, it means that we have to remember and think of everything from this world of light. That the *kawthar* that we're seeking, and this fountain of youth that people are trying to reach to, it's already there. You just open your soul to bring it in. That, *'Ya Rabbi,* let me to drink from their *Kawthar.'* This means, and that's why that *naat* was saying,  because he was sitting and drinking from the *kawthar*. And the immense beauty of what he's experiencing, and that's why when you hear these *naats* from hundreds of years ago and then been taught today, you know the path that you're on.

Because they drink in that *kawthar*, and then Allah ﷻ, 'Go out and teach. Go out and tell your students to come with a cup.' Be a student in the way to take from their *kawthar*. And be such a good student that you took, you took. You understand it, you absorbed it with your soul. Then, now you become the one whom pouring the *kawthar*. You become *saqi* (distributor), the one whom is pouring for everyone. And those whom drinking of that reality, they're drunk in that reality.

The Path of Ashiqeen Brings You Towards the Light of Love

 The *mae, maekhana* means their house and the *khanagah*. That's why we don't call it something else. The *khanagah* means in the home of the *agah*; everybody is drunk from the energy. And their home now is in any home that is watching and listening. They can reach to anyone. Anyone who opens their heart to listen, they're in there grabbing

Hidden Things Will Be Revealed Drinking From Kawthar

everyone and anything around. Even the pets are listening. Anyone has a pet, they're sitting and probably listening and watching more attuned, more attentive than even the *insan* (human being). They're dressing and blessing and saying that, 'Why you don't become *saqi* (distributor)?' And now take it so serious in your life that you want to learn it, you want to be from it, and you're going to begin to dispense it to people, this *Kawthar*.

Then describes the path is that we all come in this *chiragh* (light). We're all coming around this *chiragh* of love. We've realized that these are *ashiqeen* (lovers). Their heart is burning like a fire and their soul is sitting in the *Kawthar*. And if they opened their mouth, everything is being dressed from this *Kawthar*. They're *hayyu al qayyum* (ever-living and self-sustaining) because they speak *haq* (truth), not from the head.

Subhana rabbika rabbal 'izzati 'amma yasifoon, wa salaamun 'alal mursaleen, walhamdulillahi rabbil 'aalameen. Bi hurmati Muhammad al-Mustafa wa bi siri Surat al-Fatiha.

Guidance

SPIRITUAL INTERNET WI-FI SIGNAL FROM GOD FOR SOUL

Hadith of Voluntary Worship – Divinely Seeing, Hearing, and Speaking

First Gate of Gnosticism is That We Are Nothing

A reminder always for myself that when they talk on the subject, it requires a contemplation for a long time. It's not something that comes and goes. When they're talking from the holy *hadith* of Sayyidina Muhammad ﷺ. It's *Hadith Qudsi* where Allah's ﷻ describing, 'There's a big conveyance that the servant who completed his obligations…' Allah ﷻ is concerned only with Sayyidina Muhammad ﷺ.'

This path of ours, its first gate is that to be nothing. If I'm nothing, then I'm not looking for everything about me. I'm not reading Qur'an about me. I'm not thinking about everything about me, and me with Allah ﷻ, I'm nothing. What Allah ﷻ has to do with me? I'm nothing. That's a gate for *ma'rifah* (Gnosticism). And in that *ma'rifah*, they walk through as if they're nothing because you said at the gate, you're nothing.

Allah's ﷻ Focus is Only on Prophet Muhammad ﷺ

Then Allah ﷻ describes a holy *hadith* in which he's talking about the reality of Sayyidina Muhammad ﷺ. He wants Prophet ﷺ, 'Tell your people. They'll understand one day, especially your companions understand right away, but they'll understand the generations come later that I am the eyes in which you see. I am the hearing in which you hear. I am the breath in which you breathe.'

وَلَا يَزَالُ عَبْدِي يَتَقَرَّبُ إِلَيَّ بِالنَّوَافِلِ حَتَّى أُحِبَّهُ، فَإِذَا أَحْبَبْتُهُ كُنْتُ سَمْعَهُ الَّذِي يَسْمَعُ بِهِ، وَبَصَرَهُ الَّذِي يُبْصِرُ بِهِ، "رَوَاهُ الْبُخَارِيُّ".

"..., wa la yazaalu 'Abdi yataqarrabu ilayya bin nawafile hatta ahebahu, fa idha ahbabtuhu kunta Sam'ahul ladhi yasma'u behi, wa Basarahul ladhi yubsiru behi, ..."

"...My servant continues to draw near to Me with voluntary acts of worship so that I shall love him. When I love him, I am his hearing with which he hears, his seeing with which he sees..." (Hadith Qudsi, Sahih al-Bukhari, 81:38:2)

Everything Sayyidina Muhammad ﷺ Spoke Was Wahy (Divine Revelation) (53:3-5)

Where Allah ﷻ describes Surat al-Najm, 'He doesn't speak but that it's *wahy*', '*Uohi al Quran*'. It means everything coming out is Holy Qur'an from the heart of Sayyidina Muhammad ﷺ and he doesn't speak except that it's revelation. Even the saliva of Prophet ﷺ is from Divinely Presence.

وَمَا يَنطِقُ عَنِ الْهَوَىٰ ﴿٣﴾ إِنْ هُوَ إِلَّا وَحْيٌ يُوحَىٰ ﴿٤﴾ عَلَّمَهُ شَدِيدُ الْقُوَىٰ ﴿٥﴾

53:3-5 – "*Wa ma yantiqu 'anil hawa. (3) In huwa illa wahyun yooha. (4) 'Allamahu shadeedul Quwa. (5)*" (Surat An-Najm)

"Nor does he (Prophet Muhammad (pbuh) speak from [his own] desire. (3) He is not but a revelation revealed. (4) He was taught by one Mighty in Power. (5)" (The Star, 53:3-5)

Allah ﷻ Gave Prophet ﷺ the Authority Over Everything in Creation

Allah ﷻ is describing, 'I'm his hearing.' Not on this earth of a dot and an epsilon in the middle of nowhere. You look on the internet and you see, you zoom out, look to the milky way, the earth is – forget it, you can't find it. Imagine the inhabitants on the earth. Allah ﷻ Almighty God, you think He gave the earth to Prophet ﷺ? That's like giving nothing! I can see, you have eyes, I can see, it's nothing.

Allah ﷻ says, 'No, this entire universe! Everything created, '*Sakhkhara lakum ma fis Samawati wa ma fil Ardi jamee'an.*' I have given you whatever is in the heavens. Whatever is on the earth. And anything in between,' in case they come to argue with you later on, that Allah ﷻ didn't include this souls. No no, *jamee'an*, everything! Everything in creation, Allah ﷻ says, 'I give to you.'

وَسَخَّرَ لَكُم مَّا فِي السَّمَاوَاتِ وَمَا فِي الْأَرْضِ جَمِيعًا مِّنْهُ إِنَّ فِي ذَٰلِكَ لَآيَاتٍ لِّقَوْمٍ يَتَفَكَّرُونَ ﴿١٣﴾

45:13 – "Wa sakhkhara lakum ma fis Samawati wa ma fil Ardi jamee'an minhu, inna fee dhalika la ayatin liqawmin yatafakkaron." (Surat Al-Jathiya)

"And He has subjected/gave the authority to you [Sayyidina Mahmood (pbuh)], as from Him, all that is in the heavens and on earth: Behold, in that are Signs indeed for those who reflect/Contemplate [Meditate]." (The Crouching, 45:13)

Allah ﷻ Gave the Hamd (Praising) of All Creation to Sayyidina Ahmad ﷺ

Then the *hadith* comes because it's like a *tasbih* (prayer beads), you have to put the beads together. Allah ﷻ doesn't put it on your plate for you. He puts all in little beads. So, you attend with the shaykh, so they'll sew your beads together and give you a *tasbih* of your life so that you'll have a *ma'rifah* (gnosticism) and an understanding.

Allah ﷻ describes that, 'I have given everything to you.' Then Allah ﷻ comes back and begins to describe that, 'I am his hearing.' He hears with Allah's ﷻ power. When Allah ﷻ gave Ahmad ﷺ, he gave the *hamd*, the praise of all praising of all these universes. Allah ﷻ bestowed *alif*, his

'*asaa* (cane). He said this is my support, you are now of a category of *alif*. *Izzatullah*, where Allah's ﷻ reality is hidden and Allah ﷻ conveys the *Izzah* (might) to the *hamd* (praise) and make it to be Ahmad ﷺ.

Then (Allah ﷻ) begins to describe that your praise is the power for this entire universe and I am the *alif* in your heart. I am the power and the *qudra* (power) within your heart.

1. Divinely Senses of Prophet ﷺ

Allah's ﷻ Power is the Hearing, Seeing, and Breathing of Prophet Muhammad ﷺ

Then the holy *hadith* comes to describe, 'I am his hearing ﷺ, I am his seeing ﷺ, I am the breath in which he breathes, the tongue in which he speaks…'

…وَلَا يَزَالُ عَبْدِي يَتَقَرَّبُ إِلَيَّ بِالنَّوَافِلِ حَتَّى أُحِبَّهُ، فَإِذَا أَحْبَبْتُهُ كُنْتُ سَمْعَهُ الَّذِي يَسْمَعُ بِهِ، وَبَصَرَهُ الَّذِي يُبْصِرُ بِهِ، وَيَدَهُ الَّتِي يَبْطِشُ بِهَا، وَرِجْلَهُ الَّتِي يَمْشِي بِهَا، وَلَئِنْ سَأَلَنِي لَأُعْطِيَنَّهُ، وَلَئِنْ اسْتَعَاذَنِي لَأُعِيذَنَّهُ." [رَوَاهُ الْبُخَارِيُّ.]

"…, wa la yazaalu 'Abdi yataqarrabu ilayya bin nawafile hatta ahebahu, fa idha ahbabtuhu kunta Sam'ahul ladhi yasma'u behi, wa Basarahul ladhi yubsiru behi, wa Yadahul lati yabTeshu beha, wa Rejlahul lati yamshi beha, wa la in sa alani la a'Teyannahu, …"

"…My servant continues to draw near to Me with voluntary acts of worship so that I shall love him. When I love him, I am his hearing with which he hears, his seeing with which he sees, his hand with which he strikes and his foot with which he walks. Were he to ask [something] of Me, I would surely give it to him…"
(Hadith Qudsi, Sahih al-Bukhari, 81:38:2)

The hand means the power of Allah's ﷻ power is in the hands of the soul of Sayyidina Muhammad ﷺ. His *qadam* (footstep) and his movement in *malakut* (heavenly realm). They're only interested in the world of light. Their *tafsir* is not interested in this world of *mulk*; this means nothing. What you want to know about the *mulk* (earthly realm)? Where the pizza shop is, where the coffee store is. You're not going to find anything of value here. They're going to teach you from the world of light.

So, Allah ﷻ is now describing this world of light that this soul of Sayyidina Muhammad ﷺ hears with Allah's ﷻ hearing, sees with Allah's ﷻ seeing, speaks with Allah's ﷻ speaking, breathes with Allah's ﷻ breathing. This means *nafas ur rahmah* (breath of mercy), *rahmah*. "*Wa maa arsalnaka illa rahmatal lil'aalameen.*" His *nafas* (breath) is also from Sayyidina Muhammad ﷺ. It means he's the power that's powering everything and Allah ﷻ is on his heart.

وَمَا أَرْسَلْنَاكَ إِلَّا رَحْمَةً لِّلْعَالَمِينَ ﴿١٠٧﴾

21:107 – "*Wa maa arsalnaka illa Rahmatal lil'alameen.*"
(Surat Al-Anbiya)

"*And We have not sent you, [O Muhammad (pbuh)], except as a mercy to the worlds/creation.*" (The Prophets, 21:107)

Sleep Doesn't Overtake the Divinely Power That Covers the Universes

Allah ﷻ is the center of power of that reality that can never be seen. So, then what Allah ﷻ describes; that His power never sleeps and slumber overtakes him.

لَا تَأْخُذُهُ سِنَةٌ وَلَا نَوْمٌ ﴿٢٥٥﴾

2:255 – "*Laa taakhuzuhoo sinatunw wa laa nawm.*"
(Surat Al-Baqarah)

"*No slumber can seize him nor sleep.*" (The Cow, 2:255)

When we're talking about an authority of light that Allah ﷻ says, don't think through the body. This light that's covering entire universes, it doesn't sleep. The power of the soul, *nurul anwar wa sirratul asrar*, the secret of that light – it never sleeps, it never slumbers. It is ever-vigilant over everything. This light is vigilant over everything. We'll say just in the understanding of knowledges without going into *ayat al-Qur'an* because then they get confused.

قَالَ رَسُولُ اللَّهِ صَلَّى اللَّهُ عَلَيْهِ وَسَلَّمَ : حَيَاتِي خَيْرٌ لَكُمْ ، تُحَدِّثُونَ وَيُحَدَّثُ لَكُمْ ، فَإِذَا أَنَا مُتُّ كَانَتْ وَفَاتِي خَيْرًا لَكُمْ ،

تُعْرَضُ عَلَيَّ أَعْمَالُكُمْ ، فَإِنْ رَأَيْتُ خَيْرًا حَمِدْتُ اللَّهَ ، وَإِنْ رَأَيْتُ غَيْرَ ذَلِكَ اسْتَغْفَرْتُ اللَّهَ لَكُمْ

Qala Rasulullahi (saws) "Hayatee khayrun lakum tuhadithona wa yuhdatha lakum, fa idha anaa mutta kaana wafati khayran lakum. Tu'radu 'alayya 'amalukum, fa in ra'itu khayran hamidtu Allah, wa in ra'aytu ghayra dhalik astaghfartullaha lakum."

"The Messenger of Allah (pbuh) said: "My life is good for you, as you will relate from me and it will be related to you, and when I die my passing will be better for you. I observe the deeds of my ummah/Nation. If I find good [in it] I thank/praise Allah, and if I see bad, I ask forgiveness for them/on their behalf." [Prophet Muhammad (pbuh)]

The Soul of Sayyidina Muhammad ﷺ Carries Allah's ﷻ Power and is Our Wi-Fi Connection

Where Allah ﷻ gave us then this understanding in the world is wi-fi. So as soon as I hold up a phone, this concept of an energy, a source of power that's powering this device. And now they're becoming with actual power to charge it without a wire because that's very low and archaic understanding. They'll power this without a wire. They'll give information to it without a wire. It's wi-fi. So, the wi-fi for us is to understand that Allah ﷻ is, 'Why is this so difficult for you to understand? That in the center of all of this creation, there's something called *Muhammadan RasulAllah* ﷺ? And he's emitting a wi-fi signal for the entire of creation.' And that reality is *Hayy* (Ever-Living) and it's *Qayyum* (Self-sustaining).

This *qudra* and power that's coming out is a soul. We're not talking about a body. We're talking about a light, like a star that even we can't imagine what type of light that is and every photon of that light like a wi-fi. It's coming to you, right? It's hitting you and powering you. If that wi-fi and the signal of that drops from you, you cease to exist.

Every Cell in Creation Must Receive a Signal From Its Lord

That's why Allah ﷻ describes that *'Feekum'* (he is within you). His signal is entirely around you and in you. Everything about that light is empowering you.

وَاعْلَمُوا أَنَّ فِيكُمْ رَسُولَ اللَّـهِ ۚ ﴿٧﴾

49:7 – *"Wa'lamooo anna feekum RasulAllah"* (Surat Al-Hujurat)

"Know that among/within you is the Messenger of Allah (Prophet Muhamamd (pbuh))" (The Rooms, 49:7)

Look to one person and see that four trillion cells within your body, every cell has a signal coming. Every cell is like a mobile phone. Every cell in the body needs to know what are its coordinates. There is nothing random in Allah's ﷻ creation. Every cell needs to turn. Are we turning right, are we turning left? Are we alive or are we dying? Are we healthy or are we sick? It's in Surat al-Qadr, *'Tanazzalul malaikatu war Ruh, fiha beizne Rabbihim min kulli amr'*.

تَنَزَّلُ الْمَلَائِكَةُ وَالرُّوحُ فِيهَا بِإِذْنِ رَبِّهِم مِّن كُلِّ أَمْرٍ ﴿٤﴾

97:4 – *"Tanazzalul malaikatu war Ruh, fiha beizne Rabbihim min kulli amr."* (Surat Al-Qadr)

"The angels and the Spirit descend therein by permission of their Lord for every Command/affair."
(The Power 97:4)

Kulli amr, every single order is coming as a signal with the permission of their lord, in reference to Prophet ﷺ. And Prophet ﷺ gets permission from Allah ﷻ cause it's *'Atiullaha wa atiur Rasula wa Ulil amre minkum'*.

...أَطِيعُوا اللَّهَ وَأَطِيعُوا الرَّسُولَ وَأُولِي الْأَمْرِ مِنكُمْ... ﴿٥٩﴾

4:59 – "...Atiullaha wa atiur Rasula wa Ulil amre minkum..." (Surat An-Nisa)

"... Obey Allah, Obey the Messenger, and those in authority among you..." (The Women, 4:59)

Prophet's ﷺ Wi-Fi Signal Reaches Everything in Creation

So, it means this wi-fi signal is coming out powering everything. Every cell in the body needs to know its coordinates; every cell in the body needs to know it's alive, it's dead, it's sick or it's healthy. Every organ in the body has to know is it beating or it's not going to beat? And every moment it gets its co-ordinance.

Every ant, every sustenance, every flower. Nothing... just like if you cut this signal (of the phone). If you don't charge the phone, it's dead. Doesn't matter how fancy the box is and if it doesn't get a signal there is no video, there is no internet, there is no phone call, it's nothing. Same with the flower – the flower is need of that signal. With the signal comes the flower is growing, the flower is blossoming.

It means everything in this creation requires that signal. That signal, it's *hayy* – it's life. Allah ﷻ is not within the ocean of *hayy*. Allah ﷻ said, 'I created *Hayy o Mayt* (life and death) to test you. I'm not in your understanding of living.'

الَّذِي خَلَقَ الْمَوْتَ وَالْحَيَاةَ لِيَبْلُوَكُمْ أَيُّكُمْ أَحْسَنُ عَمَلًا ۚ وَهُوَ الْعَزِيزُ الْغَفُورُ ﴿٢﴾

67:2 – "Alladhee khalaqal Mawta wal Hayata liyabluwakum ayyukum ahsanu 'amalan, wa huwal 'Azizu ul Ghafoor." (Surat Al-Mulk)

"He Who created Death and Life, to test you [as to] which of you is best in deed – and He is the Exalted in Might, the Forgiving."
(The Sovereignty, 67:2)

When Allah (swt) loves his servant, He wants to bring them towards His *ma'rifah* (Gnosticism), realities. Not of Himself. I want to bring you towards what I love. I love *Muhammadun RasulAllah* ﷺ. I want to show you what gifts I've given to that reality and that soul.

Only Prophet ﷺ Has Access to the Knowledge of All Created Universes

So, that signal is broadcasting out, sending throughout your entire being, throughout the entire universes and what Allah (swt) describes that, 'No one encompasses anything from that knowledge unless it has permission of Prophet ﷺ.' What *ayatul kareem* says I have given you, *'La yuheetoona bishai'im min ilmihee illaa bimaa shaaa.'*

وَلَا يُحِيطُونَ بِشَيْءٍ مِّنْ عِلْمِهِ إِلَّا بِمَا شَاءَ ﴿٢٥٥﴾...

2:255 – "...Wa laa yuheetoona bishai'im min 'ilmihee illaa bimaa shaaa." (Surat Al-Baqarah)

"...They do not compass anything from His knowledge except what He wills/permits." (The Cow, 2:255)

Not the knowledge of books. Oh no, this Prophet ﷺ only knows this book and that book. No, no, Allah (swt) is saying, this knowledge of everything in this universe is known by no one. This is what we call above binary code is machine language. *Bayni Ahad wa Ahmad*, there is no intercession. There is nothing that is created to understand those co-ordinates.

The Binary Code of Heavens – On and Off is Reality of Ahad (1) and Ahmad (0)

And that's why Allah ﷻ inspired us to make computers. You understand computer language? You can go up to letters and numbers but binary code, nobody can talk or type in binary code. 1 and 0, on and off. This on and off is the reality of *ahad* and Nabi Ahmad ﷺ. The reality of Allah ﷻ 'on' and the signal continuously coming to Prophet's ﷺ reality. As a result of  receiving those signals, that is the knowledge of the entire created universe.

This knowledge is above the level of Sayyidina Jibreel ﷺ. This level of Sayyidina Jibreel ﷺ are these *tafsirs* and talks are at that level. Above this level is in the depth of the heart of Sayyidina Muhammad ﷺ which is  receiving the binary code from Allah ﷻ of ones and zeroes. It means this information that's coming that Allah ﷻ says no one has access to this information. So, it's not the knowledge of these *had dunya* (limits of material world) and the earth knowledge. It's the knowledge that everything that's being sustained. Every planet in the furthest galaxy in the furthest universes.

The Knowledge That Sustains the Souls Comes From Allah (AJ) to Prophet ﷺ Then to Angels

All of those *uloom* and knowledges that come from Allah (AJ) into the soul of Prophet ﷺ and dispersed with what; *"malaika wa ruh"* (angelic souls) is sending out this signal and illuminating and nourishing and keeping everything alive the way Allah (AJ) wanted to be alive. That is from the *haqqaiqs* (realities) of Sayyidina Muhammad ﷺ. This is what is nourishing us.

تَنَزَّلُ الْمَلَائِكَةُ وَالرُّوحُ فِيهَا بِإِذْنِ رَبِّهِم مِّن كُلِّ أَمْرٍ ﴿٤﴾

97:4 – "Tanazzalul malaikatu war Ruh, fiha beizne Rabbihim min kulli amr." (Surat Al-Qadr)

"The angels and the Spirit descend therein by permission of their Lord for every Command/affair." (The Power 97:4)

When they don't understand the importance of *Mawlid an Nabi* ﷺ (celebration of Prophet's ﷺ birth), it's not something small. It's the step in which to move towards that reality that *awliyaullah* (saints) want us to come to understand. This way of reality is something mind boggling, heart boggling that what Allah (AJ) has bestowed upon that reality. And how that reality is emanating lights and powers and *qudra*. All of those realities – that's what we're trying to reach towards that understanding, dress by that understanding.

Then Allah's (AJ) describing that is the reality of Sayyidina Muhammad ﷺ representing Allah's (AJ) hearing, seeing, speaking. What are the faculties left? Allah (AJ) saying basically my power is completely powering the soul of Sayyidina Muhammad ﷺ.

Allah is Making Zikr and Praises Himself Through Durood Sharif

Then what Prophet says, 'Ya Rabbi, nobody can praise you like you can praise yourself.'

عَنْ عَبْدِ اللهِ بنِ مَسعُودٍ رَضِيَ اللهُ عَنْهُ، قَالَ : قَالَ رَسُولُ اللهِ صَلَّى اللهُ عَلَيْهِ وَسَلَّمَ "... لَيْسَ أَحَدٌ أَحَبَّ إِلَيْهِ الْمَدْحُ مِنَ اللهِ ، مِنْ أَجْلِ ذَلِكَ مَدَحَ نَفْسَهُ" (روى البُخَارِي 4634، ومُسْلِم 2760)

'An Abdullah ibn Mas'od (ra) qala: qala Rasulullahi (saws): "Laysa ahadun ahabba ilyhil madhu minallahi, min ajli zalika madaha nafsahu, ..." [Rawa al Bukhari (4634) wa Muslim (2760)]

'Abdullah ibn Mas'od (ra) said: The Messenger of Allah (pbuh) said: "There is no one to whom praise is more dear than Allah (AJ), and because of that He praised Himself..."
(Narrated by Al-Bukhari (4631) and Muslim (2760))

It means I cannot reach a level in which to thank you or power myself for the power You have given to me. That's why when we make a *durood sharif*, "Allahumma salli ala Sayyidina Muhammad "is that Allah is making *zikr* of Himself. You're not even involved in this *durood sharif*. Allah is making the *zikr* of Himself, praising Himself, thanking Himself for this reality. The *hadith* is this description of Prophet .

اللَّهُمَّ صَلِّ عَلَى سَيِّدِنَا مُحَمَّدٍ، وَعَلَى آلِ سَيِّدِنَا مُحَمَّدٍ وَ سَلِّمْ

"Allahumma salli 'ala Sayyidina Muhammadin wa 'ala aali Sayyidina Muhammadin wa Sallim."

"O Allah! Send Peace and blessings upon our master Prophet Muhammad and upon the Family of our master Prophet Muhammad (pbuh)"

2. Divinely Senses of Awliya (Saints)

Prophet ﷺ Dresses Awliya with Divinely Power and He ﷺ Sees, Hears, Speaks Through Them

Now Prophet ﷺ is with this power hearing, seeing, speaking, touching, moving inherits that to *awliya* (saints). To their *darajat* (level), Prophet ﷺ begins to dress them as they're approaching the reality of Sayyidina Muhammad ﷺ. Prophet ﷺ begins to teach that, 'I'm going to be your hearing because you love me and I love you. You entered into my heart. I'm going to dress you with what Allah ﷻ has dressed me. You're going to have from my hearing', because you never go above Prophet ﷺ, it's *ihtiram* (respect) and *adab* (manners).

...وَلَا يَزَالُ عَبْدِي يَتَقَرَّبُ إِلَيَّ بِالنَّوَافِلِ حَتَّى أُحِبَّهُ، فَإِذَا أَحْبَبْتُهُ كُنْت سَمْعَهُ الَّذِي يَسْمَعُ بِهِ، وَبَصَرَهُ الَّذِي يُبْصِرُ بِهِ، وَيَدَهُ الَّتِي يَبْطِشُ بِهَا، وَرِجْلَهُ الَّتِي يَمْشِي بِهَا، ..." [رَوَاهُ الْبُخَارِيُّ.]

"..., wa la yazaalu 'Abdi yataqarrabu ilayya bin nawafile hatta ahebahu, fa idha ahbabtuhu kunta Sam'ahul ladhi yasma'u behi, wa Basarahul ladhi yubsiru behi, wa Yadahul lati yabTeshu beha, wa Rejlahul lati yamshi beha, ..."

"...My servant continues to draw near to Me with voluntary acts of worship so that I shall love him. When I love him, I am his hearing with which he hears, his seeing with which he sees, his hand with which he strikes and his foot with which he walks. ..."
(Hadith Qudsi, Sahih al-Bukhari, 81:38:2)

Stand behind your shaykh. Never walk in front of your shaykh. Don't think yourself to be in front of him, walk behind him. What you think about Prophet ﷺ, could you dare to walk and keep your back to Prophet ﷺ? No. How can you even talk in that sense? So, everything is always behind that; Allah ﷻ gives everything to Prophet ﷺ and we come to the door.

Praise Prophet ﷺ One Time and He ﷺ Dresses You From the Power of the Universe

That's why these *salawats* (praisings) and these *naats* are powerful. Only  through this praising, you can reach that door. You can pray all you want in your *masjid* and you'll never achieve even a drop of that reality. Because the *salah* doesn't open that, your *zakat* (charity) doesn't open that, your *Hajj* (pilgrimage) definitely doesn't open that. What opens that is *"Salli ala Sayyidina Muhammad ﷺ"* (praising upon Prophet ﷺ). It's when you get to the associations that are praising and loving and loving and loving. As soon as they enter into the door of Sayyidina Muhammad ﷺ, he's dressing them, blessing them. He's what we just described this power.

Can you imagine the hearing of Prophet ﷺ is now from the whole universe – we don't record this, we can do this for like ten years, I don't think we get the depth of what's really coming – is that this energy now begins to, like a microwave hit you at a strength that you can't imagine. It's a power of the entire universe! As soon as you praise one time upon Sayyidina Muhammad ﷺ, he asked just one time from his nation. He wants to give the greatest gift to his nation.

عَنْ أَنَسِ بْنِ مَالِكٍ رَضِيَ اللهُ عَنْهُ، قَالَ: قَالَ رَسُولُ اللهِ – صلى الله عليه وسلم -: مَنْ صَلَّى عَلَيَّ صَلَاةً وَاحِدَةً، صَلَّى اللهُ عَلَيْهِ عَشْرَ صَلَوَاتٍ، وَحُطَّتْ عَنْهُ عَشْرُ خَطِيئَاتٍ، وَرُفِعَتْ لَهُ عَشْرُ دَرَجَاتٍ.

Qala Rasulullah (saws): "Man Salla 'alaiya Salatan wahidatan, Sallallahu 'alayhi 'ashra Salawatin, wa Huttat 'anhu 'ashru khaTeatin, wa ruf'at lahu 'ashru darajatin."

Prophet Muhammad (pbuh) said: "Whoever sends blessings [Praises] upon me, God will shower His blessings upon him ten times, and will erase ten of his sins, and elevate [raise] his [spiritual] station ten times." (Hadith recorded by Nasa'i)

'Praise me one time, you don't know what Allah ﷻ dressed me with. Because Allah ﷻ will send my *nazar* to be upon you, send my soul to be upon you.' What does that mean? He said, 'My *nazar* (gaze) will be on you. If my *nazar* is on you, these eyes that power the entire created universe will be powering your entire reality.'

Ahbab Nabi ﷺ Reached High Stations Through Praising Prophet ﷺ

That's why we sing…what was that *nasheed*? They shot through the universe in their reality.

نام تیرا لے کے آقا شان اساں پائی اے
تیرے ہتھ ڈور سائیاں آپے ہی چڑھائی اے

چڑھی ہوئی گڈی نوں چڑھائی رکھیں سوہنڑیا
چنگے آں کے مندے آں نبھائی رکھی سوہنڑیا

لگیاں نے موجاں ہنڑ لائی رکھیں سوہنڑیا
چنگے آں کے مندے آں نبھائی رکھی سوہنڑیا

Naam tera le ke aaqa Shaan assaa payi yea
Teray haath dor saiyaa Apay he charhai yea

Charhai hui guddi nu Charhai rakhi soniya
Changay aa, Ke mande aa, Nibhayi rakhi soniya

Lagiya ne moja hon laayi rakhi soniya
Changay aa, Ke mande aa, Nibhayi rakhi soniya

By mentioning and praising your Name O Master, I attained this high station, My thread is in your hand and you are the one raising it higher, As you have kept my kite (soul) flying, Keep it flying higher, O Beloved. Whether we are good or bad, Keep us with you, O Beloved

Generous blessings are upon us, Keep on dressing us O Beloved, Whether we are good or bad, Keep us with You O Beloved

They reached a level that nobody could understand. They said was this from your *salah* (prayer). Was this from your *zakat* (charity)? Where was this from? My love! I praised one time and all these doors opened for me and dressed me, bless me, clean me. What my sin? They don't have any sin in the presence of that reality. How Prophet's ﷺ eyes are dressing them, blessing them. How Prophet's ﷺ hearing, dressing them, blessing them. What type of *qudra* and power dressing upon these *ahbab*, these lovers?

Awliya Inherit the Power of Divinely Seeing, Hearing, Moving From Prophet ﷺ

Then we understand now that dress is upon the *shuyukh*, the *awliya* (saints). Now what do the shaykhs have from that dress because Allah ﷻ says, '*Feekum*,' that that light is amongst everyone.

كَمَا أَرْسَلْنَا فِيكُمْ رَسُولًا مِنكُمْ يَتْلُو عَلَيْكُمْ آيَاتِنَا... ﴿١٥١﴾

2:151 – *"Kama arsalna feekum Rasulam minkum yatlo 'Alaykum ayatina…" (Surat Al-Baqarah)*

"Just as We have sent among (within) you a messenger of your own, reciting to you Our Signs, …" (The Cow, 2:151)

So, then these *awliya* (saints), they're dressed from that hearing of Prophet ﷺ. They're dressed with the eyes of Prophet ﷺ. They're dressed with the tongue of Sayyidina Muhammad ﷺ. They carry the hands and the fragrance of Sayyidina Muhammad ﷺ. They carry the *qadam* and the footsteps of Prophet ﷺ. This means everything they're doing, they're trying their best to do in the way of the *rida* and the satisfaction, *'Ilahi anta maqsudi wa ridhaka matlubi. Ilahi anta maqsudi wa rida matlubi'*. (My God, You are my aim, and Your Satisfaction is what I seek). Their whole life is we're trying our best. It's not an easy thing to accomplish.

اِلٰهِى اَنْتَ مَقْصُوْدِيْ وَرِضَاكَ مَطْلُوْبِيْ

"Illahi anta maqsodi, wa Ridaka Matlubi."

"My God, You are my aim, and Your Satisfaction is what I seek."

Awliya Have Power From Prophet ﷺ and Can Revive Us and Change Our Destiny

What they want us to know then these *awliyaullah* (saints), they have the eyes of Sayyidina Muhammad ﷺ on the earth and they're spreading that power. That's why when they describe the *qudra* and the power of *awliyaullah*, imagine when they have that type of vision, what they see. What their soul is empowering? Because their eyes have a wi-fi and they send out the signal that Prophet ﷺ wants to be sent out. That's why anything dead in their presence comes to life. That's why *Mahidh dhunubi, muhyil qulubi*. What in the *qasida* we're reciting?

Spiritual Internet Wi-Fi Signal From God for Soul

يَا مُحْيِي الْقُلُوْبِ، سَلَّامْ عَلَيك يَا مَاحِي الذُّنُوْبِ ، سَلَّامْ عَلَيك

Ya Muhyil qulubi, Salaam 'Alayk
Ya Mahidh dhunubi, Salaam 'Alayk

O the reviver of the hearts, O the eraser of the sins, Peace be upon you.

They can obliterate your sins and revive your heart. Because without a signal you're like dead filled with sins. When their eye comes and hits and scans you immediately, it can come back to life in an instant. It's not something difficult. Their hearing – dressing and blessing, their vision – dressing and blessing, their speech – dressing, blessing. Then with your *qadam* you change my whole destiny. *Agha tu ni'mate ishqi* (My master you are the blessing of love). With your hand, you change my whole destiny – how? As soon as they teach you from the heart of Sayyidina Muhammad ﷺ, your entire destiny now just changed because this knowledge will dress you and bless you and change everything about your reality. So, then they change everything with their eyes, their ears, their tongue, their hands, their feet.

آقا تو حضرت عشقی ، از ملائک بهشتی
تو با دستای مبارک سرنوشتمو نوشتی

Agha to hazrate eshghi, az malaeke Beheshti
To ba dastaye mubarak, sarneveshtamo neveshti

O my Master, you are the Master of love from the angels of paradise
You wrote my destiny with your blessed hands

Awliya Are People of the Command and in Taslim (Submission)

Now imagine that light is hitting you. Then you have to understand they're actually in you. So, how they got that? They went into Prophet ﷺ. Went to Prophet ﷺ, they surrendered, *'sallu alayhi wa sallimu taslim.'*

إِنَّ اللهَ وَمَلَائِكَتَهُ يُصَلُّونَ عَلَى النَّبِيِّ يَا أَيُّهَا الَّذِينَ آمَنُوا صَلُّوا عَلَيْهِ وَسَلِّمُوا تَسْلِيماً ﴿٥٦﴾

33:56 – "InnAllaha wa malayikatahu yusalluna 'alan Nabiyi yaa ayyuhal ladhina aamanu sallu 'alayhi wa sallimu taslima." (Surat Al-Ahzab)

"Allah and His angels send blessings upon the Prophet [Muhammad (pbuh)]: O you that believe! Send your blessings upon him and salute him with all respect." (The Combined Forces, 33:56)

Taslima, for other people to be nice and good. When they reach their

taslima, at that stage, Allah ﷻ will order them *taslim*, submit to the king. Put yourself down. I'm nothing! Repeat what the angels understood of *ihtiram* (respect) and you're nothing. *"Wa sallu ala Sayyidina Muhammad...wa sallimu taslim"* (Holy Qur'an, 33:56). *Taslima* was to make you beautiful but *ahbab*, they're *taslim*. They are *ulul amr* (People of the Command), they're waiting for the command. As soon as they *taslimed* and submitted for the order, waiting for the order, Prophet's ﷺ light has overtaken them. Pushed them out of every type of negativity and becomes their hearing, their seeing, their hands, their feet. It means the light of Prophet ﷺ is inside of them.

3. Divinely Senses of Mureeds (Saints' Followers)

If Shaytan Has Access Within Us, So Do Awliya – They are Inside Our Being

When *awliya* go out, *'Feekum'* (Holy Qur'an, 2:151) like little ships, they go out onto the earth. With what light they're coming to you? Their light  begins to enter into you and become your seeing. They see through your eyes, they hear through your ears, they can speak through your tongue, they can move through your hands, they can inspire your *qadam* and your feet. You say, 'But I want to experience it', then get yourself out of the way. They're already inside of you, but you are fighting the inspiration that's coming to you. Who is fighting? It's your big *nafs* (ego). The big *nafs* is in there, saying, 'No, I'm going to hear with my hearing and I'm going to see with my seeing and I'm going to talk definitely from my talking.' So, this is the big battle inside.

When Allah ﷻ inspires you to be amongst *awliya* (saints), through presence and through video, wherever they're reaching, it means they reached now inside of you. *Malakut* (heavenly realm), what you think you're hidden? *'Feekum'*, (Holy Qur'an, 2:151) their light is next to you. You think that they have a hard time entering within you? The door of your body is like so secure they can't? Every *shaitan* can enter inside of you.  Allah ﷻ didn't give them? It means their light begins to move inside. As soon as they come inside you, they can hear through you, whatever you're hearing they can hear. Whatever you're seeing, they can see. Then that's why the *adab* (manners) of *tariqah* (spiritual way) is to keep your vision down because they look through your eyes and they don't like what you're looking at. They can hear through your ears and they don't like what they're hearing. So, then they begin to move their energy out.

The One Who Purifies Himself Succeeds

Who's the one who fails and who's the one who succeeds? The one whom Allah ﷻ describes in Qur'an, 'The one whom purified himself truly has been given a gift' (Holy Qur'an, 20:76). Because as soon as he purifies himself, especially in the company of this reality. He watches and she watches what she hears and tries not to hear bad and begin now they can hear through the ear. Because the truth and false, they don't play with each other.

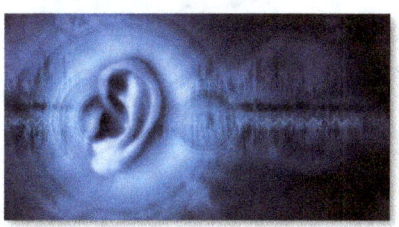

جَنَّاتُ عَدْنٍ تَجْرِي مِن تَحْتِهَا الْأَنْهَارُ خَالِدِينَ فِيهَا ۚ وَذَٰلِكَ جَزَاءُ مَن تَزَكَّىٰ ﴿٧٦﴾

20:76 – *"Jannaatu 'Adnin tajree min tahtihal anhaaru khaalideena feehaa; wa zaalika jazaaa'u man tazakka"* (Surat Taha)

"Gardens of perpetual residence beneath which rivers flow, wherein they abide eternally. And that is the reward of one who purifies himself." (Taha, 20:76)

and

وَقُلْ جَاءَ الْحَقُّ وَزَهَقَ الْبَاطِلُ ۚ إِنَّ الْبَاطِلَ كَانَ زَهُوقًا ﴿٨١﴾

17:81 – *"Wa qul jaaa alhaqqu wa zahaqal baatil, innal batila kana zahoqa."* (Surat Al-Isra)

"And say, Truth has come, and falsehood has perished. Indeed falsehood, [by its nature], is ever perishing/ bound to perish."
(The Night Journey, 17:81)

Concept of Madad – Get Out of the Way and Let Awliya Hear and See Through You

When the light of truth comes, it wants you to have clean hearing. Right? And it hears through you. When you control and clean your sight, it will begin to see through your eyes and that's the *madad* (support). You clean your tongue and what you say and how you say it, they'll become the speaking in which you speak. That's how they're doing it. Prophet ﷺ is hearing through them not because they're dirty people. But they took a life in which to clean themselves so that Sayyidina Muhammad ﷺ would accompany their hearing and say, 'Now I can hear for you, I'll give you from that gift.'

وَلَا يَزَالُ عَبْدِي يَتَقَرَّبُ إِلَيَّ بِالنَّوَافِلِ حَتَّى أُحِبَّهُ، فَإِذَا أَحْبَبْتُهُ كُنْتُ سَمْعَهُ الَّذِي يَسْمَعُ بِهِ، وَبَصَرَهُ الَّذِي يُبْصِرُ بِهِ، وَيَدَهُ الَّتِي يَبْطِشُ بِهَا، وَرِجْلَهُ الَّتِي يَمْشِي بِهَا، ...
[رَوَاهُ الْبُخَارِيُّ.]

"..., wa la yazaalu 'Abdi yataqarrabu ilayya bin nawafile hatta ahebahu, fa idha ahbabtuhu kunta Sam'ahul ladhi yasma'u behi, wa Basarahul ladhi yubsiru behi, wa Yadahul lati yabTeshu beha, wa Rejlahul lati yamshi beha, ..."

"...My servant continues to draw near to Me with voluntary acts of worship so that I shall love him. When I love him, I am his hearing with which he hears, his seeing with which he sees, his hand with which he strikes and his foot with which he walks...."
(Hadith Qudsi, Sahih al-Bukhari, 81:38:2)

So, then they say clean your speech, so that you can speak on that behalf. And that is the whole concept of the *madad* (support). The *madad* is to train in which you're nothing, to train in which you're nothing. Get yourself out of the way, get your opinion out of the way, get all your thoughts out of the way. And take a path in which to be nothing. They keep testing you to see if you have an opinion. They don't care for it nor do they want it. Because it's that opinion that got you in trouble and brought you here in the first place. It's all your character that's bad that has to be destroyed. When you have absolutely nothing left, nothing left, nothing left, and you died within yourself, then all of these faculties can come to life. Then they will give you the hearing and you hear what nobody can imagine to hear. You see what nobody could imagine to see; you speak realities that nobody can speak from that reality and that becomes the inheritance of that *hadith*, holy *hadith*. We pray Allah ﷻ dress us, bless us. These are the blessings of *Mawlid an Nabi* ﷺ and the dressings and gifts from the heart of Sayyidina Muhammad ﷺ, inshaAllah.

Subhana rabbika rabbal 'izzati 'amma yasifoon, wa salaamun 'alal mursaleen, walhamdulillahi rabbil 'aalameen. Bi hurmati Muhammad al-Mustafa wa bi siri Surat al-Fatiha.

REALITIES OF A ZAWJ (MATE) ON EARTH, WITHIN, AND IN THE HEAVENS

From Heart of Holy Qur'an – Surat YaSeen, 36:36

A reminder for myself always that we play from *ayatul Qur'an* where Mawlana Shaykh ق is giving us that reality and that light, inshaAllah. *"Subhanalladee khalaqal azwaja kulla mimma tumbitul ardhu wa min anfusihim wa mimma la ya'lamoon."*

سُبْحَانَ الَّذِي خَلَقَ الْأَزْوَاجَ كُلَّهَا مِمَّا تُنبِتُ الْأَرْضُ وَمِنْ أَنفُسِهِمْ وَمِمَّا لَا يَعْلَمُونَ ﴿٣٦﴾

36:36 – *"Subhaanal lazee khalaqal azwaaja kullahaa mimmaa tumbitul ardu wa min anfusihim wa mimmaa laa ya'lamoon"*
(Surat YaSeen)

"Glory to Allah, Who created in pairs all things that the earth produces, as well as their own kind and things of which they have no knowledge." (YaSeen, 36:36)

Sadaqallah hul azheem wa barakat Rasulul Kareem ﷺ. InshaAllah, from Surat YaSeen, Surat 36, verse 36. That Surat YaSeen is the heart of

Realities of a Zawj (Mate) on Earth, Within, and in the Heavens

Holy Qur'an and *manzil al Qur'an* (house of Qur'an) in which Holy Qur'an is emanating from the heart of Sayyidina Muhammad ﷺ. And Surat YaSeen and Sayyidina YaSeen ﷺ means every reality is flowing from the heart of Sayyidina Muhammad ﷺ. And in this understanding and in this way of *ma'rifah* (gnosticism), the importance of understanding the self, the importance of women, and the importance of our reality.

Allah ﷻ Created All Things With a Mate

What Mawlana Shaykh ق wants as a reminder for ourselves is that Allah ﷻ in this *ayat kareem* is, 'Glory be to Him.' Allah ﷻ is stressing the importance of this *ayat* (verse) by saying His *Subhan* and putting His *Subhan* (glory) upon what is about to be coming from this *ayat* (verse). *Subhana* that, 'Glory be to Him Who created all things in pairs.'

Now their English is incorrect. *Khalaqal azwaj*, it is not 'pairs of fruits.' Everything Allah ﷻ created with *azwaj*, with a mate. Everything Allah ﷻ, His *Subhan*, 'Glory be to Me that I have created everything with a mate, with an *azwaj*,' because *zawj* (mate) has a deep inner reality. 'That which is on the Earth, that which is within themselves and that which they don't know.' *Fil ardhi*, *anfusihim*, 'within themselves', and *la ya'lamoon* 'that which they don't know yet.' That is through the oceans of *ma'rifah* (gnosticism).

سُبْحَانَ الَّذِي خَلَقَ الْأَزْوَاجَ كُلَّهَا مِمَّا تُنبِتُ الْأَرْضُ وَمِنْ أَنفُسِهِمْ وَمِمَّا لَا يَعْلَمُونَ ﴿٣٦﴾

36:36 – *"Subhaanal lazee khalaqal azwaaja kullahaa mimmaa tumbitul ardu wa min anfusihim wa mimmaa laa ya'lamoon"*
(Surat YaSeen)

"Glory be to Him, Who created with a mate all things that grow on earth, and from themselves/their soul, and from that which they do not know." (YaSeen, 36:36)

We Do Not Realize We Are Oppressors to Ourselves

From that, they are pulling that reality to teach us that in this season of weddings, seasons of marriage, and all around us marriages are collapsing. When Allah (عز وجل) is describing humans, 'Verily, you are an oppressor to yourself.'

﴿إِنَّ اللَّـهَ لَا يَظْلِمُ النَّاسَ شَيْئًا وَلَـكِنَّ النَّاسَ أَنفُسَهُمْ يَظْلِمُونَ ٤٤﴾

10:44 – *"Innal laaha laa yazlimun naasa shai'anw wa laakin nannaasa anfusahum yazlimoon." (Surat Yunus)*

"Indeed, Allah does not wrong the people at all, but it is the people who are oppressor to themselves/their soul." (Jonah, 10:44)

And if we talk to people who are out and doing crazy things in life, they don't think that they are oppressing themselves at all. They actually, when you talk to them, they think they are having fun. They think that they are living life to the fullest with every crazy thing that they want to do and no inhibition, no stopping. Just do what you want, as much as you want. So, then whom is Allah (عز وجل) referring to that, 'You are an oppressor to yourself?' Allah (عز وجل) is not caring only for the physicality because the physicality goes back to the dirt. There must be something Allah (عز وجل) is concerned about. Divine Presence knows that this body – you are going to throw to the dirt and most likely I am going to send the worms to eat you.

We Have a Mate in Dunya, Within Ourselves, and in Paradise

What then is Allah ﷻ worried about? What is He warning us about? He said, 'I gave to you a *zawj*. I gave to you, for English word, a wife, a mate. It is not really a wife, but it is a mate. I gave to you from your

reality, your reality in heavens. The body is not your reality. The body is a vehicle in which you are using on this Earth and you are an oppressor to that mate.' And Allah ﷻ is giving that *ayat al Kareem* that, 'There is a mate of *dunya*. There is a mate within yourself. And there is a mate in Paradise.'

سُبْحَانَ الَّذِي خَلَقَ الْأَزْوَاجَ كُلَّهَا مِمَّا تُنبِتُ الْأَرْضُ وَمِنْ أَنفُسِهِمْ وَمِمَّا لَا يَعْلَمُونَ ﴿٣٦﴾

36:36 – *"Subhaanal lazee khalaqal azwaaja kullahaa mimmaa tumbitul ardu wa min anfusihim wa mimmaa laa ya'lamoon."* (Surat YaSeen)

"Glory be to Him, Who created with a mate all things that grow on earth, and from themselves/ their soul, and from that which they do not know." (YaSeen, 36:36)

This material world thinks the soulmate is you find somebody you love, and that's your soulmate. No, no, Allah's ﷻ *haqqaiq* (reality) is something completely different.

Admit That We Are Oppressors to Ourselves

This means we come to the *turuq* (spiritual paths) to clean ourself, to take away *zulumat* (oppression) and that, *"laa ilaha illa anta subhanaka, inni kuntu minaz zhalimeen."* That we have to admit in our life that if I am in this *turuq* (spiritual path) and Allah ﷻ guided me to this *turuq*, I am, *ya Rabbi*, Your Greatness, You are *Subhan*, but

I am an oppressor to myself. And Allah ﷻ, 'We will give them a *najat* (salvation) if they acknowledge they are an oppressor to themselves.'

...لَّا إِلَهَ إِلَّا أَنتَ سُبْحَانَكَ إِنِّي كُنتُ مِنَ الظَّالِمِينَ ﴿٨٧﴾ فَاسْتَجَبْنَا لَهُ وَنَجَّيْنَاهُ مِنَ الْغَمِّ ۚ وَكَذَٰلِكَ نُنجِي الْمُؤْمِنِينَ ﴿٨٨﴾

21:87-88 – "...la ilaha illa anta Subhanaka, innee kuntu minazh zhalimeen. (87) Fastajabna lahu wa najjayna hu minal ghammi, wa kadhalika nunjee almumineen. (88)" (Surat Al-Anbiya)

"...There is no god/diety except You; Glory to you: Indeed I have been of the wrongdoers/Oppressor to Myself!" (87) So We responded to him and saved him from the distress. And thus do We save the believers. (88)" (The Prophets, 21:87-88)

Women Have Great Importance in Islam

So, then the *turuq* (spiritual path), this is now the way of understanding that mate, and the importance of women in Islam, the importance of women in spirituality. How much Prophet ﷺ put an importance upon them, and the love and the respect upon them, and their children – their paradise is under the feet of your mother and how much it's abused now.

عَنْ أَنَسَ بْنِ مَالِكٍ رَضِيَ اللهُ عَنْهُ : قَالَ رَسُولُ اللهِ صَلَّى اللهُ عَلَيْهِ وَ سَلَّمَ "الْجَنَّةُ تَحْتَ أَقْدَامِ الْأُمَّهَاتِ

Realities of a Zawj (Mate) on Earth, Within, and in the Heavens

'An Anas bin Maliku (ra) Qala, Qala Rasulullahi ﷺ
"Al Jannatu tahta aqdamil ummahati." (Sunan bin Maja)

Narrated by Annas bin Malik that the Messenger of Allah, Prophet Muhammad (pbuh) said: "Paradise is under the feet of the mothers."

How much it is taken advantage of now, and how much people put their horrible culture upon Islam that does not have anything to do with what Prophet ﷺ brought. But what Prophet ﷺ brought for us is that before your marriage of Earth, *anfusihum* (within) – the one whom with you all the time, make that marriage work. So, lucky are the ones who come young into *tariqah* (spiritual path) so that they can make their real marriage work.

Islam Perfects the Physicality to Guard the Soul

Then the *turuq* begin to teach them that, 'Your physicality is the male aspect of your body,' for men and women, it doesn't make a difference. This is a *haqqaiq* (reality). But for us to understand that this is a *zawj*, a mate, but you translate it to 'wife' in Arabic is different. *Zawj* is a mate, it's non-denominational – it has nothing to do with male and female. But for us to understand, we have to speak in a language for people to have an understanding.

Your body, your physicality is your Islam, it's your shield. Your Islam

has to be strong, your *deen* (religion) has to be strong. The body has to have *istiqam* and firmness because it is guarding something very precious inside. It's guarding a cargo from Allah ﷻ. That is what Allah ﷻ is making reference to, 'I brought you this *deen* not to oppress other people, but to perfect this treasure I put within you, this *zawj*, this mate that I have put upon you. And you are responsible to feed her, to dress her, to nourish her, to bring her true power out.' That *zawj's* power out, the power of her soul, the power of her reality, and she will bring all *azmatullah* upon your being.

So, it means all of Islam is for the physicality, that discipline the physicality, correct the physicality. Know your boundary and your limits, and don't exceed upon them. Don't move beyond yourself to do anything and any harm. So, Islam comes to perfect the physicality.

Station of Iman (Faith) is All About Love

Then the *turuq* begin to teach that that within you and the reality of the soul, when you discipline the physicality, that is the Islam. Now bring out the reality of your soul which is *Maqamul Iman*. And *Maqamul Iman* (Station of Faith) is then the whole story of love, where Prophet ﷺ clarifies for us, 'You have to love me more than you love yourself.'

لاَ يُؤْمِنُ أَحَدُكُمْ حَتَّى أَكُونَ أَحَبَّ إِلَيْهِ مِنْ وَالِدِهِ وَوَلَدِهِ وَالنَّاسِ أَجْمَعِينَ

"La yuminu ahadukum hatta akona ahabba ilayhi min walidihi wa waladihi wan Nasi ajma'yeen."

"None of you will have faith till he loves me more than his father, his children and all mankind." (Prophet Muhammad (pbuh))

Undisciplined Physicality Oppresses the Soul

So, anybody wants a successful marriage, we are talking *anfusihum* (within yourself). The one inside first because this will also teach counter-terrorism, counter-extremism, counter crazy-ism. Because if a person goes unchecked, untrained, and becomes a *zalim* (oppressor) to himself where his physicality is oppressing his soul, is destroying his soul, no doubt that one is overcome by *shaitan* (satan) and begins his *zulumat* upon everyone. His *zulumat* (oppression) will move onto everyone. He is a *zalim* (oppressor) to himself, you don't think he will be *zalim* to everything and begin to inflict harm and pain upon all of Allah's ﷻ Creation?

So, then the cure for that oppression is to train them back, fix the *zulumat* (oppression) within ourselves. That understand your boundary and your limits. Put upon your physicality a discipline.

Anything without discipline becomes wild. It is a beast. The physicality is a beast, it has to be domesticated. Any wild beast, any horse, even when you love a horse and you want to go horseback riding, if it is not trained, that horse is going to kill you. If you domesticate the horse, it becomes a ride in which you can ride, and you can move and accomplish what Allah ﷻ wants us to accomplish.

Be Careful Who You Love

Then the discipline of the soul and the reality of the soul is *muhabbat* (love), *"Qul inkuntum tuhiboonallah fatabioni."*

قُلْ إِنْ كُنْتُمْ تُحِبُّونَ اللَّـهَ فَاتَّبِعُونِي يُحْبِبْكُمُ اللَّـهُ وَيَغْفِرْ لَكُمْ ذُنُوبَكُمْ ۗ وَاللَّـهُ غَفُورٌ رَّحِيمٌ ﴿٣١﴾

3:31 – *"Qul in kuntum tuhibbon Allaha fattabi'oni, yuhbibkumullahu wa yaghfir lakum dhonobakum wallahu Ghaforur Raheem."*
(Surat Ali-Imran)

"Say, [O Muhammad], 'If you should love Allah, then follow me, [so] Allah will love you and forgive you your sins. And Allah is Forgiving and Merciful." (Family of Imran, 3:31)

Allah ﷻ wants the greatest gift for that soul. He says this soul is so precious and now how Allah ﷻ will begin to describe, *"Qul inkuntum tuhiboonallah fattabioni yuhbibkumullah."* You want the greatest love

for that soul, I want the highest reality for that soul. Be careful, because this world, they want to love each other. And there are people who talk that, 'You are my everything. You are like my God. You are my paradise.' You are incorrect. And Allah ﷻ will grant that person what they wanted. That is the scary sadness of it all. Allah ﷻ is Great, Allah ﷻ is Just. You die and all your life was just about the spouse, and you loved the spouse as if they were everything. Then Allah ﷻ will ask you, 'What is it that you want? Are you coming?'

You Will Be With Whom You Love

And Prophet's ﷺ *hadith* comes to purify and to clarify, 'You will be with whom you love.'

قَالَ رَسُولُ اللهِ صلى الله عليه و سلم: الْمَرْءُ مَعَ مَنْ أَحَبَّ

Qala Rasulullah (saws): "Almar o, ma'a man ahab."

Prophet Muhammad (pbuh) said: "One is with those whom he loves."

Good news and a warning; warning, 'Be careful who you love,' because you will be with them. All you did was condition yourself to be with that person. As soon as you pass away, Allah (swt) will grant you, 'Be with them, good or bad, be with them.' You loved them in *dunya* (material world), your soul is attached to them – it doesn't know anything else. It is not all of a sudden going to reach to the grave and think it loves something else. What you have attached your soul to, of whatever craziness, insanity, whatever you can imagine you are attaching your love to, Allah (swt) will grant that love to you. 'Be with it!' And you will be so far from the reality.

Allah (swt) Wants the Highest Love For Us

What Allah (swt) wants for us? What Allah (swt) wants for us is the highest love. That is why *awliyaullah* (saints) come into our life and say that, 'God's Mercy is unimaginable. Be careful what you love. Be careful what you are focused on and what you are dedicating everything to. Dedicate that love and that heart to the highest which its eternity and its  reality is beyond imagination, and which eternally flows fountains of abundance upon you. The love of the Divine.'

Allah (swt) says, 'That heart of yours, I made no man with two hearts.' 'That heart of yours is the house of the soul. That wife of yours inside, that *zawj* and that mate of yours inside, teach her the correct love – not the love of physicality, not the love of people, but the love of the Divine, love of the Divine.'

مَّا جَعَلَ اللَّهُ لِرَجُلٍ مِّن قَلْبَيْنِ فِي جَوْفِهِ ۚ ... ﴿٤﴾

33:4 – *"Ma ja'ala Allahu lirajulin min Qalbayni fee jawfihi..."*
(Surat Al-Azhab)

"Allah has not made for a man two hearts in his interior..."
(The Combined Forces, 33:4)

Follow Habibullah ﷺ (Beloved of Allah) To Gain Allah's ﷻ Love

If that soul is trained to love Allah ﷻ and wants nothing but Allah ﷻ, Allah ﷻ will guide that soul, *"qul inkuntum tuhibbunallah."* 'If you want My Love, make your life *"fatabioni."*

...قُلْ إِن كُنتُمْ تُحِبُّونَ اللَّهَ فَاتَّبِعُونِي يُحْبِبْكُمُ اللَّهُ ﴿٣١﴾

3:31 – *"Qul in kuntum tuhibbon Allaha fattabi'oni, yuhbibkumullahu..."* (Surat Ali-Imran)

Say, [O Muhammad], "If you should love Allah, then follow me, [so] Allah will love you ..." (Family of Imran, 3:31)

Fatabioni, you have to be from *tabi'een* (followers) and *itibah*

(following). You give your whole life because I want your love, *ya Rabbi*. And Allah ﷻ says, 'My Love is with Sayyidina Muhammad ﷺ and he is my *Habibullah* (beloved of Allah). All Creation is looking for My Love and I am looking to please My Beloved Sayyidina Muhammad ﷺ.' All the prophets were seeking Allah's ﷻ Love. Allah ﷻ was sending His Love to Prophet ﷺ granting, 'What is it that you want, My *Habibullah*! To make you happy, to make you satisfied, I am giving you the highest of gifts. I am giving you My Divinely speech, Holy Qur'an.'

Anfusihum (Inner Marriage): Your Soul Should Be in Love with Prophet ﷺ

This means then they come to purify and perfect that this love of yours – make it for Allah ﷻ. Make that soul to understand that reality to love and to praise upon Prophet ﷺ. Then Prophet ﷺ comes into our life and teaches that, 'That soul, it should love me more than it loves you. More than it loves your body, it should love me.'

لاَ يُؤْمِنُ أَحَدُكُمْ حَتَّى أَكُونَ أَحَبَّ إِلَيْهِ مِنْ وَالِدِهِ وَوَلَدِهِ وَالنَّاسِ أَجْمَعِينَ

"La yuminu ahadukum hatta akona ahabba ilayhi min walidihi wa waladihi wan Nasi ajma'yeen."

"None of you will have faith till he loves me more than his father, his children and all mankind." (Prophet Muhammad (pbuh))

Because it is the world of light, it will attach. That light will move close to Prophet ﷺ and begin to attach to Prophet ﷺ. And that is the opening of the reality of that *azwaj*, that that soul is moving towards true love. Its true love in which Prophet ﷺ will begin to dress it. *Anfusihum* (within) is the one that should be in love with Prophet ﷺ.

When Allah ﷻ Loves You, He Teaches You the Muhammadan Reality

It is from *malakut* (heavenly realm) and everything but the Holy Face will perish, in *malakut* even. It means every reality is the dress of Sayyidina Muhammad ﷺ.

وَلَا تَدْعُ مَعَ اللَّهِ إِلَهًا آخَرَ ۘ لَا إِلَهَ إِلَّا هُوَ ۚ كُلُّ شَيْءٍ هَالِكٌ إِلَّا وَجْهَهُ ۚ لَهُ الْحُكْمُ وَإِلَيْهِ تُرْجَعُونَ ﴿٨٨﴾

28:88 – *"Wala tad'uo ma'Allahi ilahan aakhara la ilaha illa huwa kullu shayin halikun illa wajha hu la hul hukmu wa ilayhi turja'oon."* (Surat Al-Qasas)

"…Everything (that exists) will perish except His holy Face. To Him belongs the Command, and to Him you will be returned."
(The Stories, 28:88)

When Allah ﷻ loves His servant, He begins to teach them the *haqqiqat al Muhammadiya* (Muhammadan Reality). Allah ﷻ doesn't teach anything about His Divinely Presence, it is *la sharik*. Allah's ﷻ secret is for Allah ﷻ. When Allah ﷻ loves you, He teaches you the secret of Sayyidina Muhammad ﷺ.

So, the reality of the inner marriage; if someone is not taking a path in which to have a perfected inner marriage and begins to struggle with all his desires or her desires, begins to perfect their character, take away *zulumat* (oppression). And enter into the Oceans of Love, Oceans of Fragrance and perfumed love of Sayyidina Muhammad ﷺ in which Prophet ﷺ then comes and begins to open that ocean of that love.

Three Things Made Dear to Prophet ﷺ: Perfume, Women and Prayer

Prophet ﷺ, his holy *hadith* that, Allah ﷻ has made three things dear for me.

Realities of a Zawj (Mate) on Earth, Within, and in the Heavens

---

عَنْ أَنَسِ بْنِ مَالِكٍ رَضِيَ اللهُ عَنْهُ قَالَ: قَالَ رَسُولُ اللهِ ﷺ: حُبِّبَ إِلَيَّ مِنْ دُنْيَاكُمْ: اَلطِّيبُ؛ وَالنِّسَاءُ؛ وَجُعِلَتْ قُرَّةُ عَيْنِي فِي الصَّلَاةِ

'An Anas bin Malik (ra) qala: Qala Rasulullahi ﷺ "Hubbi ilaya min dunyakum: Attayib, wan Nisa, wa ju'ilat qurratu 'ayni fis Salat."

Anas bin Malik (Ra) narrated from Prophet (pbuh) "Made beloved to me from your world are perfume/Purity, and Women, and the coolness of my eyes is in prayer."
(Jami' al-Saghir, Hadith 5435. Classified as Sahih by Albani)

Pure Souls Give a Perfumed Fragrance

Allah ﷻ made *tibb*, perfume. But *tibb* is also from *ya tayba*, from purity. Prophet ﷺ is teaching us, 'Allah ﷻ made three things dear for me. When you are now moving to that *zawj*, that mate inside you, be very careful. Be sensitive with that. Allah ﷻ made this very dear for me.' And the opening to that reality is the *attar* and the fragrance, but in reality, it is *tibb* and purity. That when you safeguard its purity, its cleanliness, it's going to give you an immense fragrance.

Your soul has a fragrance. If people smell your soul, they smell roses in their home. They smell sandalwood depending upon the fragrance that that *wali* (saint) has. When people smell fragrances in their homes, these are the souls of *awliya* (saints) because Prophet's ﷺ *hadith* is teaching that, 'Allah ﷻ made it dear for me to be pure, to be clean, and the *attar* and fragrance that comes from *mutahireen*.' Be

tawabeen (those who repent) and *mutahireen* (those who purify themselves). All our *wudu* (ablution), everything we are doing, *ya Rabbi*, make us to be pure and clean, for what? Not the body. The body is going into the dirt, but the purity of the soul.

اَللّٰهُمَّ اجْعَلْنِيْ مِنَ التَّوَّابِيْنَ وَاجْعَلْنِيْ مِنَ الْمُتَطَهِّرِيْنَ

Allahummaj 'alni minat tawwabina, waj'alni minal mutatahhirin.

O Allah make me to be from those who repent and make me from those who are purified.

Women Represent the Reality of the Soul Within

Prophet ﷺ then says, 'Allah ﷻ made dear for me – women.' It is not physical. It has nothing to do with physical women but the reality of this *zawj*. That, 'make dear for me the soul'; the soul of myself, the

soul of my Companions. And one of the names of Sayyidina Muhammad ﷺ is *Abu Arwah*, the father of the *arwah* (souls). *Nurul anwar wa sirratul asrar* (light of every secret and secret of every light), that every light is coming from Prophet ﷺ. It cannot come from Allah ﷻ to go back to Allah ﷻ, *la sharik* (has no partner). It comes from the Ocean of *Muhammadun RasulAllah* ﷺ and it returns to the Ocean of *Muhammadun RasulAllah* ﷺ. 'Made dear for me this reality of souls. Keep it pure, keep it clean. Allah ﷻ made it dear for me,' and then its proof is then, 'made my *salah* to be the coolness of my eyes. That Allah ﷻ made dear for me my *salah* and it becomes the coolness of my eyes.'

Realities of a Zawj (Mate) on Earth, Within, and in the Heavens

عَنِ الْمُغِيرَةِ بْنِ شُعْبَةٍ، رَضِيَّ اللهِ عَنْهُ،، قَالَ: قَالَ رَسُولُ اللهِ صَلَّى اللهُ عَلَيْهِ وَسَلَّمَ: « جُعِلَتْ قُرَّةُ عَيْنِيِّ فِي الصَّلاَةِ » صَحِيحُ الْجَامِعِ الصَّغِيرِ وَزِيادَتِهِ ، حَدِيثُ ﴿٣٠٩٨﴾

'Anal Mughira bin Shu'bah (ra) Qala, Qala Rasulullahi ﷺ "Ju'yelat qurratu 'ayni fis salati."
(Sahih al-Jaami as-Saghir wa Ziyaadah, Hadith 3098)

Narrated Mugeerah (may Allah be pleased with him), "He (the Prophet – may Allah bless him and grant him peace) said, "The coolness of my eyes has been made in the prayer.'

Safeguard and Purify Your Soul – She will Give Fragrance

If your soul is fragranced, clean and *pak* and you clean it with *zikrullah* (remembrance of Allah ﷻ, you clean it with *durood sharif*,

you clean it with *istiqam* and the firmness of your belief. That your belief is there to keep everything of harm away from this passenger that I am carrying within me. Because we have *ghairah* (sense of honor). We are not the people who prostitute our women. You don't prostitute the most important one inside of you. When you let yourself open for everything, Allah ﷻ is asking, 'You are destroying your soul. This is a delicate being I gave to you. Your responsibility was to safeguard her, nourish her, protect her. She will be a fragrance for you. She will be the coolness of your *salah* (prayer).

يَا أَيُّهَا الَّذِينَ آمَنُوا عَلَيْكُمْ أَنْفُسَكُمْ ۖ لَا يَضُرُّكُم مَّن ضَلَّ إِذَا اهْتَدَيْتُمْ ۚ إِلَى اللَّهِ مَرْجِعُكُمْ جَمِيعًا فَيُنَبِّئُكُم بِمَا كُنتُمْ تَعْمَلُونَ ﴿١٠٥﴾

5:105 – "Yaaa aiyuhal lazeena aamanoo 'alaikum anfusakum. Laa yadurrukum man dalla iza ahtadaitum; ilallaahi marji'ukum jami'an fayunabbi'ukum bimaa kuntum ta'maloon" (Surat Al-Maidah)

"O you who believe, Guard your own souls: If you follow (right) guidance, no harm can come to you from those who have gone stray. The return of you all is to Allah. He will inform you of all that you did."
(The Table Spread, 5:105)

Because that powered soul when it prays, it's praying in Allah's ﷻ Divinely Presence. Because the body was Islam, the soul is *Iman*, the purified soul is *Maqamul Ihsan* (Station of Moral Excellence) and

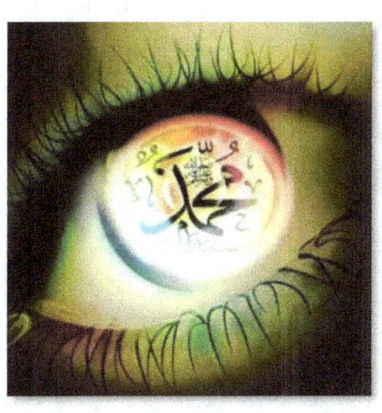

Maqamul Ihsan is that all your *ibadah* (worship) as if you see Allah ﷻ. There are *awliyaullah* (saints) who see what Allah ﷻ wants them to see, *Ahlul Basirah* (people of spiritual vision). They are not blind leading blind people; their heart is open. As a result, Allah ﷻ shows them and all their worshipness is as if they see Allah ﷻ from whatever Allah ﷻ wants to show them. And if you didn't reach there, at least know that Allah ﷻ is watching you.

قَالَ: فَأَخْبِرْنِي عَنْ الْإِحْسَانِ،
قَالَ: أَنْ تَعْبُدَ اللَّهَ كَأَنَّكَ تَرَاهُ، فَإِنْ لَمْ تَكُنْ تَرَاهُ فَإِنَّهُ يَرَاكَ

"Qala Fa akhberni 'an al Ihsan."
Qala: "An ta'bud Allaha, Ka annaka tarahu, fa in lam takun tarahu fa innahu yarak."

"Now, tell me about spiritual excellence (ihsan)."
The Prophet (pbuh) replied, "It is to serve/worship Allah as though you

behold/see Him; and if you don't behold/see him, (know that) He surely sees you." (Prophet Muhammad (pbuh))

A Successful Physical Marriage Requires a Happy Marriage Within

So, it means the successful marriage of *dunya* (material world) requires the successful marriage of your soul first. So, it means this way of *tazkiya* (purification), this way of *ma'rifah* (gnosticism) is that we  perfect ourself, perfect our character. If you are a fragrance and a person of reaching perfection, you begin to understand that that physical marriage, its importance. How am I going to safeguard now my physical marriage? If I am an oppressor to myself, I will oppress everything around me. Doesn't mean there is no struggle. Life at every moment is a struggle. Prophet ﷺ said, '*Ya Rabbi*, don't leave me to my *nafs* (ego) for a blink of an eye.'

اللَّهُمَّ لَا تَكِلْنِي إِلَى نَفْسِي طَرْفَةَ عَيْنٍ وَلَا أَقَلَّ مِنْ ذَلِكَ

"*Allahumma laa takilnee ila nafsee tarfat `aynin wa laa aqala min dhalika.*"

"O Allah! Don't leave me to my ego for the blink of an eye or less." (Prophet Muhammad (pbuh))

You don't ever reach anything until you get into the grave. This battle is continuous, this struggle is continuous and not until we enter the grave, then something else begins to open. So, it means the one who is perfecting and trying to work upon themself, they begin to understand, and they begin to perfect the marriage of their physicality. That, *ya Rabbi*, as I am safeguarding my soul, I am responsible for the soul and the physical person that I am married to. My responsibility is to safeguard them, take care of them, nurture them, treat them with respect and with honour and with dignity. And their responsibility to uphold your honour and your dignity.

Don't Dishonour Your Spouse by Speaking Negatively About Them

Tariqah comes and tells women never talk about your husband to anyone. It's *Tark al adab* (disrespect) and Prophet ﷺ became angry with you. Don't talk to anyone about your husband. Don't go from left person to right person, saying, 'This guy is crappy guy. This guy is like this, this guy is like that.' The angels will curse you. Don't talk. What you don't like, don't talk. Because now you are being pulled

into dishonouring and your half of the contract will be in trouble. Now if the person is dishonourable and the person is bad, that is Allah's ﷻ Hand upon them. But *shaitan* trying to pull you also into something bad. Rabia al Adawiya, a female *awliya*, how much she took difficulty and stayed quiet, stayed quiet. So even the *adab* (manners) they come to teach. So, then this life, you safeguard the rights. The woman safeguards the rights and the honour of her husband and the husband's responsibility is to take care and nourish and protect.

Realities of a Zawj (Mate) on Earth, Within, and in the Heavens

La Ya'lamoon – The Soulmate You Have Yet to Discover

Then the reality of the Paradise. That reality in which Allah ﷻ *"la ya'lamoon,"* that reality which you don't know and in which Hollywood comes to tell you, 'That's your soulmate. Oh, I have this person that is going to be my soulmate.' So, I marry them, and 'You are going to be my soulmate.' No, you are incorrect. You are not going to be my soulmate.

Someone came to Prophet ﷺ and asked, *'Ya Sayyidi ya Rasul al Kareem*, I married somebody and I loved him so much and he died in battle. And then I married somebody else and then he died from a sickness. Life was hard. Then I married somebody else. *Ya Sayyidi ya Rasul al Kareem*, I am married, what will be my case?' This is something like we are all forced to be somewhere where we don't want to be?

Prophet's ﷺ *rahmah* (mercy) and Allah ﷻ described Allah's ﷻ *Rahmah*, you will be free. Allah ﷻ will ask you, 'Who did you love?' Because *hadith* of Prophet ﷺ – how Prophet ﷺ brings his *hadith* to clarify issues of Allah ﷻ. Allah ﷻ will ask you, when you are raised, 'Who did you love? The first one whom you loved? And through marriage or war or conflict you had to marry different people.' Allah ﷻ will ask, 'Who is it that you love? You will be with who you love.' That is why we started with, be careful who you love. People are so free to give their heart out and you end up with them for eternity. Those whom are in difficulty, Allah ﷻ will ask them, 'You will be with whom you love.'

قَالَ رَسُولُ اللهِ صلى الله عليه و سلم: الْمَرْءُ مَعَ مَنْ أَحَبَ

Qala RasulAllah (saws): "Almar o, ma'a man ahab."

Prophet Muhammad (pbuh) said: "One is with those whom he loves."

Love Sayyidina Muhammad ﷺ, He Will Never Let You Down!

The greatest – that is why *awliyaullah* (saints) come into our lives and say, 'We are going to clarify your love – not for him, not for her – your love is for Sayyidina Muhammad ﷺ. He is never going to let you down.' Men and women, you are going to let each other down like you can't imagine. Some say, 'I would never want to be raised with that person.' And they think they are tormented. They are taught back home, 'You are there forever,' and they have been put into that  at a young age and forced. No, no, this is not the *hadith* of Prophet ﷺ. They will ask. Allah ﷻ will ask, 'Who is it that you love?'

A Wakeel Guards the Soul and Gives Permission to Get Married

That is why *awliyaullah* (saints) come and the greatness of what they are teaching. When you say a *"wali";* we went to a marriage. He is a *wali* and a *wakeel* (representative) for your soul. Your soul that is in Paradise, it wants to be married. It wants to reach towards its *zawj*, its reality. And you are about to enter the wrong marriage. You are about to love the wrong things from this *dunya* (material world). When Allah ﷻ assigned for you a *wali* (saint), an *awliya* (saint), it's like the marriage we went to. He is your *wakeel*. Immediately, he is guarding your soul and he has to give the permission.

Realities of a Zawj (Mate) on Earth, Within, and in the Heavens

---

So, when your love is wrong and your love is incorrect to what Allah wants, he says, 'Are you giving permission?' The *wakeel* (representative) says, 'No.' Are you giving permission? The *wakeel* says, 'No.' And then the testing comes down to Earth to slap this way, slap that way, slap this way, slap that way to put the person back onto the path that Allah wants. You are about to permanently lock your soul into something you can't imagine. So, Allah's amazing

Rahmah (mercy) is that a *wakeel* and a *wali* (saint) and is not something small, not something you deny in this *dunya*, but he is safeguarding that reality because the *wakeel* (representative) has to give permission. We went to a wedding this weekend. They said, 'You be the *wakeel*. Go ask. Are you giving permission that such and such wants to come to marry you?' That *wali* (pious servant) in that presence says, 'No, we are not giving permission.'

We speak on behalf of the soul that is behind us by, *"Ati ullah ati ar Rasul wa ulil amri minkum."* They have been given permission and *Izzatullah wa izzat ar Rasul wa izzat al mu'mineen*.

﴿٥٩﴾ ...أَطِيعُوا اللَّهَ وَأَطِيعُوا الرَّسُولَ وَأُولِي الْأَمْرِ مِنْكُمْ...

4:59 – *"...Atiullaha wa atiur Rasula wa Ulil amre minkum..."* (Surat An-Nisa)

"...Obey Allah, Obey the Messenger, and those in authority among you..." (The Women, 4:59)

﴿٨﴾ ...وَلِلَّهِ الْعِزَّةُ وَلِرَسُولِهِ وَلِلْمُؤْمِنِينَ...

63:8 – "…Wa Lillahil 'izzatu wa li Rasuli hi wa lil Mumineen…" (Surat Al-Munafiqoon)

"…And to Allah belongs [all] honor, and to His Messenger, and to the believers…" (The Hypocrites, 63:8)

An *izzah* from Allah ﷻ, 'Answer on their behalf. You are their *wakeel* (representative). These souls have been partitioned to you, you are the *wakeel* for that soul,' and they are not allowing that love to begin to manifest upon that soul. And that is the soul of the soulmate, that you have your reality of your soul always in Divinely Presence. If you perfect the love of this physicality and it loves whom Allah ﷻ loves, and loves Sayyidina Muhammad ﷺ.

Urs is the Blessed Union of the Soul With Its Origin

Then why we celebrate the *Urs Mubarak* (Blessed union/death anniversary), Right? *Awliyaullah* (saints), big celebration, why? They achieved. They made the perfection of their love in this *dunya* (material world) perfect the way Allah ﷻ wants it. The *anfusihum*, the one inside of them perfectly in love with Sayyidina Muhammad ﷺ. Their *urs* is their *aroosi* (marriage). Their *urs* (blessed union/death anniversary) is their marriage, that they are free from the physicality and they be will be reunited with that which they spent all their time loving, and their soul goes back into that Ocean of Love. There is no physicality, no sex involved in this. This is an Ocean of Light that goes back into that Ocean and back to where it came from.

Realities of a Zawj (Mate) on Earth, Within, and in the Heavens

We said many times before, like drops of water. You put the drop of water, drop of water, drop of water, drop of water [Shaykh demonstrates with a glass of water]. In the end, if I put ten thousand drops, its but one ocean of water. It means *malakut* (heavenly realm) is singularity, and what they are teaching is the perfection of that love, *Urs Mubarak*, their soul goes deep into the reality, into the *haqqaiq*, and into the heart of Sayyidina Muhammad ﷺ. That is why everything around them is a celebration. All of the heavens are celebrating that one from Earth reached Allah's ﷻ True Love. And now he is going to be reunited with his real love and his real *zawj* (mate), back to his origin, back to his reality.

Subhana rabbika rabbal 'izzati 'amma yasifoon, wa salaamun 'alal mursaleen, walhamdulillahi rabbil 'aalameen. Bi hurmati Muhammad al-Mustafa wa bi siri Surat al-Fatiha.

A SEED IS ANNIHILATED IN THE SOIL TO BECOME A TREE - THE TREE IS A MANIFESTATION OF THE SOIL

Plant the Seed of Faith in Rajab

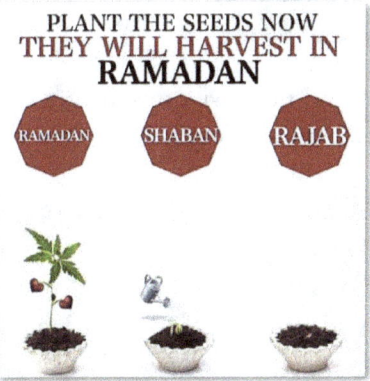

They give the analogy of Rajab, *subhana huwa man khalaq an-nur*, is a month of Allah ﷻ in which there's a seed, the seed of life, the seed of faith. And the holy month of Sha'ban, they say is like the soil and the watering. That that seed that Allah ﷻ brought from Rajab, places it within the month of Sha'ban and begins to water it with the love of Sayyidina Muhammad ﷺ. And its manifestation is the month of Ramadan. With that seed, now begins to manifest.

A Seed is Annihilated in the Soil to Become a Tree - The Tree is a Manifestation of the Soil

We Are Seeds With Immense Potential

Ahlul haqqaiq and the people of realities, their focus is on the world of light, the eternal reality, not so much that which is temporary and is passing, but Allah's ﷻ *Haq* (truth), Allah's ﷻ Oceans of Light and Realities. And they want for us to remember that our life is like a seed. And this is the month to remember before what is going to be opening,

inshaAllah, by Friday, by Saturday, the holy month of Ramadan in which

the day is to fast and the nights to pray and to be dressed by Holy Qur'an. It's that they want us to understand it's a deep reality in which we hope can be conveyed a bit of its understanding. That our existence here is not the prize only and that we are sort of content with this meager existence, this material world, and our material possessions.

But they want to remind us, you are but yet a seed, just a seed. And the potential of what we have and what Allah ﷻ has given to us is immense. And if we look at the seeds, *subhanAllah*, that there are so many different seeds and so many of them, you look alike. You can take handfuls of seeds and they all look alike, but its product is immensely different. You can have a seed this big and it can mature into a tree that is  immense and can produce millions of fruits through its lifetime. Some may be 100, 150 years old, the tree, and continuously producing fruits from one seed.

Did We Accomplish What Allah ﷻ Wants For Us?

And *awliya* (saints) come into our life and begin to make a teaching from Prophet's ﷺ teachings always and that's why, *"Atiullaha wa atiur Rasula wa Ulil amre minkum."*

﴿يَاأَيُّهَا الَّذِينَ آمَنُوا أَطِيعُواللَّه وَأَطِيعُواْالرَّسُولَ وَأُوْلِي الْأَمْرِ مِنْكُمْ...﴾٥٩﴿

4:59 – *"Ya ayyu hal latheena amanoo Atiullaha wa atiur Rasula wa Ulil amre minkum…"* (Surat An-Nisa)

"O You who have believed, Obey Allah, Obey the Messenger, and those in authority among you…" (The Women, 4:59)

They put it in a way that's so easy for people to understand. That they, if they are confused think, 'I've never heard this in Islam.' Ah, because it's coming as *ayat al-Qur'an* and holy *hadith* all packaged in something easy for you to understand, where we are just a seed. And this life of ours is still just a seed. We have many variations and this seed is not reached its potential.

And we said many times, some seeds can be very big, and they only cause harm because if you throw that seed – an avocado seed, it's like a baseball – solid wood. And we're going about our life thinking that we accomplished something. That 'Mashallah, you know, I came to Islam' or 'I'm something' or 'I'm something'. They are coming into our lives and reminding, 'Yet, but you are just a seed. You didn't accomplish what Allah ﷻ wants us to accomplish.'

A Seed is Annihilated in the Soil to Become a Tree - The Tree is a Manifestation of the Soil

The Secret is in the Teen

"Khalaq al-insana min teen"

وَلَقَدْ خَلَقْنَا الْإِنسَانَ مِن سُلَالَةٍ مِّن طِينٍ ﴿١٢﴾

23:12 – *"Wal laqad khalaqna al Insana min sulalatin min Teen."* (Surat Al-Muminoon)

"And certainly, did We create man from an extract of clay (water and dirt)." (The Believers, 23:12)

That there is a secret in *min* – *meem, noon* – this is a Muhammadan *nur* – *noon*. *Teen* – it has from *Tahir ul-Hadi*, has the *toi*, is the purified soul, purified soil. It has a deep reality, the reality of soil. Because now if you  want to understand the ocean of annihilation, which is a deep *tariqah* (spiritual path) reality, the ocean of a black hole is a deep scientific reality, and something so simple right in front of us is the soil.

And then *tariqah* (spiritual path) comes and teaches us that if we live our life as a seed, all our life will be a seed and merely never anything blossoms from a seed. You can hold a seed all you want. It never becomes the tree and never produces any fruit and most people we meet are like that. They are like a seed. They are very dry. Their understanding is very dry. Their character is very dry. There's no fruit in them and then you question yourself, 'Is this what Allah ﷻ created the purpose of that person? It's impossible!' Every seed has a purpose, whether it's to bloom as a beautiful flower or as a beautiful tree, or as a tree with immense fruits, immense blessings and benefits for people.

The Soil is the Great Annihilator

They come into our life and teach us the great annihilator is the soil. The soil is the great annihilator. It's for us to understand a deep reality. Whether you're scientific and trying to understand the black hole, whether you're spiritually trying to understand, 'Do I need to make seclusion? Do I have to seclude my life? Do I have to train myself to always do what the *nawaytul arbaeen, nawaytul itikaf, nuwaytul khalwa*, is continuous reminding of myself.

نَوَيْتُ الْأَرْبَعِينْ، نَوَيْتُ الْاِعْتِكَافْ، نَوَيْتُ الْخَلْوَة، نَوَيْتُ الْعُزْلَة، نَوَيْتُ الْرِياضَة، نَوَيْتُ الْسُلُوكْ وَالصِّيَامْ لِلَّهِ تَعَالَى فِيْ هَذَاالْمَسْجِدْ.

"*Nawaytul arbaeen, nawaytul itikaf, nuwaytul khalwa, nuwaytul uzla, nuwaytul riyada, nuwaytus sulook wal siyam, lillahi ta'ala fi hadhal masjid.*"

"I intend the forty (days of seclusion), I intend seclusion in the mosque, I intend seclusion, I intend isolation, I intend discipline (of the ego), I intend to travel in God's Path, I intend to fast for the sake of God in this mosque."

I have to seclude myself because they are going to explain now that if that seed understands its reality and its purpose, it will begin to seek out the soil. And the soil is the great ocean of annihilation.

*A Seed is Annihilated in the Soil to Become a Tree -
The Tree is a Manifestation of the Soil*

We Were Created From the Soil of Prophet's ﷺ Light

Whatever you put into that soil, its nature and its reality is to begin to break down the seed. It annihilates and crushes the seed. One of the realities and understanding of Prophet ﷺ is that – that soil. The soil in which we were created is from the light of Prophet ﷺ. The soil that's all around us as an understanding is if you put that seed into the soil, that is the ocean of annihilation. That is the ocean of annihilation.

As soon as that seed goes into the soil, the soil, its reality is to break down that seed. It begins to crush that seed. It begins to destroy that seed. It begins to send an energy to that seed that makes a plant to begin to appear. It means there's a process. If that seed is visible and continuously out in life and out and about, it never took a path in which to know itself and Prophet's ﷺ *hadith* is, 'Who knows himself will know his Lord'. How would you know yourself in the mall?

مَنْ عَرَفَ نَفْسَهُ فَقَدْ عَرَفَ رَبَّهُ

"Man 'arafa nafsahu faqad 'arafa Rabbahu."

"Who knows himself, knows his Lord." (Prophet Muhammad (pbuh))

We Will Return to Allah's ﷻ Ocean of Annihilation

It means these are *ithikaf*. These are the *khalwa* and seclusion of Prophet's ﷺ teaching; seclude yourself, for the name that people call you is of no relevance. What they know of you is a walking dead. What Allah ﷻ wants from you is a completely different reality. So, it means that *hadith* is an *isharat* (sign) for us. Take a path in which to know yourself, not by asking other people, but isolating yourself and finding your own soil because there's a soil coming for all of us. You take your last breath; you walk out the door. That may be your last breath and Allah ﷻ throws you into the Ocean of Annihilation which is the *qabr* (grave), which is the dirt.

They throw you into the dirt and put the shovels of dirt upon you and now you're in Allah's ﷻ Oceans of Annihilation. That earth will eat you. Everything inside that earth will be sent to eat you and to destroy you and from *sifat al-Qahar*, to make nothing of you to be in existence anymore. This is the oceans of understanding of *fana* (annihilation). When you want to understand, 'Why, *ya Rabbi*, why are from *ahlul haqqaiq* (people of realities) are talking about annihilation, annihilation?' And Allah ﷻ says, 'Don't you see it all around you? Don't you see that every beauty you have on this earth was from a seed that was thrown into an ocean of annihilation?'

*A Seed is Annihilated in the Soil to Become a Tree -
The Tree is a Manifestation of the Soil*

The Soil Brings Out the True Reality of the Seed

As soon as it went into the dirt and isolated itself from people and began to water it with a *rahmah* and a mercy. What power that dirt has? What power does it have that it breaks down and brings out the reality of the seed? It's Allah's ﷻ *Izzah* and Allah's ﷻ Miracle in our life.

And a deeper understanding is that when that seed begins to be crushed and be crushed and be crushed, and you come back 30 days, 40 days, however long it takes, you see something growing from the dirt. But if you dig, there's no more seed. Allah ﷻ transposed and changed something. The seed that was before, once it annihilated into the oceans of annihilation, something new came out. That which appears now is a manifestation from the soil. That which is appearing is a manifestation from what was annihilated in the soil. The seed is no more.

We Can Crack Our Seed in This Life or in the Grave

This means that, that is a very deep reality because they are teaching us that all these beautiful flowers, they are not from the seed. They are manifesting from that soil. They are manifestations of Allah's ﷻ Annihilations. That He annihilated them and that, 'You are no longer a seed and I'll bring out a completely different reality. And for everything, I created in pairs. The first one went into the dirt, the second one is now appearing from this *teen*.'

If *ahlul haqqaiq* (people of realities) and *ahlul tafakkur* (people of contemplation) understand that when they go into seclusion, there's no difference for *insan* (human being) or for a seed. Allah ﷻ said, 'Which one is harder – the seed or your *insan*? No difference, that what I created you for is not what you're running for.' But as soon as you take a path of seclusion, of *khalwa* and isolation; and that can even be 10 minutes every day, that as soon as you make your *salah*, put your Qur'an and say, '*Ya Rabbi*, before my grave, I'm intending to seclude myself.' Because the grave can be very harsh if that seed is very hard. If the seed accomplished nothing in this world from what Allah ﷻ wants, it has a lot of cracking to do.

And why Allah ﷻ inspired people towards 'build yourself.' Why? So that you can do most of that cracking in your physical world. Every day, just a few minutes of cracking the seed, cracking, 'Who knows himself will know his Lord.'

مَنْ عَرَفَ نَفْسَهُ فَقَدْ عَرَفَ رَبَّهُ

"*Man 'arafa nafsahu faqad 'arafa Rabbahu*"

"*Who knows himself, knows his Lord.*" *(Prophet Muhammad (pbuh))*

You're now cracking the seed. All the layers of this seed are its bad characteristics. But there's a flower within the heart that Allah ﷻ wants to bloom, says, 'Get rid of the outside. Get rid of all that garbage'. There's something special, the kernel, the precious force inside that Allah ﷻ wanted to grow. If that grows in that ocean of annihilation, it's now is a manifestation of that soil. Manifestation of that soil – so when you see the tree with all its fruits, it's no longer a seed. You can't say, 'Oh, this was a seed.' Say, 'No, that seed, it died a long time ago. What you are seeing is a tree manifesting from this soil and giving you fruits.'

A Seed is Annihilated in the Soil to Become a Tree -
The Tree is a Manifestation of the Soil

Through Seclusion Awliya Become Manifestations of Prophet Muhammad ﷺ

Now imagine *insan* (human being). *Insan*, if they live a life in which they continuously secluding themselves. And the greatest soil is the light of Prophet ﷺ because this dirt, this whole creation is all from the light of *Muhammadun RasulAllah* ﷺ. It can never be from *La ilaha illAllah*. There is no *sharik*; there is no partnership with Allah ﷻ. All of this is a manifestation of *Muhammadun RasulAllah* ﷺ.

So, when you go for seclusion and *khalwah*, and say, '*Ya Rabbi*, I don't want to be a seed. I'm not waiting for the *qabr* (grave) to rip everything apart. I want now to seclude myself.' And as soon as you go into that isolation and they begin to train you; keep making *durood sharif*, keep praising upon Prophet ﷺ. When *awliyaullah* (saints) go into seclusion, 40 days, 40 days, 40 days, their seed died in that seclusion. Just like Allah ﷻ put you 40 days, a seed in this soil; if you look, there is no more seed. If that one goes into seclusion and is taught and trained in an authorized seclusion, their seed died and what you see of them is a manifestation of Sayyidina Muhammad ﷺ. You understand?

Be Like the Tree Whose Seed No Longer Exists

The tree is not there. There is no seed there. If you dig under and keep looking for a seed, you will never find the seed. *Mawt qablil mawt*, all of Prophet's teaching; if you want to be like this and just a seed, you didn't achieve what Allah ﷻ wanted you to achieve. The great ocean of annihilation, the oceans of *fana* is everything is running to the love of Sayyidina Muhammad ﷺ. He's the great Ocean of Annihilation.

When you take your being and you go into that ocean, the *Haq an-Nabi* ﷺ, you take yourself into that ocean and become nothing, and become nothing and become nothing. Allah ﷻ makes you to be a manifestation from that Ocean of Light. So, whatever's manifesting in that reality is a manifestation from that Ocean of Prophet ﷺ. That is the reality of the *akhfa*. That is the reality of the *fana*, that which you *fana* and annihilate yourself in, it will begin to make a manifestation. It means your new appearance is going to appear from that reality and that's why Allah ﷻ describes the Qur'an,

"Feekum," that the light of Prophet ﷺ is amongst you.

كَمَا أَرْسَلْنَا فِيكُمْ رَسُولًا مِّنكُمْ يَتْلُو عَلَيْكُمْ آيَاتِنَا وَيُزَكِّيكُمْ وَيُعَلِّمُكُمُ الْكِتَابَ وَالْحِكْمَةَ وَيُعَلِّمُكُم مَّا لَمْ تَكُونُوا تَعْلَمُونَ ﴿١٥١﴾

A Seed is Annihilated in the Soil to Become a Tree - The Tree is a Manifestation of the Soil

---

2:151 – *"Kama arsalna feekum Rasulan minkum yatlo 'Alaykum ayatina wa yuzakkeekum wa yu'Allimukumul kitaba walhikmata wa yu'Allimukum ma lam takono ta'Alamon." (Surat Al-Baqarah)*

"Just as We have sent among (within) you a messenger of your own, reciting to you Our Signs, and purifying you, and teaching you the Book/Scripture (Quran) and Wisdom, and teaching you New Knowledge, that which you did not know." (The Cow, 2:151)

To Reach Annihilation Requires an Open Heart

In one understanding of that 'amongst you', are that all those *awliya* (saints) and all those *Ahbab an-Nabi* ﷺ, lovers of Sayyidina Muhammad ﷺ. Prophet ﷺ said, 'You will be with whom you love.'

قَالَ رَسُولُ اللَّهِ صلى الله عليه و سلم: الْمَرْءُ مَعَ مَنْ أَحَبَّ

Qala RasulAllah (saws): "Almar o, ma'a man ahab."

Prophet Muhammad (pbuh) said: *"One is with those whom he loves."*

If they annihilated themselves in the light of Prophet ﷺ, in the love of Sayyidina Muhammad ﷺ because you cannot be annihilated with Allah ﷻ. Don't confuse yourself thinking *shirk* (polytheism). There is no *shirk*. The mind is not even capable of understanding. This has to do not with worshipness and worshipping Allah ﷻ. This has to do with annihilating. And many times, we taught but you have to have an open heart to understand.

We Are Just Drops in the Ocean of Light

If I take an ocean of water and come to me and said but, 'Here, this is me [referring to a glass of tea] and this is my form and this is who I am.' And they come and teach you, no, no, this glass is nothing to do with you. It's merely a body Allah ﷻ gave to you. Why, why Allah ﷻ wants you to be buried? Why do we have death? It's the great annihilation. Those who didn't want to annihilate themself willfully will be forcefully annihilated by throwing them in the *qabr* (grave).

So, what happens if this body is lost and you go into the *qabr*? Where does your light go? Your drop of light, it goes back as a drop [takes drops of tea and puts in a glass of water]. 1 drop, 2 drops, 3 drops, 5 drops – how many oceans do you have? One. There is no two. In *malakut* (heavenly realm), there is only *tawheed*, oneness. Multiplicity is in the world of form. Singularity is with Allah ﷻ. Multiple is the world of form. When a drop of water goes into a drop of water into a drop of water, it's but one drop of water.

Seclusion Trains Us to Focus on Our Soul, Not Our Body

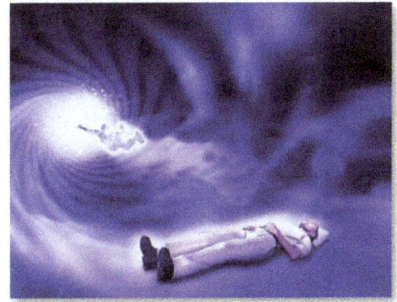

The seclusion and *khalwah* is that we're taking a path to lose our form. 'I'm not coming to you with this body, *ya Rabbi*. I'm coming with my soul.' Says, 'Then dump your body. Get rid of it. Don't put your importance upon it.' *Mawt qablil mawt*, where *Sahabi* (Companions) were trained by Prophet ﷺ. You

A Seed is Annihilated in the Soil to Become a Tree -
The Tree is a Manifestation of the Soil

want to see somebody who died before he died? Look at the great *Siddiq*, Sayyidina Abu Bakr as-Siddiq ﷺ. That they were the symbols of, 'We're not operating from our body. Our body died a long time ago. Our body desire died a long time ago.'

Allah ﷻ brought, when Allah ﷻ describes in Surat al-Zalzalah, what's a

zalzalah? Earthquake. But what Allah ﷻ describes an earthquake, 'That which is hidden and We will bring it out. That which is hidden within you, your true reality; I will crush everything and bring your reality out.' As soon as we take a path in which to be nothing, our soil, our way of entering into nothingness is in the light of Sayyidina Muhammad ﷺ, the love of Prophet ﷺ.

إِذَا زُلْزِلَتِ الْأَرْضُ زِلْزَالَهَا ﴿١﴾ وَأَخْرَجَتِ الْأَرْضُ أَثْقَالَهَا ﴿٢﴾

99:1-2 – *"Izaa zul zilatil ardu zil zaalaha (1) Wa akh rajatil ardu athqaalaha (2)" (Surat Az-Zalzalah)*

"When the earth is shaken with her (final) earthquake. (1) And the earth discharges its burdens (from within) (2)"
(The Earthquake, 99:1-2)

The Light of Prophet ﷺ Destroys Everything Incorrect Within Us

If you take yourself back into that ocean, he is the great Annihilation, he is the great Annihilator which crushes and destroys all form. Everything incorrect will be destroyed by the light of Prophet ﷺ, to perfect you, to bring you to true *tawheed* and oneness and present you to Allah's ﷻ Divinely Presence. As a result, if you achieve that and lose everything and be *ashiqeen* (lovers), your manifestation is from where then? You are manifesting from the *Nurul Muhammad* ﷺ.

So, they're like flowers. Why are they so fragrant? Why do they have so much *juzba* and attraction? Because they are manifestations of the light of Sayyidina Muhammad ﷺ and Allah ﷻ says at all times, *"Feekum"* (Holy Qur'an, 2:151). That light is amongst you, purifying you, teaching you, cleaning you, guiding you. Why? Because they are manifestations of the oceans of Sayyidina Muhammad ﷺ.

*A Seed is Annihilated in the Soil to Become a Tree -
The Tree is a Manifestation of the Soil*

The Black Hole is the Reality of Sayyidina Muhammad ﷺ

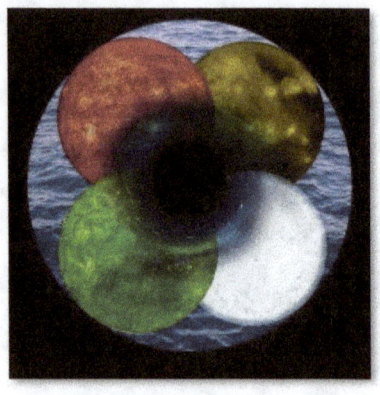

And only now they understand at the higher levels of the *akhfa* (most hidden), the black hole. They say, 'What is a black hole?' And only now they are getting an understanding that these suns that you see; you saw the diagram of the *lataif* (subtle energy points) of the heart. There is a yellow sun, there is a red sun, there is a white dwarf sun, there is a pistol star – and the center of the *lataif* is the black hole. It means the black hole and the ocean of annihilation is the reality of Sayyidina Muhammad ﷺ, the great annihilator. That anything coming for its final completion, that the black hole destroys and crushes everything. We're not talking about destroying and crushing as in a violent act, but not allowing anything to manifest in the presence of Allah ﷻ, to bring it to be *khashi'a*, to be dust.

That in which Sayyidina Musa ؏ asked, '*Ya Rabbi*, let me see You.' 'How you're going to see Me? Look to the mountain. I'm going to send you the light of My Annihilator.' This means that light of Prophet ﷺ appeared and Nabi Musa ؏ was out, then came back.

وَلَمَّا جَاءَ مُوسَىٰ لِمِيقَاتِنَا وَكَلَّمَهُ رَبُّهُ قَالَ رَبِّ أَرِنِي أَنظُرْ إِلَيْكَ ۚ قَالَ لَن تَرَانِي وَلَٰكِنِ انظُرْ إِلَى الْجَبَلِ فَإِنِ اسْتَقَرَّ مَكَانَهُ فَسَوْفَ تَرَانِي ۚ فَلَمَّا تَجَلَّىٰ رَبُّهُ لِلْجَبَلِ جَعَلَهُ دَكًّا وَخَرَّ مُوسَىٰ صَعِقًا ۚ فَلَمَّا أَفَاقَ قَالَ سُبْحَانَكَ تُبْتُ إِلَيْكَ وَأَنَا أَوَّلُ الْمُؤْمِنِينَ ﴿١٤٣﴾

7:143 – "*Wa lamma jaa Musa limeeqatina wa kallamahu Rabbuhu, qala rabbi arinee anzhur ilayka, Qala lan taranee wa lakini onzhur ilal jabali fa instaqarra makanahu, fasawfa taranee, falamma tajalla Rabbuhu lil jabali ja`alahu, dakkan wa kharra Musa sa`iqan, falamma afaqa qala subhanaka tubtu ilayka wa ana awwalul Mumineen.*" (Surat Al-A'raf)

"And when Moses arrived at Our appointed time and his Lord spoke to him, he said, "My Lord, show me [Yourself] that I may look at You." [Allah] said, "you will not see Me, but look at the mountain; if it should remain in its place, then you will see Me." But when his Lord manifested His glory on the mountain, He made it as dust, and Moses fell unconscious. And when he awoke/recovered his senses, he said, "Glory be to You! to You I turn in repentance, and I am the first of the believers." (The Heights. 7:143)

Companions Are Manifestations in the Garden of Prophet Muhammad ﷺ

It means that light of that reality is the *akhfa* reality and only now they are getting an understanding that that sun that is appearing to you, what if it's a manifestation from the black hole? And that which came into the black hole and that which you're seeing, you call a star because Prophet ﷺ described his companions, they are all manifestations of his garden.

So, the black hole is a symbol for us, is the garden of Prophet ﷺ. The garden like the *min teen*, that anything that comes into that will be completely annihilated. The stars that manifest, they are a manifestation of *nurul anwar wa sirratul asrar* (light of every secret and secret of every light). And all his Companions, they are manifesting from his *akhfa* reality, the great Annihilator, that all his Companions became stars.

*A Seed is Annihilated in the Soil to Become a Tree -
The Tree is a Manifestation of the Soil*

He said, 'All my Companions are stars; any one of them you follow, you will be guided'. And only now they are understanding that sun, if they look, you can enter into it. Its manifestation is from where that is appearing to you as a star?

أَصْحَابِيْ كَالنُّجُـومْ بِأَيْهِمْ اَقْتَدَيْتُمْ اَهْتَدَيْتُمْ

"Ashabi kan Nujoom, bi ayyihim aqta daytum ahta daytum."

"My companions are like stars. Follow any one of them and you will be guided." (Prophet Muhammad (pbuh))

Subhana rabbika rabbal 'izzati 'amma yasifoon, wa salaamun 'alal mursaleen, walhamdulillahi rabbil 'aalameen. Bi hurmati Muhammad al-Mustafa wa bi siri Surat al-Fatiha.

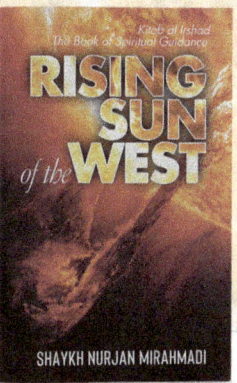

Featuring over 1,000 full-colour images including custom teaching diagrams!

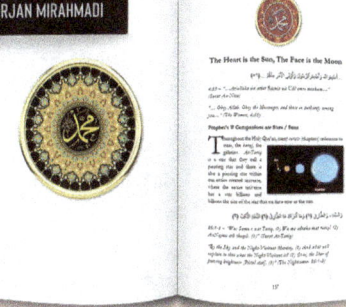

Kitab al Irshad
The Book of Spiritual Guidance

RISING SUN of the WEST

FIVE STAR REVIEWS
By Amazon Reviewers
★★★★★

ABOUT THE BOOK

Rising Sun of the West is an essential spiritual guidebook filled with invaluable knowledge of the elements within our cosmos. The author presents inspiring discourse, supported with full-colour images and custom diagrams, guiding the student through a comprehensive program of spiritual development.

The journey examines the Divine's (Allah ﷻ) most powerful sun of all universes, Prophet Muhammad ﷺ, and progresses to an insightful overview of the stars, represented by the Holy Companions. These symbols of guidance lead us on the path to enlightenment and by applying the disciplines of the star, the willing seeker can unlock hidden realities of the soul.

This book encapsulates the importance of following the full moons, the spiritual guides, who dedicate their lives to reflect the sun and exemplify the best in character. It is ultimately through their guiding light that the student transcends life on earth and moves closer to realizing true cosmic awareness.

"I brought this book to help develop my spiritual understanding and practice - I got a lot more than I thought! In over 580 pages the book is packed with incredible knowledge, quotes, stories, diagrams and metaphors.

This book advances both scientific and spiritual understanding. Where ancient Arabic text is referenced to demonstrate points, it follows with clear and inspirational English translations and application. The use of small colourful pictures to bring complex concepts to life is excellent for visual learners. I love the diagrams!

It's a powerful book; educational and full of learning that can be easily used in all aspects of life, family and work. It is rich in guidance. Worth re-reading to help protect and perfect self-behaviour and character.

It is one of the best books I've ever purchased and I have already ordered another book from the same author!"

DIVINELY PRAISING UPON THE PEARL OF CREATION
HUB-E-RASUL

YASEEN
PROPHET ﷺ IS THE WALKING QURAN

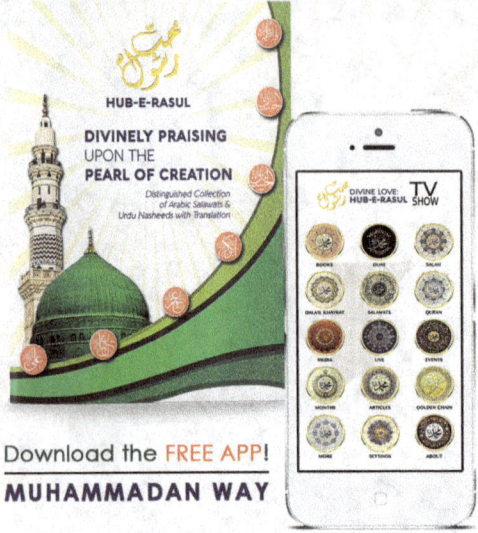

ABOUT THE BOOK

A distinguished collection of supplications and praisings upon the Prophet Muhammad (pbuh). By sending salutations the reciter builds a tremendous light and energy within their heart and soul while increasing love and gratitude for all Prophets and the Divine. Salawats carry an immense power and provide healing and relief from ailments and difficulties.

ABOUT THE BOOK

Prophet Muhammad ﷺ has been granted the highest of stations by Allah (the Divine) and nowhere is it clearer than in the heart of the Holy Qur'an, Surat YaSeen. It is through Prophet Muhammad's ﷺ light that all of creation came into existence and it is through his heart that the Holy Qur'an was revealed. As the chief of all Prophets, he is the literal Walking Qur'an, conveying the sublime realities of Allah's Holy Speech to all.

FIVE-STAR REVIEWS
By Amazon Reviewers ★★★★★

"A beautiful compilation of Praisings on the master of Prophets. Transliteration provides an easy way to recite for anyone. Translation gives the reader glimpse of beauty and depth of these poems and praisings. A MUST Have."

"A blessed and amazing treasury of praisings! Truly appreciate having this book available on the **Muhammadan Way app** - so easy to use from anywhere!"

FIVE-STAR REVIEWS
By Amazon Reviewer ★★★★★

"This is yet another amazing book from Shaykh Nurjan. His knowledge is without limit and his delivery is digestible to the well versed and the initiate. Illustrations are beautiful and fill this book from the first page to the last."

"Author's heavenly knowledge touches the heart and feeds the soul. If knowledge is power, then can you imagine what heavenly knowledge is? Empower your soul and buy this book."

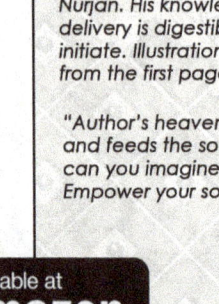

ORDER YOUR COPY TODAY!

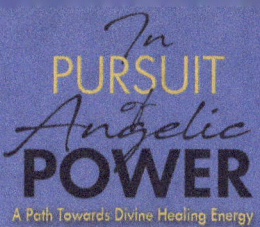

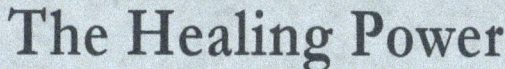

ABOUT THE BOOK

As heavenly beings, our souls are eternally in pursuit of healing energy through Divine and Angelic Power. By understanding the origins of energy through light and sound, the seeker learns to attune to the guides of heavenly knowledge and discovers essential techniques to acquire and increase positive energy within our beings.

ABOUT THE BOOK

For those who have reached a level of understanding of the illusory nature of the world around us and seek to discern the reality that lies behind it, Sufi meditation (muraqabah) is the doorway through which we can pass from this realm of delusion into the realm of realities. Through meditation the seeker has a means to return to his or her perfected original self.

FIVE-STAR REVIEWS

By Amazon Reviewers

"This invigorating book broadens and promotes a knowledge of the affinity and interactions between Angels and Humans."

"A must have in every home, "In Pursuit of Angelic Power" serves to mankind an introduction and insight to our illuminating friends."

FIVE-STAR REVIEWS

By Amazon Reviewers

This is a one-of-a-kind book by an actual authorized teacher of Sufi meditation. Not only it details the methods of meditation, but it also gives the practical advice regarding everything a seeker needs in order to pursue such a journey, first of which is to have a guide!"

"The book is rare gem in English language, providing the much needed instructions of Sufi meditation in a clear way. It contains some extra-ordinary illustrations, which is a huge plus for a beginner.

ORDER YOUR COPY TODAY!

LEVELS OF THE HEART
LATAIF AL QALB

SECRET REALITIES OF HAJJ

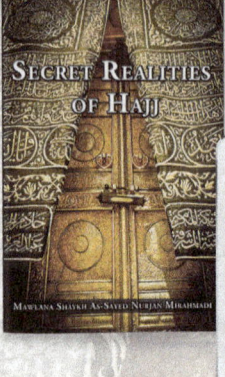
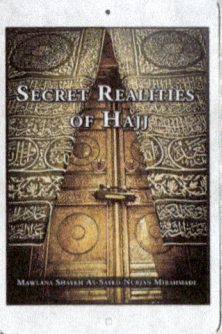

ABOUT THE BOOK

There are subtle energies and realities that are dressing the heart – these are the Levels of the Heart (Lataif al Qalb). Shaykh Nurjan has composed an exceptional work on the map of the heart, intertwining the teachings of its spiritual attributes and how they affect every aspect of a seeker's path.

ABOUT THE BOOK

Secret Realities of Hajj features invaluable teachings and spiritual insight into the Islamic holy pilgrimage of Hajj. From the historical references of holy prophets to the remarkable scientific explanations of the circumambulation, this book provides a deeper understanding of this important pillar of faith.

FIVE-STAR REVIEWS
By Amazon Reviewers
★★★★★

"I've learned more about Islam in 6 months than in 20 years reading Shaykh Nurjan's books, reading the articles on his app and watching his YouTube channel videos. His teachings transcend the worldly divisions we've created and helps unveil our deeper spiritual and universal realities within."

"To finally have all this information in one book is simply incredible. It is an ocean of spiritual knowledge."

FIVE-STAR REVIEWS
By Amazon Reviewers
★★★★★

"Amazing! A rare jewel filled with illuminating knowledge. Highly recommended for non-Muslims and Muslims equally, as the secrets referred to are, in reality, secrets related to creation itself, and the inner reality of the human heart."

"A must-read for people interested in the spiritual dimensions and secrets of the Hajj. The author has intimate knowledge of the topic from a long lineage of Sufi Masters. Pick up and enjoy, I did."

ORDER YOUR COPY TODAY!

NURMUHAMMAD.COM

A comprehensive website covering the deep realities of classical Islam.

- Watch the Latest Videos
- Connect to Live Zikr
- Listen to Sufi Radio 24/7
- Divine Love: Hub e Rasul TV Episodes
- Read the Latest Articles
- Enjoy Nasheeds - Naats
- Free Library of Resources

Join 20,000+ Active Users!

THE MUHAMMADAN WAY APP

Comprehensive Islamic Guide

DOWNLOAD NOW!

Available on the App Store · GET IT ON Google Play

- Awrads
- Salawats
- Multimedia

- Wazifas
- Special Duas
- Works offline!

CHECK US OUT ON SOCIAL MEDIA!

Shaykh Nurjan Mirahmadi

The Muhammadan Way

shaykhnurjanmirahmadi

Shaykh Nurjan Mirahmadi

The Muhammadan Way

WhatsApp

SMC MERCHANDISE

SUFI SUNNAH APPAREL
NO FEAR COLLECTION

ACCESSORIES
UNIQUE ITEMS WITH ORIGINAL CALLIGRAPHIC DESIGN

SUFI ESSENTIALS
TAWEEZ / PRAYER BEADS STICKERS AND MORE

BAKHOOR AND PERFUMES
BLESSED SUFI SCENTS FEATURING PREMIERE ARABIAN BRANDS

WELLNESS TEAS
CUSTOM-BLENDS WITH HEALING PROPERTIES

LIMITED EDITION PRODUCTS!

VIEW THE FULL SELECTION OF ITEMS AT
SMCMERCH.COM

Inspired from Traditional Islamic Armor and Protection with Qu'ran Ayat, IsmAllah and Ism Rasul

GIVE THE PERFECT GIFT!

SHOP ONLINE TODAY!

"Give charity without delay, for it stands in the way of calamity."
— Prophet Muhammad ﷺ

nurmuhammad.com/donate

General Donations

You may donate to many different projects.

You can add a dedication or prayer (du'a) requests you have.

Sadaqah

Please add a note on which Sadaqah the payment is for and prayer (du'a) requests.

Sadaqah Nafilah
Sadaqah Wajibah

Zakat

Please add a note on which type of Zakat payment is being made.

Use the online calculator for current values.

The collected funds will be paid to specific recipients of the Muslim community in accordance to zakat principles.

Help Those in Need

Fatima Zahra Helping Hand volunteers prepare and distribute meals on a monthly basis.

Clothing and other basic necessities are collected or purchased and distributed to the less fortunate including the Orphan Donations Program in Pakistan.

Mawlid

Donations go towards Mawlid Events such as the Annual Grand Milad un Nabi ﷺ.

These are special programs to commemorate the life and times of our Holy Prophet Muhammad ﷺ.

"Give charity without delay, for it stands in the way of calamity."
— Prophet Muhammad ﷺ

Support is the Way of Love - Donate Today!

Qurban / Zabiha

Payment for any program requiring Qurban offerings including Udhiyyah for Eid ul Adha sacrifice.

Khums / Hadiya

Khums = one-fifth
Hadiya = gift

Please add specific note whether payment is for khums or hadiya.

Please also add any prayer (du'a) requests you have.

Canada
Sufi Meditation Center Society

CRA no. 856872817 RR0001

*Also for donations from United Kingdom, Australia, New Zealand & Other Commonwealth Nations

United States
Mystic Meditation

Zelle Direct Deposit - No fees
donation@mysticmeditation.org

EIN No. 84-2681459
* Also for International donations but will not get non-US tax receipt.

Pakistan

For

Fatima Zahra Helping Hand in Pakistan
&
Orphan Donations Program in Pakistan

www.ingramcontent.com/pod-product-compliance
Lightning Source LLC
Chambersburg PA
CBHW071947070526
44583CB00015B/1097